LAST TRAIN TO TORONTO

ALSO BY TERRY PINDELL

Making Tracks:
An American Rail Odyssey

LAST TRAIN TO TORONTO

A Canadian Rail Odyssey

TERRY PINDELL

HENRY HOLT and COMPANY
NEW YORK

Library of Congress Cataloging-in-Publication Data
Pindell, Terry.
Last train to Toronto : a Canadian rail odyssey / Terry Pindell.—1st ed.
p.   cm.
Includes index.
1. Railroads—Canada.   2. Railroad travel—Canada.   I. Title.
TF26.P56   1992
385′.0971—dc20   91-39748
                                                       CIP

ISBN 0-8050-1574-4

Henry Holt books are available at special discounts
for bulk purchases for sales promotions, premiums,
fund-raising, or educational use. Special editions
or book excerpts can also be created to specification.
For details contact:
Special Sales Director, Henry Holt and Company, Inc.,
115 West 18th Street, New York, New York 10011.

First Edition—1992

Map by Arnold Bombay
Printed in the United States of America
Recognizing the importance of preserving
the written word, Henry Holt and Company, Inc.,
by policy, prints all of its first editions
on acid-free paper. ∞
1   3   5   7   9   10   8   6   4   2

Grateful acknowledgment is made for permission to reprint the following: Excerpt from
The Poetry of Robert Frost, edited by Edward Connery Lathem; copyright 1934, © 1969
by Holt, Rinehart and Winston; copyright © 1962 by Robert Frost; reprinted by
permission of Henry Holt and Company, Inc. Excerpt from "Ballad of Springhill" by
Peggy Seeger, copyright © 1960 (renewed) by STORMKING MUSIC INC.; all rights
reserved; used by permission. Excerpt from "Helpless" (Neil Young), © 1970 Cotillion
Music, Inc., and Broken Fiddle Music; all rights on behalf of Cotillion Music, Inc.;
administered by Warner-Tamerlane Publishing Corp.; all rights reserved; used by
permission.

*For Nancy—"When I have the words,
I don't have the chance; when I have
the chance, I don't have the words."*

Acknowledgments

I would like to thank the following people who helped make this book possible:

—Ernest Hebert, novelist and assistant professor of English at Dartmouth College, who spotted and helped me correct fundamental flaws in the early drafts.

—Bill Coo, Canadian railwayman, writer, photographer, and historian extraordinaire, whose guidance with the research and the drafts helped make it possible for an American to presume to describe the Canadian railway landscape.

—Rob Saunders, my Canadian publisher at Douglas & McIntyre of Vancouver, B.C., whose interest and advice helped make this a truly "North American" book.

—Paul Raynor, Director of Public Relations for VIA Rail, whose letters of introduction and hinted insights helped me to ask the right questions and to put myself in the right places at the right times.

Acknowledgments

—Bernie Goedhart, contracting writer for the VIA employees' newspaper, for her help in the "Last Train" chapter and from whom I borrowed one of its stories.

—Linda Eakeley, my expatriate college classmate who offered her Montreal home and knowledge of her adopted land to provide me with an ambassadorial gateway to the country.

—Bill Strachan, my editor, who took me and my book with him to Holt and enabled me to carry on through a change in publishers without disruption of my work.

—Joe Spieler, my agent, who besides performing the expected service of selling the book (twice), put me on his "analyst's couch" and drew out of me what I really wanted to write about in this and subsequent projects.

—Craig Nova, novelist, whose appreciation for my first book helped shape the tone of this one.

—Jane Perlungher and the staff of the Keene Public Library, whose help with interlibrary loans again enabled me to do a book like this from the comfort of my small New England city.

—VIA employees named throughout the book, who, during very trying times for them, performed their duties and infused my story with heart, as if I were documenting the grand beginnings of their world, rather than its possible demise.

—Proprietors and employees of various trackside establishments, also named throughout the book, who cooperated magnanimously with a foreigner carrying a notebook.

—The scores of fellow travelers, mostly Canadians, who so generously and fearlessly allowed a foreigner into the truth of their experience. In some cases I have changed names to protect their privacy.

—And finally, my family—Nancy, Molly, and Katie—who tolerated for a second time a year of my wanderings abroad.

Contents

Contents

Part Three   *Up North*

Prologue

I decided to travel through Canada by train because of the experiences I had riding thirty thousand miles of my own country's passenger rail routes. On the tracks of America, I put the ghost of my father to rest and searched to connect past heritage and present community. I was fleeing the modernity of our age that seemed so stale—interstate highways, airports, fast-food chains, shopping malls, crowded cities, and lifeless suburbs. I sought old things that, being unfamiliar, would seem new, and to which might cling a richer culture and a warmer human fellowship. I ended those journeys enticed by the thought that there was more to be found elsewhere in North America—even farther down the tracks.

I had heard intimations from fellow travelers that Canada, being more sparsely populated and of a different historical lineage, offered the possibility of an alternative North American way of life, close enough for kinship and far enough from the fast lane to satisfy my yearning. When I learned that Prime Minister Brian Mulroney's government had prompted a national convulsion by proposing drastic cuts to VIA Rail, the Canadian national passenger system, I set out to ride the steel of Canada while I still could. I spent a year traveling Canada by rail, often following train companions into their communities to glimpse a view of our neighbors that I don't believe many Americans have known and sometimes to experience that rare traveler's delight—to find exactly what I came looking for.

To a visiting American, Canada seems to work so well. Its cities and towns are clean, civil, and so crime-free that I eventually developed the Canadian habit of leaving my bags unattended in stations. Canadians enjoy a quality of life that has made their half of the continent a dynamic crossroads for international travelers, especially the young. Something there attracts as no other advanced nation does—and it's not just scenery or the connections of old empire. There is an innocence in Canada, a freedom from the stifling historical baggage that haunts so many of the world's great nations—and from the corrosive consequences of crowds and chaotic change that dominates life in my own country. Sometimes the train in Canada was a time machine to an earlier, simpler place; elsewhere it leapt the harried present to a regime of lucidity and sanity.

Yet Canada's future may be as unsettled as that of places far less tranquil. The history of Canada is one of a continuing struggle to forge a viable, unified nation from a mosaic of diverse peoples in the economic and political shadow cast by the United States—a struggle that after 130 years is still in flux. While I traveled, politicians wrangled over the now defunct Meech Lake accord, separatists in Quebec and the western provinces schemed secession, and native peoples armed themselves for violent confrontations with provincial authority. And I saw for myself places where the Canadian idyll simply does not work.

This book is the record of my Canadian rail journeys, interwoven with the history that helped me to make sense of them. It is a story of a people blessed in a union they don't always appreciate, who face the prospect of dissolution and separation. My mode of travel, currently in danger of extinction in Canada, is more than symbolic. Canada's inception coalesced not around war or political revolution, but around a single monumental undertaking of human bonding and community—the building of a transcontinental railway.

Ah, when to the heart of man
Was it ever less than a treason
To go with the drift of things,
To yield with a grace to reason,
And bow and accept the end
Of a love or a season.
                              —ROBERT FROST

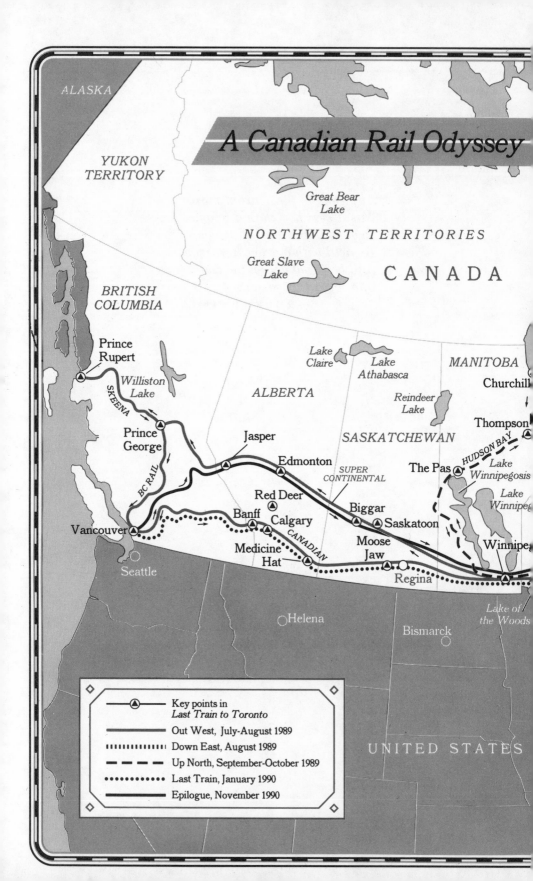

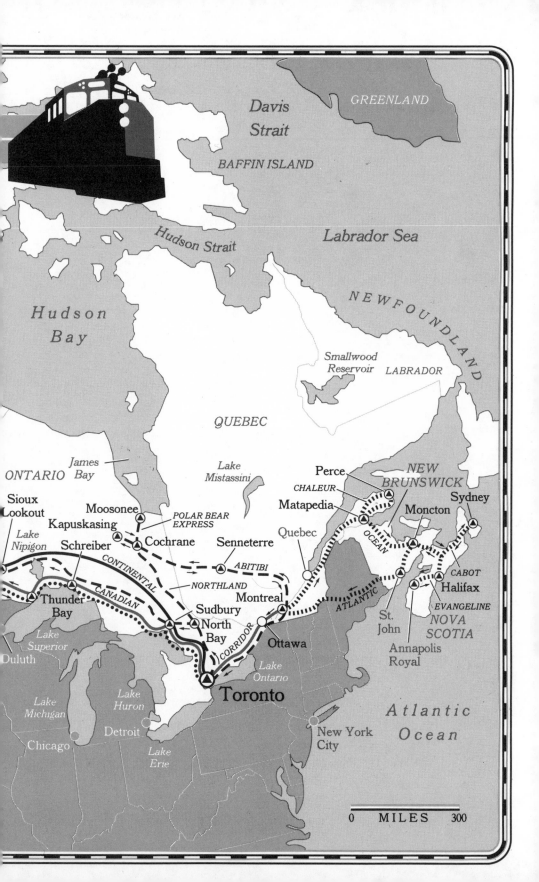

Introduction

THE *CAVALIER*

THE train comes to a halt just a few minutes out of Montreal's central station. As I peer from my sleeping compartment into the midnight darkness, it's clear we can't even be out of the yards yet. I can see the black rectangular shapes of boxcars beside us and the winking of trainmen's flashlights below my window. It looks like trouble. Just settled into my bed, I hadn't thought to go to work so soon, but off come the covers, and in bathrobe and loafers I venture to the open door at the rear of the car and down the steps to trackside.

Immediately I'm blinded by a flashlight in the face and a gruff voice of authority asks me what I'm doing off the train. But then the conductor recognizes me and relents, "Oh, come along, you'll hear all about it in the morning anyway."

I follow him and two other trainmen up the dark corridor between the passenger and freight trains. A heavy smell of diesel exhaust hangs in the still summer air and a few sleeper windows cast glimmers into the murk. The conductor's radio crackles, "Not so bad as we thought. Might be able to make it by. You'll have to really walk that track carefully and take it easy going through."

1

"I'll need authorization," answers the conductor.

"You walk it and say it's okay, and we'll get it for you."

"My responsibility, eh?"

"If you want to get to Toronto tonight."

He points up ahead in the glow of the flashlight to where the two trains appear to be even closer together and mumbles in explanation to me, "Freight derailment. This train right here split a switch. We don't know if our track is clear."

Beyond the grumbling engine at the head end of our train, more flashlights flit along the tracks of the freight. I can make out the derailed cars, two boxcars off the tracks to our side with their wheels down on the ends of the ties. Ahead of them, in the light cast by our diesel's headlamps, I can see the freight engine tilted off the tracks at the switch.

Our conductor greets the engineer of the freight by name and joshes, "Well, you fucked us up pretty good here."

The engineer answers, "You'll get home tonight. I'll have the roadmaster and super waiting for me at the end of my division. I missed a slow order on that switch—gonna be hell to pay."

The check of the tracks is thorough and careful, and it does appear we can get through, provided our weight doesn't make the freight lean too much toward us. It will be very slow going till we are clear. On the way back to board the train, I ask the conductor how bad it will be for that freight engineer. "Aw, he'll be okay. He's a good man and they know it. They could make him face an inquiry and fire him, of course, but they won't do it because of his record."

Back in my sleeping compartment, as the train slowly eases by the derailed freight, I toss and turn and finally give up on sleep when we have cleared the trouble and the eighty-five miles per hour clickety-clack fails to sedate me. I drag out one of the dozens of Canadian histories that will stuff my baggage during the coming months. I already know that Canada is a land whose geographical extremities made the building of a transcontinental railway perform virtually the same function in its founding as the Bill of Rights did in ours. The railway was the promise that brought in the diverse fringe provinces: the Maritimes and British Columbia. It is instituted in the articles of government and enshrined in the slogans on coinage. It dominates Canadian history since home rule—a story of how a handful of men of vision and opportunity patched together a nation, in defiance of geography, climate, ethnic differences, economics, and the pressure of its powerful southern neighbor's "manifest destiny."

But the roots of this relatively modern story run back in time even further, and I have lots to learn.

Aside from Viking explorers, there were English fishermen from Bristol off the shores of Newfoundland in the 1480s, a dozen years before Columbus. The Frenchman Jacques Cartier discovered the St. Lawrence in 1528 and first heard the word *Kanata*, which he took to be the Indians' name for the place to which they pointed, though it is more likely that the word meant simply "a collection of huts." Champlain founded the French enclave at Port Royal in today's Nova Scotia in 1605, later discovered the lake in today's Vermont that bears his name, and sided with the Algonquin Indians in a dispute with their blood enemies, the Iroquois, that made the latter eternal allies of whoever opposed the French. He sent the eighteen-year-old Etienne Brule on a mission to explore a route to the Pacific and the young man reported the first white man's crossing of the great Canadian shield to his superior before he was summarily cooked and eaten as punishment for his promiscuity with young Indian maidens.

By the 1630s, French woodsmen with a penchant for living amid the native Indians established the fur trade that dominated northern American history for two centuries. First there were the voyageurs, canoemen, who traveled with natives to the rich fur grounds to the northwest. When the Iroquois began their blockade of the territory, the *coureurs de bois* learned Indian ways to run the blockade and keep the trade alive.

Ville-Marie (Montreal), initially a monastic center, became the capital of this trade and the premier city of the future nation. There was never the same fervor among European Frenchmen to emigrate to the New World as there was among the English. With the country populated primarily by soldiers and fur traders (all male), the king decided to export young single women, usually from desperate straits in France, to populate the realm—the *"filles du roi,"* whose progeny formed the bulk of the largely homegrown French population in Quebec that still exists today.

Meanwhile the fur traders, Radisson and Groseilliers ("radishes and gooseberries" to generations of Canadian schoolchildren), discovered the land approach to Hudson Bay and explored the territory between the bay and the Great Lakes. After being dismissed by their French superiors, they approached the English with their proposal to develop a vast fur trade deep inland that could use the bay as a shipping route to Europe. Prince Rupert welcomed their scheme and so was born the Hudson's Bay Company and Rupert's Land. Rupert's Land was defined to consist of the entire watershed of Hudson Bay. Neither Charles II nor anyone else had any idea of just how vast that tract would turn out to be when he granted title to all of it, with the single requirement that members of the royal family be given the skins "of two elkes and two black beavers" whenever they visited North America.

Thus began years of intense rivalry between British and French interests for the fur trade. The English had the better route out of the country, through the bay. The French had the advantage of their voyageurs' natural instinct for living among and communicating with the native Indians. The English had cheap rum, the French the appeal of their Roman Catholic religion.

By the mid-eighteenth century, when the conflict between the English and French began to involve the nascent colonies on the southerly Atlantic Coast, French voyageurs had penetrated deep into the Canadian prairie, many settling with Indian wives in the Red River Valley around today's Winnipeg. Their offspring were called the Metis, and no one at the time took much notice of them while more tempestuous storms raged nearer the Atlantic Coast, but for Canada their presence in what would become Manitoba later made them agents of history.

In 1744 the series of wars that Americans know as the French and Indian War commenced. The atrocities that are ingrained in American lore were grisly and real; the ways of the Indian frontier that the French had adopted included the ritual dismemberment of captured prisoners. During the Seven Years' War, General Montcalm himself, a French regular army man rather than a frontiersman, sometimes had to ransom English and American prisoners from his own Indian and Quebec allies to halt the hideous screams that soured his savoring of victory.

With the defeat of the French by Wolfe on the Plains of Abraham, the British were faced with the fact of a large settled constituency of French-speaking Catholics. Under the liberal terms of the peace and the later Quebec Act of 1774, the language and religion of the defeated were guaranteed in perpetuity. The relatively peaceful accommodation in subsequent years is not so remarkable as it may seem. The French of Quebec were monarchists who felt more affinity to the crown of Britain than to the mob of revolutionary France or America.

By 1776, the loyalties of the French to the crown were strong enough that it took only a little bungling by the thirteen rebellious colonies to ensure Quebec's neutrality in the revolution. Sam Adams and John Hancock attempted in 1775 to persuade French Canada to join the Continental Congress but were foiled by the Congress's inflammatory denunciations of Catholicism in response to the Quebec Act. When a congressional army under David Wooster urinated in Catholic shrines and roughed up priests, it was the last straw and even the efforts of Ben Franklin himself could not bring the *Canadiens* in. Upper Canada (today's Ontario) was royalist through and through. Nova Scotia absented itself largely because of the presence of the royal fleet in Halifax. Thus thirteen colonies rebelled and three didn't. The first basis of a Canadian nation was founded.

After the war two things happened that colored Canadian political psychology for a century. The first was the immigration of committed Tories from the rebellious colonies, who brought with them their strong anti-republican and pro-royalist convictions. Second was the shabby treatment of Canadian territorial interests by the British negotiators in the Treaty of Paris. No one articulated it at the time, but here were sown the seeds of an eventual Canadian identity—defined by an abhorrence of the rowdy character of the former colonies to the south and the need to defend its own interests within the empire to which it wished to remain spiritually and politically loyal.

The night train I am riding from Montreal to Toronto, named with typically Canadian diplomacy the *Cavalier*, features a takeout counter in one of the coaches that stays open all night. Still unable to sleep, I find myself drawn toward it like a city insomniac hanging out at an all-night grill. Here a few night owls gather to nurse the beer they have bought before the bar service closed at 1:00 A.M. or the coffee that the attendant continues to pour: two rowdy working girls, a French-Canadian farmer, a businessman, and a young freight engineer deadheading back to his home in Kingston.

The two young women, flirtatiously flipping their long hair as they kneel and lean over the backs of their seats, revel in the male audience they have before them. Though several of the men in the group are old enough to be their fathers, they seem quite at ease bantering wittily and seductively with strange men.

The freight engineer wants to know how soon they have to be back home in Hamilton. "Not for another couple of days," smiles one of the girls. "Who cares anyway?"

"You wanta get off with me at Kingston, see the Thousand Islands?"

"Here we go again," laughs the other. "Michele, you old whore, you're good, you are. Right on." Indeed they do detrain with the freight engineer at Kingston while we older fellows left behind shake our heads and mutter. "Kids," marvels the businessman. "God, they know how to live."

"Oh, they do more living in their early twenties these days than a lot in my generation do in a lifetime. I could write a book about the tales they tell me," says the attendant at the counter. "It's one of the things I'll miss the most when Mulroney cuts this train."

There it is—the reason I am here. "VIA was a crippled child when it was born," he explains for my benefit. "No legislative mandate to do its job, and it had to absorb the costs of old equipment and stations that nobody else wanted. Listen to this. Since we're late, VIA will owe CN a penalty for disrupting its route schedule, even though a CN derailment was responsible. And if we arrive on time, we pay CN a bonus for getting us there."

The Frenchman worries that dismantling VIA will fuel separatist sentiment in his province. "Many of our elderly don't drive. Most of our college kids don't have cars yet. How is everyone going to get to Quebec City or Montreal? People will say, if the federal government won't do it, then the province will have to. It's just one more way that we'll have to fend for ourselves, and separatists will argue we may as well go all the way."

"Oh don't worry, Bourassa's friend Mulroney will take care of you," argues the attendant, referring to the influential premier of Quebec and his ally the prime minister. "You know about the nine routes they say they're going to protect? Well, three of them are in Quebec, eh?"

Shortly the Frenchman goes off to bed and the attendant confides, "They always take care of Quebec, you know—the squeaky wheel gets the grease. But some of the other provinces, especially B.C. and Alberta, have started to catch on to the Frenchmen's old trick. They're talking separatism out there now that they have all that oil money and aren't too pleased about seeing big chunks of it go to prop up the basket cases in the Maritimes. Down east, where everybody's so poor, they extort help from the government by talking about how they'd be better off as states in your country. And now even the Indians are raising hell. It's going to fall apart—and then one of these years we're all going to be voting for the American president."

That fear is Canada's story. In the years between the American Revolution and the Civil War, the American concept of "Manifest Destiny" dominated North American history, inexorably driving out or buying out the British, French, Spanish, Russians, and Mexicans until halted by the Canadians, who managed to draw a line and hold it at the 49th parallel.

By the War of 1812, there was intense fur-trading competition in the northwest between the Russians, John Jacob Astor's Americans, and the rival Hudson's Bay and North West companies of British North America. In the east the shooting war was a pretty incompetent affair, but when Wellington burned Washington in response to the Americans' razing of York (Toronto), Canadians paid the price. In the ensuing settlement, it was largely British outrage at the burning of archives by its own troops that brought about the generous terms for the Americans and the loss of more territory for the Canadians.

Canada never had a fully developed Civil War, but in 1837 it experienced the first of several rebellions ignited in part by republicanism spilling over the border. William Lyon Mackenzie of Ontario conspired with Louis-Joseph Papineau of Quebec to revolt and establish an American-style republic. The movement was put down bloodily by British troops, especially in Quebec where the issue was largely French independence, and the foundation for generations of hate was laid.

Britain sent Lord Durham to the colonies to study the causes of the disturbances. His report contained the famous sentence, "I found two nations warring in the bosom of a single state; I found a struggle, not of principles, but of races."

The resulting British Colonial Union Act of 1840 was little more than a cosmetic attempt to force the union of English and French, which still remained elusive. The first massive emigrations to New England by French-Canadians, unable to make a living and unimpressed by the Union Act, began. The British Governor-General Charles Bagot attempted to assuage the growing pro-American feeling among French-Canadians by appointing them to key posts in government, establishing a perennial tradition of Canadian politics.

But French politics had its own schisms. The radical heirs of Papineau's *"fils de la liberté"* came to be known as the *Rouges* and the more conservative faction, supported by the Church, the *Bleus*.

While Canadian parties were forming and jockeying for power, the American threat emerged again in Oregon. Again Britain gave away great chunks of potentially Canadian soil, in the Treaty of 1846, and reversed its policy regarding trade tariffs between British North America and the United States. Now "reciprocity" (free trade) was in the air as a result of the perception that tariffs were a cause of continuing bad economic times. Railroad builders came forward with schemes to improve the colonies' wretched transportation and enrich themselves in the process with subsidies from the government. Both issues, railroads and free trade, would still dominate the newspapers in my travels through Canada 150 years later.

By the time of the American Civil War, the political physiognomy of the unborn nation was formed, with the *Rouges* and the *Bleus* competing in Quebec, and Tories versus Reformers and "Clear Grits" (who refused to accept alliances with the French) in English Canada. In 1856, a curious partnership of the Tory John A. MacDonald and the anti-American French *patriote* (thus neither *Rouge* nor *Bleu*) Georges Etienne Cartier founded the Liberal-Conservative party. The hurly-burly of politics was beginning to accomplish what British legislative fiat had failed to do a decade earlier.

By the 1850s it was clear to Britain that if there was to be a British-aligned entity in North America to counter the fractious Americans, it would have to be an autonomous nation. In 1857, John Palliser was sent to see just what kind of expanded realm might be carved out of the Hudson's Bay Company's old western domain. He reported that while there might be fertile territory in a crescent running north and west from the Red River Valley (from today's Winnipeg to Edmonton), the area south of that was a northerly extension of the uninhabitable Great American Desert. He concluded that because of the obstacle of the rocky Great Shield north of Lake Superior, settlement of the northwest would always be by way of travel through the States. If a nation wasn't established and extended to the northwest quickly, the Americans would use that advantage to acquire the northwest and the Pacific Coast by default.

While Americans engaged in their Civil War, Canadians used the breathing space to hammer out national confederation. By the late 1860s even the "Clear Grit" George Brown temporarily joined the alliance of MacDonald and Cartier in that effort. After many false starts, the thing was done, roughly giving a large degree of local control to provinces and power over interprovincial matters to a federal government, with Britain retaining authority over provincial-federal (constitutional) disputes and foreign policy through retention of the aegis of the crown. The British Parliament passed the British North America Act, officially to take effect July 1, 1867.

John MacDonald became prime minister, and a name was chosen—the Dominion (rather than kingdom, to avoid unduly upsetting their republican neighbor) of Canada. The Quebecois were pleased; the Maritimes were not. The first acts of the legislatures of Prince Edward Island and Newfoundland were to secede. Nova Scotia threatened to do the same. The new province of British Columbia promised to form an independent nation or join the United States if the government didn't build a transcontinental railway. Manitoba, the first piece of new land carved from the old HBC empire, was crawling with American agents from Minnesota looking for a new northward dimension of Manifest Destiny.

Meanwhile, on the prairie west of the Great Shield, the ancient Metis, isolated descendants of the voyageurs and native peoples, worked their farms just as their French ancestors had for generations in Quebec. In the spring, they massed with military precision for the traditional buffalo hunt, just as their aboriginal ancestors had on these very lands for eons. None suspected that decisions regarding stewardship of their land made two thousand miles away would change their lives forever. No one in the capitals back east could imagine that through these same Metis, history would twist a way to save their national dream.

In the morning, I am wakened by the sleeping car attendant who brings a continental breakfast to my roomette. As the train rolls through the prim Toronto suburbs, where the warm June sun steams the streets still wet with a passing shower, he lingers at my doorway: "Don't get many Americans riding this overnight run." I explain my intention to catch the *Canadian* out of Toronto for Vancouver as the first leg of a quest for remnants of a North American way of life that were hard to come by in my own country.

"Well, you better get right on that train, because you won't find what you're after in Toronto. Most American city in Canada."

Toronto Station, still a classic stone edifice with a cavernous main hall connected by aerial walkways to the modernistic Canadian National Tower and the Bluejays Skydome, bustles with commuters and intercity travelers when I arrive. But those in the queue, which soon stretches from gate 7 all the way through the concourse and up the ramp into the waiting room, stand out because of the large amount of carry-on baggage that attends them. There are young people, families, elderly, working stiffs and businessmen, single men and single women, people in suits and people in denim. Some sit in tight circles on the floor playing card games, some pace and fidget, some perch on their suitcases holding places for others who sit in the lounges by gates at the side of the concourse. These are the westbound riders of the *Canadian*, besides the *Orient Express* perhaps the world's most famous passenger train. I join the queue with more than just the anticipation of a transcontinental train trip, I mean to ride all the way into the life of a foreign country.

We Americans think we know Canada. We speak (mostly) the same language, buy the same brand names, watch the same movies and TV programs, listen to the same music, and live under superficially similar democratic institutions. But this is a country whose political institutions have quietly evolved from very un-American origins in Tory loyalty to an even more un-American form of democratic socialism. Canada has "big government" by U.S. standards, including outright ownership of some of the most important national corporations (crown corporations), womb-to-tomb health care, heavy regulation of business and industry, and social welfare benefits beyond the wildest dreams of American liberal Democrats. In cities and towns across the country, the second- or third-largest employer is usually the government, federal or provincial.

Canadians tolerate authoritarian powers that would make American liberals and conservatives embrace each other in shuddering horror. The Royal Canadian Mounted Police can search without warrants, arrest on suspicion, hold without habeas corpus, wiretap without a court order, and open mail. Whereas American institutions are shaped by the right to "life, liberty, and the pursuit of happiness," in Canada it's "peace, order, and good government."

Canada has experienced the world's second-largest influx of immigrants. Here the model for assimilation is not the "melting pot" but rather the "mosaic"—the concept of a national patchwork of ethnic entities that retain their national cultural heritage within a loose social confederation. Climate, geography, and a sparse population have molded the character of communities and individuals here into shapes that, to an American sojourner, are refreshingly novel.

Though I don't know it as I queue up for the *Canadian*, the government's cutbacks in rail service will include canceling this train. Most of the other routes will be preserved with thrice-weekly service, including a transcontinental run by a different route. But the train over the route that founded the country will make its last run from Vancouver to Toronto on January 14, 1990. I will be on it for that run, and by that time I will believe that separate evolution from a common ancestry has ironically realized in this country some of the best lost dreams of my own. Like this train, they, too, are threatened with extinction.

PART ONE

―――

Out West

We have no blood in our history—no searing civil war, no surgical revolution. We are the only nation in the world created non-violently by the building of a railway.

—PIERRE BERTON

1

Voyageurs

THE *CANADIAN* TO WINNIPEG

BOARDING the *Canadian* in Toronto at noon on a warm June day, I contemplate the nature of heaven. Two thousand eight hundred eighty-seven miles lie ahead of me—the longest train ride in North America, the second longest in the world after the *Trans-Siberian*. Three days and three nights to Vancouver with nothing to do but read, eat, sleep, watch the passing landscape, and talk to people. There will be no telephone calls, no mail, no TV, no traffic, no supervisors. There will be no appointments, no social entanglements, no family responsibilities, no community obligations, no promises, no identity save what I create out of whole cloth during this passage. If not heaven, this is at least the opportunity to be temporarily born again.

As a veteran American rail traveler, my first instinct on getting settled into my roomette on the *Canadian* is to make comparisons. These cars remind me of the rebuilt 1940s and 1950s vintage equipment in Amtrak's eastern *Heritage* fleet, but the accommodations seem a bit more elegant and antique, which indeed they are since they have never been rebuilt, as have Amtrak's. The budget-busting cost of maintaining forty-year-old equipment is one of the reasons VIA is in trouble. But it is also part of the charm of Canadian trains—the toilet is porcelain rather than steel, the sink is a handy fixture in the corner of the roomette rather than a convertible piece of the wall. The bed is meticulously sheeted and tucked so that it flops down properly made when lowered rather than requiring re-making. Traditional royal blues and dark reds color the carpeting, seats, and curtains rather than the mustard earth tones prevalent on American trains. It's all charming and a little threadbare, like a venerable old inn.

As we pull out of the Toronto yards, I take a train-walk and discover once again that any transcontinental North American train is really a traveling village. The *Canadian* is still the standard of this phenomenon—indeed it was designed that way back in 1955 when the Canadian Pacific Railway was trying to stem the tide of travelers turning toward the airlines. Up front is the powerhouse, where one of the engines generates steam for heating, followed by warehouses (baggage cars), and the post office in the mail car. Linked to the industrial side of town are the working-class neigh-borhoods, the coaches, five of them this trip. The regime of the train is good to its modest class, whose coach seats recline fully and have leg rests; pillows and blankets are available so that a reasonable facsimile of a bed can be made. One of the coaches features a fast-food joint—a takeout counter with coffee, drinks, snacks, hot dogs, hamburgers, and sandwiches.

Following the coaches rolls the neighborhood bar—the Skyline Dome car, whose lounge features publike fixed tables and booth-style seats. There is an observation bubble up a little flight of steps, which on starry or aurora-lit nights offers all the advantages of a drive-in theater. The bartender's station is in the middle of the car, under the dome floor, and here hamburgers, pizza, and snacks are served as well as beverages. At the other end of the car there are tables with freestanding chairs where the conductor and crew hang out and hold court (sometimes this section is used as a truncated diner when the train doesn't carry a separate dining car). Thus city hall and the police station are conveniently located adjacent to the place where authority is most likely to be needed.

Behind the Skyline car one enters a more affluent neighborhood of three sleeping cars. Sleepers on the *Canadian* have three kinds of accommodation: first-class single roomettes (private rooms with a bed, toilet, and sink), first-class bedrooms (two beds, upper and lower, with the toilet facilities in a tiny separate room), and second-class sections in which one can enjoy a comfortable address at modest cost (couches by day, by night the old movie-style upper and lower berths, with no private toilet, separated from the corridor by thick curtains).

In the middle of this neighborhood there is a fine restaurant—the dining car, with glass partitions etched with Canadian birds, curtains at the windows, fixed tables, and freestanding chairs. Behind a corridor at one end of the car, a real chef and a dishwasher work in a tiny galley to prepare meals that are nothing like airline food. Passengers from the coach section are allowed to pass through the first group of sleepers to patronize the dining car, where offerings are just expensive enough that few coach passengers avail themselves of the opportunity.

Following the diner, there are three more sleepers and finally the "Park car" (each one in the fleet named after one of Canada's national parks), which contains a few bedrooms whose addresses are the peak of train society; a classier lounge with murals painted on the walls by members of the "Group of Seven" and a bar that you can actually lean on; a separate carpeted observation parlor with cushioned freestanding chairs and curved, curtained windows looking out on the tracks behind, and above, another bubble dome. The Park car is forbidden to coach passengers and exudes a clubby ambience, while the Skyline car often roars like a corner bar.

The social conventions of any small town apply here. Just as many coach riders never see any of the train aft of the Skyline car, many sleeping-car passengers never see any of the train ahead of the diner. I prefer to be located in that first set of sleepers, ahead of the diner at mid-train, where I enjoy mobility and contact with all the train's social milieus.

"Whoa, have another one to get yuh feet under yuh," shouts a stocky woman who raises a glass in a mock toast amid a circle of drinkers in the Skyline bar as I lurch with a roll of the train almost into her lap. The woman wears a black leather jacket, a neckerchief, ragged denims, and heavy black boots. Her hands are heavy with bracelets and rings and her blue eyes glint with mischief in a face that is tough and scarred yet nevertheless young. Her hair contradicts her otherwise rugged, intimidating features. It is tawny blond, clean, straight and long over her shoulders. She tosses it with the elegance of a proud thoroughbred and then belches loudly and spits on the floor.

"Yeh gutta say theas woom'n. Checkit aht, might," says the young Australian who makes room for me to sit beside him in the corner booth. He is an agricultural exchange worker from the land Down Under, and I can hardly understand a word he says.

Meanwhile the rowdy blonde wants to know why I carry a notebook and write things down. "I got a brother would take that notebook and make you eat it if you was writing things about him. I ratted on him once and if I saw him on the street in Sudbury tomorrow, I'd run the other way."

Genafer Beaulieau is thirty-five years old, married to the leader of a motorcycle club, and a substantial citizen of Whitecourt, Alberta, where she works as a French interpreter for the RCMP. She introduces herself as a reformed hell-raiser, adding that the motorcycle club was once a gang, and that her introduction to the institution she now works for was adversarial.

She carries on a bantering repartee with several Sudbury natives in the bar. She lived there fifteen years ago, is returning for the first time for some unspecified reason, and wants to know what has become of some of her favorite spots—a bar, a restaurant, a club, a hotel, a gym. One by one, each of her memory spots has become the victim of fire.

"Like I'm some kind of witch. Every place I ever cared about burned. I'm a troublemaker without even trying."

She can recall times when she did. She was in high school during the peak of the Quebec separatist movement of the seventies and couldn't get in the day the radical French students occupied and closed the school. Voices of reason arranged a meeting of concord in the school gymnasium for the following Saturday night.

"Three nights I had to wade around in the muck of Sucker Brook Swamp, but my friends and I finally got a hundred of 'em—one hundred fat juicy frogs that we let loose in the middle of the meeting." The French accused the English of setting up a public insult. Genafer laughed and laughed during the ensuing riot.

Today she pounds down the beer and passes pictures of her kids, her house, her horse, and her Harley around the bar car. "I'm settled and civilized," she says. "I even run in the civic marathon for crippled kids. But I still know how to drink and party." She gets up and does a song and dance routine—a sort of super-androgynous Mick Jagger, complete with teasing tosses of her magnificent hair across the faces of the gawking beer drinkers in the bar car. The bartender eyes her stonily.

After running through a stretch of prosperous-looking corn, alfalfa, dairy, and vegetable truck farms that reminds me of Ohio, the train suddenly bursts upon the expanse of Lake Simcoe, about an hour and a half out of Toronto. I have departed the Skyline car for the Park car dome at the rear of the train and have just settled in to an expectation of wilderness, the vast forested and belaked wilds of the Great Precambrian Shield. Instead, to the left stretch acres of cars and campers, and to the right, the blue of the lake is criss-crossed with the white wakes of powerboats, jet-skis, and sailboats.

Behind me a young woman in an orange sweater explains to a small audience of men and women much older than herself that this is Toronto's playground. She apparently is some kind of tour guide and her group intrigues me—my first chance to find out who travels the rails over the old voyageurs' route across the Great Shield.

"Americans are always so surprised to see such a crowd of people as they ride the train through here," she says. "They have this idea that Canada is a vast, sparsely populated wilderness. And they're right, but Lake Simcoe is typically Canadian. You see the same thing out west at the Calgary Stampede. You see it at the ski resorts in winter. Canada's small population tends to gather in dense knots at recreational places. Canada is really a handful of crowds separated by light years of emptiness."

During a pause in her monologue, I turn and ask why she pitches her description to an American traveler's viewpoint and she answers that most of those in her tour group are retired Americans. Would I like to meet them? I demur. I did not come to Canada to talk to Americans.

This train and its route have always had a fascination for Americans. They know that Canada's Rockies are younger and thus more vertical and ragged than our American version, that Canada's plains and prairies are colder and bigger, and they've heard something about a great geological monstrosity, the Great Shield, which stands between the east and these other sights. It's the first wonder of the journey, just as it's the first fact of the Canadian experience.

To an American being initiated into the culture of Canada, the Great Precambrian Shield sprawls across both geography and history to an extent for which there is no native frame of reference. It is almost like what Americans would have faced if the Great Basin Desert had occupied all of the map between the Appalachians and the Missouri River. But it's even more than that, because the task of building any kind of reliable transportation system over the shield was far more daunting

19

than doing so over a desert. A brakeman on the *Canadian* puts it this way: "God took a long, cold, sparsely populated country stretching four thousand miles from Newfoundland to Vancouver and plopped a thousand-mile-wide boulder right in the middle of it just to see how strong was the human need for community."

Geologically the shield is simply a huge outcropping of the oldest and hardest rock on the planet, extending from Labrador to Manitoba, the remains of super-solid cores of ancient mountains. The crests of the shield are soilless, diamond-hard granite ridges, and the depressions are muskegs, bogs of hoary, decayed vegetable matter and silt—huge bowls of pudding, often covered with a layer of water creating lakes with no bottoms. The shield was scored by the glaciers so that its rivers run south-north rather than east-west, as do most of those in other parts of the continent.

No one would have dreamed of attempting to take a Conestoga wagon across the shield, so no waves of settlers from the east poured into the Canadian prairie over some northern equivalent of the Cumberland Road. Instead there were just the handful of voyageurs and their epic treks by canoe over a thousand unconnected waterways and lakes.

Shortly beyond Lake Simcoe we are into it. The tracks now wind and bend, and the train runs at a considerably slower speed than it did before. With no level ground anywhere, the tracks run over cuts and fills and bridges—the necessity of a level roadbed in this terrain is an engineer's nightmare. Outside, the topography resembles a storm-tossed sea, with waves of rolling granite that tower above us one moment and then fall away leaving troughs of muskeg below. Frequently there is real water, like splashes left from some ancient cataclysm when the gods petrified this geological typhoon—enough streams and little lakes to make this part of the Canadian geographical horror a prosperous resort region. The barroom levity going on in the Skyline car seems almost a sacrilege to the memory of the voyageurs who trekked this way on foot carrying canoes. The men who thought they could build a railway across this country at a time when Canada's population was one-tenth of America's when that country built its first transcontinental must have been crazy.

That's exactly what the parliamentary opposition called it when Prime Minister John A. MacDonald promised in 1871 to build a transcontinental railway: "An act of insane recklessness."

MacDonald, the man who occupies the same place in the Canadian historical pantheon as George Washington does in that of the States, was initially skeptical about the rail-building enterprise that would eventually come to be so closely identified with him. His true passion, aside from strong drink and hearty fellowship, was his Liberal-Conservative party, the Tories. If he could bring the new province of British Columbia into the confederation—at the time consisting only of Ontario, Quebec, and the wavering Maritime provinces—his Conservatives would win elections for years to come, riding the resulting wave of national pride and dealing a blow to the hated Yankees, whose "Manifest Destiny" foretold a different future for the western regions.

But British Columbia demanded a railway linking it with the east as the price for handing MacDonald this partisan triumph. Thus MacDonald came to assume its necessity, eventually becoming the vision's spokesman and architect. British Columbia was simply too good a political opportunity.

There was also a political liability with which to contend. For half a century the fertile Red River region around today's Winnipeg had been settled by the Metis, who laid out their homestead plots in the characteristic French-style strips running back from the river's edge and carried on the traditional Indian buffalo hunt. When the Hudson's Bay Company was finally prevailed upon to turn over the first chunks of Rupert's Land to form the province of Manitoba, surveyors from Ottawa arrived unannounced to lay out boundaries along the lines of traditional English townships without regard to the Metis squatters' deep strip farms.

On October 11, 1869, a passionate twenty-five-year-old Metis put his boot upon a surveyor's chain and said, "You shall go no further." The man was Louis Riel. To Tory English-Canadians, he is still today a rebel, traitor, and murderer; to French Canadians and native peoples he is a national hero.

Brought up and trained under the extravagances of a mystical Catholicism, Riel's powerful intelligence and eloquence were warped by a fanatical sense of self as divinely charged, which led him eventually into insanity and tragedy. Initially Riel and his followers merely wanted to negotiate the terms of their entry into the dominion.

Riel took over Fort Garry, raised a Metis flag, and declared his own independent North American nation. He barred the new governor from entry into the province, established contacts with annexation-minded Americans, imprisoned members of the small local Tory community, and drew up a very moderate list of demands—squatters would not be put off their lands and their Catholic religion and schools would be preserved.

The government sent out an HBC man, Donald Smith, as special commissioner of Canada to preempt the rebellion by tardily assuring the Metis that their rights would be respected. Thus, along with MacDonald and Riel, Smith became the third of the unlikely trio of men whose destinies would entwine to ensure the founding of a continental Canadian nation. Beside the passionate Riel or the convivial MacDonald, the character of Smith reminds one of a great hunk of that Canadian Precambrian granite.

As Americans revere George Washington through the story of the cherry tree or Lincoln through the legend of the rail-splitter, Canadians define the character of Smith with the story of his thousand-mile snowshoe journey. He once suffered a severe attack of snow-blindness at his HBC station in Labrador. With two Indian guides, he trekked 550 miles to HBC headquarters in Montreal to find relief, but there he was harangued and abused by the tyrannical HBC chief, George Simpson, for leaving his post and was hastily sent packing. The return journey was so ghastly that the two Indian companions died before Smith crawled to the door of his outpost. The ordeal nearly killed him, but it crystallized the unyielding character that would serve Smith so well in subsequent years, when he would have more than most mortals' opportunities to demonstrate his ability to endure bitter adversity.

Meanwhile in 1869, Riel became increasingly inebriated with his newfound power. He waxed into towering rages and tried to suppress Smith's presentation of the government's benign position. But Smith, under house arrest, would not be intimidated and shrewdly negotiated a public proclamation of the government's intentions with Riel acting as interpreter. The gathering rejoiced to hear the terms offered and Riel shifted to a more moderate stance. Nonetheless he still stubbornly insisted on recognition of his provisional government during the interim period. With a peaceful settlement in the offing, he was granted his wish, and then all hell broke loose.

Some of the violent Orange Manitobans Riel had imprisoned escaped and initiated an armed counter-rebellion. When a retarded Metis boy shot and killed an armed English settler who had accused him of being a spy, the Orangemen hacked the boy with an ax and dragged him to his death behind their horses. Now there was blood on the snow and the rebellion took a fatal turn. Riel's men rounded up the perpetrators and, after summary court-martials, sentenced one Thomas Scott, with a reputation for particularly violent bigotry toward the Catholic Metis, to be shot. Perhaps, as Riel said himself, someone had to pay for the Orangemen's traditional dismissal of the Metis. Perhaps a sacrifice was needed to satisfy Riel's increasingly bizarre ego. Whatever the cause, Scott was shot by a firing squad of six and fell bleeding in the snow on March 4, 1869. Someone finished him off with a pistol, and with that one act, Riel guaranteed the founding of a transcontinental nation with a terrible, possibly fatal flaw.

MacDonald could have ignored the other acts of rebellion and negotiated with an obscure local leader to establish an amicable compromise, but the death of Scott made Riel a villain in the eyes of the Ontario Orangemen, who formed the backbone of MacDonald's political coalition. While granting most of the rebels' demands in the charter for the new province of Manitoba, MacDonald was forced to mount a major military expedition from the east to pursue Riel and avenge Scott. Several of Riel's lieutenants paid with their lives while Riel himself escaped and lived in exile in Montana, waiting in vain for the amnesty and vindication that never came. He was elected a member of Parliament from the Manitoba riding of Provencher but was never able to take his seat due to the price on his head. Believing himself to be a betrayed martyr, he wallowed in mystical delusions and waited for the day when he knew God would call him to continue his mission.

While the military expedition against Riel was successful, its tortuous and costly transit of the Great Shield showed how impotent the new government might be in the face of a serious threat by a sturdier military power—from, say, Minnesota. A railway across the shield could have had those troops on the scene in days rather than weeks.

Thus MacDonald's resolve was sharpened by the twin bludgeons of opportunity and threat—B.C. and Manitoba. By the end of 1871, the Canadian Pacific survey was in the field and the Conservatives had staked their future on the Pacific Railway. An expedition under Henry Hind confirmed the existence of a "fertile belt," an area running in an arc along the Saskatchewan River north of the desolate Palliser's Triangle. For ten years, Sanford Fleming's Pacific Survey focused its efforts on the mountain passes and Pacific harbors easily accessible to this northern route. But nothing turned out as initially planned. If ever there were a classic case of the false start, this was it.

I know people who will drive two hours and spend $50 to dine at a particularly charming restaurant. I would ride a train carrying a diner with a real chef to do the same thing and spend about the same amount of money. I could board just before dinner with a $30 round-trip coach ticket to someplace about two hours away, have a full meal with a cocktail, soup, salad, entree, dessert, wine, and coffee for under $20.

I like the diners on any train, but the one on the *Canadian* offers touches of elegance. The tablecloth is white linen, and the meals are served on real china (except for the salads in plastic bowls). With its art deco glass partitions, curtains, and steward's station, the decor seems rich—more like a traveling hotel restaurant. There are fewer menu selections, only two, and the price of dinner is about $3 more than on Amtrak (and isn't complimentary for sleeper passengers, as it is on Amtrak, even though the cost of a sleeper is only a little less). The diner crew provides a level of service that Amtrak and most airlines can't touch.

Broccoli soup is included (Amtrak serves soup only at lunch) and tonight's entrees are salmon or Cornish hen. The salmon, with a Bearnaise sauce, is excellent and my dinner companions are convivial. I am seated with a college-age couple and the tour leader I spoke to earlier in the Skyline car. She is Linda Melillo, of Vancouver, and she works for University Tours Limited. The couple is Tim, on holiday from university in England, and Katrina, a traveling backpacker from Germany.

Tim and Katrina met on the train from Halifax to Montreal. Each was traveling alone and they combined resources to travel together for the duration of their odyssey through "beautiful Canada." She is fairly well fixed for cash (dinner tonight is her treat); he has a well-annotated notebook containing phone numbers and addresses of relatives and friends across the continent.

"Why Canada and not the U.S.?" I ask without telling them where I come from.

"Too dangerous," says Katrina without a pause. "I travel to get away from gang violence and drug dealers and terrorists. Why would I want to go to America and worry about getting raped?"

Tim, who recognizes that my English is not quite Canadian, is a little more circumspect. "America just doesn't have the same glitter for young European travelers as it used to. I think we still admire America, but there's no reason to go there now."

"Canada has what people used to go to America for," adds Katrina. "Lots of unspoiled wide open spaces and the friendliest people in the world."

"For me it's a little more complicated than that," says Tim. "Maggie's England is a rubbish heap. I can't imagine being happy with the life I'll settle for there. Post-Reagan America seems headed down the same road. But there's still hope for Canada. Here's an English-speaking nation that has a chance to learn from the follies of her older relatives. I'm here to see what life might have been like in England without the hangover of a dead empire or in America without the cold war and cost of its military machine."

Meanwhile the granite ribs of the Great Shield roll past in the sunset gloaming outside the train. Periodically the sound of the tracks becomes hollow and steely as we pass over one of the scores of bridges the railroad had to build to cross this rugged landscape. I picture the early voyageurs sweating and freezing in their canoes in their epic journeys. Just as Americans trekked west for gold, Canadians chased furs. Yet the two nations turned out so different. The black ridges of the oldest rock on earth roll past, one on another without a sign of human habitation, just a few hours away from Canada's largest city.

After dinner Tim and Katrina return to their coach seats while I linger over coffee with Linda. "You never told them you were an American," she says.

"I suspect if I go around advertising that too much, I'll never learn anything," I answer.

"You're right. People are uneasy with Americans. They're mistrustful of your power and money, they fear you want to run everything."

"How do you feel about us?"

"Well, I meet more Americans than most people, with my job. But what I see—Americans don't know how to have a good time. They're uptight. They go through one of these trips with me gritting their teeth and taking pictures and worrying about whether everything will go smoothly. And when it doesn't, some of them just lose it. Fortunately I laugh a lot, and I've learned to just roll with what comes. Like when the train is late and we miss connections as we are going to now."

Approaching Sudbury in the Skyline bar after dinner, the spirits of most of the beer drinkers steadily lighten. John is still here carrying on in incomprehensible Australian English. Genafer, the rowdy blonde, now seems heavier with each passing mile. When the conductor announces ten minutes to Sudbury, she disappears into the bathroom and shortly emerges wearing a white shirt, black tie, and jacket. She orders a straight shot of vodka, and, tipping it, says, "This is for Judy, rest in pieces." Genafer cries, shouts, and sobs on shoulders. She latches on to the assistant conductor for the last few miles into Sudbury and simply won't let go.

When the train pulls into the station at 8:30, she leans on him all the way to the vestibule and down the steps to the ground. I follow, and out on the platform she explains in a wet gush, "It's my sister. I'm going to a funeral. She was on her Harley riding to White River. The guy going the other direction pulled out to pass, never saw her, I guess. She went right through his car, the front and back windows. It's been ten years since I last saw her. I always thought she was the straight arrow of the family— never even knew that she had a bike. I'm sorry I made an ass of myself, but what else is there to do but get drunk?"

Perhaps MacDonald's judgment was affected by his addiction to strong drink. He was known to show up on the floor of Parliament so inebriated that his fellows had to lift him from his chair. When MacDonald was once so drunk that he vomited during an opponent's speech, he recovered by joking that the words of the opposition can't help but turn a man's stomach. He once advised another government souse, D'Arcy McGee, "Look here, McGee, this government can't afford two drunkards and you've got to stop." He summed up his idiosyncratic popularity when he said, concerning his bitter rival and leader of the Liberals, the aloof and unsociable George Brown, "Better John MacDonald drunk than George Brown sober."

Yet even his detractors had to admit that his political judgment was usually crystal clear and his performance in great moments of parliamentary drama spectacular. An opposition member told the story of how, upon his entering the house chamber, the leader of his own party brushed him off as irrelevant due to his long absence in Europe but MacDonald wrapped an arm around him and said how good it was to have the man back to vote against him. When he was out of power, MacDonald once encountered the Liberals' Prime Minister Alexander Mackenzie outside Parliament in a state of extreme physical distress over the pounding he had just taken inside at the hands of MacDonald and the opposition. Genuinely concerned for the well-being of his old antagonist, MacDonald accosted him, saying, "Mackenzie, you should not distress yourself over these things. When I fell . . . I made up my mind to cease to worry and think no more about it."

Mackenzie responded, "Ah, but I have not that happy frame of mind."

Here was the secret of his success. MacDonald had a variety of mechanisms for setting aside trouble. The bottle was one of them; so were his camaraderie and his "yellowbacks"—lurid horror novels which he devoured during times of stress. Politically, he seemed to follow an unspoken maxim: when you know exactly what to do, act immediately and decisively; when you don't know what to do or dislike all of the alternatives, act not at all. Thus MacDonald earned the nickname of "Old Tomorrow" for his penchant for avoiding or putting off action when a profitable course did not present itself.

MacDonald never profited personally from his work in government, spending much of his life in debt, and behind the public life lurked a personal one of tragedy and disappointment. His first son died at the age of two, and his frail wife, to whom he was devoted, languished in his shadow, an invalid. The man who was so busy building a nation spent much of his time during the critical years caring for his second baby boy as his wife became increasingly helpless. The more one reads of John A. MacDonald, the more one wonders, where have such leaders gone?

Nonetheless, there is this aberrant point of record. During the time when his drinking escapades were at their peak, his government entered into arrangements for the building of the Pacific Railway, which, in effect, would have handed the project over to the hated Yankees.

It wouldn't have been so bad if the American involvement had been merely a political embarrassment to Yankee-baiting Tories. But through the Canadian capitalist Sir Hugh Allan, MacDonald became entangled with Americans whose goals were nothing less than the annexation of the Canadian northwest. Behind them was Jay Cooke, builder of the American Northern Pacific Railway, whose scheme was to promise an all-Canadian route and later renege on the critical section north of Superior. Then western Canada would fall into American hands as Oregon had done without a rail connection, fifty years earlier.

To make matters worse, Allan funneled huge sums of American

money into conservative coffers for the elections of 1872, employing them in particular to subvert the constituency of MacDonald's Quebec ally, Georges Etienne Cartier. After the election, Mac-Donald lamely announced that the Pacific Railway would not be awarded to any party with American connections. But his secret agreement with Allan, who was inextricably entangled with the Americans, still stood.

On New Year's Eve, George McMullen, a Chicago financier associated with Allan who was clearly cut out of the deal by MacDonald's announcement, arrived at the prime minister's residence with a packet of letters. These detailed the already established connection to American interests as well as Allan's monetary suborning of Cartier and the election of 1872. Old Tomorrow shrugged off the blackmail attempt, somehow believing that he could weather the coming storm.

For a year the Pacific Scandal consumed Parliament and the Canadian press. Yet when it came time for MacDonald to defend himself on the floor of Parliament, the entire capital, indeed the nation, stood at attention when the word went out, "Sir John is up." Despite the evidence, MacDonald's great speech, pulling all the emotional strings of a nation that had known no other leader, turned the tide. Normally no boaster, he catalogued his accomplishments as a nation builder and concluded with words that even his enemies could not challenge: ". . . there does not exist in Canada a man who has given more of his time, more of his heart, more of his wealth, or more of his intellect and power, such as it may be, for the good of this Dominion of Canada." He sat down at the end amid roaring cheers and was followed by Edward Blake of the opposition. Blake carefully listed the facts of the scandal point by point. The effect was to sober some of the nationalistic intoxication of MacDonald's speech. Yet despite the damning facts, the contest at that moment would have been a draw.

Then Donald Smith, the Hudson's Bay Company official and Labrador fur trader who wrangled with Riel and whose career would interweave with Canadian destiny throughout his life, rose to speak. Regarded as a government supporter and potential beneficiary of the Pacific Railway, Smith was expected to boost MacDonald's case to victory over the scandal charges. In his speech, he insisted that MacDonald could be guilty of no corruption but had countenanced a "very grave impropriety." He could not, in good conscience, vote with the government.

MacDonald resigned the next day, adjourned the house, and then went home to his bedroom beside his invalid wife. "Well, that's gone along with," he said to her evenly. "The government has resigned. It's a relief to be out of it." With that he opened one of his yellowbacks and placidly began to read.

In the ensuing election, Alexander Mackenzie's Liberals prevailed. The common wisdom held that MacDonald would languish into drunkenness and obscurity, that Mackenzie would preside over the building of some watered-down version of the Pacific Railway, that Americans would never again have any hand in the project, and that the traitor, Donald Smith, would be banished from all contracts with any future Conservative government. It was noted with profound headshaking that the project MacDonald initiated to ensure his party's survival outlasted him. Again the gods of irony laughed and flexed their sinews across the Canadian historical landscape. Absolutely none of it would turn out that way.

The *Canadian* normally makes a half-hour stop at Sudbury while riders of the connection from Montreal change trains. But tonight the stop will be even longer because the Montreal train hasn't arrived, delayed somewhere near Ottawa. Like Canadian stations everywhere, Sudbury station, with a little restaurant attached, buzzes with the sounds of teletypes, ringing telephones, baggage handling, and boisterous traveler and visitor conversation. Canadians never got out of the habit of gathering at their rail stations, as Americans did, and thus all across the country an American visitor is surprised that rail stations are still vital and integral parts of so many communities, large and small.

Outside it's getting too dark to see much of the famous Sudbury landscape. This mineral-rich hump in the rock of the Great Shield has been so scoured by decades of open-pit smelting that it resembles a lunar landscape—enough to lure NASA here to test its lunar rover during the Apollo missions. I can see the winking red lights on International Nickel's 1,250-foot superstack. Since the stack was built the local landscape has slowly begun to come alive, though downwind to the east, Ottawa Valley residents are embarrassed by this significant source of acid rain that can't be blamed on the Americans.

"Ay might, let's ehva pop et the bah across the straight," chirrups John Smith, who has been leaning against a post under a platform lamp smoking a cigarette and draining the Labatt's Blue he bought in the bar car before detraining. Across the street, the plain red neon sign of the Ledo Hotel flickers over a street corner. The men entering and leaving the place look hard, and I recall hearing Linda telling her elderly charges not to go there. But John's a pretty sturdy fellow and this is Canada, where you're supposed to be able to walk into any bar anywhere without fear, so I accept his invitation.

The lobby is littered with debris and a broken pay phone dangles from the wall. John opens a makeshift plywood door and we step into the smoky purple-pink haze inside. Across the room is a small platform stage decorated with blinking lights like those that people use at Christmas. Around the stage at little tables sit maybe thirty or forty loud rambunctious men, in knots of various sizes. To the left, and strategically near the door, stands the bar where John and I take up perches on tall stools. Loud rock music charges the place so that talking requires shouting.

"Just in time for the show," says the woman behind the bar.

"Ohroyt," shouts John. All eyes are turned toward a tall woman with teased blond hair who wears a long, heavy purple robe and fiddles with the cassette machine in a shadowy corner near the bar.

Kathy Stack, local alias Superstack, stage name XTC, walks to the middle of the stage and begins to sway back and forth in her long robe as the music starts. She smiles and laughs and looks at the men, sitting at the tables less than ten feet away, right in the eye. Then off comes the robe and a collective male gasp gives way to rousing cheers and whistles. Now she wears a sheer blue veil, transparent enough that one can see the tiny bra and G-string underneath.

" 'Oly Jaysus," leers John on his stool beside me. Kathy's dance isn't particularly flashy or sophisticated, just a graceful display of a perfect body in motion. It isn't long before she has shed the veil, the bra, and the G-string. She makes no obscene gestures, there are no raunchy pelvic thrusts, but make no mistake, she displays everything. Despite the makeup and the teased hair, she is animated without seeming stagy. She maintains eye contact with her audience, smiling and laughing; her naughtiness is like the girl next door, come over to play doctor while Mom is out shopping.

Then she comes down from the stage. She buries one man's face in her substantial bare bosom and he flops back in his chair pretending to have died and gone to heaven. She sits on the lap of another and blows in his ear, and he gives a creditable acting performance of a man having a tearful nervous breakdown. She passes from table to table teasing and touching, but amazingly the men never make the slightest move to touch her. Even the shouts of encouragement avoid the obscene language that one might expect.

"How come she doesn't get molested? There aren't even any cops in here," I ask the bartender. She points to a table where four beefy men sit silently with Cokes in front of them.

"Nobody ever touches a nude dancer, eh?" she says.

After her dance, Kathy Stack puts on her robe and comes over to speak to the bartender. Up close now, I can see that she is sweating heavily from her exertions and her makeup is smudged and streams in blue and pink gobs down her face. But still she charms, so what is this magnificent woman doing here? John speaks to her, gesturing to me, "'Ay's a Yank wroyta, talk to 'im and 'ay'll make yuh fighmous."

"Hi, I'm Kathy, but I don't mind if you call me XTC," she says without hesitation, and as she reaches out to shake my hand her robe parts for a moment.

"You're talking to Miss Nude Canada. She already is famous," says the bartender. Then in a conversational duet she and Kathy explain that in Canada, competitive nude dancing has become a tremendous national fad. The main attraction for free-spirited young women is the competitive pageants where prizes and endorsement opportunities mean good money. Dancing in bars like this keeps them in practice and shape and helps with the cash flow between big events. Many dancers are college students working to pay their way through school; some are young mothers, and some, like Kathy, gave up office jobs simply to make more money. Prostitutes are rare, and strict laws forbid "insertion routines" or "reciprocal contact" with the clientele.

I ask Kathy why Miss Nude Canada performs in a small hotel across the street from the railway station in Sudbury, Ontario.

"Well, for one thing, my boyfriend runs the place. But this would be a pretty good location anyway—only a day's train ride away from Montreal, Toronto, and Winnipeg. A lot of us nude dancers travel by train. It's so much cheaper than air and so much safer and less of a hassle than buses. And right here at the Ledo I probably get seen by as many people from different parts of the country as I could in Toronto. It seems like everybody passes through Sudbury either on the Trans-Canada Highway or by train."

The bartender gets a telephone call from Archie, the station manager, advising her to announce the imminent departure of the train to any rail riders who might be present. "I'll accompany you out the door, if you don't mind," says Kathy. "I don't like to walk in or out of here alone."

"Ohroyt," says John, and so our fellow train riders waiting at the station across the street gawk at the sight of John and me emerging from the Ledo Hotel walking Miss Nude Canada to her car. "Eat yer 'arts out, mights," says John, as we board the *Canadian* at 10:30 to continue our voyage across the Great Shield.

Long before the railway, the land was traversed by the French voyageurs, whose mores, formed amid the realities of the frontier and living among the native people, shocked both the Catholic Church and later the British officers of the HBC. The voyageurs brought no white women into this land, choosing instead from native maidens in rituals at least as bawdy as what I witnessed at the Ledo Hotel. Without benefit of clergy or magistrates, marriages were considered formalized by the simple act of consummation; divorce was executed by walking (or canoeing) away. Yet most of these marriages stood for life. The voyageurs were often family men, and it was their children who eventually settled in the Red River Valley. Though the HBC tried out "good Protestant men" from the Orkneys, one officer dismissed the abortive experiment saying, "Five of [the voyageurs] with one canoe will carry as much goods as ten of the Honorable Company's can with five canoes."

By tradition and later company regulation, the voyageurs were never more than five-foot-two in height (more room in the canoe for freight) and had to be able to carry at least two ninety-pound packs across portages up to ten miles in length. Voyageurs needed endurance to sustain them over the eighty-five portages and eight hundred miles that existed between Montreal and Grand Portage on Lake Superior. There the freight was transferred to smaller canoes with new teams of voyageurs for the western third of the trek, across the shield north of Superior to the Red River. Their lives were hard and mean, with ambush, drowning, exposure, scurvy, starvation, and syphilis guaranteeing that few lived past thirty. But fur traders were unanimous in the report that the voyageurs seldom complained of their lot, so complete was their adaptation to this land only they seemed to love.

No one else took the route over the shield to the west. The first surveyors found difficulty just getting into the heart of the country through which they were charged to route a railway. Yet, despite horrific struggles with ice in winter and fire in summer, they ran their lines and eventually railway construction began.

Though the first rails of the Pacific Railway were laid north of Superior, much of the route over the shield was the last to be completed. First there were the muskegs to contend with. Construction crews poured solid fill into them until they realized with horror that a few hundred feet of swamp had swallowed fill intended to cover ten miles. They tried driving piers or pilings in search of bedrock. Because the muskeg increased in density with depth, sometimes trains would be sent out on newly completed pilings in the belief that bedrock had been found only to disappear—tracks, trestles, engines, cars and all into the bottomless muck. In winter the muskegs disguised themselves as solid ground and tracks laid across them were swallowed up when spring thaw melted the frost. Even when all the muskegs were filled, at staggering cost, the ooze tended to permeate and lubricate the fill so that when trains crossed, the tracks inched forward, causing damage somewhere down the line.

Then there was the granite. Old-fashioned blasting powder had been replaced by the far more powerful and dangerous liquid explosive, nitroglycerin (dynamite was still untried). The evil reputation of nitro is well earned. Chemically it gets its explosive power from the fact that the bonds holding its molecules together are only minutely stronger than the powerful mutually repellent forces of the molecule components. As long as nitro remains liquid at a moderate temperature, the free molecules cushion the tremendous protesting energies stored in each one, and it won't explode.

The trouble comes when any condition impedes this cushioning effect. Thus frozen nitro may explode with the slightest jar. Many men died when the weather turned cold and someone forgot to take the precaution of keeping the nitro warm with hot water. Even when the nitro was liquid, anything that could create a shock wave or form droplets small enough to lose the cushioning effect would send careless handlers sky high. Nitro could not be carried in bouncing wagons; it had to be carried in clean tins on individual packers' backs. Grit, dust, or sand in the nitro, or rust or scratches on the inside of the container, spelled doom for the packer.

In standard practice, holes drilled in the granite were first filled with water to insulate the nitro against the roughness of the rock. Then the heavier nitro was carefully poured in and set off with a fuse. One of the greatest causes of casualties was small quantities of nitro spilled on the ground or rocks that did not initially explode but would, sometimes days or weeks later, when a horseshoe or even a man's boot scuffing grit across it set it off. The stuff's capriciousness resulted in most of the deaths; a practice that did not cause an explosion one time would cause one later. Laborers, traditionally fast learners about safety shortcuts that caused no harm the first time, frequently died as a result of paying more attention to the school of experience than the cautious instructions of their supervisors.

Small wonder that the men who worked the shield north of the Great Lakes took so readily to another fluid that could be explosive— alcohol. Though the government established Prohibition along the line, in the wilds of the Ontario shield enforcement was flimsy. Life was too hard. Supervisors, judges, and constables had their daily glasses, and everyone knew it. Smart construction bosses adapted by ignoring the whiskey peddlers except when well-announced pushes of work requiring extended shifts were in the offing. Then there would be arrests and severe punishments. Peddlers and drinkers quickly learned the rules and accommodated themselves.

Nonetheless, the little settlements that popped up at the end of track spawned an alcohol-inspired violence seldom seen in the relatively peaceful history of Canada. Rat Portage (today's Kenora) in particular was a hellhole because of conflicting authority. Since no one knew whether the town was in Ontario or Manitoba, constables from both provinces fought each other as well as the hoodlums until 1884, when the railway was finished and the town was officially declared part of Ontario.

In 1879, two whiskey peddlers, Dan Harrington and Jim Mitchell, brutally beat up a constable who tried to serve them with a warrant and escaped to Rat Portage. There a magistrate under their control went through the motions of fining them and then sent them off armed with a letter of discharge and two pistols. They headed for the railhead with fifty gallons of whiskey but were arrested near Hawk Lake by a Constable Ross and his deputy. Mitchell escaped into the woods and Harrington asked to be allowed to enter a brothel to wash up. He returned with a pair of pistols but was felled by shots from the quick draw of Ross. Ross's deputy advised that it wasn't necessary to fire again, that the bullet had done its damage; Harrington, bleeding on the ground, answered, "You're damned right it has taken effect, but I'd sooner be shot than fined." Then he died.

In later travels through the northern shield, I was to find that the closest thing in Canada to the American-style legacy of the lawless West still lurks in the land of the muskeg and granite ridges. The Canadians eventually built three railways across it but never tamed it. Much of the shield is still a land beyond the pale.

Tonight the Park car lounge contains a quiet parlor gathering of Linda Melillo's American charges playing cards and checkers and knitting and reading. Linda is herself subdued because the conductor has informed her of a further delay—something about a bridge repair.

But in the Skyline bar, a gathering of young international travelers keeps the barman busy. Tim and Katrina are here, huddled with a young man from New Zealand and two young women from Switzerland. John is here, too, and he and the New Zealander have made a truce in the traditional animosity which exists between the inhabitants of the two lands by sitting at opposite ends of the group. Most of the others in the Skyline bar are young Canadian working men and women or students. The one exception is a leather-faced, gray-bearded man with pale blue eyes who wears a black cowboy hat, boots, and a denim jacket and jeans. He sits in a corner stolidly nursing bourbon and speaking to no one.

The youngsters move upstairs to the dome. Someone has found a guitar, which Tim plays rather well. The beer flows, the voices croon, and time passes. Outside the northern lights dance wildly and one of the youngsters lights up something that is not a cigarette and says, "Toasties?"

The fellow is passing it around when the conductor appears at the top of the steps and speaks with searing authority, "You've got marijuana up here, I want to know who's responsible."

The silence is heavy. He waits and then says, "I'm gonna put you all off at Biscotasing and call the constable." More agonizing silence. Then, "If the one that's responsible speaks up, I'll let the rest go." After more tension, finally the fellow who produced the stuff steps into the aisle.

"It's mine. I'm responsible. The rest here had nothing to do with it." It's the New Zealander.

The conductor orders the rest of us back to our seats. "And I don't want to see you again till I get off at the end of my division," and with a great scurry, we're all gone. In my room, behind the closed door, I realize with horror that I left my notebook in the Skyline dome.

There's not much in it yet, but a principle is involved here. If I can't keep track of my notebook this early in the journey, what's going to happen later on? I creep back to the scene of the crime.

The conductor has just finished with the New Zealand miscreant—I can see him heading up the corridor of the coach just ahead. When I enter the lounge and turn toward the steps, the conductor halts me. "I told you I didn't want to see you again." I explain my predicament and that I'm not really part of the youngsters' group, but he's not buying it. Why didn't I show him my letter from VIA earlier?

Maybe it's the beer, maybe something else, but my feet are suddenly carrying me up the steps. I imagine myself a *coureur de bois* delivering a desperate message to homesteaders threatened by hostile Iroquois. There on a seat in the dome is my notebook. The conductor is approaching the bottom of the steps, his face puffed and red, just as I scramble down and, almost brushing him, burst past him and run all the way through three cars back to my roomette, where I close and lock the door and wait. No one comes. I splash in the sink, pull down the bed, and crawl in. It whirls.

Beware of the first night on a transcontinental train ride. There are sirens, potions, smiling ministers of doom, and a fatal spell of enchanted motion that has hexed this rail traveler every time without fail. Barriers of age, wisdom, and time itself tumble as the mooring tether is stretched. Maybe it's the tactile feeling of the earth passing underneath, but nowhere else do home and good sense seem so far away. The distance intoxicates; it transfigures. By the end of the journey, the solo traveler is a bigger, richer, freer being, but that first night he flirts with hideous transformations.

All morning the *Canadian* winds along the spectacular shore of Lake Superior. To the right is the immense emptiness of the Great Shield, rock without end only partially overgrown with ragged forest that struggles vainly to set down roots and veined with rivulets of water running south. To the left is the blue of the lake stretching to three horizons with sizable white breakers crashing on the rocks just below the railway grade. How the voyageurs must have welcomed their first glimpse of the water after nearly a thousand miles of streams and portages from the east. And how they must have yearned to be free of it after a week of storms and wetness, rounding each point of land only to confront another vast expanse of blue and another point on the far horizon.

At 11:00 A.M. we pull into the station at the tiny town of Schreiber, just inland from the lake shore. Linda Melillo's advance intelligence was correct. The conductor passes through the train informing everyone that we will stand here for several hours until Canadian Pacific Railway crews finish some work on a bridge somewhere down the line. John and I hop off the train to explore the town.

It doesn't take long—just a couple square blocks, a few dozen houses, a garage, and a tiny general store across the street from the train station. It's chilly even on this summer day. We join a group of fellow passengers milling around in the warmth of the little store, where there is a little poolroom and the biggest display is rental video tapes in well-worn boxes.

"Ighn't much for pupple to do 'ere but watch the bloody telly," observes John. I notice that the classiest of the titles are things like *Nightmare on Elm Street*, *Friday the 13th*, and *Rambo*. I buy a Coke and ask the guy at the counter about his video tape rentals.

"Oh no, this isn't a violent town," he insists. "But it's pretty lonesome here, eh? People need a little excitement."

In the store, in the street, and on the platform at the station, knots of travelers coalesce with locals who pepper us with questions about the journey thus far—"Why are we so late?" "How far are we traveling?" "Have we seen any wildlife?" "How do we like their town?" I will discover throughout Canada that communities like this one have a fascination with travelers. Unlike so many small towns in America where the traveler is a figure of suspicion and distrust, the villages of Canada welcome him with open arms. They want to talk to him, feed him, drink with him, and offer him a place to sleep. Perhaps it's a vestige of the community of the frontier; perhaps it's just loneliness.

Our interruption of Schreiber's isolation doesn't last long; suddenly the diesel's horns make the two short blasts that signal imminent departure. Passengers come scurrying from their strolls and the conductor and service crew make a big deal of counting heads so that no one is left behind. It seems the CPR's work on the bridge is going faster than anticipated and the train will head on down the line in hopes that they are finished by the time it gets there. If not, we will wait at the bridgehead.

After lunch in the diner, I ride for a while alone back in the Park car dome. I'm impressed by the number of islands and bending peninsulas just off the shore of Superior. Unobstructed views of the expanse of the lake are actually rather rare. And at Thunder Bay I am surprised to see a thriving city rather than the remote outpost I had envisioned. This is Canada's western port of the St. Lawrence–Great Lakes Seaway. The skyline here is dominated by huge grain elevators and paper mills, which are the reasons for this place's existence.

After the tracks leave the shore of Superior, the route, now double-tracked to carry the huge cargoes of grain from the prairie to the elevators at Thunder Bay, plunges into some of the most rugged country of the entire shield. Like a spasm of geographical cussedness in the last stretch before the prairie and Winnipeg, the granite ridges here are higher (some actually sport ski slopes) and the muskegs broader and deeper. With the city of Winnipeg now only a few hundred miles away, one sees occasional signs of human habitation, usually in the form of lonesome sportsmen's camps along the shores of otherwise uninhabited ponds and lakes. Despite its particularly harsh terrain, this country always was the most heavily traveled section of the shield. These tracks were the first of the Canadian Pacific Railway to be laid.

After canoeing over the eastern shield and then traversing the horizonless expanses of the big lakes, the voyageurs faced the trek across the western shield from Lake Superior to the forts in the Red River Valley. Winter blizzards and swarming summer black-flies added to the misery of the passage. The soldiers sent through here to quell the Riel uprising in 1869 built the Dawson Route, a crude corduroy road consisting merely of round logs laid perpendicular to the direction of travel over the rock and muskeg. Later, steamers built on the larger water sections brought the route to its greatest level of utility in 1872. Still, the now booming commerce of the fertile Red River area passed instead primarily through Minnesota.

For five years the Mackenzie government presided over half-hearted efforts to build this section of the great railway, and construction actually began in 1875. But Mackenzie was stymied by a constellation of hostile conditions. First was his own Liberal philosophy. In those days it was the Liberals who distrusted "big government" expenditures on great projects, because all too often the beneficiaries were the barons of private enterprise. Railway building was particularly suspect, so Mackenzie dramatically scaled back the commitment to the Pacific Railway and, in longstanding Liberal tradition, insisted that what remained of the plan be built and run by the government as a public work. The hard-nosed Donald Smith, disappointed by the decision but impressed by this show of conviction, said, "He is a noble man."

Second, MacKenzie had the ill-fortune to take power just as the continent was gripped by a severe depression, ironically caused by the collapse of Jay Cooke's American railroad empire. By 1877 grain prices had foundered and the lumber and mining industries were stagnant. The United States, experiencing its own version of the depression and violent strikes along its railroads, desperately dumped millions of dollars' worth of goods on the Canadian market at cut rates.

Despite Mackenzie's Liberal philosophy and credentials as a noble man, his government quickly became mired in its own style of corruption. In making the railway a public work, it contracted construction on a piecemeal basis to outfits that would have no responsibility for running the finished railway. The result was a feeding at the public trough by contractors having no commitment to building a useable line. Costs were huge, waste was rampant, and construction was a pale imitation of the Union Pacific standard that conquered the American half of the continent.

Meanwhile, the man who brought down the MacDonald government, Donald Smith, figured in the fall of its successor. The issue was control of the "Pembina route," a branch line built by Mackenzie's government from Winnipeg to the U.S. border. Smith had an interest in the line, and when he promoted it in Parliament, the House exploded like nitro contaminated by a noxious abrasive.

Conservatives had never forgiven Donald Smith. During the elections of 1874, he had stood in his stoic manner while enraged crowds drenched him with rotten eggs and tomatoes. Now, with the Liberal government beholden to him but wishing to avoid a risky blowup with conservatives in Parliament, Mackenzie attempted to shepherd through a bill that would give Smith and his partners a lease on the Pembina route without actually naming Smith.

MacDonald, knowing of Smith's involvement and of the unpopularity of the monopoly of trade that Smith's associates enjoyed in the Red River Valley, smelled blood and moved in for the kill.

On the last day of Parliament's sitting, Smith rose to defend himself against MacDonald's charges. As the messenger from the governor-general tried to enter and begin the formalities closing the session, MacDonald and his ally Charles Tupper engaged in a shouting match with Smith that replayed the treachery of 1874. Smith protested that he had never promised to support Mac-Donald's government in the Pacific Scandal vote. Tupper screamed that he had. MacDonald shouted that Smith's betrayal was done for personal profit. Smith retorted, in a thinly veiled reference to MacDonald's drinking, that MacDonald possibly didn't know what had passed between himself and Smith in interviews before the vote. The speaker called for order, but the house was now out of control.

"Coward, coward, coward," cried Tupper and the Conservative opposition took up the chant. As the speaker finally concluded the rituals of closing the session, MacDonald roared, "That fellow Smith is the biggest liar I ever saw," and with Tupper and several other Tories, rushed at him, fists raised, amid the continuing chorus of "Coward, coward, coward!" Violence was avoided, but with the Liberal government already a quivering house of cards, the upshot was the fall of Mackenzie and an unexpected landslide for MacDonald and his Conservatives in the ensuing election.

This time MacDonald presented the electorate with a true vision, "national policy," which consisted of three tenets: completion and maintenance of a transcontinental railway; aggressive recruitment of immigration for settlement of the west; and tariff barriers to prevent American dominance of the Canadian economy. The goal was a true Canadian nation, capable of guaranteeing its own independence. The policy has been a recurring theme of Canadian politics through changing leadership up until the Conservative government of Brian Mulroney, which has finally abandoned all three elements. I will discover in my travels that he did so at his peril.

MacDonald took office with no Canadian capitalists with the money, experience, and motivation to take on the task of the Pacific Railway. But the gods of irony made Canada their playground. The syndicate that would become MacDonald's and Canada's salvation was already aborning. Its first shared purpose was a railway linking Manitoba over the Pembina route to the trunk lines of the enemy to the south. Their prime mover was an American—and a Canadian expatriate at that. One member was an official of the Hudson's Bay Company, whose influence over the west the government had worked so hard to curtail. One was a president of the Bank of Montreal, whose connections to French and Liberal Canada were sure to make Tories squirm. And one was, in Conservative eyes, the devil himself.

You don't get an epic sense of travel riding by rail across the eastern United States. The miles and miles of New York or Pennsylvania, Ohio, and Indiana are so tamed that you must wait till after the Missouri crossing to feel what I am feeling as we approach Winnipeg. Near Dryden, a remarkable transformation in the landscape begins. There are a few fields tucked in amid the forest and the terrain gets flatter. Houses pass often enough that one stops remarking on them. Then the rock, muskeg, and stunted forest suddenly diffuse into memory as prosperous farms of wheat and alfalfa stretch to the horizon—the Canadian prairie.

There is a story of the Pacific Railway surveyor, Sanford Fleming, and several assistants who had stopped just short of the sudden transition to prairie because of rain, the lateness of the day, and dwindling light. After their meal of bacon and beans, the surveyors pushed on just to see this thing they had never seen before. When they stepped out of the woods, they sensed a vast opening, but it was still raining so they retired to a nearby HBC store to sleep. In the morning they looked out on the sunswept prairie and marveled at "a sea of green, sprinkled with yellow, red, lilac and white. . . . As you cannot know what the ocean is without having seen it, neither in imagination can you picture the prairie."

Canada's topographical transitions are stark and sudden; there is no slowly changing spectrum of landscape as in the United States. The same thing will happen again a thousand miles down the line when prairie gives way to mountains and again near the coast when glaciered ranges end abruptly at the Pacific shore.

At Winnipeg station there is a sorting out of passengers who have made acquaintants on the journey. My young international friends get off here to see Winnipeg. The New Zealander whose "toasties" gave us all such a fright is okay; the conductor got off at the end of his division without doing anything about it. Linda Melillo and her tour group are off for a flight to Edmonton tomorrow.

Back on board, the Skyline bar is nearly empty as we await the influx of new passengers boarding at Winnipeg. John Smith is still here and so is the leather-faced, cowboy-hatted fellow. Ignoring John's incomprehensible banter, his pale blue eyes blaze at something out there as passengers board, as the train pulls out of the station, and as the lonely lights pass in the prairie darkness west of Winnipeg.

2

Palliser's Triangle

THE *CANADIAN* FROM
WINNIPEG TO VANCOUVER

A CANADIAN expatriate, James Hill, who came to St. Paul, Minnesota, in 1856 with a passion to become a trader with the Orient, quickly recognized that the Minnesota-Manitoba area was a breeding ground for transportation empires. Like Cornelius Vanderbilt in New York, he started with steamboats.

For a century, transportation between the Red River and the Mississippi had been the monopoly of the Hudson's Bay Company. When Hill launched his steamboat operation, his project brought him into conflict with the tough-minded chief commissioner of the HBC, Donald Smith, the same man who brought down two Canadian governments. The story looms large in Canadian legend of how the two met by accident on dogsleds in a blinding blizzard in 1870, somewhere in the vastness between St. Paul and Winnipeg. There is no record of what they said to each other as they encamped and ate pemmican while the storm raged, but both stated in later years that each recognized greatness in the other and that nothing ever transpired to change that opinion.

By 1871, each also recognized that the other would never yield in their economic war, so they agreed to join forces in secret behind the facade of a steamboat company run by another Hudson's Bay official, Norman Kittson.

But boats were already fading in the mind of James Hill, who recognized that an obscure, undervalued railway, the grandiosely named St. Paul & Pacific, would someday replace the river. With his partners Smith and Kittson, he laid plans to take possession of it.

Donald Smith had a cousin who happened to be president of the Bank of Montreal. Entertained by the passionate Hill during a visit to Minnesota, George Stephen saw for himself the excitement and energy of a community of settlers at the end of track. That did it. With the backing of Dutch financiers, Smith, Hill, Kittson, and Stephen bought the St. Paul & Pacific and turned it into a gold mine.

With their control of both the river and rail connection between Winnipeg and St. Paul, the group held a monopoly of the only viable transportation to the Canadian west. Its critical link ran through the United States and its rates quickly became exorbitant. Pressure mounted on the newly reinstalled MacDonald government to expedite the building of an alternative all-Canadian rail route.

Now MacDonald had a group of experienced and successful railway builders he could turn to, ironically the very men whose monopoly provoked this latest thrust to the Pacific project. Advised to "catch them before they invest their profits," MacDonald snatched their promise to build the Pacific Railway in ten years for less than Hugh Allan had proposed.

The contract negotiated in 1880, which was tortuously pushed through Parliament over the opposition of the Liberals, established a pattern of government involvement in realms Americans regard as the province of private enterprise that has colored Canadian history and institutions ever since. As a factor in the evolution of the two great North American nations, it stands in relation to the British North America Act as the Bill of Rights does to our American Constitution—it is the post-constitutional document most responsible for the Canadian side of the difference between the two nations today.

Like the first American transcontinentals, the Canadian Pacific Railway would receive $25 million and 25 million acres in government subsidy. But the contract went on to turn over to the CPR the lines already built by the government, to exempt the CPR from import duties on materials and from property taxes, and to prohibit the construction of any competing line between the CPR route and the U.S. border for twenty years. In America, the rail monopolies that evolved from the original government contracts without these extra provisions eventually provoked an adversarial relationship between government and big business. In Canada, despite populist disenchantment with the CPR's monopoly clause, the contract stood as the model for how government and big business would collude to get things done in a nation handicapped by geography, population, and the threat of being overwhelmed by its neighbor.

Ironically, when the nation-shaping language of the contract was being written, MacDonald was much more concerned with the makeup of the syndicate. He calculated that the Conservatives could live with the Hudson's Bay Company and Bank of Montreal connections, and even the involvement of several Americans and the expatriate Hill. But Smith was too much. His involvement would have to go unacknowledged. Yet, five years later, when it came time to drive the last spike and photograph the "great Canadian portrait," it would be Donald Smith who would wield the hammer.

Tonight out of Winnipeg, I settle into the Skyline bar for what's left of the evening. John Smith proposes cards. I have noticed the signs displayed over the toilets in French and English that specifically identify gambling and spitting as offenses punishable by federal law on trains in Canada. John, of outlaw Australia, sneers at my allusion to those signs and the fact that I had a brush with the law last night and don't wish to offend again. So the game is poker and the stakes are merely our purchases from the bartender—no money on the table. John, an earnest working fellow named Dean Parkinson, and I are in. A blond woman about my age spectates while the man in the black cowboy hat continues to stare out the window.

Dean Parkinson says there is a long tradition of Americans getting away with stuff in Canada that would put them in jail at home. He is riding to Moose Jaw, where we are scheduled to stop at 4:00 A.M. and cheers every delay that might help move his debarkation into a more civilized hour of the morning.

According to Dean, Moose Jaw became the home away from home of Al Capone during the most violent years of U.S. Prohibition. Capone bought a big house there, and whenever the heat was on in Chicago he would show up in Moose Jaw—via the CPR and James Hill's connection roads to the Windy City.

45

"Capone never broke a law in Moose Jaw. In fact, he was a model citizen, supporting all the right causes and donating money to charitable aid. He was a bit of a ladies' man and had women all over town waiting for his call. A few of them still survive today and insist that he was the finest gentleman they ever knew."

But Capone did use Moose Jaw as a marshalling center for the good Canadian whiskey that fueled his mob activities in the States. That same train to Chicago that made Moose Jaw such a convenient getaway for Capone also carried his illicit product. In earlier times the problem flowed the other way and Canadians railed in high dudgeon against it; in Capone's time "folks enjoyed sending the Yanks some of their own favorite medicine."

Throughout our game, the blond woman has kibitzed over our shoulders and been downright friendly. Her name is Donna Hansen and she lives in Red Deer, Alberta. When my card partners tire and slink off to their seats after midnight as the bartender closes up, it's just me, the bearded man in the black hat, and Donna Hansen. Now he stirs and speaks to her.

"So you're from Red Deer—home of Canada's most beautiful women," he says with a slow, careless drawl.

At first I'm embarrassed to hear what sounds like a really lame come-on line, but Donna responds, "Yep, that's what they say about us. But with every birthday it gets harder for me to keep up my contribution to the legend, eh?"

It turns out that the little Alberta city of Red Deer really does have a reputation all over Canada for its beautiful women. Some say it's the sun and wind of the prairie that give a burnished glow to feminine skin. Or maybe it's the water. Some say it's the particularly strong strain of native blood in many Red Deer women, descended from marriages in which Indian wives were chosen by their white mates for possessing striking beauty. One man will insist that it's the location, midway between the populous cities of Edmonton and Calgary, where jealous men with particularly beautiful wives sequester themselves out of fear of competition from the bright lights of the big city. Whatever the explanation, I will meet half a dozen different women from Red Deer without ever having cause to doubt the legend.

The man with the black cowboy hat is John Solaris, a rancher from Strathmore, near Calgary. He is on the train because of the government's threat to cut the passenger rail service. "The calves are all in and things are slow at the ranch. So I got a Canrail pass and started riding, to do as much of it as I can before it's gone."

It's not really trains he's after but his country. "I'm not a rail buff; I never even rode a train before this summer. But I know my history. Never mind what Canada looks like on a map. It's really nothing but a thin string of places connected by the railway, places that wouldn't have given a damn about each other without the railway. Canada and the railway, since John A. MacDonald it always was one and the same thing."

John's grandfather immigrated from Latvia in the late 1890s, and John has always felt a special pride in his country because his grandfather chose it over others. "There were all sorts of promotions for immigrants in those days—from the U.S., from Australia, even from India and Africa. But my grandfather chose Canada and I always thought he made a good choice. I've flown over it, I've driven over it, but I hadn't really seen it till I did it this way."

What he has been staring at outside the window is trees. "I don't think I'll ever be really happy out on the prairie again without those trees. You grow up out there and always feel there's something missing, something that a living creature needs that ain't supplied. And then you travel east and find out what it is—trees, man, evergreens and oaks and maples and birches—the most blessed things that God ever put on this earth."

But he's not sure he could ever live way east. "In Toronto, everywhere I went people would look at my hat and beard and turn away. Unfriendliest people I ever saw. People say that Toronto's where you get a taste of what life is like in the United States. Well, I'll stay here, thank you."

When I leave to go to bed, John is describing to Donna his process for making ranch beer. The key, he says, is the stirring of the brew with a red hot poker before bottling. I initially dismiss his method as bar-car baloney. But subsequent inquiries confirm that such a step, while boiling some of the alcohol, would probably burn off all the vinegar and aldehydes that compromise the beneficial effects of alcohol and promote the hangover effect.

There was intoxication and lawlessness aplenty in the west before the coming of the railway. When the expedition against Riel had completed its task, a cadre of officers was left behind to determine what sort of military force might be needed to pacify the country west of the shield. The major problem was American whiskey traders who had established a network of forts, such as the infamous Fort Whoop-Up, flying the Stars and Stripes and peddling alcohol to Indians. The booze—a vile blend of whiskey, red pepper, ginger, and hot water—along with smallpox and the dwindling of the buffalo herds, had brought the country to an incendiary state of debauchery and desperation. The lawlessness at Fort Whoop-Up was epitomized by a now legendary letter sent to Fort Benton in Montana:

Dear friend:
My partner Will Geary got to putting on airs and I shot him and he is dead—the potatoes are looking well—
Yours truly,
Snookum Jim

In a dispute over stolen horses, a drunken group of Americans from Fort Benton set upon an Indian encampment in Cypress Hills and raped and killed squaws and children. Something had to be done.

In one of his final acts during his first term in office, John MacDonald authorized the creation of a military force, at least one third to be mounted, and labeled "police" to avoid a challenge to the U.S. cavalry south of the border. The police's original purpose was specifically to "rid the plains of Americans" north of the border. The first unit of the North West Mounted Police (later renamed the Royal Canadian Mounted Police) were issued British-style red jackets and black breeches and American-style Texas Stetsons and moved west in 1874 by the only route then available, a train through the United States. On board they had to travel unarmed in civilian clothes, with their weapons packed in crates in the baggage car.

Beyond the railhead in Minnesota, the Mounties rode in their own epic trek to the western prairie. At first they were mocked as greenhorns, but the denizens of Fort Whoop-Up fled as news arrived that a serious military force was approaching. Colonel James McLeod established a fort near the Blackfeet and imprisoned a few American whiskey traders and poured their wares on the ground. When news of this action reached the wise chief of the Blackfeet, Crowfoot, he was impressed and rode to the fort to announce that "The law of the Great White Mother must be good when she has such a son as you." The Blackfeet had despised Americans ever since the killing of two of their ancestors by the Lewis and Clark party in 1805.

McLeod built another fort at a place he called Calgary and continued to impress Crowfoot by prosecuting those of his own men who trespassed against the Blackfeet. When Sitting Bull asked for Blackfeet to join him in the conflict that led to the Little Big Horn, Crowfoot refused saying instead that, if need be, he would defend Canadians against the Sioux.

After the massacre of Custer and his men, Sitting Bull and the Sioux fled to the Cypress Hills in Canada where they encountered a lone white soldier accompanied by a Blackfoot scout. It was Mountie James Walsh who rode into their camp and offered them protection if they obeyed the laws of the Great White Mother. He was given a lodge to sleep in but was awakened during the night with questions—"What are the laws?" He answered that killing, raping, stealing, giving false testimony, and injuring people or property were forbidden and went back to sleep.

Eventually the Mounties rounded up some of the American perpetrators of the Cypress Hills massacre. Though American courts let them off easy in the extradition process, the legend spread that "the Mounties always got their man." The Indians took note and remained obedient to a force a fraction of the size of the U.S. cavalry, which failed to win the respect of their brethren to the south.

That same force from the south wanted the Sioux who had wiped out Custer. In the latter 1870s the Mounties walked a shaky tightrope between the armed Sioux encamped on their side of the border and the U.S. cavalry that threatened to come and get them. Eventually, with the disappearance of the buffalo herds caused largely by the building of transcontinental rail routes in the United States, the Indians began to starve. In its own most shameless episode of Indian relations, the Canadian government withheld food until the Sioux departed for American reservations and the Canadian Indians accepted terms relegating them to Canadian reservations. When the tracks of the CPR began to creep into the western prairie, the country was pacified—Americans and Indians were out of the way.

In the morning I have breakfast with Donna Hansen as the dry Saskatchewan plain drifts by outside. We have passed through most of the grain country during the night, and now, as we approach Maple Creek, the livestock ranches of the high prairie country begin to appear. To the north, we can see small bodies of sparkling blue water surrounded by what appear to be shorelines of crusty snow. These are the prairie sloughs, and the "snow" is the mineral deposits of sodium and calcium sulfate that are left behind as the shorelines contract from summer evaporation. To the south, we can see a bluish skyline of low mountains, the Cypress Hills, an anomalously forested range poking its hard caprock above the glacier-scraped flatness of the prairie.

The train stops briefly at Maple Creek, where whitewashed buildings line Main Street. Donna is in high spirits. She is returning to her home in Red Deer by her favorite mode of travel after a visit to her family in Kirkland Lake, in northern Ontario. She says she doesn't know where the government gets its figures showing that relatively few Canadians travel by train. Everyone she knows in Red Deer and Calgary uses the train to visit relatives in the far-flung corners of the country. "People will take a bus as far as Edmonton [three and a half hours]—that's about the limit, but no one would think of traveling that way to Vancouver or Toronto. And in the winter you just don't drive those distances. You can fly, of course, but it's so damned expensive."

Throughout the Canadian prairie, the railway is still associated with family, hearth, and home in a way that is hard for Americans to imagine today. Despite the fact that the majority of American settlers of the wide-open western spaces got there by train, our national mythology fixates on the earlier wagon trains as the national symbol of homesteading. Canada never had a wagon train era; most of its western settlers traveled by train and their descendants still do. Settlements grew up in thin corridors following the westering railways. Despite Canada's vaster area and significantly smaller rail network, a far greater percentage of Canadians live near a working railway station today than do Americans. In the Canadian prairie, it is the link of the railway that continues to make it possible for people to live in such wide-open spaces so far north.

Donna owns a beauty salon in Red Deer and her husband is a thriving seed and feed merchant, but her route to this station in life deviates from that of the typical American businesswoman. When she first tells me about it this morning over breakfast, I think I have met a Canadian sport. Eventually I will come to recognize her tale as an archetype of a life path uniquely Canadian, uniquely shaped by the limitations and opportunities provided by Canadian geography.

Donna's mother had ten kids in Kirkland Lake. Life was plain and hard there, but Donna was taught that her parents chose life in a remote shield town because it was safe; cities were dangerous and unfriendly. Folks living amid the lakes and granite hills knew what was important—family and community, the changing seasons and the lessons of the natural land.

Donna knew there had to be more excitement in the world, and at sixteen she ran away to Toronto to seek her fortune as a model. "There were a lot of girls like me rebelling against that parochial Canadian upbringing. Read Margaret Atwood and you'll learn that in Canada the angry young rebel is female." In Toronto she found a handful of modeling jobs and a husband who, after she bore him a child, turned out to be a wife-beater. She got a divorce and headed for Baffin Island for a new life.

There, with child in tow, she worked as a cook for a construction crew building a dam, then moved on to work at Baker Lake in the Northwest Territories. Her ingrained memory of those years is of sun dogs, those spectral columns of light that frame the sun in far northern climes. She recalls that their image reflected the quality of her life in the far north. "Nothing made any sense in those days. You Americans were supposed to be fighting Communism in Southeast Asia but the only Americans I ever saw were draft dodgers, who were good fine people."

She had a boyfriend in her construction team, and at Baker Lake, an Inuit chief made the traditional offer of a swap of his wife for her. When she and her boyfriend declined, the effect was to spur the man on to a campaign of courtship. He offered fish, sealskins, bear claws, whalebone. He was particularly enamored because she resembled so closely his favorite model in a year-old fashion magazine. Donna's boyfriend finally got a look at the model in the magazine and it was, of course, Donna, in one of the few spots she had wrangled during her days in the Toronto modeling scene. Finally the chief's frustration reached a point where Donna's presence in Baker Lake came to be a problem and she left, with her son, for Kirkland Lake.

Nothing had changed there. "I thought it would be this fantastic homecoming—the return of the prodigal daughter. But I found out you can't go back. Everything I had done since I left was suspect. I couldn't breathe there." She headed west with a man who told her about the freedom of the prairie.

She married the man and settled in Red Deer. Today she laughs that some of her attraction to Red Deer is the same as her parents' for Kirkland Lake. "Life is simple and elemental on the prairie. Sun, sky, earth, weather, friends, family, work." And she has watched her story begin to repeat itself with her sixteen-year-old son, who has just left home with his girlfriend without finishing high school. "It started out with some pretty scary satanic stuff, but I think that was just a phase. Now they're in Calgary making their own way." Donna cares but is not devastated. She believes you can do better than your parents did, but you probably can't get it right within one generation. "You just can't live for your kids—and if you have your own life, maybe you won't have time to screw theirs up too much."

Outside the train we can see tumbleweeds blowing in the hot summer wind. Donna remembers her first trip out west by car when, despite her adventurous travels up north, she felt like a neophyte voyageur gushing over the "real tumbleweeds" and antelope.

John Solaris slouches into the diner and joins us over coffee. "No more trees," he grumbles. As we approach Medicine Hat, we can see a perfectly defined thunderstorm on the horizon with its anvil-shaped cloudtops. Dull flickers of lightning pulse within it like a flashing light inside a brown paper bag. "Now if we had trees on the prairie, a fellow could find shelter from those sons o' bitches," says John. I remind him that standing under a tree is the worst place to be in a thunderstorm and he looks at me with that "you are an idiot" look he does so well and says, "Why?"

Suddenly I realize that, living all his life in a place without trees, he honestly doesn't know what I am talking about. I explain and he says, "Bullshit. If you're not under a tree, you're the tallest thing on the prairie, so what the hell." And then he confesses his fear of lightning. Once he and two of his ranch hands were bringing in some steers on horseback when a sudden thunderstorm exploded out of the dusty wind without warning. "One minute it was hot and dry with the dust so thick you couldn't see the sun and the next minute the sky went from brown to black and the air just went wet." There were no warning thunder rolls but the cattle were spooked. "They all laid down and then my buddy and his horse just went off like a giant flashbulb. There was a kind of quiet pop a split second before the thunder crack and then they were down on the ground steamin'—stone dead, both of 'em."

That was the only time John ever saw anyone struck by a bolt, but he has been "bitten" by electrical storms himself a number of times. "The clouds roll by about a hundred feet off the ground just cracklin'—biting you on the ass with little jolts all the time. You just tell yourself that you'll never feel the big one."

Donna concurs with John that thunderstorms are only one of the things that make prairie living so tough. There are also the periods of drought, when prairie people would gladly accept the risk of lightning just to see some precious moisture. In winter, of course, there are the blizzards and in spring the mud, "like quick-drying black concrete." Both agree that the railway men who correctly foresaw that this land could be settled and profitably exploited must have been half-crazy or divinely inspired. Certainly it might never have been inhabited without them.

For twenty years, the Pacific survey had based its explorations on the legacy of John P. Palliser and Henry H. Hind and Sanford Fleming, who established the northerly route through the fertile belt of the Saskatchewan Valley and today's Edmonton. A half-dozen passes and routes to different Pacific termini were charted, all assuming the fertile belt route along the North Saskatchewan River Valley across the prairie. In British Columbia, the debate over routes became so heated that the island of Vancouver almost seceded from the province, which was threatening to secede from the confederation. Through all of this a southern route, close to the U.S. border, was rejected because of the belief that Palliser's Triangle, an arid area bounded by the U.S. border, the North Saskatchewan River Valley, and the Rocky Mountains, was an uninhabitable desert. Southern passes through the Rockies were neglected despite explorer Francis Moberley's serendipitous discovery of Eagle Pass through one of the westernmost ranges and his prophetic carving on a tree, "This is the route of the Pacific Railway."

Accompanying the surveyors on some of their journeys was a botanist, John Macoun, whose crossing of Palliser's Triangle during a relatively wet period convinced him it was not the desert that everyone thought it to be. He became a fanatic on the notion of a southerly route and in James Hill in particular found a receptive audience. On the strength of Macoun's testimony, Hill sent an American surveyor, Major A.B. Rogers, to search for southerly passes overlooked by previous surveys. But even before Rogers's return, Hill declared to his colleagues that the route would cross Palliser's

Triangle and the Rockies through as yet undiscovered passes. With that decision, twenty years of surveying were discarded and the shape of Canada was fundamentally altered.

Historians debate the motives behind the fateful change of route. Reasons put forward include: that the new route was shorter than the original; that there was a fear of penetration by American lines into the southerly prairie; that a route across the triangle would create its own communities dependent on the railway while the northerly route would serve already established towns; that the southerly route would tap coal deposits in Alberta. Probably all of these played a part, but considering the fact that it was James Hill who promoted the change, another possibility emerges. Hill became a Canadian expatriate who eventually built his own American transcontinental, the Great Northern, just as close to the border on the U.S. side. Perhaps he was a forerunner of today's global business magnates to whom national boundaries are not obstacles but arenas of opportunity.

However motivated, the change of route is responsible for the string of prairie towns just north of the border—Brandon, Regina, Moose Jaw, Medicine Hat, and even Calgary. As the railway pushed west during the early 1880s, immigrants from Scotland, Ireland, and England answered the call. Land speculators swarming over the prairie just ahead of the workers quickly learned about one of the advantages to the CPR of the new route across virgin land—through the siting of tracks, stations, and services, the railway could make or break them. Paralleling the successful towns lies a string of ghost towns just off the line, founded by real estate sharks who thought they could anticipate the exact route and thus demand high prices from the railway for land. In case after case, slight adjustments to the route left the high hopes of its would-be manipulators flapping in the dusty wind at isolated spots just a few miles away from places that became booming towns.

Americans who have read in high school English classes O. E. Rolvaag's tragic novel of life on the northern prairie, *Giants in the Earth,* cannot look on these empty lands without hearing echoes of the prairie woman's desperate cry ". . . nothing to hide behind." Prairie Canadians harken to a different legacy of the prairie woman, set down in the memoirs of May Clark Davis, who immigrated from England to Regina with her family at the age of nine. Regina was then nothing more than an encampment of tents amid mud, but still this was not the place. Her father dragged his family thirteen miles farther into the open prairie, where he nearly killed himself attempting to build a log house. There were times of terror, such as the night her parents got lost in the prairie and the six terrified children huddled in their windblown tent for twelve hours, never expecting to see them again. Sometimes subsisting on shrubs and wild berries, the children seldom had enough to eat during those first awful years. The first winter sent the family staggering back to Regina to join a seasonal crowd of settlers who couldn't yet make it on their homesteads.

But somehow the family eventually prospered and Mrs. Davis's memoirs record the reverse image of Rolvaag's dark prairie woman. When she published them at the age of eighty-one, they revealed a lifetime of love for the scenes of the prairie—the wildflowers exploding like fireworks from the spring grasses, the promise of infinite possibility in the huge sky, the mornings like an invitation to participate in the beginning of the world. There were thousands who came to see Palliser's Triangle that way, and despite the eventual building of the northerly route through the more fertile Saskatchewan valley, many are still here.

At Medicine Hat, the train makes a short refueling stop and Donna, John, and I step off to stretch our legs. Like so many prairie and shield stations along our route, this one bustles with activity as the fuel trucks pull up beside the engines. There aren't really many people getting on and off, maybe a half-dozen each way, but a lot of mail seems to be handled at these places and there are always another dozen or more folks who just stop by the station for a cup of coffee, a smoke, some local gossip, and a moment of contact with the rest of the world as the *Canadian* makes its stop. They all seem to know the train crew personally and are full of inquiries about the state of things out on the line. "Any trouble with livestock on the tracks back at Maple Creek?" "Have they finished with that trestle yet?" "Heard there was a fire on Main Street in Swift Current, eh?" "How many grain cars did you pass yesterday?"

I assume that most of these people's work has something to do with ranching till John explains, "No, most of 'em grow flowers and vegetables." He gives me a minute to wonder how anyone grows flowers and vegetables out on the dry prairie before explaining that one of Medicine Hat's biggest industries is greenhouses, watered by a tremendous underground aquifer of cool water that runs just beneath the town's hot, dusty streets.

Donna reminds me to set back my watch an hour, so it's only 9:30 in the morning and already it's hot here. Because you set back your watch three times (four if you begin on Atlantic time in Nova Scotia) in the transcontinental trek, the days seem to grow longer and hotter as you travel west. I imagine that, by Vancouver, my night owl habits will finally coincide with the routine of the rest of humanity.

We haven't time for much of a stroll around the town, just the rail station neighborhood, which comes to be so standard in all these towns that they blur together in memory. The street the station is located on is seldom the main drag; it usually runs a block away or else intersects with the railway front street at right angles near the station. The downtown bustles with prosperous shops carrying the familiar brands I might find in my own town back in New Hampshire. The mix of autos on the street differs little from what I might see in any western American town—Chevy and Ford pickups, four-wheel-drive Jeep wagons, lots of Japanese cars, maybe fewer Audis and BMWs and more well-maintained big American sedans from the sixties and seventies. Across the tracks, the switching operations of the CPR freight division enlivens the railyards to a degree not seen in many U.S. towns. No rusted tracks here. The cargo is mostly grain, and some carloads of Japanese cars and western lumber. Towering over everything a quarter-mile down the line are the ubiquitous Canadian prairie grain elevators.

"Welcome to Alberta," says Donna as the three of us take turns posing for pictures with the elevators as backdrop. I hadn't thought of that. Somehow it seemed that we would have to be in Saskatchewan till we reached the mountains that one usually associates with Alberta. Alberta turns out to be Canada's most varied province—the eastern half prairie, the western mountains, the southern half hot and arid, the northern cold and arctic. Much of it is fundamentally rural, yet it is the only province besides Ontario that boasts two cities the size and significance of Calgary and Edmonton. There are still prairie homesteads here where farmers scratch out a meager living, and yet the economy is dominated by big ranches, the boom in oil, and some of Canada's richest men. Dry alkali lake beds and glistening, eternal glaciers; lonely high plains dirt roads and skyscrapered Calgary streets; cattle dust and skiers' powder; leathery ranchers and three-piece-suit yuppies; grim-faced native people and the ravishing women of Red Deer—Alberta defies characterization with a single image.

Back on the train, John, Donna, and I settle into the rear Park car lounge for the last of the run into Calgary where they will detrain. The rear brakeman, a young fellow with long sideburns and loud opinions, declaims that the essence of Alberta is rebellion. "Westerners don't like most things handed down from the federal government—'looneys' [dollar coins featuring a loon in the design], motorcycle helmet laws, seat belt laws, taxes, special treatment for Catholics and Indians. Once a nation becomes a nation, all you need is a postal service, a national transportation system including good railroads, a communications system, paper money, and maybe an army. Today Mulroney wants to back out of all those things and just give us the things we don't want."

The approach to Calgary reminds me of Denver, Colorado. John says the skyline just sprouted when the oil boom began. "Half the people here are transplanted easterners who came here thinking the streets were lined with gold. Then there was the Olympics. Now we're just getting back to reality."

"And what's reality?" I ask.

"Well, that the oil money couldn't solve everybody's problems— the winter still rolls in, people still get divorced, friends die, taxes go up, and there still ain't any trees."

As the train wends through the Calgary yards, there is a bustle on board as a large number of passengers prepare to detrain. Walking the length of the train, I hear one conversation played over and over by people rubbernecking at the windows—all commenting on the newest additions to the skyline.

In the station, I get off to say farewell to John and Donna. Donna invites me to stop in for a haircut in Red Deer sometime; John Solaris reminds me that this is a short stop for him to check up on his ranch. He'll be out on the rails again in a few days. We compare itineraries and discover that there is a good chance we'll be riding the same train from Winnipeg to Edmonton about a week from now. When I take my leave from them, John is offering, for the tenth time, to show Donna his ranch and how he makes his high-test ranch beer.

In 1875, before the coming of the railway, Mountie Colonel McLeod chose a site for a post, first called Fort Brisebois and then Calgary, after a Scottish island castle. The name in Gaelic means "clear running water," and early settlers rhapsodized about the first place of beauty they had seen in over a thousand miles. At the fork of the Bow and Elbow rivers just beyond the end of Palliser's Triangle, Calgary in those days had clear water and trees, "thick woods bordering the banks of both streams," according to an early settler, and heavier timber rising up the foothills to the snowy peaks of the Rockies. For nearly a decade, Calgary flourished as a center for Mounties, HBC traders, and missionaries working among the Indians ravaged by the Americans' rotgut.

By 1883, all that had changed as the railway approached. The woods were cut down and the place was quickly turned into the latest of the series of grim mud and tent cities that sprang up across the prairie in front of the railhead. When the man who would become Calgary's first mayor arrived to set up a harness shop, he complained of the lack of trees for lumber and the isolation of this place at the very end of the earth. An era was ending and the first harbingers of the new one to come were less than promising—especially for the oldest inhabitants of the region.

The native peoples of the northwest had lived through nearly a century of contact with white men. It is little remarked these days that those were their best years—nostalgically remembered by later generations and often mistakenly ascribed to the last generations before the coming of the white men. The horses and the weapons introduced by the whites established the brief golden age of the native North American peoples.

But even without the ravages of the Americans' whiskey, the disappearance of the buffalo and the division of the prairie by the railway in the 1880s would have reduced the tribes to a state of desperate starvation. As it was, starvation was accompanied by the inevitable disintegration of tribal values and authority brought on by alcohol.

With the hindsight provided by the earlier dismal experience of the Americans south of the border, the Canadian government at least had a plan. For a time it would be necessary to feed the native people as a public program. Eventually, it was hoped, they could be taught an agrarian life-style on reservations in the fertile lands north of their traditional hunting grounds. The program had little chance of success.

Yet it almost worked, largely due to the emergence of two native leaders of far-seeing wisdom—Poundmaker of the Cree and

Crowfoot of the Blackfeet. Watching the railway approach from the east, Poundmaker declared to his people in 1881: "It is useless to dream that we can frighten [the whites]; that time is past. Our only resource is our work, our industry, and our farms. Send your children to school . . . if you want them to prosper and be happy." Crowfoot, who still commanded the strongest Indian fighting force in the west, took a tougher stance, ordering the railway builders to stop work when they encroached upon Blackfeet lands. The CPR turned to Father Albert Lacombe, the Catholic missionary whose work among the Blackfeet had earned their trust for more than a decade. He spoke to Crowfoot and his council, arguing that the railway answered to the just law of the white man's chiefs and that the governor himself would come out and listen to the Blackfeet's grievances. If his offer of compromise was unsatisfactory, that would be the time to order the railway builders off the land.

Crowfoot responded, "The advice of the Chief of Prayer is good. We shall do what he asks." Meanwhile he took the audacious step of personally asking a trusted NWMP colonel what he thought of the Blackfeet's chances of fighting off the railroad. When the colonel responded that it would be like trying to hold back the waters of the Bow, Crowfoot kept his armed braves in place but palavered with the government and CPR officials. Thus Crowfoot became the only chieftain who ever earned for his people a significant grant of land from a railroad beyond the reservation lands of government treaties.

The Canadian government never deliberately went to war with its Indians as the Americans did. There is a temptation for a visitor to credit the Canadians with too much enlightenment—the Canadian native peoples also had the gloomy lessons of the violent conflict to the south to learn from, and they were occasionally deliberately starved when they proved recalcitrant—but there can be no question that the Mounties engendered a different order north of the border. When the last desperate spasm of violence finally did come, a groundwork had been laid for its resolution.

Sam Steele and his men were the quintessential representatives of the Mounties' moral force during these years. As acting adjutant for the district from Fort Qu'Appelle to Calgary during the westward march of the railway, he came to epitomize, along with Walsh and McLeod, the image of the Canadian west and its association with law and order rather than the anarchy of the American west. His mandate made him arresting officer, prosecutor, judge, and jury, yet his reputation for fair play rose above this deviation from Anglo-Saxon concepts of fair jurisprudence.

The story is legendary of how two of Steele's sergeants rode into the camp of the Cree, Piapot, which was deliberately set astride the right-of-way of the approaching tracklayers. One of the sergeants announced that the Indians had fifteen minutes to move. When time was up and young braves were galloping about firing rifles into the air, the sergeant dismounted and kicked in the struts of Piapot's teepees. The Indians offered no fight and another image was added to the Mounties' scrapbook of scenes of invincibility. Yet the story, hallowed in Canadian literature of the west, is really tragically atypical. It would not be long before such conduct with the increasingly desperate and emboldened tribes would become unthinkable. More often the Mounties earned the Indians' respect with just dealings and by joining them in common cause against the whiskey-peddling enemy.

A new flood of American liquor kept Steele's Mounties busy during the 1880s. Hidden in wells, abandoned steam engines, the nitro cans of navvies carrying the red flag, carcasses of dead horses, eggshells, imitation Bibles, vegetable tins, and, in at least one case, the false pregnancy of a prairie woman, the stuff poured in. Mounties themselves were expected to bring "some good rye" back for their fellows from visits to the wet towns back east, and permits were obtainable for a gallon or two for "medicinal purposes."

Sam Steele enforced Prohibition, and thereby earned the continuing respect of native chiefs who saw in demon rum the ruin of their people. But he resented it profoundly and became perhaps one of North America's first outspoken anti-Prohibitionists, arguing vehemently that "the prohibitory law made more drunkards than if there had been an open bar and free drinks at every street corner." He further feared that in making illegal a natural human inclination, the government was creating an unnecessary incitement to lawlessness. In this Steele was years before his time, describing conditions that did not truly obtain until twentieth-century Prohibition and anti-marijuana laws, but in his own era, historians are unanimous that Steele's reluctant war on whiskey helped the CPR to accomplish its task in half the time promised under the contract.

Back on the train after Calgary, I sit with the young Australian, John Smith, in the observation dome of the Skyline car for the ride into the Rockies. I haven't seen much of him for nearly a thousand miles because he has been nursing a furious hangover from last night, after Winnipeg. "Didn't miss moech, did oy—jes a feeyoo moyles o' droy empty spice—gutta lutta that in Ahstrighlyuh." But he's excited about the climb into the Rockies and so is a young English traveler he has made friends with who sits across the aisle from us. Sheila, of Nottingham, is appalled by what we have just crossed.

"I thought we'd never get to the end of it," she groans. "I don't care if they grow enough wheat there to feed the world; people weren't meant to live on the moon." She says that the saddest thing she ever heard was a story the service chief told her about a dying woman who once rode his train to Medicine Hat. The woman had lived for twenty years in Toronto when she contracted cancer. It was detected early so her doctors thought they could beat it, and she spent a year on chemotherapy. When the doctors decided they were losing the battle and gave her a few weeks to live, she started dreaming of Medicine Hat every night. She had no family there anymore, but she told her daughter to take her on the train to Medicine Hat to die. Her daughter and other family members tried to talk her out of it—what was in Medicine Hat now that the family had all moved to Toronto? She had grown up on the prairie and wanted to die there.

The service chief remembers her boarding the *Canadian* in Toronto with her daughter and her oxygen machines. In Sudbury, they tried to take her off, because she had had convulsions and they didn't want her to die on the train, but she fought to stay in her bedroom. She spent much of the first night retelling events from her childhood on the prairie to anyone who paused at her open door. Her recollections, filtered through several tellers of the story, remind me immediately of the raptures of the prairie woman, May Clark Davis—the warmth of the rich soil under bare feet at midday, the shimmering veils of an approaching summer squall line, the sound at night of lonesome horns of CPR freights. At Thunder Bay, the woman lapsed into unconsciousness and again the crew wanted to put her off the train. This time the daughter barred the bedroom door and tearfully threatened violence to anyone who tried to move her mother. By the second evening in Winnipeg, the woman had rallied and listed for her daughter the places she wanted to see in Medicine Hat, but in the morning, she was ashen and couldn't breathe. She died just after Maple Creek, less than fifty miles from her home.

The story casts a pall of gloom over the exuberance John and I were feeling about the approach of the Rockies, and even the weather seems to respond. Outside, low clouds thicken as we climb higher into the mountains. By the time we reach Banff, the murk is so dense we have given up any hope of seeing the magnificent vistas for which this train is famous. I console myself with the thought that after a day in Vancouver, my itinerary calls for me to ride back this way to Winnipeg. Surely the weather will have cleared by then.

Though we have left Palliser's Triangle behind, it still dominates conversation in the rear Park lounge during the evening ride through the cloud-shrouded mountains. Several of the passengers here are former prairie dwellers transplanted to Vancouver, returning home after visits with relatives. Our service chief, J. B. MacLean, is also a prairie native now residing in Vancouver.

"There's less and less to go back to in Saskatchewan every time," says one of the passengers. "Houses that were my best friends' homes are now abandoned and boarded up. Seems like everybody with any spirit or initiative has moved out."

Another agrees. "I had to be dragged by my husband kicking and screaming. But he was right. Back on the prairie I just had no idea how much more there could be to life in a place like Vancouver."

Nods all around the room. "I don't even go back for visits anymore," says J.B. "Too depressing. Last time I was in Maple Creek, the pastor in church offered a prayer for more people to move into town. I just said my own little prayer asking for more of the people I cared about in Maple Creek to come out and join me in Vancouver."

There is more discussion of the advantages of Canada's great Pacific city over the prairie, then one of the passengers who has remained silent speaks up. "But you know, sometimes when we've had a lot of rain and I get tired of looking at city streets, I dream about a sunny prairie morning, with the wheat all golden and the sky so big you think you can do anything."

The comment brings everybody up short. After a momentary silence, J.B. confesses, "I guess we all know that one."

As we approach Vancouver along the broad Fraser River in the morning, I am struck by the color of the world outside the train windows—a deep almost electric green. After the crossing of the arid prairie, these pastures and vegetable farms look unreal, as if local agricultural boosters had applied a heavy green transparency over the windows of the train during the night just to impress us with the lushness of their world. But the contrast with the purple and gray mountains that rise above the delta valley in the distance testifies that this is indeed real—and that it is a place a transcontinental traveler cannot help but instantly love. No wonder John A. MacDonald moved heaven and earth to tie it to his new Canadian nation.

Soon the rural fields give way to the streets and buildings of Vancouver but still the green persists. Never have I seen a city so infused with trees, shrubbery, grass, and gardens. Surrounded by water and towering mountains that are never out of sight, Vancouver makes one imagine that here one could live the life of a city dweller without ever losing touch with the earth.

So finally I detrain to the CN Main Street station after the three-thousand-mile trek across the continent. The station is a fitting monument to the end of the journey, a vaulted hall dominated by a magnificent brass clock hanging over the information desk in its center. Though it only serves four trains daily—two arrivals and two departures—it bustles at train time with activity. At one end a little restaurant serves diner-style meals; there is a newsstand, a barbershop, a traveler's assistance center, and the traditional hard wooden highbacked benches for waiting passengers.

Outside a line of taxis idle, ready to whisk passengers to downtown hotels. From the curb I can see a city skyline that is impressive without being intimidating. Construction cranes testify to growth and nearby a modernistic elevated light rail commuter line contrasts with the antiquated rail equipment I have just traveled on. In the distance the peaks of the Coast Mountains tower above everything, their white tops just peeking through breaks in the clouds.

I've experienced a variety of feelings stepping from long train rides in strange cities, ranging from disorientation to exhaustion to anxiety to outright revulsion. This morning I'm cheered to find this bustling green place at the very end of the continent, and when I spot J.B. coming through the doors, I tell him so.

"I hear that a lot, you know. What it is about Vancouver—here it is all by itself out here beyond the mountains, north of your border, and it's big enough, warm enough, civilized enough, and lively enough that you feel like you don't need the rest of the world. Vancouver's got everything that Toronto or Montreal has, probably most of what New York has, without the crime, the rush, and the dirt. You want me to show you some of it tomorrow? I could pick you up at your hotel."

So it is that I spend a day in Vancouver driving around with a train companion as a tour guide. The streets are wet from one of Vancouver's ubiquitous showers and people carry umbrellas, even though now the sun is out. Our first stop is Granville Island, a historic area recently developed as a traditional market. Though people come here to shop, gawk, and mingle as they do at a mall, there are no sprawling parking lots and few amenities for the automobile-bound. Most of the people come here on foot or by mass transit. The developers have eschewed the sterility and orderliness of a modern mall for the communal anarchy of a county fair. There is no Muzak but the hubbub of the crowds and the voices of hawkers. A variety of sometimes confused aromas—at one point incense mingled with fried foods—assault the nose. Underfoot there may be gravel, pavement, tile, or dirt. Shipments arrive by the front doors so that one sometimes has to maneuver around piles of cartons and boxes. J.B. couldn't have picked a better starting point for a visitor in search of a change of scene.

We drive across the bridge over False Creek and cruise the high-rise area of the West End, which J.B. explains rivals Manhattan for population density. I notice a tremendous racial and ethnic mix in the fashionably dressed people walking the streets.

In the lovely Stanley Park, located at the western extremity of the peninsula of Vancouver, I see scores of lone joggers on paths winding into dense woods—anyone doing the same thing in New York's Central Park would have to be crazy. Along English Bay, where families and couples have spread their blankets on the still damp grass for picnics, we spot half a dozen huge ships out in the harbor. Down Georgia Street past the pricey hotels all the way to Gastown, I begin to marvel at the display of affluence and ask J.B. if Vancouver has become a two-class society with no comfortable middle, as has so much of America.

In response, he drives south on the Granville Bridge back over False Creek and into the vast residential areas extending from here all the way to the University of British Columbia south and west of English Bay. For block after block we pass through the tidy neighborhoods of Kitslano, Arbutus, Shaughnessy, and Dunbar. The streets are tree-lined and the houses surrounded by hedges, flowers, and well-groomed little lawns. The bungalows display a fantastic range of styles and designs, yet all have two things in common—they are not new and they are impeccably maintained. Mothers stroll their young and gather in little knots of neighborliness at corners. It's an idyll out of a children's book of neighborhoods.

"Who can afford to live here?" I ask.

"Teachers, cops, assembly-line workers, reporters—and even VIA employees like me." Then he makes a turn and points out the charming pink stucco bungalow just visible between tall hedges and bushes that is his home.

In the afternoon, J.B. takes me to the VIA maintenance yards where workers virtually put the old *Canadian*'s cars back together after every westbound run. As we stroll around watching men make frantic repairs to air-conditioning units, toilets, steam lines, and galleys, J.B. tells me how he came to live in Vancouver. "I grew up in the flatlands of Saskatchewan. Took my first trip to Vancouver on the train when I was twenty-one and it was like in the movie *The Wizard of Oz*, when everything went from black and white to color once you were out of Kansas. It wasn't any one thing—the warm climate, the friendly neighborhoods, the good food, the symphony, the gardens, the international ambience, the pretty girls in their fashionable clothes—it was how all of those things combined to make the place almost magical. This is home now."

J.B. drops me off at the station a couple of hours before the departure of my train headed back to Winnipeg. As a parting shot he tells me a joke about the pastor complaining that it's hard to motivate Vancouverites with the promise of heaven—they think they're already there.

After he's gone, I park my bags in a locker and set out on foot toward a highway overpass about two blocks away from the station. Out of sheer cussedness, there's something I want to see if I can find. It doesn't take long. Under the bridge, three or four sleeping street people lay sprawled in the shade during the warmth of afternoon. You can see the same people on any street of San Francisco and Seattle, but here I had to look to find them. One of the men sits up and panhandles me for a dollar. I oblige and in return have a question for him. "How did you come to be here?"

His hair is graying and his face is dirty, but when he speaks, a glint of intelligence sparkles in his eyes. "I guess you'd call me a drifter. Walked away from a Saskatchewan farm, a lot of us did that, you know. Never could hold a job. Moving west is all I'm good at—and from here ya can't go any further."

3

Centrifugal Force

Vancouver to Winnipeg
on the *Canadian*

ASTERNERS don't give a damn about this train. That's
why we might lose it," says Brent, a young man who runs a
pizza business in Vancouver, to the gathering of travelers settling
comfortably into the cushioned chairs of the Park lounge as the
Canadian pulls out of Vancouver bound east. Besides the usual
handful of traveling retirees, the group tonight includes two college
students from Switzerland, Nicole and Karin, who are crossing the
continent in a round-the-world "young voyageurs" trip. Three young
Muslim women from Kenya and Tanzania who have been studying at
the University of British Columbia are delighted to make two
friends from their favorite European country, and they form a
fivesome that is indivisible, despite Brent's best efforts to seduce
the Swiss. There is a middle-aged forester from Lillooet returning
to visit his family in Qu'Appelle, and a young man and a woman who
seems to be his only slightly older girlfriend. She is tall and ath-
letically built with tawny skin, wide-set greenish eyes, and long,
thick dark-reddish hair. The prominent cheekbones make me think
"Metis" every time I look at her.

The forester agrees with Brent and adds, "B.C. ought to consider secession if they cancel this train."

The conductor has just come through and, apparently already acquainted with the forester, reacts to the allusion to secession. "Here you go again," he says. "People are always getting on my train to go see people they love in other parts of Canada and then start talking about secession. We got the best standard of living in the world, we can finally start standing up to the Yanks—apologies to any present—and all Canadians want to talk about is breaking it all up and giving it all away. Give me a break."

"I know, I know," says the forester, "but what about Quebec, you're not going to say we should give away the store to keep them in, are you? And that's just what Mulroney's done at Meech Lake." At the aspersion to the French, I think I see a flush color the tawny features of the woman with the young boyfriend and I think again, "Metis?"

"Okay," says the conductor, "let Quebec go if we have to. Let the Yanks have 'em, with maybe an international corridor across the Eastern Townships or something. But besides the Quebec foolishness, the rest of us ought to be able to get along together."

"Provincial autonomy, eh?" growls Brent. "Special deals for Newfoundland and Nova Scotia, too. That's all that is. It's not just Quebec. They're telling us that we westerners have got to help pay for the basket cases down east."

The "Metis" woman leans forward to speak, and instantly all eyes and ears are intent upon her. She speaks in a fluid, mellifluous voice without hesitation or deference before this company of opinionated men. "The problem is that Canadians in all the different provinces don't really like each other very much. We're like a couple in a failing marriage too timid to either declare our love or make the break."

Silence. The simile is a little too intimate and an unspoken recrimination implies that she has hung out too much dirty laundry before the curious eyes of foreigners. To establish her point, she rhetorically asks, "What happened when God sliced up the brain of a Frenchman singing '*Auprès de ma Blonde*'?" Three male voices chime almost in unison, "The guy started singing Newfie drinking songs."

The woman has broken the awkward spell and made her point in one deft gesture. For the remainder of the hour until the call to dinner, the conversation degenerates into the telling of the intraprovincial jokes that Canadians delight in as Americans revel in ethnic jokes.

Indeed, Canada's centrifugal tendencies seem as strong as ever. Except for the Civil War, Americans have never experienced the feeling of tenuousness of the union that Canadians chronically do. In my travels over the next six months I will encounter again and again provincial intramural hostility that goes well beyond the well-known English-French schism. Every province has grievances against some other, and all distrust the dominant Ontarians. Everyone picks on everyone else, with poor Newfoundland at the bottom of the heap. All across Canada I will hear that Quebecers are arrogant and parochial, Prince Edward Islanders are supercilious and irrelevant, Nova Scotians and New Brunswickers are lazy, Ontarians are ruthless and greedy, Saskatchewanese are hicks and too many don't speak English or French, Manitobans overestimate their importance and mistreat their Indians, Albertans are rich and selfish upstarts, British Columbians are disloyal and crazy as Americans, Indians and other inhabitants of the northlands are drunks, and Newfies are stupid. There's only one neighbor that unites Canadians in a national prejudice—Americans. We are mean, rapacious despoilers of the continent—somewhat akin to Ontarians.

A *MacLean's* poll addresses the issue head on. In response to the question of whether respondents held stronger allegiances to province or nation, only Quebec and Newfoundland showed outright majorities for the province. But hefty minorities in the 30 to 40 percent range—especially large in Nova Scotia, Alberta, and B.C.—favored their province. A question about Quebec offered three possible responses: forcing it to stay, encouraging it to stay, and letting it go. Large pluralities, again particularly in the western provinces, responded that Quebec should be let go (ironically, Quebec itself recorded not only the largest plurality for letting it go but also the largest percentage of those who would force it to stay!). In the same poll, 75 percent of Canadians felt that losing VIA Rail would be a bad thing because of its historical role in unifying Canada, though less than 5 percent actually ride on its trains.

At dinner I find myself seated with the "Metis" woman. Her name is Molly Hobbes, her young companion is her fifteen-year-old son, who is forgoing the dining car for a burger with some other youngsters in the Skyline car. She is thirty-three, divorced, and descended from several mixed marriages of Cree women and

Irishmen. She lives, of course, in Red Deer and is getting off at Calgary tomorrow.

She was pregnant with Chris, her son, during her senior year and so never finished school. Her mother, a full-blooded Cree, never let her forget that she was the first in several generations to drop out of school, and as a result, she became an avid reader and eventually earned associate degree credits from the University of Calgary for independent study. She later married an accountant and went to work as a secretary. "Starts out as an Indian success story, doesn't it," she says as we struggle to keep our dignity while wrestling with the delicious slabs of barbecued ribs we are served.

But she had a brother who couldn't stay out of jail. He piled up a string of small offenses till a judge finally gave him a maximum term. "And he had finished college—so much for the theory that education guarantees success." There was a fire at the jail where he was incarcerated and he was killed. All the prisoners in his section were Indians and no one even tried to get them out. No one had taken such rudimentary precautions as installing fire alarms in his section and there was a scandal after his death. "They tried to cover it up, but we wouldn't let them. It just showed once more that Indians don't count, especially if they're in jail."

Molly threw herself into an activist movement to find some remedy for her brother's death, and that was the beginning of the end of her marriage. "For so long my husband—a son of England, the first any of my family had ever married—was proud to have such a domesticated Indian for a wife. But then my work protesting the jail fire made me seem undomesticated, I guess. I became an embarrassment for him. He thinks that's why we got divorced, but I see now that the marriage was already on the rocks." Then she stops talking, discomfited perhaps that she has said too much. For the rest of dinner, we chat about the Fraser Canyon scenery passing the dining car windows in the dimming sunset light.

During soup we pass the green dairy farms and profuse growths of wild roses in the broad and fertile lower Fraser Valley that I saw on the morning of my arrival in Vancouver. By dessert we are into the territory I slept through before. The valley has narrowed and tightened to become the fierce, barren canyon of explorers', miners', and railroaders' legend. Clinging to the nearly vertical canyon wall, the track winds through tunnel after tunnel. Looking across the gulf above the rushing waters is like looking in a mirror, because the opposite wall carries the tracks of the CN where a freight train just about matches our progress. At Hell's Gate, the waters boil through a small opening between columnar rock formations that once must have formed a natural dam. A suspension bridge and an overhead aerial tram complement the two railways in a tableau of the human assault on this hostile topography. Nowhere I have traveled has there been such a striking juxtaposition of ferocious natural obstacles and ingenious human inventiveness in conquering them.

Andrew Onderdonk's conquest of the Fraser Canyon in the early 1880s is often overshadowed in the histories by the later stories of the triumph over the Great Shield or the taming of Kicking Horse Pass. But here the rock was just as hard as that north of Lake Superior and the canyon walls more vertical than anything the CPR had encountered in the Rockies. Perhaps the challenge has been underestimated by the fact that there was already a wagon road here, the Cariboo Road to the gold mining country, running along the top of the two-thousand-foot cliffs. But for much of the route, Onderdonk had to blast out a ledge on the face of the nearly vertical precipice far below the road that was his source of supply.

For four years the canyon reverberated with continuous explosions. A factory cranked out powder and the newfangled and dangerous nitroglycerin on a scale never before attempted. Men had to be lowered on ropes down the walls to drill holes for the charges in the flat face of granite and quartz. Often after setting the charges, they didn't make it back up in time. At the approaches to some of the tunnels, it wasn't enough to carve a ledge into the rock. In these places, a gallery, like a roofed porch indented into the mountain face, had to be painstakingly blasted out without bringing down the overhanging rock and disrupting the entrance to the tunnel. Casualty rates were horrendous. All the horrors of work with nitroglycerin described earlier were present here, along with the added hazard of working on sheer granite drops above a boiling river.

Where there wasn't rock to be blasted, the tracks had to be laid through thin air. Millions of board feet of lumber had to be hauled up the Cariboo Road and lowered into the canyons where trestles and bridges were built. In places the line would hang over the waters below on "grasshopper trestles" built out from the wall.

Finding men to do the work was a problem from the start. Many of the most influential founding fathers of the province were rabid

Anglophones, horrified at the possibility that B.C. would be inundated with Chinese as had California with the building of the first American transcontinental. To appease them, Onderdonk initially promised to employ only local white labor until greater numbers were needed, then Americans, then Irish imported from the east, then French-Canadians, and finally native Indians as necessary. Chinese would only be employed when the other sources of labor were exhausted. That happened very quickly.

It turned out that the Indians were the best for the terrifying work of drilling holes and carving out footholds in the solid rock face while suspended by ropes from summits high above. Americans with experience building their own transcontinental railroads dominated the corps of foremen, but the labor force was soon inundated with the Chinese. What made the Chinese so effective was their ability to maintain themselves independently. They had their own system of organization and authority. When orders were given, supervisors did not have to worry about how to sort out instructions for each individual coolie. They could travel and be settled into a work site in huge groups in a day, where it might take a similar group of white men a week. And they would work for a dollar a day while white workers expected twice that. Only the most die-hard racists could not see that the Chinese were essential to an effort that was arduous enough even with them.

For their part, most of the Chinese came to Canada to earn the three hundred dollars it would take to own their own farms and achieve financial independence back in south China. But winters were a deterrent to many of their dreams. The Chinese Achilles' heel was their inability to withstand severe cold. Whole groups were let go when their productivity declined after December, and when the work was completed, those who had come over most recently were left short of their financial goals. At the completion of the Onderdonk contract, over five thousand Chinese who never intended to settle in North America were left without the money for passage back home.

Besides rock walls and labor, the biggest problem facing Onderdonk was supplies. The huge quantities of food, lumber, and steel needed for the work quickly clogged the old Cariboo Road, and rivermen had long viewed the barrier of Hell's Gate as impassable by water. Onderdonk thus built a steamboat that could force its way up through Hell's Gate and operate regularly in the canyon above it.

On May 17, 1882, pilot Asbury Insley attempted the feat. All day long Insley struggled to breach the gap, but on every try the waters forced him back. When he declared the task impossible, rivermen gravely informed Onderdonk that they had told him so and the effort was assumed to be ended.

But Onderdonk, originally an American from San Francisco, knew of men in Idaho who had accomplished a similar feat on the Snake River. He recruited them for a second attempt and imported an audience of spectators to witness the event from flatcars parked along the completed section of track high up the cliff wall. Betting was a hundred to one against the effort. After ten days of futile struggle, Onderdonk had ringbolts installed in the canyon walls through which huge ropes were run from the boat's capstan to a steam winch and 150 coolies up on the ledge. Finally, nearly a month after the spectators had all gone home, the *Scuzzy* got through. She went into regular service and had to be patched after almost every downstream run, but now the materials needed to complete the job could be delivered.

As the project of conquering the canyon began to show signs of ultimate success, the towns that sprang up along the route gave themselves over to spectacular celebrations of great holidays— Chinese New Year, the Queen's Birthday, and the American 4th of July. But July 1st, the Canadian national holiday, passed here almost unobserved. In British Columbia, the date would have little meaning until the completion of the railway all the way to the east.

In the later evening, the Skyline car comes alive as some of the younger members of the group I met earlier join with coach passengers to generate the tone of a singles bar, with Brent buying drinks for the Swiss, Karin and Nicole, and a tough-skinned, long-haired, beady-eyed trucker named Wesley coiling up with Molly. He's not very pleased at first when she asks me to join them. Brent's not doing so well either as his companions want to talk about Canadian writers whom Brent has never heard of. Two high school boys are gnashing their teeth that they can't get a tall, pretty blond girl up in the coach to come back to the bar and join them in passing for eighteen. They content themselves by leering at the long-black-haired Filipino-Canadian named Cherrie who works as bartender in this car. The spell of romance hangs in the air like the curls of cigarette smoke because of the whispered rumor that a couple who met here earlier are passionately ensconced in the last seats of the darkened dome upstairs.

"Make-out heaven up there," says Wesley with a watery leer toward Molly, who sips her drink and fidgets with her straw.

"You're married," she reminds him and he grunts toward me, "See what a man gets for being honest with women?" and then back to her, "What do you know about being married?"

"I've been there twice," she says with a smile that suggests she doesn't really mind the direction of the conversation.

"Oooh," whistles Wesley. "Then I shouldn't have to explain a thing to you now, should I, honey?"

Wesley is not behaving offensively and Molly is not altogether uninterested. I will witness scenes like this again and again on trains in Canada, where passengers often take quite literally the phrase "romance of the train." This flirtatious repartee is standard fare in the bar cars. Wesley is a good practitioner of the art.

"Traveling all the trains till you run out of track, eh?" Wesley says to me. "I wrote a poem you might like." He scribbles it in my notebook.

ENDLESS JOURNEY

On this trail leading to nowhere,
How far till your road will end?
Stop and take a look around,
Who am I, maybe a friend?

How could you not know me?
If there were no laws, no time or death,
We'd ride on from here together,
There'd be no last breath.

The poem's not really for me; it's for Molly and she knows it. It doesn't matter that his verse will win no awards or even that it is presented ruthlessly as a means for seduction. Under the rules of the game, Wesley has extended himself and made himself vulnerable. That's what counts and Molly responds by speaking intimately to us of marriage.

"I don't know what either of your marriages is like, but I bet the odds aren't good. I'm an expert on marriages where the odds aren't good."

I open my mouth to protest but she hushes me, with that same authority of voice that she used in her coup in the Park lounge this afternoon, and says, "It's okay, I just mean that every marriage has times when it must end or be born again. Both of mine had to end, though I have seen it work the other way. Think about it. When you get married and swear eternal love and fidelity, what you're doing is promising that you will never grow or change in any independent way."

Wesley thinks about it and nods. She continues, "So one of two things happens. Either you stifle yourself and become a frustrated person fixated at some point in your past that you no longer really care about, or you let yourself grow and realize you don't fit into your marriage anymore."

"What about that business you mentioned about being born again?" I ask.

"It happened with my friend. And I've heard of it happening with others. You have to go your separate ways and then rediscover each other." Her friend, a teacher, was married to a rancher who loved the rodeo. As the years went by, he spent more and more time traveling to rodeos, until that's all he wanted to do. She in the meantime went beyond teaching as merely a job to supplement the family income. She took graduate courses and had ambitions about school administration.

"As long as they were still living together, neither one liked the new person the other was becoming. She thought he was frivolous, he thought she was a tight-assed schoolmarm." They tried marriage counseling, but the sessions merely served to highlight the fact that the marriage had already died of the syndrome of familiarity and estrangement.

"They were simultaneously bored with each other and not interested in getting to know the new person the other was becoming." So they split up but didn't get divorced. "During that year, each had lovers and discovered sex—that's so common, you know—people not experiencing good sex till they get away from their first marriage partner." Wesley nods and winks at me; he likes the direction this monologue is running.

After two years of separation, the husband wrote and suggested that they see a lawyer about an amicable divorce. "When they met at the lawyer's office, he was tanned and fit and wearing clothes that she had never seen before. His hair was longer and his arm was in a sling from a rodeo accident." She had lost weight in an aerobics program and, now an assistant administrator of a middle school, had developed an ability to walk into situations like this with a sense of command. "They went through the motions of the meeting with the lawyer, but both were champing at the bit to go out for an evening together afterward. They dated half a dozen more times and never went back to the lawyer. And they didn't even have sex till the fourth or fifth date."

It was an evening when they took a group of kids from her school to the rodeo. Afterward they drove around drinking a bottle of wine and laughing about stupid things they had done to each other in their years together as if they were talking about two strangers. Then they went back to her house and made love successfully together for the first time ever. I remember her telling me about the arched backs and sweat on her forehead."

Wesley whistles heavily and Molly gives him a playful pat on the cheek. "So they got back together?" he pants.

"Yes, they did, and they're one of the few happily married couples I know."

"What about children?" I want to know. At this Molly adopts a stern tone and almost lectures me.

"Kids are better off in a family where Mom and Dad really please each other. They're resilient, they recover from divorces, but they never recover from growing up with unhappy, unfulfilled parents. And they think that marital deadness and sexlessness is the norm so they become that way themselves and wonder why life is so much less than it ought to be. Don't talk to me about keeping bad marriages together for the children's sake!"

"Take that, asshole," laughs Wesley in an ironic tone that shows he is just as chastened by Molly's passion as I am. "I guess I'm a bit of a preacher about that issue," Molly confesses. "Chris has had two fathers and several 'Mom's boyfriends.' But he's got a better shot at being a man who can make a good marriage himself, because he's never lived with the model of a dead marriage for long."

At Kamloops we step out into the midnight air and though we can't see the mountains, we can smell them—like a mixture of pine boughs, wildflowers, and wet earth. Wesley slips his arm around Molly's waist and she lays her head on his shoulder. When we reboard, they head up the steps for the dome even though the moon still has not appeared. This time Molly does not invite me along.

During the night we begin the climbs over the mountainous portions of the route that early surveyors considered impassable. When

Jim Hill convinced the syndicate to take a southerly line across Palliser's Triangle, he sent an American major, A. B. Rogers, to find a corresponding route through the mountains. It wasn't a pass over the Continental Divide that posed difficulties. Kicking Horse Pass, named for an incident in which Palliser expedition member James Hector was kicked in the head by his horse, was well known. The problem was the Selkirk Range, an unexplored region of unusual pyramidal peaks lying west of Kicking Horse Pass between the main spine of the Rockies and Moberley's Eagle Pass through the westerly Gold Range.

Rogers arrived at the western slopes of the Selkirks with his nephew, Albert, and ten Indian packers in the late spring of 1881. He studied Moberley's journals, which revealed that a possible route up the ravine of the Illecillewaet River might have been abandoned due as much to problems with weather and fallen timber as to actual topography. To lighten the packs, Rogers made the fateful decision to carry minimal provisions, assuming that game could be shot along the way.

The climb up the canyon was a killer. The snows were still yards deep, and in the warmth of the day, the crust softened so that the men foundered in the drifts. Only by climbing in the shadows or in the very early morning could the surveyors count on firm footing on a frozen crust. In some places they were forced to belly-crawl gently across natural snow bridges over the river to follow a shaded route.

When Rogers found a broad snowfield at whose verge a brook seemed to split and flow in two directions, east and west, he thought it might be the summit of the long-sought pass. Since mountains still towered in all directions, he could not be sure, so he led his men up one of them in hopes of finding a vantage point that would confirm a pass. The men had been on half rations for days as a result of the surprising discovery that the Selkirks were weird in ways beyond geology—there was simply no game in this region. Weakened, they overextended themselves in the climb to a summit where there was little time to appreciate the spectacular view. During the night, the explorers had to beat each other with ropes to keep the blood circulating in the mountaintop cold. After the ordeal of the night on the peak, Rogers thought he saw an opening to the east that appeared contiguous with the river and the broad snowfield below, but he could not be sure. With food running short, he could go no farther and had to call off the expedition.

With his first chore unfinished, Rogers turned to his second.

Kicking Horse Pass had never been fully explored since Hector had crossed it from east to west. Now Rogers sent his nephew, Albert, up the Kicking Horse River on the west side, while he himself circled around to the east side by a southerly route. Albert was being sent on a route that was steeper, rockier, more prone to slides and more strewn with tangled, fallen timber than any of the other known passes. The Indians believed it was impassable.

When Rogers and his group arrived at the summit from the east, there was no Albert. The men were ordered to fan out down the westerly defiles in a desperate search, firing pistols as they went. Two of them worked their way down the terrible pitch that the railway builders would someday be expected to conquer with blasting powder and nitro. Halfway down, they found Albert—starving, exhausted, and out of his mind. He had survived the last two days on the raw meat of a porcupine.

That night on the ridgepole of the continent while Rogers made notes in his tent, the men of his surveying group initiated one of those precious little rituals of the bond between Canadian geography and Canadian community. Gathered around the campfire, smoking their pipes and drinking their tea, twenty men speculated on this lonely, awesome place which no white men but Hector had ever explored. Someone proposed an oath, and the twenty stood to swear that they would reunite yearly henceforth, no matter where destiny might take them. For forty-five years, almost all the participants in the "Pledge of the Twenty" stayed true till death intervened. Finally only two were left in the first years of the twentieth century, Albert Rogers and the man who found him lost on the terrible western slope of Kicking Horse Pass.

The following spring, Rogers tried the Selkirks again, this time by way of the Beaver River up the eastern slopes. Despite floods of spring waters, the dense, virgin underbrush, and blackflies and mosquitoes that tormented exposed flesh, he pressed on. Finally he spotted weird pyramidal mountains that looked familiar, though now from an eastern perspective. On July 24, 1882, in a place seemingly enclosed by mountains on all sides, he stood on a broad snowfield bordered by a creek that split and ran in two opposite directions.

What had made the pass so maddeningly difficult to confirm was that it ran at right angles to the river canyons approaching it from both sides—the resulting route in the shape of a Z. Thus, from no single perspective was it possible to see a gap through the Selkirk divide. Yet now there was no mistake—Rogers would have his immortality; and Jim Hill and the syndicate, with hundreds of miles of track across the prairie committed to its eventual discovery, could breathe a collective sigh of relief.

When larger surveying parties arrived to confirm and lay out the line over the mountains, the devastating west side descent of Kicking Horse Pass that had nearly killed Albert Rogers came to be known as the Golden Stairs. Much of the route was a zigzagging ledge, in some places no more than eighteen inches wide, hanging nearly a thousand feet above the river. An encounter with a patch of ice, a small landslide, or a hornet's nest could create moments of sheer terror. Sanford Fleming himself had worried that all the nitro in the world might not be able to maintain the required 2.2 percent grade down this furious chasm. As it turned out, he was right.

By the summer of 1884, members of the Twenty would hardly have recognized the site of their pledge, now overrun by mobs of surveyors, construction workers, scientists, and even sightseers— the mountainsides ablaze with forest fires set by the builders and scarred by the continual avalanches provoked by blasting.

Down the west side and the horrific Golden Stairs, Rogers had laid out a route that indeed kept to the ruling grade of 2.2 percent, but it would require blasting on a scale never before attempted. The fateful decision was made to abandon the requirement and build a "temporary" line on a grade of 4.5 percent. Thus was born the infamous "Big Hill."

The expedient of the Big Hill got the line built, but for twenty-five years it remained a dangerous obstacle on the CPR route. The very first train to try it ran out of control and plunged over the edge at a curve and into the canyon below. Special braking regimes were instituted to prevent runaways, and safety switches leading to uphill sidings were installed every two miles. Still, runaway tragedies occurred. In 1889, the engine of a fourteen-car train went over the side into the canyon, killing its engineer and fireman. It was eventually retrieved and put back into service as a pusher for the uphill climb, where it promptly blew up due to weaknesses in its damaged boiler, thus killing another engine crew.

And in 1904, the engineer of a descending freight train noticed that his air brakes weren't working properly, nor could he reverse the engine. He whistled for the crew to apply hand brakes and, strangely confident that he could regain control, whistled for the first safety switch to be set open so that he could come through. At the second safety switch, he still thought he could bring his speed down and signaled the switchman to let him through this one, too. The switchman, seeing the speed of the onrushing train, tried to turn the switch back to the safety siding at the last minute, but the train roared through before he could move the bar. He telephoned the keeper of the third and last safety switch with the frantic warning of a runaway train, but the train had descended so fast that the third switchman got the switch turned only halfway before the engine rattled through it and derailed, crashing with a terrific explosion into a rock wall. No shred of the overconfident engineer or his fireman was ever found.

By 1907, the CPR had had enough. Uphill operations, while not involving the spectacular runaways, required so many helper engines and proceeded so slowly that the line here was little more serviceable than would be a shuttle road linking two ends of track. Something had to be done.

The solution became one of the world's rail engineering wonders—the Spiral Tunnels. To lengthen the line enough to achieve a 2.2 percent grade, two climbing spiral tunnels would be carved into the bowels of Cathedral Mountain and Mount Ogden, creating an elongated figure-eight in the route. It took ten thousand men two years with a million and a half pounds of dynamite to carve the great "pretzel route" into the rock under the old Golden Stairs. Today, though the run through Kicking Horse Pass still presents the railway with a continuing struggle to hold this weakest link in the continental transportation system together, the grade is one of the least of the roadmaster's and engineers' problems.

In the morning, I'm up for the stop at Golden by the Columbia River, between the run over the Selkirk Range and the climb up Kicking Horse. At breakfast, service chief Brigit McDaniels is intrigued by my quest and arranges for me to ride in the cab with the engineers from Field to Banff—the most spectacular stretch of the west side climb.

For the ride from Golden to Field, I park myself in the Park car dome, crowded already with so many early-rising sightseers that some stand in the aisle. Up the steep grade of Kicking Horse Canyon, the *Canadian* grinds its way toward the Continental

Divide. We cross the river seven times and plunge into five tunnels and a deep cut that was once a tunnel until falling rock forced the railway to remove the top of the mountain and open it up.

At Field, the train crew changes and Brigit takes me out on the platform to meet engineer Edwin Washbrook and assistant Larry Buchan. I clamber up the ladder after them into the cab for my head-end ride over the top of the Rocky Mountains.

Larry, who is training to be an engineer on this division, drives, with Edwin kibitzing as we begin the climb whose 2.2 percent slope I can feel immediately out of Field. The old 4.5 percent grade must have been dizzying. Though the diesel engines are roaring at full throttle just a few feet behind us, the sound insulation in this brand-new General Electric F-40 is so effective that we can talk at reasonable levels. Ironically, VIA has taken delivery of an order of these new engines just as the decisions are being made about drastic cutbacks to the system.

Edwin is keen to show off his new wheels. The controls are incredibly simple—basically four levers on a panel in front of the engineer's seat. The one on the left is simply forward and reverse. Next is power, now open all the way for the climb. It controls the rpms of the diesel engines that drive the generators that pump electricity into the electric motors on the wheels. Then comes the dynamic brake, which uses the electric motors to put a drag on the wheels during downhill runs. And finally, at the right, is the lever that controls the air brakes on cars throughout the train. The horn and bell are square green buttons. Gauges show speed, rpms, voltage, and various other engine conditions. In addition, a large square box with a lighted incremental dial hangs down almost in front of the windscreen to show track speed, so critical when the power is available to pull the train faster than track conditions will safely allow. To the left of the engineer's seat hangs the radio telephone, which is a key tool in modern railroading.

Edwin points out the spot where the old 4.5 percent grade veers off to the right and straight up the pass; much of the old line now lies under the pavement of the Trans-Canada Highway. The power we are carrying today, the three-thousand-horsepower F-40 and an old fifteen-hundred-horsepower B unit, would never make it up that grade. Even on the new grade we can't get above twenty-five miles per hour at full throttle. "But that's the speed limit on this stretch of track today anyway. There are track crews up ahead—we may even have to stop," Edwin explains.

In confirmation, we round a curve and face a double-red signal. As we are stopped, the radio crackles with communications from the roadmaster and the track crew. Apparently the roadmaster is going to hop on and ride with us when we stop again up ahead. "Hope he doesn't mind that we got company up here," says Edwin, referring to me. "You got a letter from VIA, eh?" Again the radio crackles with instructions to take the siding at five miles per hour, the work crew will handle the switches manually. Shortly we have pulled alongside the ground crew and the work train and stop again. The work train includes a machine called an undercutter, which lifts the track and clears out the old punky ballast underneath in preparation for the laying of new ballast. Louis, the roadmaster, climbs on board and greets me with a friendly hello. Apparently my presence is to be no problem.

More instructions come in over the radio. The signal is still against us because of the work train, but we are being given an authorization to proceed past a double-red. It's called Rule 264 and requires a special instruction number from the dispatcher and the copying and repeating of the specific orders: ". . . proceed on main track at ten miles per hour. Switch need not be placed in neutral position."

"So we're away," says Larry. Shortly we cross what looks like a recent avalanche path, yet the tracks are straight and true through this swath of destruction.

"It's the glacier up on Mount Stephen that keeps Louis busy. This isn't just a recent avalanche path, it's a continuing avalanche path. Louis's boys work year-round to clean up after the mess that glacier makes." Now I can see payloaders parked along the tracks—frontline equipment in the battle against the glacier.

Ahead of us now the black hole of the lower spiral tunnel approaches. Crossing above it from left to right slope the tracks we will run on after we have passed through. Crews in the caboose of a long freight can view their engines passing overhead from this spot.

You can't appreciate a railway tunnel from the vantage point of the passenger cars. But here on the head end, I am surprised and impressed at the roughness of the rocky tunnel walls. It's wet and dank. Edwin says that often he has seen mountain goats huddling against the walls as the train passes through. Great hunks of ice hang from the ceiling.

We emerge from the twisting hole and cross forty-five feet above the portal we entered a few minutes ago. Above and ahead of us loom the crags of Cathedral Mountain, whose bowels we will shortly enter in the upper spiral tunnel. But first we encounter another double red. There's a work train up ahead of us and we have gained on him.

Throughout the ride, Edwin has coached Larry on handling the controls for specific idiosyncrasies of the route. Now, after we receive our 264 authorization to pass the double-red, Larry releases the air brake and then increases the power. Both men laugh at Larry's rookie error as the train rolls slightly backward and Larry has to apply the brakes again. On this kind of an uphill grade, the power must be applied before releasing the brake since there is a lag between opening the throttle and the development of effective horsepower. Larry does it just right the second time and Edwin compliments him.

At the entrance to the upper tunnel, a sign warns of the necessity for carbon monoxide testing as the train runs through the tunnel. Edwin explains, "This one doesn't have ventilator fans, and if you have to stop in here, the fumes can get to be dangerous." Indeed, shortly after we plunge into the hole, we are nearly gagging even up on the head end because of the fumes of the work train that has passed through ahead of us. It must be really bad back in the passenger cars where our fumes are added to the foul mix. Edwin confirms with mild understatement, "If we had to stop in here now, we'd have a problem."

When we emerge from the second tunnel, we run along a high cliff with a yawning gulf to the left. More tunnels, snow sheds, and avalanche warning fences testify to the continuing struggle that Louis and his crew carry on here beneath another glacier on Cathedral Mountain. After another double-red, where Louis gets off to join the work train that is stopped on a siding, we see mountain goats and antelope in increasing numbers. Ospreys rise from huge nests perched on telephone poles as we approach them. Eventually the river and the valley floor catch up to us, and by the Stephen division and the crossing of the Continental Divide, we ride through a broad saddle of little lakes and wildflowered grassy downs—the site of the Pledge of the Twenty. This is the highest point on the CPR line, just over a mile above sea level.

At Lake Louise, the station is a magnificent log structure with leaded-glass windows, built in 1909. High overhead to the south hangs Victoria Glacier and to the north tower the crags of ten-thousand-foot Mount Richardson.

The last thirty-five miles to Banff along the Bow River is a parade of mountains lovingly named and catalogued by Edwin as we roll along. A few are named for their appearance: Pinnacle Mountain, Castle Mountain, Storm Mountain, Massive Mountain. Others are named for men and women out of CPR or Canadian history: Mount Cory, Mount Whymper, Mount Edith. A few are named biblically: Mount Ishbel, Mount Babel, Mount Sheol. And one, Mount Eisenhower, is named for an American president. The pyramid-shaped Pilot Mountain is named for its role as a site for mountain-climbing surveyors who exploited its eagle-eye view to survey the line up through the Bow Valley.

Edwin points out the green turrets of the Banff Springs Hotel rising above the treetops and soon we're slowing for the stop at Canada's greatest resort. It was Queen Victoria herself who established the park after hearing of the hot sulphur springs that bubble up from these rocks. When I climb down from the engine to return to the passenger cars, I wish I were getting off here, but my itinerary doesn't allow for a Rocky Mountain stopover until I reach Jasper, up north on the CN *Super Continental* line. I chose Jasper because Americans always go to Banff. The distinction seems silly—the air here is cool and fresh and dry. There's a spirit of ease evident among the tourists on the platform that is infectious. Again I am struck, as I was frequently during my travels in the United States, at how some of the scenes of North Americans' greatest struggle and pain become settings of ease and amusement in latter days. Reluctantly I board and am immediately cheered by the aromas wafting from the galley. It's lunchtime.

The turmoil of the Pacific Scandal, the granite of the Great Shield, the Americans with their Manifest Destiny and whiskey, the rampages of the Sioux, the desolation of Palliser's Triangle, the chasm of the Fraser Canyon, the undiscovered Selkirk Pass, and the drop off the west side of Kicking Horse—none of these things halted the inexorable drive of the Canadian Pacific Railway to make a nation out of a geographically divided subcontinent. But in 1884, the project lay dying due to an invisible obstacle—money. For five years George Stephen had successfully moved heaven and earth to keep the cash flowing. Now it became increasingly difficult to meet the huge payrolls that came due every month, and a massive dividend needed paying off early in 1885. Stephen wrote anguished letters to

MacDonald urging him to speed the payment of government subsidies, and he and Donald Smith began dipping into their private fortunes to stave off disaster. They both hailed from a region of Scotland where a great rock, once used as a site for lookouts, stood as a symbol of rugged defiance and endurance. The rock was known as Craigellachie, and after one brief financial coup, Stephen sent Smith the shortest and most famous telegraph in Canadian history. "Stand fast, Craigellachie," was all it said.

Still the CPR rolled toward financial disaster like a runaway train. But in northern Montana, a half-breed dreaming mystical delusions stirred—Louis Riel, who had inadvertently midwifed the CPR in its birth, was about to step forward to revive it from death.

By the 1880s most of the Metis displaced by the settlement of Manitoba, the province Riel founded, had moved to the upper Saskatchewan Valley east of today's Edmonton, where they struggled to continue their ancient way of life. Here, too, were the reservations of the native peoples, now totally dependent on the white man for food, and new settlements of whites who felt dispossessed by the choice of a southerly route for the CPR and the government's benign neglect of the far northwest.

In 1884, harvests were poor and MacDonald was warned by the Mounties of potential unrest. The native tribes faced starvation in the coming winter and Metis and English settlers alike worried about the consequences of continued government neglect. The settlers sent Gabriel Dumont to Montana to bring Riel back to work his province-making magic again.

But Riel had changed during the seventeen years since his first triumph. Goaded by a monumental sense of personal injustice, he had visions that God still held a "mission" for him to found a great Catholic nation of Indians and Metis. When Dumont arrived in Montana to find him living the humble life of a schoolteacher, it was clear to Riel that this was the call. He returned with Dumont to Batoche in Saskatchewan where he sat in state as the loyal Metis, now allied with the Cree, gathered around him.

His first actions seemed reasonable enough. He issued a proclamation demanding that the Metis be given deeds to their farms, that the tribes be supplied with food, that treaties with them be honored, and that Saskatchewan be recognized as a French-speaking province. Riel at first organized the same kind of cautious escalating measures that he had employed in Red River. But he also sent a personal letter to MacDonald promising to leave and drop the whole thing if he were paid $35,000 in reparations for the loss of his farm and the pains of his unjust exile. One Mountie officer later wrote to MacDonald that the Northwest Rebellion probably could have been avoided with the payment of a few thousand dollars. Still MacDonald did nothing.

In the spring of 1885 at Duck Lake, a combined force of Metis and Cree faced a Mountie detachment and shooting erupted. When it was over, twelve of the police lay dead and so did the myth of the invincible Mounties. Cree Chief Big Bear promptly brought Riel a force of a hundred braves. Poundmaker encamped nearby with another two hundred in war paint. By now the Catholic hierarchy had abandoned Riel due to his increasingly bizarre claims of prophet status. In response Riel renounced Catholicism and told his followers that he would be their priest. He took to eating nothing but blood cooked in milk. Now with bloodshed and the cutting of the leader's last ties to established authority, the Northwest Rebellion exploded in earnest.

Finally MacDonald responded. He sent Father Lacombe to the west to try to keep Crowfoot and the Blackfeet out of the uprising. He sent Colonel Middleton to determine the military needs for an expedition in force. If only MacDonald could find a way to get enough troops out there quickly.

While the government was rousing itself to action, the CPR continued to slide toward insolvency. Stephen and Smith, in a last desperate effort to stave off disaster, pledged their entire worth to keep it afloat—all their financial and personal material possessions were signed away. Though Smith remained staunch through these trials, Stephen began to crack. He penned a letter to MacDonald, admitting defeat, and began to square away his affairs.

General Superintendent William Van Horne was in Ottawa in early 1885 and was the first to spy the opportunity to save the CPR. With experience moving troops by rail during the American Civil War, he knew more than anyone what could be done with a railway and an army. He announced that if the government would vest all authority for executing the operation in himself and the CPR, he would have troops on the scene in the northwest in ten days.

Men scoffed. The road still had numerous gaps in it, the operation was untried, the proposal was a cheap publicity stunt for the railway. But MacDonald asked, "Has anyone got a better plan?" No one did.

The public announcement that the CPR would move troops to

fight rebellion in the northwest created a fever of nationalistic cele-
bration overnight. For the troops, however, the fun ended soon
enough as the trains reached the first gaps in the line in the Great
Shield country, where cold, snow, and ice marked another in the
legends of great Canadian treks. But when the exhausted army
reached Winnipeg, it could collapse in a great collective sleep in the
warm cars of the trains, which from here ran uninterrupted all the
way to Saskatchewan.

Still, MacDonald, absorbed now by the crisis out west, could do
nothing financially for the CPR. At railhead in Beavermouth, B.C.,
the famous Mountie Sam Steele was beset with bad news from all
directions. The Metis, the Cree, and even English settlers were in
outright rebellion. The Blackfeet threatened to join. Now CPR
workers right outside Steele's bedroom window rioted over lack of
pay. And Steele, who had for so long been the central force holding
things together in the west, lay seriously ill with Rocky Mountain
spotted tick fever. He sent from his sickbed severe warnings of dire
consequences to the strikers. Still the strikers carried on, taking
over the line and stopping all work. Gunplay erupted and Steele
ordered arrests that were rebuffed by the strikers. At that, he
roused himself, called for his copy of the Riot Act, and marched
forth with a rifle and eight armed officers to face down the mob at a
bridge. Threatening to mow down those who persisted in taking
advantage of the fact that an insurrection had broken out, he read
them the Riot Act, which allowed officers of the law summarily to
shoot anyone who refused a direct order. The crowd dispersed,
Steele arrested more leaders, and peace returned to the line. Here
the recently discredited Mounties not only made their finest stand
but also coined a phrase that became an idiom in English-speaking
nations everywhere.

The expeditious arrival of troops in Saskatchewan quickly
brought the rebellion to heel after some initial military bungling,
which was not without further bloodshed and pitched battles.
Poundmaker backed off, Big Bear was defeated, Dumont fled to
Montana, and Riel was eventually captured. It was truly a small
war, but the feared Indian general uprising never materialized.

Back east, times had changed. The CPR had become a corporate
national hero for its role in challenging the rebellion. Despite continuing carping from the opposition, a bill providing whatever assistance the CPR needed to complete its task now twisted its way
through Parliament. Stephen rallied, though he swore that as soon

as possible the CPR would have no further truck with the government.

On November 7, 1885, a gathering of men stood where the last rail was to be laid in the Gold Range near the spot where Moberley had once carved in a tree, "This is the route of the Pacific Railway." The spot had been dubbed Craigellachie even before Stephen's famous telegram to Smith. Major Rogers cut the last rail. In the crowd were his nephew Albert Rogers, Sam Steele, William Van Horne, and Sanford Fleming. There was little of the elaborate ceremony arranged by the Americans for the driving of their golden spike on the completion of the first transcontinental railroad. A plain iron spike was placed into the last tie and Donald Smith, for so long exiled to the shadows of the great project, picked up the hammer. A photographer snapped his camera as Smith, now an old man with long flowing white whiskers, pounded the spike. Canada finally had its railway and its great national photographic tableau. A conductor on the waiting train called out, "All aboard for the Pacific."

Nine days later, Riel was hanged as a traitor in Regina and Quebec erupted in riots with the cry "Our language, our religion, our race," which has never been stilled since.

At Calgary, Molly Hobbes and her son are among those getting off the train. Back on board in the Skyline lounge, Wesley says, "What a woman. God, it warms the heart to know there are still women like that out there. I wouldn't trade a couple of hours with her for a year in heaven. What's your wife like?"

When I describe her, he says that he and I don't have a lot in common. "You're either a fool or a lucky man. There's no in between for guys like you. I'm not lucky and I ain't no fool. I got a wife who stopped being a woman years ago. I don't beat on her, but I sure cheat on her."

"Why don't you get divorced?"

"Why indeed. Let me tell you something, sometimes it's easier to get what you need out of life by not rocking the boat. You hear what I'm saying? Maybe I don't have as much guts as that Molly. But I'll bet I hurt the people around me a lot less with my little white lies than she does with her brave honesty."

"I thought you liked her."

"I do. I'd worship the ground under her feet if she gave me the chance. But I couldn't live her life."

Later in the evening, after I tire of a series of desultory conversations with rail buffs deploring the decline of the railways, I set out in search of Wesley's spirited company. I find him in the Skyline lounge laughing roaringly with a young brunette who boarded at one of the prairie stops.

"Can I tell him?" he asks her as I sit down with them.

"Sure," she says. Then he asks me if I ever met a nude dancer before.

"Well, as a matter of fact . . ." and I tell him about the Ledo Hotel in Sudbury and Kathy Stack.

"I know her," says the brunette, whose name is Shannon Wakeley. "I've competed against her. You must have seen her just before the Miss Nude World competition in Toronto this weekend. She's sure to be there."

Shannon has a title herself, Miss Nude Molson. Her stage name is Marie Kendall, and for her, nude dancing is a temporary stopoff between college and a career as a model. She doesn't look like a nude dancer—has a wholesome "kissin' cousin" look. When I mention this, she smiles and says, "Good, I want that look. I never bleached or permed my hair, I don't wear a lot of makeup and I don't do the raunchy stuff—no glitz and frizz. Every dancer has an identity, that's mine."

As the evening conviviality in the Skyline bar rolls on, Shannon becomes the center of attention, defending her current calling against the insinuations of several other drinkers. One, an earnest straight-arrow fellow, insists that it must be degrading. She counters, wondering if it's degrading for boxers to get into a ring nearly naked to batter each other's bodies, or for an actor and actress to portray a romantic sex scene in a movie, or for an artist to paint nudes. Another fellow, with a less moral bent, sees her as fair game to be the butt of several obscene sexist jokes.

Ignoring him Shannon explains that in Winnipeg, where she is heading, there are probably fifty bars hiring four or five dancers each. And that's not to mention the traditional dives hiring old-time strippers, though those places are dying out due to government restrictions intended to protect the legitimate dancers. "A lot of people wondered how serious the government was about its rules—no insertion routines, no prostitution—till they banned the American Mitzi DuPris and her ping-pong balls and cucumbers." Shannon has her own self-imposed rules as well. "When they start hollering, 'Show us some pink,' I stick out my tongue."

At 11:30, Wesley detrains at Moose Jaw and Cherrie closes up the bar. The patrons clear out, but Shannon, who says she is a night owl, wants to hang out and talk. She seems compelled to make someone understand how she has come to do what she does. She asks if I've seen the movie *An Officer and a Gentleman*. She's seen it twelve times and says it portrays her story. She grew up a poor girl in a neighborhood on the wrong side of Winnipeg. Her family are strict Mennonites who left the farm, so she had neither roots in the earth nor the colorful, rowdy side of the working girl's life to look forward to—her future looked gray. But she was smart, did well in school, and was able to go to college on a scholarship. There she met middle-class girls doing nude dancing to earn some extra money and was spellbound by the glamour of it all. "I suppose there was some rebellion in it, too. You know Mennonites aren't allowed to drink, smoke, or dance at all—never mind dancing nude. You know why Mennonites don't make love standing up?"

I don't.

"Someone might think they're dancing."

College showed her that she wanted to fly as far as she could from that poor Mennonite background and never go back. She took a year and traveled to New Zealand and returned bitten by the voyageurs bug. Then she traveled all over the United States, where she gained the courage to begin her forbidden career.

But soon this, too, seemed like a kind of trap. "You heard the attitudes of those guys earlier tonight. I hear that stuff all the time. There's a bar in a place called the Grant Hotel in Winnipeg, where working-class girls hang out hoping to get picked up and carried away by one of the guys from the nearby military base. They call those girls 'Grant-hogs.' I was one of them till my lieutenant came along. And he carried me right out of the place just like in the movie." She is returning to Winnipeg from a visit with him at his current base in Calgary, where he offered her an engagement ring.

"Did you say yes?"

"No."

"Why not? Do you love him?"

"Yes, I think so. But I've struggled so hard to get free, I just panicked when I realized what his offer meant. Plus I don't want it to be like in the movie, where she was just a nothing—what do you think that marriage was going to be like, with him the shining master and she on her knees grateful to him for the rest of her life?" Following the ethic that has motivated so many working-class young men, Shannon told her lieutenant that she couldn't marry him till she had succeeded in establishing herself in a modeling career.

I had already noticed a small, recent scar on her chin, now she shows me a long ragged one at the side of her cheek that she has kept hidden under her hair. She says there are more on her shoulder and knee under her denim. "It was the last night we were out before I was supposed to take the train back to Winnipeg. A truck pulled out in front of us and everything went black. When I came to, I was on a stretcher and the car was totaled. He wasn't hurt badly, but I'm all scarred. I spent two extra weeks in Calgary recovering and wondering if I should have said yes when I had the chance. Now I don't know if I'll get a shot at modeling."

In the morning after breakfast a subdued little gathering hangs out in the Skyline lounge as we approach Winnipeg. The Swiss are both reading books by Canadian author Farley Mowat. Cherrie rummages through her stock taking inventory and listens intently as Shannon points out the familiar images of homecoming and talks about the Mennonite family she misses and still loves, staying young, preserving her dignity, making friends from fresh walks of life, and keeping Canada beautiful. I ask her what would she think if her country ever split up into different states? The Swiss travelers look up from their reading, shocked to hear that such a thing is a possibility. Shannon responds in terms familiar from her own life. "It sounds like such a bad thing, but it's just like with individual people—maybe some of the provinces feel trapped and need to be able to go their own way. But we'd still all be Canadians at heart."

Cherrie, who has performed her duties without comment ever since Vancouver, speaks up. "I don't think it would really change anything."

4

Right On

WINNIPEG TO JASPER
ON THE *SUPER CONTINENTAL*

W E pull in to Winnipeg station at 10:00 A.M., nearly on time. I have the day here since my train back out west via the northern route through Edmonton and Jasper doesn't leave until ten this evening. My luck isn't quite so good as it was in Vancouver; no one I meet on the train offers to give me a tour of the city. But in the station, Cherrie Gosselin, the bartender, sketches a walking tour for me on the back of a VIA napkin.

"Winnipeg isn't like Vancouver or Montreal," she says. "People aren't gonna jump up and down to show you how wonderful their city is." It's not that residents don't love or take pride in their city— but Winnipeg has had a hard history. It was here that the first Riel rebellion began. Here Canada experienced its most devastating boom-and-bust economic cycles and its first modern slums. Here was the site of Canada's worst general strikes and bloody confrontations between workers and police. Though Winnipeg is experiencing a wave of redevelopment and economic growth today, too much of its history has been a record of stagnation. And there is the climate, which batters residents with possibly the worst extremes of any big

91

city in the world, from fifty below zero cold, howling winds, and six-foot snowdrifts in winter to scorching hundred-degree heat and drought in the summer.

The station fronts directly on Main Street and the high-rise downtown area, with the Red River and the fork with the Assiniboine River at its back. I hike toward downtown along a street named Broadway with a grassy tree-lined median. People bustling about their day sport the same cosmopolitan dress and bearing as those in any big city, though perhaps with a little less color than in Vancouver. A few blocks from the station the Louis Riel Hotel stands adjacent to York Street, and I'm reminded, despite the dominance of English in the talk I hear, of just how far we are from Ontario, where a hotel with such a name would be like having a Hotel Robert E. Lee in Boston or a Hotel Benedict Arnold anywhere in the States. A cop on the corner explains that the primarily English-speaking mainstream I see on the streets downtown does not represent Winnipeg as a whole. "It's a city of minority neighborhoods—Metis, Indians, Frenchmen, Jews, Ukrainians, Poles, you name it."

"Like Chicago?"

"Well, yes, if that's what Chicago is like, eh?"

Yet despite its longitude, its ethnic mix, and its role as a transportation hub, Winnipeg is not like Chicago. Winnipeg is a true prairie and river city, more like St. Louis or Kansas City. Its most important street is not Main but Portage Avenue, which intersects with Main a few blocks from the railway station at what locals call "the coldest street corner in the world." Today it's pleasantly warm and sunny as I turn the corner of Portage and Main and cross the bridge over the Red River.

Wandering the streets of Provencher, Cathedrale, and Tache east of the river, I hear more French than English. There's a touch of Montreal in this part of town, and since it's lunchtime, I stop in at a little diner on Tache. But my waitress, who looks like a high school cheerleader, pops her bubble gum and asks, "What'll ya have?" with an accent that could be right out of Iowa. With fond remembrances of delis in Montreal or Vancouver, I order a smoked meat sandwich. "Gravy on yer mashed?" the waitress queries between pops of her gum. I didn't know mashed potatoes were ever served with a Canadian smoked meat sandwich.

After lunch I recross the bridge and spend a somnambulent few hours in The Forks National Historic Park on the west bank of the river. There's a dockage here for pleasure boats, an outdoor amphitheater, a tour boat that cruises the river, and a concrete promenade along the waterfront. But the best thing about the park is a large sweep of well-maintained lawn, which, separated from the downtown by the low profile of the rail yards, offers a striking view of the city skyline. Here as I doze in the sun mothers entertain their toddling children, well-dressed businesspeople take their brown bag lunch break, and gaggles of tourists try to picture scenes out of six thousand years of The Forks' history as a meeting place on the empty prairie. Native hunters, fishermen, and traders met here for eons before the relatively modern parade of French explorers, Metis, Scottish Selkirks, Hudson's Bay Company men, Nor'westers, soldiers chasing Riel, riverboatmen, railway builders, immigrants with their dozens of European languages, union organizers and socialists and contemporary city-builders, which has continued and now hallowed the tradition.

At the very spot where the waters of the Assiniboine meet those of the Red, there is a small roofless gazebo where visitors stop to take the obligatory pictures. Some bend down and stare into the murky water itself, as if somewhere in its depths they might glimpse the ribs of a bark canoe, a trapper's cache, or a native warrior's tomahawk. When I look there is nothing but prairie mud and a waterlogged page of the *Winnipeg Free Press*. It's the real estate page and it advertises prairie farms at fire sale prices.

For half a decade after the driving of the last spike and the hanging of Riel, John A. MacDonald struggled to overcome the fractious centrifugal force of the nation whose geography he had welded together with the CPR. Nova Scotia considered a separatist bill, New Brunswick howled over the decline of its lumber economy, Manitoba was near revolt over the CPR monopoly, Ontario experienced renewed Clear Grit agitation, and Quebec's Parti Nationale openly dreamed of a separate French nation in the aftermath of Riel's execution. And by 1891, after winning one last election, Sir John lay dying.

It began with a quirk in his speech and then a tic in his face. When Sir John refused his physician's advice to rest, he was stricken with a stroke, then another that paralyzed him, and finally one that killed him. For five years since the triumph of his Pacific Railway, he had tried unsuccessfully to rally Canadians to a sense of national unity. His death accomplished that feat, if only for a moment. The young nation that had known no other leader stilled its tempestuous quarrels as his body was carried to Kingston aboard a CPR train and laid to rest. Even to his opponents, Sir John represented a focal point, an axle around which to revolve—to embrace or to rebel against. With his passing, the nation was momentarily unified as never before, by the loss of its center.

In his quest to conquer Canadian geography MacDonald left a profound imprint on his country. He forged an enduring party and built a railway that became a national symbol of geographical unity and independence of the Americans. His personality—his nonconformism, his iconoclasm, even his bottle—established a strain of tolerance and earthiness in the Canadian national character that persists to this day. But he never overcame the centrifugal force in the demographics of the country. That task would be left to another leader, another party, and another railway.

During MacDonald's waning years, the next great Canadian leader was gathering his colors in a pattern just as unconventional as Sir John's. With his vociferous support for amnesty for Riel, the Catholic Liberal Wilfred Laurier carried sound French-Canadian credentials. But in the *Rouges* tradition, he opposed the arbitrary power of the Church and so earned the enmity of the bishops. Thus the Church supported the Conservatives in the 1896 elections, declaring that a Catholic vote for Laurier was a sin. French-Canadians, finally bridling at the Church dictating their politics, followed Laurier and gave him the votes that guaranteed a Liberal victory. With this masterstroke, the gods of irony broke the power of the Church in Canada forever and created a leader who could bring the nation together—a Catholic, a French-Canadian, a Liberal.

The root of much of the disunity that preceded Laurier was an intractable economic depression that caused each province to view its own hardships as the result of the pernicious influence of some other. Laurier, on taking office, quickly saw general economic recovery as the key to national unity and saw further that Canada already possessed the means to effect it. As far back as 1842, an Ontario farmer had discovered a strange strain of hard red wheat that ripened up to two weeks faster than the varieties widely in use. By the end of the century, cereal research on Red Fife led to the discovery of Marquis, which shortened the growing season by another week. The result was the breakout of wheat growing from the arid southern expanses of Palliser's Triangle into the friendlier northern prairie of the fertile crescent.

Laurier also perceived that wherever the rails went, communities came alive with enterprise and commerce. In the northern prairies were nearly a million square miles of sparsely settled land that could be developed into a national engine of prosperity with wheat and railways. All that was needed were settlers.

Laurier recruited Manitoban Clifford Sifton to manage the greatest immigrant search the world had yet seen. Sifton's plan began by making it easier for homesteaders to stake claims, then he went on the road—to England, to eastern Europe, and even to America. He distributed thousands of pamphlets in the world's first million-dollar advertising campaign and brought hundreds of journalists to tour the new lands. He encountered a stroke of luck in America where frontier lands were just petering out, and for the first and only time in North American history, more immigrants poured northward over the border than southward. Everywhere the cry was "Settle—right on!"

By the first decade of the twentieth century, two million newcomers had swelled Canada's population by nearly a third. They were generally better fixed and more knowledgeable than the earlier pioneer homesteaders, so they put down roots quickly and deeply. And then they began to demand railroads, perhaps even another transcontinental—or two.

Back in Winnipeg station, waiting for the departure of the westbound *Super Continental* for Edmonton and Jasper that evening, I am fascinated by an elaborate display of artifacts and photographs of the great immigration. The station is actually a little museum dedicated to the Canadian mosaic, with the distinctive communities of Jews, Scotsmen, Hungarians, Russians, Irish, Ukrainians, as well as Metis and native peoples well-represented. One photograph focuses my attention. It portrays a homesteading family of seven standing in the midst of tall prairie grasses. The father and the two youngest children display the characteristic stern, grim visage so familiar in pioneer photos and memorialized as *American Gothic*, but the mother and the other three children are all smiling rapturously.

While I have been admiring the display, passengers detraining from the westbound *Canadian* have arrived. I hear an outburst of some very foreign language just to my left. There stands a young man in denims and boots, gesticulating haplessly to a pretty, short-coiffed young woman who appears to be trying and failing to understand what he is saying.

"He's from Poland and doesn't speak any English," she explains to me as I turn toward them. "He was on the same train I came in on from Toronto and I think he's going where I'm going—Edmonton. All I know is his name is Mark, eh? I'm Connie."

She speaks in an exuberant, laughing, western Canadian accent and seems to feel that efforts—and failure—to help Mark are great fun.

"Friends . . . telephoning . . . Mark," he says again with rolling eyes and shrugs of exasperation.

"Maybe he wants to call somebody," she says.

Earlier in the day, I had noticed a friendly looking restaurant and bar called Grapes just across the street from the station.

"Let's take Mark over to Grapes, have a bite to eat, and help him out," I suggest.

"Right on," says Connie.

After some refreshment at Grapes, Mark begins to relax and actually smiles. He has a Polish-English dictionary, and with its help, some "Pictionary" work on napkins, and lots of hand language some things become clear. Mark is a refugee from Poland where Solidarity has just triumphed over the Communist establishment. He writes the name *Lech Walesa* on a napkin and then thumbs through his dictionary till he finds the word *compromise*. He pounds his finger on the napkin and the entry for *compromise* in his dictionary. He writes *Solidarity = Communists* and says, "No good also." Then he draws a quick map of Poland on the napkin and violent, billowing scribbles whose meaning is clearly that Poland is going to blow up. He has friends in Edmonton who immigrated last year and he has come to join them.

So far he doesn't like Canada. "Is boring," he says. Connie thinks it's hilarious that someone from Poland would find Canada boring, but further questioning reveals what he really means. "Rules," he says, and pulls out a pack of Marlboro cigarettes. "No smoke . . . too many places."

"Amazing," says Connie. "His first impression of the free world is not being free to do something he takes for granted."

I want to know where he got the Marlboros. Traveling on trains in Canada, where Mark's complaint notwithstanding it seems everybody smokes, I have suffered a relapse into the habit and have been frustrated all across the country by the difficulty of finding any American cigarettes besides Salem Menthols and Winston Lights.

"Black interest," he says. "Eighty cents." He offers me one and I accept. By the time I have finished it, and with more map drawing on the napkin, it emerges that he has come to Canada via Italy where he bought the Marlboros for eighty cents American on the black market—U.S. military PX stuff.

Connie shows Mark how to use a Canadian pay telephone and he succeeds in placing his call to the friend in Edmonton. Meanwhile the D.J. has taken his place at the wheel of a cutoff Buick, which is his console beside the dance floor, and the driving beat of the Cars' "Summer" provokes Connie to step lively toward the floor, gesturing for me to follow. A wave of inhibition quickly rises and passes. If you're going to travel and not be an accidental tourist, you have to be a participant.

When Mark finishes his call we head back across the street to catch our train. It turns out Connie's roomette is next door to mine, but since Mark is traveling alone in coach, we hike to the front of the train to join him in his car for the rest of the evening.

We find him waiting for us in one of the seat groupings where two pairs of chairs face one another. Mark doesn't want to talk. He just wants to listen to others speaking English, so Connie obliges him while, outside the train, mechanics wrestle with some problem that has delayed our departure.

Connie is another "voyageur." After graduating from university in Edmonton, she taught first grade for a year, hated it, started traveling, and was hooked. "I'm a terminal travel addict," she says. "In Edmonton, life was getting boring. So I just took off with a girlfriend for Australia."

She and her friend hitchhiked all over the country, working as waitresses when they needed more money. Australia was especially appealing to this Canadian who hates cold—"It's big and sparsely populated just like Canada, but it's warm."

Traveling taught her that she wasn't as weird as her settled family and friends back home thought. "We're all over the world, us travel addicts. Just like drugs, many started out trying to escape something bad and then just kept going. With some, it's a really particular thing like a bad marriage, or a cruel family, or trouble with the law or something, eh? But with me, it's a general thing—I just didn't want to live by the norm, follow the rules, do what you're expected to do. My mom thinks I'm irresponsible." Now she's headed home for a spell and is happy about it.

Connie is intrigued to meet an American who really wants to hear about her country, and she is blunt: "I don't mean to be rude, but I really don't like Americans very much. Nobody does. The Americans you meet traveling are obnoxious, self-absorbed, and they never listen. I've seen English-speaking travelers who aren't Canadian put Canadian flag stickers on their backpacks so people won't think they're American."

The train has finally pulled out of the Winnipeg yards and into the inky night of the empty northern plains. Outside, the sky mysteriously brightens, almost like the hour before sunrise, but it's midnight and the gathering glow is whiter, more electric than sunrise. When the conductor dims the cabin lights, the night sky looks like a violent electrical storm, frozen in mid-flash. It's the northern lights, in a display like nothing I have ever seen, even in northern New England. Mark, who has never seen them before, is dazzled. Connie smiles placidly in the electric glow and stops her chuckling banter. There's nothing you can say in that light that isn't stupid.

The first large group of travelers over the route of the *Super Continental* were not seeking homes—they were after gold. In 1862, long before the coming of railways, a group that came to be known as the "Overlanders" conceived the fantastic project of crossing the continent by land to partake in the Cariboo gold rush in British Columbia. In June, having already endured two months of rail and river steamer travel from the east to Winnipeg, the Overlanders embarked on another of those epic Canadian treks. With horses, oxen, and Red River carts, they set out along the Carleton Trail over the tall grass prairie, where only a handful of white men had ventured before, for the Yellowhead Pass nearly two thousand miles away.

The Red River carts, which also played a significant role in the Metis migrations, were the closest symbolic equivalent in Canada of the covered wagons of the United States. They were two-wheeled contraptions built entirely of wood and buffalo hide—no metal parts whatsoever. With no bearings on the axles, wood just rubbed on wood; they emitted an awful characteristic screech that became the sound of migration on the prairie.

The easterners learned to eat pemmican, the staple of the plains. It was made from the lean meat of the buffalo, cut into strips, cooked, dried in the sun till brittle, and pounded into powder. The fat was melted down and combined with the powdered meat in sacks made from the buffalo hides. Sometimes berries or currants were mixed in. The resultant mass of concentrated food would keep for years and yielded adequate nourishment for those with stomachs to eat it.

The trek provided a fine example of mobile democracy. Councils were held along the way and resolutions passed, most of which dealt with maintaining amicable relations with the Indians. The party was blessed with several good diarists, who wondered at the rolling expanses of tall grasslands, so like the sea itself. They delighted in the immense flocks of ducks and geese that descended en masse on the sloughs and rose as with one body in flight. But there was unpleasantness, too. The mosquitoes were "like swarms of hummingbirds" and wolves were constant companions. Rains swelled rivers so that bridges had to be hastily constructed and tents became cold bathtubs at night. But the party made it to Fort Edmonton, where some wrote that they might be tempted to take up residence if not for the diet of pemmican and potatoes. The place was surprisingly well supplied with handsome women.

The Overlanders continued beyond Edmonton to greater travails in the crossing of the mountains. Once they were saved from starvation by trading with local Indians for salmon and mountain sheep meat. Finally, after harrowing rafting down the Thompson and Fraser rivers, the survivors made it to British Columbia. There, a year and a half after they set out, they found frustrated miners fleeing for the ports who told a story that must have made their blood freeze. The creeks were overstaked and overclaimed; there was little or no opportunity for newcomers. In the end, none of the Overlanders found gold. Some went south to the United States, some went home, but most found new lives and became citizens in the nascent communities of the west. Their quest became a legend and their route would one day echo with the sounds of the railway and the energy of immigration.

In the morning, I am awakened by a rap on my door. It's the service chief and he wants to know if I'd like to ride in the engine cab for a while.

The train has stopped at the Saskatchewan prairie town of

Biggar. A sign by the little white clapboard station reads, NEW YORK IS BIG, BUT THIS IS BIGGAR. The dominating feature is the huge grain elevator down the tracks that is the reason for this town's existence. I hike up the platform outside the train to the engine and clamber up the ladder into the cab.

Inside, engineer Sam Riley and assistant Neil Berkman are having coffee and greet me with friendly handshakes. When refueling is completed, Sam releases the airbrake, which lets out a loud gasp, and then pulls on the power lever. I can hear the deep, rising, bone-humming violence in the engine room behind me. Here on the flat straightaway of the Saskatchewan prairie, this baby gets from zero to sixty in about six minutes and when the speedometer gets up above sixty, seventy, eighty, I am surprised by how rough the ride is up here and how noisy the tracks are underneath. The engine bounces up and down and slams back and forth. A passenger in the well-cushioned cars has no idea of the rampaging forces involved in transit and it's just as well. At eighty-five miles per hour over what I'm told is very good track, a rider in the engine feels about as secure as, well, an airline passenger at that scariest moment of maximum acceleration on takeoff—continuously. In the engine you become sensitized to subtle grades that are imperceptible in the passenger realms. The engines buzz the bones a little more deeply on gentle upgrades. The sandpaper blast of the engineer applying the air brakes announces downgrades.

I am surprised to see that the country along the route we follow today, historically the "fertile crescent" that the CPR passed up when it made its decision to take a southerly route, looks to me even more arid and uninviting today than the Palliser's Triangle country I rode through a few days ago. The towns of Landis, Scott, and Unity remind me of stunted trees that fail to thrive in high altitudes because of the harsh environment. The little lakes and sloughs we pass are shrunken and bounded by white rims of mineral deposits. Most of the land is dedicated to pasture—there are few of the well-cultivated grain-producing fields I saw along the CPR route—but Sam and Neil explain that this is due to the railway surveyors' mandate to build a fast, straight, direct route through here. The fertile valleys of the Saskatchewan and tributary rivers wind and meander in these northern prairies, but the CN's beeline from Winnipeg to Edmonton traverses northern fingers of Palliser's Triangle that are some of its worst regions. The only tangible sign of the overall fecundity of this region is the huge grain silos at even the smallest of whistle-stops.

Sam and Neil enthusiastically bombard me with observations about VIA's current crisis. When the Liberals cut this train in 1976, Jasper lost 25 percent of its tourist revenue and the Conservatives promised it would never happen again. The train carries sixty thousand Japanese and American tourists per year; VIA pays CN $1.35 per axle mile to use the tracks. But it's worse on the *Canadian* route, where the CPR charges VIA twice what it pays the crews who run the train—a 100 percent profit. CN trainmen are afforded the opportunity to cross over permanently to VIA as in the highly successful job-swap program of Amtrak and the American railroads, but the CPR wouldn't allow it for their crews. Sam and Neil, in company loyalty that I hear often on CN trains, have a lot of nasty things to say about the rival CPR. CPR crews do not tend to return the insults—almost as if the CN is beneath their notice. Sam confirms, "Well, yeah, the CPR is bigger than the CN, not track-mileagewise, but powerwise. You've heard that the government runs CN, well, CPR runs the government."

Beyond Unity, there are wheatfields, blighted by drought in this dry year. And north of the tracks, Sam points out a huge lake, Manitou, striking for the absence of trees along its shore. In the cuts through rises in this stretch we see piles of chopped-up railroad ties. Sam explains that it's against Canadian environmental rules to burn the old creosote-soaked ties, but that they are always neatly stacked up along here by daylight and gone the following morning.

During this cab ride, I have tried to keep my mouth shut, in hopes that I might be able to observe the normal conversation of the head-end crew. Eventually the routine of the job and the landscape lull Sam and Neil into talk about their families, about divorces, women, and Jim Bakker, the American fundamentalist preacher who got caught with his pants down. "He was changing more rubber than just his tires," jokes Neil.

Just as I begin to feel that I have become invisible, we approach a switch and a work crew about a half-mile ahead of us. We're really rolling now, eighty-five miles per hour, and Sam remembers my presence and begins talking to me about the problem of vehicles at grade crossings. "They know about the slow freights that run through here. They should know that fast VIA trains come through, too. But there's a tendency these days to see a train coming and assume that it's poking along. They misjudge the speed of the approaching train, pull out into the grade crossing, and get whacked. Even these track workers up here, they should know better, but look how slow they are gettin' out of our way."

Now we blast through the switch where the crew has been working. At the last moment some of them scurry off the tracks, look up at us, and make gestures saying, "What the hell?"

Sam slaps his forehead as we rattle over the switch and says, "Oh, shit!" He looks at the clipboard on the panel in front of him and says to Neil, "Slow order for that switch, ten miles per hour." Neil whistles and rolls his eyes as the radio crackles and sputters. First it's the foreman of the crew: "Number three, what are you doing? Aren't we on your list?"

"Yes, we know, sorry, guys," says Sam. The radio voice crackles again: "You're lucky to get through okay, one rail was just tacked in place." Neil whistles again.

Now the radio sputters with a woman's voice. "The dispatcher," says Sam with a groan. "Yeah, we're hearing about it," explains Sam to the voice. "We'll make a report."

The voice talks in a code that I can't fully understand, but Neil explains that it means there will be hell to pay at the end of their run with written depositions and possibly even drug tests.

At Wainwright, the end of their run, Sam and Neil bid me goodbye, a little embarrassed. Seeing me descend from the cab, a CN railway man hanging out on the platform who has heard on the scanner of the misadventure accosts me and explains what could have happened. "Ya coulda killed one o' the workmen. But fuckin' A, yer lucky that rail stayed in place. At eighty-five, ya woulda made a helluva show."

I'm a little rattled. I've come to feel so secure traveling by train that I make these journeys without even a trace of the angst that sours air travel for anyone with a touch of imagination. I tell the guy how easily it appears such a mistake can be made and he reassures me that the reason he and a half-dozen others are here is that such an error is so exceedingly rare it's newsworthy. "And besides that, trains have a pretty big margin for error," he insists. "I've heard of trains rolling over spots where a rail has been entirely missing and nothing happened. There's just so much momentum in the right direction, the odds are that the train will go where it's supposed to go." Pretty fair consolation that, but nonetheless, from the day of my cab ride out of Biggar, a little thought, like an itch at the back of the heel, rides with me wherever I go.

When Prime Minister Laurier announced the Sifton Plan to populate the northern prairies, it didn't take long for railway promoters to begin scheming new ways to assist him in getting people to their new homes. Manitoba was rabid about breaking the CPR's monopoly and about establishing its own seaport on Hudson Bay. Enter William Mackenzie and Donald Mann. Having collaborated on contracts for sections of the CPR, they knew how to grease politicians to finance their projects, even in the cleaner age of Laurier. And they knew how to make their railways beloved by the locals as the CPR had never been.

They began by entering into agreements with the Manitoba provincial government to build the line to Hudson Bay in 1896, but Mackenzie and Mann never had any thought of actually building across the Arctic to the bay. Instead they turned the line westward toward the expanses of the fertile belt. Shortly they also began building in the opposite direction, from Winnipeg toward Port Arthur on Lake Superior. Despite their manipulation of the Hudson Bay project, Manitoba saw what was happening and was delighted. Mackenzie and Mann were rapidly breaking the monopoly of the hated CPR.

The railhead of the now-named Canadian Northern rapidly moved west across the prairie. Never has the building of a railway been so integrated into the local life of the communities through which it passed—like a community barn-building, according to one historian. Materials were bought locally and farmers turned out to work on the construction. End of track looked more like a community picnic than the hell-on-wheels assembly of most other railway projects. Mackenzie and Mann never missed an opportunity to cultivate the locals with gifts of wheat, assistance with other community projects, and staunch support of local councils, schools, churches, and road committees.

Meanwhile Prime Minister Laurier began to think seriously of a second transcontinental railway. The Canadian Northern was the obvious partner for such an enterprise, but its organization and financing were chaotic and Mann brashly declared that if he and Mackenzie wanted to be part of a transcontinental project, they would do it on their own. Instead Laurier began looking to the Grand Trunk, the great system well established in the east. The Grand Trunk management and stockholders were more interested in dividends than in risky investment, but general manager Charles Melville Hays thought he spied a way to please both stockholders and the government. If the Grand Trunk could take over the Canadian Northern and combine the CNor's western lines with its own in the east, a second transcontinental would already be more than half done.

Mann and Mackenzie were not expected to be cooperative, so Hays hit on the further scheme of attempting to bluff them into coming to terms. The ruse consisted of no less than a proposal for a complete Grand Trunk transcontinental extending from sea to sea, following the original Sanford Fleming Pacific route just south of and parallel to the Canadian Northern as far as Yellowhead Pass. From there the line would be extended all the way to a Pacific port somewhere near the Alaska boundary. With the mighty Grand Trunk threatening to parallel their main line with tracks connected to both oceans, surely Mann and Mackenzie would come to terms.

The bluff played out in the worst possible manner—the prime minister fell for it, and Mackenzie and Mann didn't. The latter, with their own promises of subsidies from friendly politicians in hand, played hardball. They were ready to duplicate the route themselves if the Grand Trunk didn't agree to a purchase price twice what the Canadian Northern had cost to build. Surely the government would never assent to the cost of two transcontinentals, and the infamy would all come down on the Grand Trunk's head.

Caught bluffing, Grand Trunk officials sat down with the government for serious negotiations on a second transcontinental. The western division would become the Grand Trunk Pacific, the eastern division would eventually be operated by the government as a publicly owned enterprise. The entire project would constitute the National Transcontinental Railway.

It was the worst possible outcome for both the Grand Trunk and the Canadian Northern. Now Mackenzie and Mann were forced to make good on their threat to build from sea to sea in order to compete. Thus without ever intending to, the Canadians built two more transcontinentals.

In August 1905, the Grand Trunk Pacific began construction west of Winnipeg over the route I am currently riding. Except for the Saskatchewan capital of Saskatoon, the line ran through country far less settled than that of the CPR to the south or the Canadian Northern to the north. To compete, the GTP management was determined to build a higher quality railway that could carry more traffic faster and to found townsites along the route that would act as magnets to attract settlers. In the first undertaking, the GTP succeeded spectacularly. The same engine could haul six times the tonnage over the GTP route as it could over the CPR and three times the tonnage of the great American transcontinentals.

The campaign to establish townsites was so orderly that streets were laid out before the first settler arrived—a considerable advantage to immigrants, who were pleased to have an address rather than a nameless spot on the prairie. But despite the founding of prosperous communities such as Wainwright, the Grand Trunk arrived late in the game and never developed the traffic of either of its competitors. A CPR spy once reported, "The Canadian Northern has lots of traffic and no railway. The Grand Trunk has a good railway and no traffic. God help us if they ever get together."

Though the Grand Trunk Pacific would go on to reach the Pacific at Prince Rupert and the Canadian Northern would reach Vancouver, the projects would eventually bankrupt them both. But what is bad for a railway or two isn't necessarily bad for a nation. By the 1920s, both railways became components of the Canadian National, the largest railway in the world and a major cornerstone of the Canadian success story of the twentieth century. But that's a story for another chapter.

As a gratuity for taking her camera to the front and getting her some cab-view pictures, Connie Roch treats me to lunch in the dining car. Normally this train carries a Skyline car where the tables at one end serve as diner, but the Skyline car was taken off last night for repairs. In fact the entire consist is different from that on the CPR route. There is no rear lounge, bar, and dome car. Instead, runs on the CN routes often utilize an intriguing piece of equipment that combines the features of all of them, minus the dome, in one car. At one end, there is a small bar-lounge area, partitioned off from the corridor that passes through along the windows on one side of the train. In the middle there is the tiniest galley and then a lunch counter with six revolving stools. At the other end are six tables for traditional dining service.

The lunch menu is the same as on the full-sized dining cars, and the galley crew complains about having to put out the same service in such a tiny work space. But the ambience is intimate, and with folks sitting at the lunch counter reading newspapers picked up in the last station, the effect is a curious twist on a twist—a train diner resembling the highway diners set up to resemble train diners.

For lunch, Connie and I are seated with a talkative couple traveling to Edmonton. Sandy Schultz, a barrel of a fellow who looks like one of those guys on muscle-building shows on TV, is a roustabout for an oil company. His wife, Ina, looks like a *Playboy* model—blue-eyed, platinum blond, and everything about her bigger than life.

They're also environmentalists. Toronto, from whence they are returning, was a horror, they say. "The sky's the wrong color, even on clear days," says Sandy. "And when I went fishing, I saw more dead ones than live ones. I threw out the line I used so I wouldn't contaminate anyplace back home."

Despite his calling, Sandy seems sincere when he says that he lives in Alberta because of its good environmental record rather than for the money he makes working for an oil company. "Our energy boom happened after everybody else's and we learned from their mistakes. There's not a polluted river or lake in the province." But he worries about pulp mills, which in Canada have a dismal history of being the one industry that is immune to the nation's strong environmental conscience.

Connie asks Ina what she does for work and the couple exchange a glance of conspiracy. "Can I tell them?" says Sandy. I think, "Where have I heard this before?" She shakes her head and whispers between her teeth, "You don't know how people will react, come on—don't embarrass me."

But he's bound and determined to do just that. "You're having lunch with Miss Nude Universe, eh?" Sandy announces.

Three nude dancers in three train rides! But it's true, they have the trophies back in their roomette to prove it. Ina has just won the pageant that nude dancer Shannon Wakeley told me about on the last train I rode.

Ina knows Kathy Stack, has just beaten her for the Universe title after losing the Canadian title to her last year. Ina has only been in the business for three years. "I had heard about nude dancing, but I always thought the girls who did it must be kinda weird." She worked as a computer programmer for an insurance company where two of her friends quit to go into nude dancing.

"Soon they were making more money than I was and they weren't weird. So that did it."

Ina confirms much of what I've already heard from Shannon Wakeley and Kathy Stack. Echoing Shannon, she says that most successful dancers have some kind of stage identity. "My thing is dramatics—I use a lot of props and dance out little scenes." Her equipment includes an onstage shower, a baby bassinette, a beach ball, and lots of towels.

After lunch, the four of us move to the other end of the car and sit and smoke in the lounge. Here Mark from Poland passes out Marlboros and service chief Jerry Poole holds court. In the corner seat, staring out the window, sits John Solaris, the Alberta rancher I met on the westbound *Canadian*. He seems not at all surprised to see me again and gives me his withering "you are an idiot" look when I make a big deal out of the coincidence of meeting up with him again.

Jerry Poole is certainly the largest man I have ever seen on a train—a jolly three-hundred-plus pounds. This trip he is waging a losing battle against failing equipment with the water out in the car that replaced the Skyline, and toilets in several cars are clogged up, but he refuses to lose his good humor. "I got onto the train when I was a kid and it was so much fun I never got off. It gets in your blood, the clickety-clack, the rockin' and rollin', the days off. I'm not going to spoil it by fretting over what can't be helped now." The one equipment failing that does bother him is the lack of a public address system. "We haven't had working P.A. systems on these cars in years. That's why we do the calls for dinner sittings by sending the steward back through the train. People think it's a charming personal touch, but it's really just old equipment."

There ensues the standard discussion of the fate of VIA, and at this John perks up. So does Connie. "They can't cancel any of our trains," she says.

"Why the hell not?" growls John.

"It's just talk," she answers firmly. "Everywhere I go, people always talk about how it's the last chance to ride this, or to see that or to go there. But it never happens. People just keep on roaming."

As we approach Edmonton, Connie urges me to make an unscheduled stopoff there and let her show me the city. Sandy and Ina concur; if I want to know western Canada, I really need to see Edmonton. In my U.S. train travels, I always stuck to my itinerary, largely due to the fact that sleeping accommodations are usually so heavily booked, but this time I'm going to throw caution to the winds.

As it turns out, I don't have to risk losing my sleeping car digs. At Edmonton, Jerry announces that departure will be delayed while VIA deals with equipment problems. Connie's sister has brought her car to the station—I have two hours to see Edmonton.

Mark is met by his Polish friends at the station, and Connie promises to call him to help him settle into his new home. Sandy and Ina pose for farewell pictures—clothed—and urge me to come see Ina do her show sometime.

Nudity has not always been so acceptable in the Canadian prairies. Among the groups pulled in by Sifton's net was a Russian sect known as the Doukhobars. Having endured generations of persecution in their native land, these Christian pacifist "Sons of Freedom" attracted the attention of no less a figure than Count Leo Tolstoi. Impressed by their rejection of all authority and convention but for that of God residing in their own individual consciences, Tolstoi and others petitioned the Czar's government to allow them to emigrate to Canada under the Sifton Plan. In 1899, over seven thousand Doukhobars settled west of Saskatoon with a promise of exemption from military service.

Though they were hard workers and became immensely successful settlers, trouble ensued quickly. Despite Canadian philanthropic intentions, the Doukhobars continued in their new homes to acknowledge only one source of authority—the God-man, a reincarnation of Christ himself. This man, Peter Verigin, commanded them to forgo education, registration of homesteads, the oath of allegiance, and a handful of other processes in which all immigrants were expected to participate. The authorities made demands, and though Verigin tried to rein in his more radical followers, arson and vandalism erupted in response.

Then in May of 1903, the citizens of Yorkton, Saskatchewan, were shocked to see a column of naked men filing down the road into town. The Mounties were called and clothing was quickly donated by confounded townspeople. Police and citizens surrounded the nudists and struggled to clothe them as they held their bodies rigid. They were arrested and sent to jail for indecent exposure.

Another such parade, in a town far from Yorkton, included women as well as men. The Mountie sent to deal with them fared better. He lured them into a house for the night where he hung a lantern in the doorway and removed the door. It was a good night for mosquitoes, and in the morning the Doukhobars had put on their clothes.

But the increasingly frequent nude protests of the Doukhobars befuddled the Mounties as no miscreants ever had before. Winter brought no relief. The nude parades continued with even more public impact when the temperature dropped below zero. It became common in Saskatchewan to see men or women, when challenged by police on other grounds such as loitering or spitting, tear off their clothes in the middle of the street, sometimes continuing to remove them and strewing pants, socks, skirts, garters, and underwear along the way as constables hauled them to the police station.

Eventually the government responded by reclaiming huge portions of the lands given to the nonconformist sect. But in 1909, Peter Verigin had communal funds enough to buy lands in remote British Columbia. Descendants of his followers still reside there today and are blamed for mysterious fires in schools and sabotage of railway tracks. And nude parades that are not part of any competitive dancing still mark the quirky life of Canada's most nonconformist province.

As one of the most garishly colored patches in the quilt stitched by the Sifton Plan and the railway colonization of the upper-western prairie, the Doukhobars pushed the concept of the Canadian mosaic beyond the limit. More commonly the idiosyncrasies of the different immigrant groups flourished in a nation whose demographics were not blended into a melting pot of monolithic national identity. No one ever planned it this way, but Canada's weak sense of national identity made it the world's first truly international dominion—and also one of its most strifeless nations in the bargain.

"What do you want to see?" Connie Roch wants to know as we drive away from Edmonton station. "The West End Mall or Fort Edmonton?" Edmonton's mall is the world's largest, enclosing an entire theme park as well as the usual shops and stores, but I choose the fort and a chance to see a slice of Alberta away from the tracks.

Edmonton is a city of beautiful, sparsely traveled parkways, rivers, lakes, and rolling greenery. The buildings are new and as tall as they need to be, without attempting any kind of skyline statement. The place is fresh—that's the word—and, for a city, uncrowded. At one point Connie apologizes for traffic that to me looks like what would be left on American freeways "the day after." We stop at one of the riverside parks and soak up the sun for a few minutes while kids float toy sailboats and fly kites. Connie says this is the one season she likes in the place she lives; she hates the winter cold and believes that's what drove her to become a travel addict. "There are probably more of us in Canada than anywhere. I've never wanted to move anywhere else. It's such a good place to live, but you just have to get away from the cold."

At the fort, in the park, and at the downtown convenience store where I stock up on beverages, cheese, and crackers, I am struck by the ease, civility, and friendliness of these Edmontonians. I hear snatches of conversations in a variety of languages—French, Chinese and Japanese, Slavic, Yiddish. The city is not as regular a stop for American tourists as are Vancouver, Calgary, and Banff. I can't even find Winston or Salem cigarettes, but I feel more at ease here than I've felt in Massachusetts towns a half-hour from my home. Take one of the coldest and most northerly forts of the old British empire and import people from all over the world. Who would predict that this pleasant metropolis is what you would get? I suppose it helps that they found oil here, but still—sunny Beirut, eat your heart out.

Back at the station, Connie advises me about my destination, Jasper. There's a place there called the AthaB, which is a mecca for international voyageurs, and there is a man who frequents the joint whom I must seek out. His name is Bob Barker and it should be easy to find him because he is a world-class dancer and a local legend known by everyone in the Jasper region.

John Solaris meets us on the platform as Connie bids me farewell and suggests that we'll probably all meet on a train again sometime.

"If they don't cancel them all," grumbles John.

"They won't; it's just talk," Connie insists again.

After dinner on the *Super Continental*, Jerry Poole lets John and me hang out at the open vestibule window as we wind into the Rockies. To the south, the Athabasca River, surprisingly placid for a watercourse this close to the Continental Divide, meanders and occasionally widens into pristine blue lakes. Beyond it towers a striated hunk of rock, the Roche Miette, with a tree line that seems unusually low till I recall just how far north we are. In fact, what recommended this route originally to Sanford Fleming was its relatively low altitude; the Yellowhead Pass itself is only a little over three thousand feet high. But the mountains along the pass loom as high as those down south at Kicking Horse. With their low tree lines and great vertical drop, they present a towering world of rocky crags which is austere and alien.

It is said that while the CN route has the grades, the CPR route has the scenery. Approaching Jasper through a wide valley, John and I try to analyze just why the Kicking Horse route is considered better scenery despite the Yellowhead's lower tree lines and greater vertical drops. The answer is obvious: the wide, flat valley of the Yellowhead route diminishes its impact—the sheer drops are farther away from the tracks. In the narrow Kicking Horse, the train crawls right along the edge of precipices that here appear at a distance. Riding on this gentle grade into Jasper, I see why Sanford Fleming and the fur traders before him favored this gap two hundred miles farther north. It's one of the few places in Canada where nature provided a friendly gateway to east-west travel.

At Jasper John Solaris and I part company. He is continuing on the *Super Continental* to Vancouver and then across the strait to ride the train on the island. "There's talk that the *Canadian* will be the first to go," he says standing by my roomette door as I gather up my stuff. "Will you be riding the last run?"

"If it comes to that, I will," I promise.

"See you then," he says.

I hit the ground in Jasper near sunset. The place has the instant feel of a heavily touristed town—the streets busy with people toting cameras and wearing souvenir hats and tee-shirts—but it's not unpleasant because there is no oppressive sense that the place is designed for tourists exclusively. Half of the valley is taken up by the extensive CN railyards. This is the junction of the old Grand Trunk route to Prince Rupert with the Canadian Northern route to Vancouver. Nowhere in North America have I seen such extensive rail yard operations amid such imposing mountains. Towering over the town looms the rock of Whistler's Mountain and its dizzying cable car ride. To the west, a dip in the skyline is Yellowhead Pass itself, and beside it rises the ice-draped peak of Mount Edith Cavell.

There is a huge green lawn across the street from the station where dozens of voyageurs lounge with their backpacks. Beyond that I can see the Athabasca Hotel where I am booked. And there, as part of the hotel, is Connie's AthaB bar. My room turns out to be just upstairs from it.

After check-in, I confirm Connie's report on the AthaB. The place is really two bars. The inner bar, with its own door to the street, is a dance place, and it isn't long before the floor that circles around the live band is packed with very young singles. The outer bar, adjoining the lobby of the hotel, is the hangout for a slightly older and more worldly gathering—serious voyageurs. Within a half-hour I meet a man from Guyana currently living in London and traveling "beautiful Canada"; a young woman from Australia who was headed east but never made it past Jasper; another young woman from New Zealand; a fellow from France; and an American from Exeter, in my own state of New Hampshire, who wants to know if I have any coke to sell. The Australian says that Jasper is like a thorn bush, which snares passing spores blowing in the wind.

It doesn't take long to find Bob Barker, dancing western-rock style with everyone else standing back as audience in the inner bar. I ask him to meet me for lunch tomorrow, and he says, "Right on," and goes back to dancing.

In the morning, I meet Bob Barker for lunch at the pancake house across the street from the Athabasca Hotel. Bob looks like a cowboy—he wears boots and jeans with a huge belt buckle, a flannel shirt, and a white ten-gallon hat. He confesses that he's over forty, but you'd never guess it. He is divorced and beginning his second life, full of energy and not missing a moment of it. During lunch a procession of folks stops by our table to establish what looks like a daily ritual of contact with the town's closest thing to royalty. The big subject is the indoor rodeo scheduled for next week, of which Bob is an organizer. The other topic is grizzlies. Bob is a warden for Jasper Park and has just returned from a week in the bush checking on bridges, cabins, and trails.

In response to my question about his celebrity, Bob laughs and says, "Well, I've lived here for thirty years. Just stay put in one place long enough and you become a legend these days." The population was only 1,800 when he came here as a boy. Today it's grown to 4,500 and is swelled by many thousands more during the tourist seasons (winter and summer).

When I make a comment comparing the tourism of the town to Banff, he patiently explains that the two places are not to be compared. "Banff is strictly a tourist spot. But with the CN junction and the rodeo, we got a real town that'd be here even if there weren't no tourists." Jasper became a rodeo capital because until recently the railroad had extensive stockyards here. Now most of the freight is potash, lumber, coal, and, of course, grain. Bob believes the tourists "come here for nature that is really unspoiled. You have to watch out for Thumper and Bambi just driving around the streets. And you get just a mile out of town and you're in real wilderness."

After lunch, he takes me in his pickup out along the Yellowhead Highway to the Miette Hot Springs. On the way he points out the mountainside scars of deliberate burns he has taken part in. "Sometimes nature doesn't make enough fires on her own to keep the ecology as rich as we like it to be in a national park. So we step in with a little jellied gasoline dropped from helicopters." It's a hazardous undertaking because "once you've got the fire going it tends to burn with a mind of its own." Bob shows me a ridge in the Colin Range where he had a crew working above a fire that he thought was confined to the north face of the slope. From his supervisory post in the valley he began to see puffs of smoke rising above the ridge behind the crew and to the east. Suddenly he realized that the fire had spread around the base of the mountain and was coming up behind his men, surrounding them. They had to be pulled out by helicopter.

I ask Bob about the little red flags I've spotted along the verge of the highway. He explains that they mark spots where wild animals have been killed by autos. They're part of a wildlife memorial campaign to cut down on the serious problem of road kills. "The animals in Jasper Park have no fear of man. They've never been hunted and the human beings' little corner of the park is so small that they disregard it. They're as fearless today as when the first white men came through here a century and a half ago." Elk, wolves, bighorn sheep, deer, and sometimes even bears have been killed along the highway at a rate of about fifty a year since 1970.

As we drive, Bob slows to check out gatherings of picture-takers stalking an elk, or a sheep, or in one case, a bear. "Look at those idiots," he groans. "We get a few people hurt by animals every year, because they just insist on getting too close." And then there is the problem of poachers. Bob directs my attention to "fingers" of green sweeping down from the cliff faces rising above us. These are great grazing areas for goats, and with goat skins commanding big money on the black market, the poachers pick them off with high-powered rifles from down here and then go up and drag them out. A $100,000 fine has recently been instituted, and Bob hopes it will serve as a deterrent.

At Miette Hot Springs, I'm disappointed to see parking lots and large modern buildings in this wilderness place. Bob says, "It's worse than that. To get the volume of water needed for the big pools, they actually heat up ordinary spring water and add it to the flow." He gestures for me to follow him up a path along the stream and says he'll show me the real thing. It's a pleasant hike, with spectacular views down the canyon toward towering peaks. Along the way we are entertained by whistlers, fearless little creatures that look like oversized chipmunks and dart out at us looking for a handout and posing for pictures.

Halfway up the ravine we find the ruins of the original establishment. Built of stone, brick, and wood, this was a structure worthy of the site. Surrounded by several levels of verandas and patios, the old pool is rather small, and the forest grows up to the very foundation of the structure. Here those taking the waters must have found truly intimate contact with nature and with each other. Bob explains that at this site, cold spring water had to be mixed with the hot springs to bring it down to a temperature that wouldn't poach the bathers.

Several hundred yards beyond the old spa, we find the natural outlet of one of the springs. A heavy sulphur smell is in the air, but it's not unpleasant, not like rotten eggs. Clouds of steam rise from a bright yellow grotto where the hot water bursts out of the side of the mountain and splashes into a boiling pool. "Well," says Bob. "Are you going to take the waters or not?" So off come the shoes and pants and tentatively I submerge a toe, then a foot. The water is excruciatingly hot, but finally I am standing in it, my legs red like lobsters. Veils of steam drift between me and Bob, who is crouched beside the pool. Whether it's because of the sound of the rushing waters or the pleasant buzz that rises in my head from the back of my neck, I can no longer hear what he is saying. But this feels great—better even than the rock and roll of a train or the warm glow of champagne.

Afterward as we hike back down to the parking lot, I feel as though I'm pleasantly coming down from some blessed opiate. Bob says it's the gases, or maybe the hot sulphur getting into the blood, but that's what people come here for.

Later in the afternoon, Bob takes me to the home of his friends Rick and Sharon. Rick is also a warden for the park, and over chips and beer, they talk shop: trail blow-ups, guys who are bad luck to go out with, the occasional modern-day bandit, and, of course, bears.

There are also Bob's plans for an officious partner he has to work with sometimes. "I'm going to take that asshole out in a river and drown him." There's a lot of talk about horses, how easy they are to hurt, how they don't bounce back from injury when you push them too hard; and Bob's promise to ride again in the rodeo despite several injuries he's received. "You boys," says Sharon, "you just have to get that big ole belt buckle."

I'm not in any hurry to leave this pleasant little abode nestled amid birches and pines under the cliffs that tower above the Yellowhead Highway, but Bob wants to get me back to town with time to properly anticipate the next leg of my journey. "You have to sit and wait for a train—see who's coming along to ride with you—and look around at the place you're leaving and think about it," he explains when he drops me off at the station.

When he's gone I park myself on the lawn across the street from the station with some backpacking voyageurs from Germany and Finland who sit hunched up in blankets as the night air cools. There are stars overhead and a thin sliver of a moon setting in the western gap of Yellowhead Pass. But it's not these sights that mesmerize the voyageurs. It's the restless energy out in the rail yards—hundreds of grain cars, slamming and banging in switching operations, a long CN lumber train pulling out with a raspy echo toward the prairie, and my VIA train with a half-dozen blue passenger cars steaming and poised for the Pacific.

5

Work and Drink

JASPER TO PRINCE RUPERT
ON THE *SKEENA*

THOUGH treated as a separate route by VIA Rail, the *Skeena* line to Prince Rupert, Canada's most northerly Pacific port, was originally the westernmost leg of the Grand Trunk Pacific in the National Transcontinental system built during Prime Minister Laurier's regime. Today's *Super Continental*, which I have taken from Winnipeg to Jasper, makes a turn just west of Yellowhead Pass and heads southwest over the old Canadian Northern line to Vancouver. With apologies to Mackenzie and Mann, I plan to miss that stretch in my travels. For weeks I have been imagining the ride on the *Skeena* through a great blank spot in my mental map of North America to a port that's almost in Alaska. Northern British Columbia is a place I never thought I would see, especially from the comfort of a sleeping car on a train.

The evening ride on the *Skeena* out of Jasper is quiet, no rowdy singles scene in the bar, no poker, no loud storytellers. Two men about my age sit and talk quietly in the otherwise empty lounge. They are old friends, returning from a Jasper fishing trip to their homes in Prince George. I overhear just enough of their conversation to understand that one of them fears his wife is planning to leave him and that this has been the main subject of their talk throughout the vacation.

"She's still a damn good woman, looks ten years younger than thirty-eight, doesn't she?" The friend nods in agreement.

"I look at her and get turned on like crazy, but by the time I get around to doing anything about it, I just want to get my rocks off and go to sleep. Why does that happen?" Friend shrugs.

"She says all I know is 'work and drink, work and drink.' She wants more out of a man—and she's going to find it."

The next morning, I am surprised to see fields, tractors, and grain elevators outside the window of the dining car as I order breakfast. We have crossed the spine of the Rockies and passed Prince George during the night, and before we wend our way through the Coast Mountains there is a stretch of little-known agricultural land in the heart of northern British Columbia. I am seated with a woman in her fifties and her twenty-five-year-old companion, who study the passing landscape with more than voyageurs' interest. Charlotte Dubois and Krista Mack are mother and daughter beginning a second life together and looking for a new place to call home.

There was trouble in the family during Krista's teenage years, and she ran away from home. Now she and her mother are reunited after ten years. "She showed up on my doorstep in Ontario after my divorce and said, 'Mom, let's go west.' So here we are," explains Charlotte. They did it Krista's way—no itinerary, no reservations, just two Canrail passes, good for a month on the trains.

Following the Nechako River, a tributary of the mighty Fraser that runs down the center of British Columbia, we soon leave the agricultural area and enter forested mountains, which remind me of my home in New England, except that all the flora are different. Along Fraser Lake we are treated to a display of huge wildflowers— magenta, golden, electric blue—unlike any I have seen before. Krista Mack and her mom are glued to the window, rapt with thoughts of home-founding in an unspoiled frontier.

But at Burns Lake we see scars on the mountainsides—clear-cutting operations. We pass lumberyards with piles of tree trunks bearing the telltale green color of chemical pressure treatment and I'm reminded of burning piles of railway ties in Saskatchewan. Canada has a reputation as an environmentally progressive nation, especially along the thin strip contiguous to the United States, but in remote regions where the economy struggles, environmental horrors are perpetrated. Northern British Columbia turns out to be one of those places. Besides fish and timber, the traffic has never lived up to the economic hopes of the railway and government officials who brought the Grand Trunk here in the first place. Thus those two resources are exploited to extremity in what should be Canada's most pristine land.

Despite the fact that the scheme to build a transcontinental through this country was initially a bluff and finally a financial disaster, the Grand Trunk had good reasons to believe that it could actually be a success. The route had been seriously considered by Sanford Fleming for the first Pacific Railway because of its easy grades. The Japanese current guarantees ice-free harbors and a surprisingly mild climate along the coast even this far north. Any new port located near the Alaska boundary would be considerably closer to Japan and the Far East than the CPR's terminal at Vancouver, which had already become a booming success.

In addition to these inducements, northern British Columbia seemed to offer something else the dominion desperately needed—economic variety. So far the west had generated only one commodity, wheat. British Columbia offered gold and silver, halibut and salmon, cedar and Douglas fir, and eventually a cornucopia of fruit and other agricultural products, due to its mild climate. And then there was electricity, known in Canada as hydro, because the country is so blessed with waterpower that no other source is needed. Surely a province so well endowed with natural resources and having a seemingly unlimited source of energy could support another great Pacific seaport and accompanying transcontinental railway. Grand Trunk President Charles Melville Hays developed a scheme that transformed a bluff to a dream of a new transportation empire in the age of grand undertakings. Fittingly, he was one of those aboard the *Titanic* when it went down. The plan went forward without him, but his fate might have been taken as an omen for what was ahead.

In the autumn of 1908 at the specific request of the always prickly B.C. leadership, construction began from the west eastward. On the advice of the British admiralty, a fine harbor was chosen out of cannon range of the Alaska border. Sheltered by an offshore island and located on an island itself, the new port of Prince Rupert was founded with visions of its becoming a second Vancouver.

Following the Skeena River, the railhead soon encountered the narrow canyon known as the Hole in the Wall of the Coast Mountains. Here engineers wrestled with many of the same challenges faced by the CPR in the Fraser Canyon, only this time there was no road already in place and the scale was larger. Thus the task was not so much a matter of innovative engineering (the experience of the Fraser already provided the know-how) as it was sheer, brute labor.

Historian William Hard's description of the legendary Swansie the Tireless Swede illustrates the challenge. He describes the subcontractor who knows he can make men work but needs "station men" like Swansie to make them work hard enough to kill them, which is what it takes to get the job done: "The station man goes and gets a bunch of fellows as dippy as himself and they make a gang who . . . say, 'We will chew the rock out of this hill and chuck it into this mighty river for so many cents a cubic yard.'" Since they work by quantity rather than time, they labor at all hours, their lanterns shining in the small of the night and meals consumed at the task. Their only requisition is for meat. "'Got to work,' says Swansie. No time to boil porridge or make bread. No time to suck water with a carrot or tomato flavour, which is all a vegetable is. Give him meat, every ounce the solid, right stuff." When they come down with scurvy, Swansie orders a barrel of lime juice and makes them drink it till they're sick. And when the job is done, they get paid, often under Swansie's supervision, enough to buy a farm in Saskatchewan and settle down.

By the muscle of such men, the Skeena River section of the route was built at a cost below that of any comparable stretch before or since. The section over the Rocky Mountains was considerably easier to build than the CPR's Rocky Mountain crossing due to the excellence of Yellowhead Pass, but near Jasper, the construction crews encountered an obstacle that would not yield. Along the route through the wide valley were ponds that had to be drained when they stood in the way of the approaching railhead. By the day following a draining operation, the ponds would always be back at exactly the level of the day before drainage. Jasper's native engineers, the beavers, simply would not be out-engineered or out-labored, repairing their dams faster than the railwaymen could wreck them. The railway acknowledged defeat and relocated the line.

In the spring of 1914, nine years after construction began, the National Transcontinental opened for traffic from Quebec to Prince

Rupert by way of the GTP in the west. After an initial flurry of high-stakes real estate speculation, residents and property owners in Prince Rupert settled down to await the tide of commerce that would flow over the railway to their deep-water harbor and transform their little island into another San Francisco, Seattle, or Vancouver.

Seventy-six years later, they are waiting still. Again the gods of irony must have giggled when the railway itself funneled B.C.'s natural resources away from Prince Rupert to the east and Japanese shippers replaced British dominance in the Pacific, shunning Prince Rupert for Vancouver in order to maximize the length of the seagoing journey (and thus their profits) and minimize the length of the ensuing rail journey to eastern destinations. The occasional B.C. earthquake might just be the gods' belly-laugh at the fact that today the *Skeena* passenger route is listed by the government as a heavily subsidized "protected route" serving a remote and isolated community not otherwise accessible.

During lunch in the diner, we are treated to the beginning of the spectacular run through the Coast Mountains. The tracks aren't located high on mountain walls as they are in Kicking Horse Pass, but the views are just as impressive. Winding along the Bulkley River, the route presents varying perspectives on the glacier-draped peaks that rise abruptly from the verge of the flat valley. Just after Smithers, the train runs so close to Kathlyn Glacier that crews hang out the open vestibule doors to catch a whiff of its exhilaratingly cool breath. No fleeting distant view of a little piece of snow high on a peak here; the massive ice seems to roll down between two mountains, all the way to the valley floor.

My companions for lunch are a tough lumberjack and his teenage daughter. They aren't very sociable, but I can't help but overhear the daughter ask her father in whispers questions like, "Where does meat come from, Dad?" His answer is even more skewed, "Well, I guess horses, buffalo—sometimes dogs."

The girl fiddles with the salad dressing packets wondering what they are for. Dad encourages her to find out by ripping one open and tasting what's inside. She struggles to read the menu and wonders what seafood is. Patiently Dad explains that, well, it must be some kind of food from the sea—like fish.

When she turns her attention to me and wants me to confirm that her hair color is the most beautiful thing in nature, just like a squirrel's, Dad intervenes, telling her to be still and asking me to forgive his daughter's strangeness. "She's not quite right, you know. Mother died when she was a littl'un and, well, we live pretty far out in the bush and I never had the time to really raise her right. Had to work."

The man is a jack-of-all-trades mountain man. He traps furs in the winter and hires out as a tree cutter to lumber operations in the summer. The girl has grown up in the woods—never saw another child her own age till a couple of years ago. Now they are returning from Prince George and a session with a psychologist-counselor who is trying to compensate for years of developmental retardation. "The social worker came out to see us and said my daughter was suffering from some kind of mental disease that was my fault for being a bad father. But he was decent to me, said I didn't know any better. They let her stay with me if I promised to take her to Prince George once a month and do this and that. So we go on the train. I don't mind. I get pretty thirsty out where we live, if you know what I mean. There's a lot of things you can't buy anywhere near us, but Prince George—well, I tell you, that's some town."

Apparently his daughter's questions are the result of the psychologist's counseling. "He tells her to ask questions about everything. Keeps me on my toes, I'll tell you. F'rinstance, she knows about meat—from the game I shoot. But things like that neat little hamburger patty the waiter brings really cross her up."

After lunch, I take my coffee down the hall to the lounge, where I'm joined by a large, robust woman who sat across the aisle from me and the woodsies during lunch. "I hope you don't think everybody in northern B.C. is like them," she says. Loretta is returning from a family reunion in Dome Creek to her home on the Queen Charlotte Islands, across the strait from Prince Rupert, where she is a janitor in a public school. Despite her opening statement, Loretta confirms that it's not the first time she has encountered some pretty strange birds from back-country riding this train. "See a lot of drunks, too, usually loggers or down-on-their-luck Indians. Northern B.C. is a hard place for some people."

"But not you. Why?"

"Well, it's different out on the islands. We live what you would probably call 'an alternative life-style.' We don't need a booming economy to get by. There are just enough back-to-the-earth folks with a little money to keep my town of Tlell going." There are only fifty families in Tlell, working at carpentry, a little farming, some fishing. A rare breed of modern homesteader has settled there for the kayaking, the hiking, the horseback riding, and the peace that comes from living far from the haunts of men.

And there are native tribes. The Haidas on the Charlottes are politically well organized and aggressively defend their way of life in concert with the environmentally oriented whites like Loretta. "Their leader, Miles Richardson, has done more to keep out the lumber companies than anyone. Now he wants to make whites get a kind of passport to be able to come out to the island. I wouldn't mind that. There are an awful lot of mainlanders here who just don't understand how things are out on the Charlottes. Now they want to bring us a gold mine and an oil rig. The gold mine would make mercury tailings. The oil rig is unspeakable."

The Charlottes have survived as an unspoiled place because they are isolated from an isolated place. The strait between Prince Rupert and Queen Charlotte Island is shallow and among the most hazardous in North America. But the pressure to exploit the economic bonanza of northern British Columbia that has never fully ripened continues, with the islands as its most recent target.

Joined after lunch by Charlotte Dubois and Krista Mack, we ride all afternoon in the lounge while outside pass glaciers that you don't see from trains anywhere else. Some are like hanging waterfalls and some are massive white snowshields. Closer to the tracks at Kitwanga we see occasional totem poles and, more curious, little graveyards with white picket fences around individual graves. Loretta explains that these are for Haida families, who believe that walking on the dead is absolutely forbidden.

The scenery on this train ride builds from modest beginnings to these spectacular ice mountains, and just when you think that the show has peaked, the Skeena Valley tightens, the cliffs move closer to the tracks, and the train is enclosed in a true fjord. The only marks of man are the railway and the Yellowhead Highway, carved into the rock walls and built on fill out over the river shallows. Occasionally we stop at tiny clapboard station post offices where someone comes to collect the mail for communities of less than a score of inhabitants. After dinner, the river widens and the silver light of the late northwestern sun spangles it like foil while huge birds cruise alongside the train, matching our speed so that even the clumsiest photographer can get great pictures of them.

"Those aren't bald eagles?" I ask Loretta.

"That's what they are," she says. "We'll see them all the way to Rupert now. They're considered common here—don't be offended—but here they're just garden-variety pests, garbage scavengers."

Finally, after 7:00 P.M., the river widens and a smoky fog filters the evening sunlight. Standing at the open vestibule door with Charlotte and Krista, I can smell the sea in the cool moist air. We cross a bridge onto Kaien Island and roll along a widening strait to our left. The first sign of Rupert is a huge grain elevator, and then piers and fishing boats and finally streets with houses and little factories. I'm surprised not to see any large rail yards here at the end of the CN line, and the train rolls into a small station right at water's edge with no more than a half-dozen sidings.

It's a far cry from the transcontinental arrival at San Francisco or Seattle or Vancouver. As we detrain Krista is disappointed at not being able to see the Pacific—an island blocks the view. And we can't see much of Rupert either since the town is located up a steep slope above the station. Loretta and most of the other passengers know where they are going and disappear quickly. As we three newcomers trudge up the hill with our baggage to find lodgings, there's a peculiar anticlimactic silence in this arrival at the end of the line. Charlotte seems put out that she has been dragged three thousand miles to such a lonesome place. The loudest sounds we can hear are the cries of seagulls.

Prince Rupert looks like a prosperous town; it just never grew much. With a population of nearly twenty thousand, it's about the same size as my hometown of Keene, New Hampshire. But while we have only a half-dozen motels, restaurants, and churches, Rupert has more than a dozen of each—including places of worship for Sikhs, native Revivalists, Mormons, Mennonites, and Jehovah's Witnesses, as well as the usual Catholic and Protestant denominations. There's one golf course and a gondola ski lift; the harbor hosts cruise ships and ferries to Vancouver, Victoria, and Alaska. The largest local industry is fishing, followed by the pulp mill and finally the commerce of the port.

Walking the streets of a warm summer Friday evening (the sun stays out till nearly eleven in this latitude), you see mostly native kids hanging out in little groups on the street corners. They are not surly or unfriendly, but they don't seem to know what to do with themselves. I discreetly follow one of these groups of teens around for a while in their seemingly aimless pursuit of amusement. They are mostly of the Tsimpshian or Haida tribes, are well dressed and speak English, good English. I don't hear any of the profanity that I would if I followed a similar group around my own hometown.

Yet as the evening darkens, I encounter the lone wolf Indian drunks that Loretta has told me about. The kids give them a wide berth as they stagger by with glazed eyes. The bars are warming up and muscular bouncers stand at the doorways of each.

Besides native people, there are also Asians and whites out in the early evening, but as the sunlight dims, they become increasingly scarce till after dark, when the streets are left almost entirely to the tribes. Still I feel no sense of danger and, after meeting up with Charlotte and Krista, we set out for a night on the town.

At a place called Bogie's, there's an extremely good rock band, but it's just too loud for talk and there is no sense of a regular local clientele. We move on to a place next door, which seems a bit rough for Charlotte. Finally we encamp at the Surf Club where a local Haida rock band plays good dancing stuff and the air is just as full of good barroom talk. It's not long before a friendly fellow has bought us a round and strikes up a conversation.

His name is Dave Anderson and he runs a marina. He spotted us for strangers as soon as we walked in. "Basically everybody in Rupert knows everybody. And this is a real locals place so you three really stood out."

Dave explains that Rupert isn't a particularly happy town right now. A long strike in the fishing industry has just been settled and the fishermen lost $20-$30,000 each by missing the sockeye salmon run. The timber and pulp industries are hurting, too, as environmental concerns increasingly hem in their freewheeling operations in northern British Columbia. "Rupert's not much of a place in good times," he confides. "But recently it seems everybody has to work harder to just get by. The only ones doing well are the people who run these bars."

"Work and drink?" I venture.

"Exactly. You know, everybody back east always talks about our Indians' alcohol problems. But it's not just the Indians. It's everybody. A friend of mine who works for the government here says that northern B.C. has the world's second-highest rate of alcoholism after Russia. Work and drink. That's really about all there is to do here."

I wonder if I would find people around town who would disagree strongly with his decidedly non–chamber of commerce viewpoint.

"Oh, I'm sure you would. We got old families here who think that

Rupert is the center of the world. We got people involved in the tourist trade who make a good, exciting living off of what a beautiful place this is. And we got alternative life-style types, especially out on the islands, who scream bloody murder if you change one foot of their coastline or mountain. It's the ordinary working people who don't do so well."

Krista wants to know if it's the northerly climate that does it. "No, it's not bad here, you know. You look at a map and it seems so far north. But the Japanese current keeps it warmer year-round here than Toronto by far. No, it's isolation. In the east a town of twenty thousand is usually not far from a city of two hundred thousand. Even on the prairies there are little communities of several thousand all over the place that add up to a lot of company. But here we are the big city and the outlying communities have populations less than a hundred."

"So the railway is pretty important here," I suggest.

"I guess. In the winter it's often the only way out. The weather can get pretty bad for flying and it's a long boat ride to Vancouver. And the Yellowhead Highway is closed sometimes for months."

"Snow?"

"No, black ice. It just freezes right out of the fog on the pavement for hundreds of miles. They don't even attempt to sand that much road when it gets bad. You know that the town was built to give the railway a place to go to. Well, today the railway is what keeps the town going."

The Surf Club is lively tonight, the dance floor full. Two female dancers in particular attract a lot of attention. The younger one, a wispy, long-haired blond waif who can't be out of her teens, frequently shouts to the older one, who might be forty, "I love yuh, Mom."

Dave confirms that they are mother and daughter and well-known drinking buddies in Rupert. The daughter is nineteen and married to the guy that both have been telling to get lost all evening. He's supposed to be home with the baby on girls' night out. As the hour gets later I can see the wild sheen that burns bright in the daughter's eyes as she puts down the beer at a rate I can't begin to match. Mom gets sloppy, eventually declaiming loudly again and again, "Am I gonna get laid tonight or what?"

In deference to them, Dave revises the slogan to "Work and drink and fuck." He has a son at home himself. The boy's mother split for California a few years back so Dave is a single parent. He takes his son to Vancouver or Edmonton on the train as often as possible to make sure he doesn't suffocate in the isolation of Rupert. They enter fishing contests together and spend a lot of time exploring the channels with a friend who keeps a lighthouse. "I hope I'm giving the kid a good life," he says as we pay our tabs and head for the door.

"You don't like Rupert very much. Why do you stay here?" I ask before heading back to my hotel.

Dave pauses in front of the entrance to the Surf Club and stares for a minute out toward the harbor before answering. "I used to say it was the money. When you've got steady work in Rupert, the pay is good, better than for similar work in places less isolated. And if you don't blow it in bars, you can save a lot fast. But I don't care about the money anymore. I guess I feel more isolated in Vancouver with a half-million people where I don't know anybody than I do here in Rupert where I know everybody. It's home."

When he's gone, I walk Charlotte and Krista back to their hotel. Charlotte says, "Well, it's not going to be our home," and Krista agrees. They're going to meet me in the station in the morning to ride the very next train right back out of here.

In the morning the stationmaster sums up the paradox of this place. "The railway wouldn't be here anymore if it weren't for Rupert and Rupert wouldn't be here if it weren't for the railway. CN has been keeping this place on the map for a long time. It's more than just tracks and trains. It's a welfare service."

Though the CPR dominated the first half-century of Canada's history as an independent dominion, the Canadian National dominated the second, largely by providing services to far-flung communities that only a government-sponsored enterprise would offer.

Just when both the Canadian Northern and the Grand Trunk had finished construction of their transcontinental lines and needed stability and prosperity to reduce their huge debts, World War I dried up the money supply. In 1917, Conservative Prime Minister Robert Borden was forced to take over the bankrupt Canadian Northern. With government already in the railway business along the line linking Nova Scotia to Quebec and east, Borden's ministers realized that the takeover of the Canadian Northern and its huge debts would prevent the emerging public system from ever becoming viable without the acquisition of an eastern network to complement its new holdings in the west.

Simultaneous with these developments, the war ended and Canada found itself swept by a tide of nationalism that it had never experienced before. Canadians had sacrificed their blood on the fields of France on a proportionate scale not matched by their neighbor Americans until the next war. Long disregarded in the power politics of the world, Canadians now enjoyed the acclaim of their allies and commonwealth nations around the globe. Railways had come to be seen as essential instruments of national security, and Canadian railwaymen, who had managed much of the railway work in Europe during the war, now sat in positions of influence in the government. Over the increasingly minority voices of a few die-hard free enterprisers, the pressure built to create a comprehensive nationalized system by taking over the Grand Trunk, probably North America's best-built railway and one which no doubt could have fended for itself. By 1920 the deal was done and the world's largest railway, the Canadian National, was born.

In 1922, as Lenin and Stalin were obliterating communities in forced collectivization, CNor President Henry Thornton began showing the world how a government-run enterprise could sustain communities and make itself a pillar of a free country. The challenge was to avoid the crippling political entanglements and "trough-feeding" that traditionally hobble publicly run enterprises. It called for a grand vision, and Thornton provided one.

He believed that, besides being efficiently run, public enterprise must be "untouchable"—so visible and valued by the public that the light of popular affection would banish demagogues and meddling politicians to the darker recesses of the body politic. Perhaps Thornton's only model of such an enterprise on the North American continent was the U.S. Postal Service.

Thornton already had the rudiments of such a program in the inherited goodwill of westerners toward the Canadian Northern and of Ontarians and Americans toward the Grand Trunk, whose shortcuts to Chicago had done so much to break the eastern monopolies of the Vanderbilts.

Thornton moved quickly to exploit new technology. Radio was the novelty of the day in 1923 and, after discovering that signals could be received well on trains, Thornton began broadcasting programs for his passengers, offering a service no other carrier could

match. Quickly the system became the dominant network throughout Canada, and in 1924 it inaugurated the national media event
that still entertains Canadians every Saturday evening—"Hockey
Night in Canada." The network eventually became today's CBC.

In 1926, Thornton introduced "school cars" for children in remote
northern regions. Equipped with chalkboards, libraries, the traditional desks, and living quarters for the teacher, these cars brought
learning to a rural public that came to have the highest literacy rate
of such people anywhere in the world. Red Cross cars, equipped for
surgery and dental care and manned by doctors and nurses, criss-
crossed the sparsely inhabited country. Besides the traditional telegraph service, the CNor brought in telephones. And cementing the
loyalty of the prairie west once and for all, the CNor finally built the
prairie dwellers' pipe-dream line to a Hudson Bay port.

Eventually the political hurly-burly, from which Thornton successfully shielded the CNor, brought him down during the years of
the Great Depression, but his vision outlasted him.

This was the era of the freight-riding hobos who congregated
in British Columbia, the fallen businessmen and professionals selling apples on street corners for a nickel in Ontario cities and young
girls selling their bodies for two dollars in prairie towns. Initially
the policy of Conservative Prime Minister Richard Bennett was
to ask Canadians to "bite the bullet" and passively await some
change in the economic cosmos. The Agricultural and Colonization
Department of the CNor thought it could do better than that. Even
before Roosevelt's New Deal began to transform the economics and
politics of the continent, the CNor was offering free grain, livestock
artificial insemination, and technical assistance, and founding Boys
and Girls clubs that looked toward a better future. A program was
initiated to relocate farmers who had lost their land to abandoned
farms. In non-English-speaking communities, the CNor sponsored
ethnic revivals of art and folklore. The railway even sponsored the
building of hockey rinks along its routes to provide employment and
the healthy diversion so necessary to maintain a positive public
psyche during hard times.

When Roosevelt began to broadcast his messages of hope in
America, they were received by Canadians who had already had a
taste, through the CNor, of what good government could do for
people. When Mackenzie King's Liberals returned to power in 1935,
one of their first acts was to repudiate the $15 million debt the
CNor still carried.

Over the ideological howls of Conservative business interests, the Canadian government's incursion into the domains of private enterprise was complete. Entanglement of government and private enterprise had been a staple of Canadian economics since the contract for the CPR; the expansion of the role of government through the CNor was inevitable.

Eventually the CNor expanded onto pavement, real estate, the seas, and the air (Air Canada)—becoming arguably the world's most successful public enterprise. Then World War II showed what a nationwide railway under government management could do to hasten troops and materiel to the ports.

Though the war effort involved railways nationwide, nowhere was the conflict closer to home than on the old Grand Trunk Pacific line to Prince Rupert. After the Japanese attack on Pearl Harbor, it appeared that one of the Japanese goals was the conquest of the Aleutian chain, Alaska, and the coast of the Pacific Northwest. For the five years of American participation in the war, northern British Columbia was the only part of North America besides Alaska and the military seaports that was actually in a war zone. The CNor began construction of a two-thousand-mile branch line into Alaska, and the Americans moved into Prince Rupert en masse to defend against the anticipated invasion. The harbor was netted and mined, and an armored train patrolled east of the port. Eventually nearly a hundred thousand Canadian and American soldiers were carried to Prince Rupert by the CNor for passage to the Pacific theater.

The CNor emerged from World War II established as one of the footings on which a healthy, vital society rested. Though certain divisions, like the CBC and Air Canada, were eventually vested with their own public identity as "Crown corporations," CNor remains a model for free-world governments courageous enough to subordinate private wants to public needs.

Perhaps I should have spent more time in Rupert, but the rail's-eye view fades when the feet are too long on the ground. So it's with a long backward glance that I board the eastbound *Skeena* out of Prince Rupert in the morning with Charlotte and Krista. They're riding back to Jasper where they will catch the *Super Continental* for Vancouver. I'm going to get off at Prince George for an overnight stay and then take a daylight ride on the British Columbia Railway down the Fraser Canyon to Vancouver.

The early morning run up the Skeena River fjord presents a different spectacle from yesterday's ride. A layer of cloud hangs less than a hundred feet over the water, and above that a solid bank of higher clouds obscures the tops of the peaks and the sun. From time to time, raindrops streak the windows and the quiet mood of a rainy day percolates even inside the train. It seems everyone aboard has a book open and no one wants to talk. So I dig out my Canadian history books and get into the spirit till after supper, when I'm interrupted by a loud crash outside my doorway.

"Bloody fucking Christ," grumbles a young man wearing a leg cast who is sprawled with his crutches on the floor of the corridor. I help him to his feet and he collapses into the seat in my roomette. His name is John and he is a student at the University of Durham in England taking a semester off to travel "beautiful Canada"— another voyageur. "Got anything to drink," he asks. "It hurts. I broke it playing football." I send the attendant off to the bar for scotch, and he returns with Krista Mack tagging along, now *sans mère*. In my crowded quarters, we spend an hour evaluating the contributions of various nations to the culture of the world. Largely in unspoken deference to Krista, John and I deplore the arrogance of Brits and Americans. John boosts the French and I think of some nice things to say about Asians, but finally we come around to reconsider our own heritage. "Some of the most decent things in the world have come out of the Anglo-Saxon tradition—popular government, trial by peers, and great pubs," says John. "Our problem is how we lose those things when we try to bring them to benighted places—remember *Heart of Darkness* and Vietnam and 'the white man's burden'?"

John was on his way to the rear platform of the last car when he crashed by my doorway. You're not supposed to go out on the rear platform, but the door is often left unlocked and, led by a fellow on crutches now fortified with spirits, the three of us head for it when the crew are out of sight. Once we are there, we sit out of the line of sight through the glass door and continue our conversation. It's a little hard to hear—the sound of the wind and the wheels on the tracks is stiff competition—and it's too dark to see anything. It's a little like falling down a long, dark tunnel.

John is the most articulate yet on the subject of what motivates the young voyageurs like himself. "Older people always seem so envious of the freedom, but we're not happy travelers, you know. For most it's not some joyous, experiential thing. It's disaffection, alienation, more like the sixties than anybody realizes. Your generation experimented with drugs and took to the streets to protest wars and racism. My generation travels—aimlessly, pointlessly."

Krista agrees, talking now for the first time without her mother around. She left home as a teenager to roam and remembers "the hell of those years. There's just nothing parents can do right, it's only a question of which mistakes they'll make." She thinks that by going off on her own, she was lucky. "If you don't have a curfew, there's no reason to self-destruct staying out late so you can break it."

"Parents get all the blame whether they deserve it or not. But they're as helpless as we are," John argues. "It's the ills of Western culture—the pressure for unobtainable success, the social competition, the lies and hypocrisy, and the fact that all of the decent things you might like to do with your future have been co-opted by the corporate empires." John cites as an example an ad current on American and Canadian television recruiting idealistic young people to work for Dow Chemical—"Dow makes you do great things." "So if you want to help discover a way to feed the babies in Ethiopia or cure cancer, you have to work for the people who sell napalm."

"What are you going to do when you finish at university?" I ask him.

"Go into the Royal Navy. Might as well face the beast head-on. My family's not well off. What else am I going to do in Maggie Thatcher's England if I don't want to be poor?"

Krista thinks he might be coming down a little hard on his country and tells him about the dismal prospects of some of the young men she talked to in the Surf Club last night. "They have a phrase out here for the life they have to look forward to—'Work and drink.' "

" 'Work and drink'? You think northern B.C. has a corner on that slogan? What do you think I have ahead of me in England? England's gone, trashed—has been since the Second World War and Maggie's finished it off. England's just a dirty kitchen sink. And Vietnam and Reagan have sent the Americans headed down the same road." He pauses for a moment as the winking red lights of a grade crossing flash by and recede into the darkness. "There's just you Canadians. You're all we've got left."

6

Another Country

PRINCE GEORGE TO VANCOUVER ON THE BCR *CARIBOO DAYLINER*

AT Prince George I tumble into my hotel bed exhausted—no evening out on the town tonight—but the air is hot and close, so before going to sleep I open the windows of my room.

In the morning, I wake with my nostrils burning and then nearly gag. My first impression of Prince George is that a drunk has somehow stumbled into my room in the night and vomited on my bed. But that's not it. A heavy fog lies across the city this morning and the driver of the van that takes me to my train says that all three local pulp mills have been going all night. When the air is saturated with moisture, this is what happens. "You learn to live with it. After all, it's the smell of money."

The shuttle van that serves the railway station circles to all of the major hotels before 6:30 A.M. to gather passengers and then takes them a few miles out of town to the British Columbia Railway yards for the 7:00 A.M. departure. Only fleeting impressions adhere to that sleepy, foggy, odoriferous ride. The streets seem to be unusually empty, even for the early hour. Maybe when the pulp mills exhale on a morning like this everyone stays home. Despite a few high-rise buildings, the predominant architecture is that of a sprawling, low-skylined, old-style western town. I don't know that there really are hitching posts along the streets, but in murky memory it seems so.

The BCR yard is a busy place. Rows of mile-long lumber freights remind me of the similar pageant of grain cars I saw at Jasper. The station is a flat-roofed modern building testifying to the fact that the BC Rail is one of North America's newest systems. In their stainless steel and green-painted livery and with their diesel engines grumbling, the three RDC cars of the *Cariboo Dayliner* stand waiting on the tracks by the platform.

The RDC (rail diesel car) equipment was developed in the fifties for intercity day runs in which light traffic made long passenger trains inefficient. Each car contains its own diesel engines linked to the wheels by mechanical transmissions, as in automobiles, rather than by electrical generators and motors, as on regular North American diesel engines. Thus efficient use of trains as short as one car is made possible, and up to twelve cars can be coupled together.

When experienced rail travelers encounter RDCs these days, the usual expectation is of a truncated form of day service little better than that on commuter trains. But boarding the *Cariboo Dayliner*, I can see that is not to be the case here. A green carpet welcomes riders to the immaculately clean and well-maintained interior. Lighting, seating, and decor generate an effect totally different from both VIA and Amtrak. Everything seems brighter, fresher. There's a sense of entering a hotel lobby with potted plants (there aren't any; it's just the green in the decor). But the train isn't really any better equipped (though it is cleaner) than Amtrak or VIA, and as it rockets out of Prince George it's clear that what I am enjoying is just the variety of a different train environment. This is what riders experienced in bygone days of competition among dozens of carriers across North America.

There is no dining car on the *Cariboo Dayliner*, but there is a first-class service in the third car where meals are served airline-style at your seat, and a takeout counter for the coaches. There are no cozy sleepers, though the coach seating is especially comfortable. With open platforms, walking in between the cars is not for the faint of heart. What is really striking within the first half-hour is the obvious care and pride the crew takes in running a good train. As the only passenger train on a line owned and operated by the people of British Columbia, the *Cariboo Dayliner* is valued with civic pride by the crew and passengers. The interaction between crew and passengers is more like what you might expect to find on an intimate, expensive luxury cruise. No effort is spared to make sure that the trip is as smooth and pleasant as possible—and I'm only traveling in coach.

It wasn't always that way. BC Rail was originally established as the Pacific Great Eastern in 1912. With the CPR, the Canadian Northern, and the GTP all east-west routes that drained as much of the province's freight to the east as they brought to B.C. ports, the independent-minded British Columbians thought they ought to have their own internal north-south railway. After two years of construction, twelve miles of track were laid between North Vancouver and Horseshoe Bay. A strange little gas-electric train, called the *Doodlebug*, made commuter-like trips back and forth over the route as real estate along the way was developed into suburban neighborhoods. But a backlash came and the line was reviled as a route that began and ended nowhere. With World War I the financing needed to conquer the difficult cliffs above Horseshoe Bay disappeared and this portion of the line languished till 1928, when it was abandoned entirely.

In the meantime the PGE had been living up to its reputation elsewhere. A rival bankrupt railway had completed ten miles of track north of Squamish, which lay twenty-eight miles away from the end of the first stretch of track. The PGE bought this line in 1912 and began building northward. Running all the way from Squamish up the towering Fraser Canyon and along the old Cariboo Road route as far as Quesnel, it halted there in 1921 due to the expense of constructing a bridge over the Cottonwood River. The PGE had done it again—another line running from nowhere to nowhere, but this time it was a big, expensive, spectacular one.

A fourteen-mile link was built south from Prince George to the Cottonwood and then it, too, stopped. In the 1920s it was possible to travel from North Vancouver to Prince George over a line with two gaps where passengers were ferried between trains. This was the least of their troubles. Sometimes known as the "Past God's Endurance" or the "Prince George Eventually," the rickety trains subjected passengers to such inconveniences as a stroll through the men's washroom to reach the diner and rain that poured in through leaky ceilings. BC Rail crews had a rare concept of timetables in those days, stopping the trains to pick berries or shoot game on a whim. Sometimes they would blast through scheduled stops at high speed past people waiting with their baggage if the crew felt they had enough passengers on board already. When a train pulled into a station seemingly on schedule, delighted awaiting passengers were often told that this was yesterday's train and their tickets were not good for this ride.

Weird accidents were common, and their reputation on a line that ran much of its length along the brink of sheer cliffs might have something to do with the pockets of intensely religious folk that prevail in British Columbia to this day. When Premier John Oliver came to inspect the line in 1921, an unmanned locomotive rolled down a siding and arrived at the inspection site moments before he did, derailed, and flipped over into a hayfield. Track workers hastily covered the engine with hay just before his arrival, and he paid little heed to the huge haystack that caught fire and burned as he passed. On another occasion an inspection crew was stranded when their train broke down high on the Fraser Canyon wall. They spent a cold day and night huddled without food or water in the baggage car around a bonfire fed with the wood paneling of the inspection car.

In 1928, the comedy came to a temporary end when those first twelve miles were abandoned and the tracks torn up. For twenty years parts of the route carried local freight service and much of it was used as a road, but there was nothing like regular passenger service. In 1952, with the postwar demand for B.C.'s raw materials running high, the bridge over Cottonwood River was finally built, tracks were relaid, and trains began running from Squamish to Prince George. In a typical B.C. departure from both Canadian frugality and American extravagance, the last spike was neither iron nor gold—it was silver.

Still the passenger service was a trial of travelers' patience. It began with a five-hour cruise from Vancouver up Howe Sound to Squamish, since the tracks had been pulled up from the first twelve miles and the next twenty-eight never laid. The consist was a ragtag collection of other railways' castoffs linked to freight cars that had to be cut out at various places along the run. At Quesnel, despite the completion of the bridge, passengers still had to transfer to buses for the final leg to Prince George. The run took thirty-four hours when it was on schedule. As late as 1960, an engine fell through a wooden trestle over the Fraser Canyon, which was weakened after sparks from brakeshoes had set the timbers afire. The PGE had a way of living up to its reputation even in later incarnations.

But by 1955, the PGE began to get serious about railroading. Tracks were finally laid at huge cost over the gap between Horseshoe Bay and Squamish. Neighbors along the route of the first twelve miles from North Vancouver to Squamish had "squatted" on the abandoned grade with vegetable gardens, flower trellises, and patios, but undeterred, the PGE relaid its original line exactly as before, through the clotheslines and between houses and their backyard garages. When trains abruptly began running they were cheered with curses and gunshots from homeowners whose parlors lay a few feet from the tracks. It didn't help when those same homeowners picked up their newspapers and read of the $400-million debt the line had laid on taxpayers' shoulders.

Yet this would turn out to be the last time the PGE would be a subject for Vancouver cartoonists. By 1972, when passenger lines all over North America were failing, the PGE became the British Columbia Railway and today preserves the continent's longest and most successful non-nationalized passenger service. The railway that once set a standard for haphazard operation has become a pioneer of modern technology including head-end power, microwave dispatching and operating, and radio-controlled diesels. And of particular concern to this rider, the modern BC Rail boasts one of the continent's best safety records despite running over a line that, from the window, looks downright dangerous.

Throughout much of the morning, the *Cariboo Dayliner* clips along the upper Fraser Canyon across the high plateau of the Chilcotin country that separates the Rockies from the Coast Mountains, with occasional crossings of deep ravines sculpted into the earth by rowdy streams. Then, after Whiskey Creek, the route veers away from the Fraser to the east. Sometimes this country looks like barren high plains and elsewhere it is dense forested wilderness, but it is the emptiness of the long stretches between logging operations and ranches that impresses. Like much of British Columbia, it is modern frontier, where refugees from the busy world who are serious about getting away from it all can really do so.

"You're not a regular, are ya," says a stocky, bearded man in boots, denim, and a Yankees baseball cap who has been watching me press my face to the glass. His name is Bobby Moleska and he is one of those refugees, returning today from a trip to Prince George to his mountain cabin in the Camelsfoot Range. "I used to be an

American—Hartford, Connecticut. This cap's about all I have left of that life and I don't miss it one bit.

"There are a lot of us expatriates in B.C., you know. It's a very American place for people who are sick of America. You can get land cheap and do your own thing. It's frontier, and life is a hell of a lot freer here than it is back in Connecticut."

Bobby was an actuary for an insurance company in Hartford when his two junior high–age daughters started coming home from school in tears. First it was not having the requisite boyfriends, then it was failure to make the cut for the softball team, then it was lack of an invitation to a sorority-like club, and finally it was the continual barrage of the nightly news. "My oldest would cry at the news and ask, 'Why is the world so bad, Daddy?' And through it all it was just the cruelty of American kids brought up on a diet of sex, violence, and vicious soap operas whose idea of life was 'Do unto others before they do unto you.' I finally told my wife, 'Fuck this shit.' The whole goddamn American dog-eat-dog pile of crap."

Ever since high school Bobby had been haunted by a story in a book called *Crusoe of Lonesome Lake*. It was the autobiography of Ralph Edwards, an American who carved out a home for himself and eventually a family in B.C.'s remote Tweedsmuir Park early in the century. "When I made up my mind to get out, I realized I had been fantasizing about Ralph Edwards all of my life. When I had trouble sleeping I would imagine scenes from the story with me in his boots."

Bobby began taking his family on vacations to British Columbia. They hiked, fished, hunted, rode horseback, and camped. "I'll never forget how the spirits of those two kids rose as the vacation week approached. And when I finally told them that we were going to move, they didn't complain and never looked back." The family started out renting an apartment in North Vancouver while Bobby took a job as an accountant in a Vancouver firm and used all his spare time to scout out a place for a homestead in the Camelsfoot Range. With the sale of his Connecticut house and some stock in the insurance company, he was pretty well fixed to start a new life.

He found a piece of land northwest of the Fraser Canyon, bought it, and, armed with a chainsaw and a trunk of hand tools, took the train to Lillooet with his wife and two teenage daughters in the spring of 1981. "We weren't going to be fanatical purists about this. I don't know how people do it without that chainsaw." By the end of the summer he had built a comfy four-room log cabin with plumbing fed by a spring, which bubbled uphill from the house, and a stable for four horses. Gardening was less successful that first year and the Moleskas were far from self-sufficient, but their new roots were established.

The girls rode their horses to school ten miles away but were none too assiduous about it, truancy not being well policed in remote regions. Bobby stocked the house with books to take up the educational slack. "We wouldn't have made it through those first couple of years without books. I read all the 'how-to' stuff I could find and the girls became hooked on history and nonfiction. My wife had her novels and all of us read those books about people who had already done what we were doing as if they were books of the Bible." In the early seventies, there was a plethora of accounts published of latter-day pioneers in the B.C. wilderness with titles like *Running Toward Life, Wilderness Wife, Silence Is My Homeland*, and *The Broken Snare*.

"You've heard the message a hundred times since Henry David Thoreau—about how life takes on new meaning when you have basic reasons for everything you do, making shelter, feeding yourself, keeping warm, and entertaining yourself with the best show in the world—the changes in the land, the water, the weather, and the wildlife around you." The Moleskas thrived in their wilderness life, and the girls are grown now. One is engaged to a rancher near the town of Exeter and one is studying forestry at the University of British Columbia in Vancouver. Bobby and his wife continue their life in the Camelsfoot Range and, thanks to the train, see their children "more often than many folks who live a few blocks away from them in a city."

I wonder if he doesn't miss the sense of community that is such a feature of Canadian life in less remote parts of the country. "If you mean neighbors, I can do without that just fine. If you mean something bigger, well, first there's my family, then there are the good folks over in Lillooet. And finally there's the province. It's like a little country, you know, not quite Canadian, not American, but really another country entirely."

Bobby is proud of his adopted country. Sheltered by mountains and sea from close connection with the North American behemoths, it's a place where the cultural mosaic achieves its most explosive panoply. "We got Japanese and Chinese, Americans, British, Australians, Jamaicans, Russians, Indians, Mexicans—you name it. And though they don't always get along together so well, they all come here for the same thing I did—freedom, real freedom. I think B.C. has the kind of community of individualism that America once had before we blew it."

And then there's politics. "No farting around with hypocritical timidity here, they go all the way—left with the NDP and right with Social Credit. I like 'em both. The right-wingers here aren't like those so-called conservatives in America. Here they're really committed to individual freedom—they're not going to meddle in your personal life and they're not going to assist the corporations to screw you like they do in America. On issues that matter, like the environment or guaranteeing the opportunity to live the good life, both sides achieve the same ends, they just do it by different means."

But Bobby does see threats to this life and, of course, they come from America. There's television, which you can avoid by not having one, and there's America's insatiable appetite for B.C.'s resources: timber and hydropower in particular. "The province grew up with a gold rush mentality. And America is all too willing to pump in that kind of money in return for cutting all our forests and damming all our rivers."

Since World War II, millions of acres in British Columbia have been deforested through clear-cutting, and two major river systems, the Nechako and the Columbia, have been diverted and dammed. In the process whole native tribes have been decimated and the salmon industry threatened. Bobby believes that the provincial government wised up just in time when it began a mandatory program of reforestation and drew the line on damming at the Fraser River. Yet the struggle continues between a muscular provincial environmental movement and equally powerful interests that can't envision prosperity without feeding America's appetite for power and paper. Bobby worries about economics despite his self-reliance in the Camelsfoot Range. "One of these days, I'm afraid a recession will tip the balance toward the exploiters."

Bobby sees a third more subtle threat in religious camps, which are proliferating and becoming increasingly difficult to avoid. British Columbia has a long tradition of providing refuge to idiosyncratic religious sects, from the ancient Doukhobars to the modern day Emissaries of Divine Light. "But it's the fundamentalist wackos that bother me. They're not content to find a place where they can do their thing undisturbed. They're looking for a base for empire. They have big money and can buy influence. And they bring in hordes of those narrow-minded people who are bent on taking away the freedom that I came here for."

I suggest that some of the most profound stories in the tradition of those doing what Bobby has done emanate from the pursuit of deep religious convictions. "I know it," says Bobby. "A lot of people find God in the mountains. But I never met a fundamentalist yet who could shut up long enough to hear the whispers of nature. Fundamentalism is the last gasp of a primitive instinct toward all the wrong things. They have failed in the face of reason, evolution, and popular trends. So they pervert religion as the only way to bypass humanity, since every decent instinct rules out things like beating children, manipulating women's bodies, fighting wars, executing criminals, persecuting minorities, all that brutal fun stuff that fundamentalists really love. I hope B.C.'s big enough for all of us, but if not, we're going to have to fight those people some day."

At the Flying U Ranch, one of dozens of thriving dude ranches in the central Cariboo area, people arrive at the stop (there is no station) on horseback. One of the women boarding sits in front of Bobby and me and in her conversation with her seatmate uses the phrase "when I got saved" several times. Bobby says, "There you go," and moves to a different seat so I can talk to her without him going thermonuclear. The woman is an American mother from Seattle who brings her daughters to the Flying U every summer while their father goes on an annual business trip to the east. "People come from as far away as Switzerland just for the riding." All of the staff play instruments, and hootenannies, hayrides, and square dances round out the fun.

Without any cue from me, she eventually adds, "Plus you meet a lot of people who are also saved in this country. By the way, are you saved?"

I confess that I'm not and then I'm surprised that, instead of haranguing me about my soul, she just breezily comments, "You really oughta get saved sometime," as casually as if she were recommending a new diet or exercise program. Then she goes back to boosting the Flying U.

So it's I who bring her back to the subject I had thought I might politely have to back away from. I want to know how she got saved.

"Well, my kids did it, really. They started hanging around with a guy they met here every time we came who turned out to be a speaker at a nearby Christian camp. He saved them during one visit and by the next one they had talked me into it."

Bobby's description of fundamentalists doesn't quite fit this particular woman. Except as a reference point in time, like "when I got my hair dyed," she isn't obsessed with talking about her own or anybody else's salvation. She's fascinated by the scenery passing by and the whispers of nature.

British Columbia was born in response to the challenge of empire-building Christians from America and later was weaned amid a scourge of American worshipers of Mammon. The wagon train immigration to Oregon began with American missionaries appalled at the empire established by a handful of Hudson's Bay Company men in this vast northwest region. These British seemed intent upon plundering the Indians of their furs with total indifference to the state of their souls. The Americans thought they could do better, offering spiritual salvation to the natives in return for the plundering of their furs. On the heels of the missionaries arrived wagonloads of settlers who established homesteads that would eventually run afoul of HBC or British (or later Canadian) authority. The settlers would howl of tyrannous mistreatment and call for help from Washington; troops would be sent and annexation demanded. British and American statesmen would then solve the problem to the Americans' liking by redrawing the North American map without concern for the interests of Canadians. That's how it was done with Oregon in 1846.

While his superiors were busily bungling the American challenge in Oregon, young HBC chief factor James Douglas began preparing for the day when the little skit might be reenacted farther north. It was he who chose the site of Victoria on Vancouver Island as a bastion out of reach of the wagon trains. In the towering bulk of this huge, stubborn man, the irresistible force of American Manifest Destiny met its immovable object.

With just the handful of company fur traders and the occasional Royal Navy ship that called in the harbors occasionally to show the flag, there was little hope for seeing any immediate substantial British immigration, so Douglas concentrated instead on creating the illusion of a well-established British enclave. By 1850, he had overseen the founding of a lumber trade, seven farms, and a coal-mining operation. The few who made their homes here came directly from Britain. They found a gentle, wet climate and natives firmly managed by the authority of the venerable HBC. Free of the horror of the continental winter, this was a kind wilderness of flowers, towering trees, plentiful fish and game, and fertile soil. And the place was an island, where an islander's mentality of security and isolation could allow a newcomer to re-create the amenities of life back on the home island. As in England, events such as school examinations became public ritual with parades through flowered arches, twenty-one-gun salutes, and high tea. In 1856, with the Americans preparing to chew each other up, it seemed this idyllic life might go on indefinitely.

But on a cloudless, summer morning on the mainland that year, American prospector James Huston roused himself in his camp on Tranquille Creek, near the junction of the Fraser and Thompson rivers. With a handful of other miners discouraged by the end of the rush in California, he had come to the Fraser following a will-o'-the-wisp rumor of gold north of the border. No substantial strikes had been confirmed, but Huston had arrived late in California and missed the action, and so on a hunch he had come north. There might not be gold here, but if there was, he wasn't going to miss out on it.

After a breakfast of flapjacks, coffee, and salmon netted in the river, he bent over the waters with his pan. One wonders at the thoughts of a man on the verge of history. Did he dig his pan into the sand with relish, hoping to find the tiny glittering golden grains in that very first dip? Or did he stolidly foresee a long, arduous process of back-breaking pains and frustration?

The pan must have met grating resistance beneath the layer of sand and come up heavy. Was he awake enough to sense already what he had found? For when he had sloshed away the sand and the murk from his first dip, his pan was full of large hunks of shining yellow metal—nuggets bigger than marbles.

By late 1857, Douglas saw what was coming, formed a police force, and braced himself for the spring onslaught. On foot, in ox-drawn wagons, on horseback, and in ships crammed to the gunwales, they came, mostly from America. Victoria's population of two hundred was soon overwhelmed by twenty thousand rough gold-seekers whose manners had been learned in the California rushes. All were in a lather to get to the Fraser River as soon as possible. Douglas was eager to oblige them as long as they understood that they were guests of the British Empire and the HBC and would have to abide by British law.

Douglas was fortunate to have several Royal Navy men-of-war in port throughout this time. With the illusion of authority they conveyed, he maintained order with another hoax. Legally he had no authority over the mainland, since it was not yet a colony, but nonetheless he issued a proclamation requiring all miners to purchase licenses from him on behalf of Her Majesty's government. In return the HBC provided safekeeping of gold, coordinated the delivery of supplies, and even organized nightly dances at Fort Langley, which were conducted with British decorum.

Still the hordes poured in and when they inevitably clashed with Indians and when an agent provocateur of U.S. President Buchanan arrived inciting riots against Douglas's rule, he had the trouble he had so long anticipated. Again without any legal authority, he appointed a Justice of the Peace and informed the Americans that the law would protect Indians and white men equally and reminded them of the prohibition against selling liquor to Indians.

But Douglas's greatest coup was in road building. The miners were most rambunctious when high waters idled them in the spring and supplying the camps became increasingly difficult. Douglas hit on a scheme to solve two problems with one master stroke. He convinced the miners that they needed a road and that the only way they were going to get one was to build it themselves without pay. Thus Douglas built the first leg of what would eventually become the great Cariboo Road—108 miles from Harrison Lake to Lillooet.

In November of 1858, Douglas presided over ceremonies at Fort Langley instituting the new mainland province of British Columbia, whose name had been chosen by the queen herself. The HBC relinquished its hold on the huge territory and Douglas became its first governor.

Through his fearsome chief justice, Matthew Begbie, Douglas now had real authority to continue his iron rule over the rowdy mobs. Often acting as prosecutor, defense counsel, and judge, Begbie never could accept the hair-splitting verdict of manslaughter and the attendant required sentence of life imprisonment. If a man killed someone, that man must hang. When juries occasionally brought in verdicts of manslaughter instead of murder, he would harangue them, on one occasion threatening to charge each of the jurors with murder himself. When a jury once went so far as to acquit a man he considered guilty, Begbie, enraged at having to release the prisoner, advised the man to be sure to choose a member of the jury as his next victim. When a gang of trigger-happy gunmen arrived in the Kootenay region from Oregon Territory, one of Begbie's associates assured them that, "Boys, if there is shooting in

Kootenay, there will be hanging in Kootenay." Execution of Begbie's sentences were usually not long delayed, sometimes occurring from the tree nearest the roadside court where the itinerant judge passed judgment.

But Begbie was jealous of his authority and when vigilantes attempted to circumvent it by lynching miscreants, he and his officers would face them down with their own nooses. Murder was murder, though the victim himself might be a killer. Under such a regime, hangings were actually rather rare because killings were rare by the standards of the North American west. Douglas and Begbie, through sheer force of character, tamed the miners as no force in California ever had.

When new strikes farther north inaugurated the Cariboo rush in 1860, the gold-seekers came from all over the world, and some of them, the Overlanders, even came by land from eastern Canada.

An extended Cariboo Road to the new site was needed to ensure that Americans didn't dominate the Cariboo trade with an alternate route down the interior Okanagan Valley to Oregon Territory. Long before the coming of the railways, Douglas conceived the fantastic plan to carve 385 miles of road out of the rock walls in a province with little ability to pay for such work. By 1864, he had done it again, paying the $1.25 million bill largely from tolls. Portions of the routes of today's CPR and BCR follow that unlikely road.

By the time of confederation, the handful of British Columbians had held off the Americans and created a fiercely independent enclave, with political clout totally disproportionate to its population. Gold had given economic importance and geography had bestowed imperial status, and so it was that British Columbia was able to call the shots over the issues of confederation and the building of a transcontinental railway. By then Douglas had given way to a colorful newspaper publisher and opposition politician who called himself Amor de Cosmos (Lover of the World).

As we approach the division where the tracks run along the precipice of Fraser Canyon, the conductor invites me to ride with the engineer. The front half of the first car contains a baggage room and a little galley where the crew hangs out. Beyond that lies the tiny cubicle of the cab, where engineer Carl Leidenius allows me to sit in the assistant's seat for one of the most spectacular train rides in the world. We round a bend and suddenly there it is—the hazy empty gulf of the Fraser Canyon, with the river nearly three thousand feet below us.

Words and figures crumble in the attempt to describe this sight. The tracks run along the upper wall of the canyon, continually curving with the undulations of the contours so that in front of the cab there is either empty air or rock walls. The sheer size of the canyon must be understood; the opposite walls are five miles away. The mighty Fraser River appears as a thin meandering line in the haze beneath us. Nothing of our side of the canyon can be seen between the dusty verge next to the tracks and the river far below. Perhaps the only comparable spot in North America is the Grand Canyon of Arizona, but there is no railway running along its walls.

For a while I sit as one walks on a high bridge, afraid to move too forcefully for fear of pitching the whole train into the gulf. There are places where the tracks hang on wooden trestles out over the drop, plunge into tunnels and then emerge into sunny empty air again. Around sharp curves, the engineer's cab, ten feet in front of the wheels, hangs out over the side. But as my confidence builds, eventually the little roadbed ledge comes to feel secure. We pass a northbound freight at a siding and the routine radio talk and hand-waving between crews furthers my sense of security. At another siding we meet the northbound passenger train and the two trains stop to exchange takeout counter provisions and crew members. All the while the microwave voice transmission system keeps Carl in touch with other trains and the central dispatcher. Twice we meet "speeders," the little gasoline-powered cars that patrol the line looking for rock slides.

Carl Leidenius has worked the line for forty-two years and has never seen a serious accident along the cliffs. It all began with a honeymoon trip from Vancouver to Lillooet on the train. He and his young wife liked Lillooet so much that they stayed longer than they had planned and ran out of money. "We didn't even have the railfare to go running back to our parents, so I took a job with the railway." He liked the work enough that he has stayed with it and lives in Lillooet where he and his wife manage the Mile-0 Motel.

Carl is no newcomer to British Columbia. His Lithuanian family has been here for three generations. I ask him how established British Columbians feel about the recent influx of American expatriates. "You probably know that Canadians don't like some of the Americans who come here as tourists very much, but those who settle in B.C. are a special breed. They're displeased with the same things about America that we don't like, so they're welcome as far as I'm concerned."

As we approach Lillooet, the river is closer, the sky farther than when we began this carnival-ride descent down the wall of Fraser Canyon. Carl points out bright orange and blue camping tarps set up along the river. "Those are the people who really belong here." Under constitutional mandate, the native people are still allowed to net salmon and they dry the fish under these tarps. "They're not content to let the white man dictate what's going to happen to their land anymore. They got lawyers all over the place fighting the lumber and mining companies and trying to save the rivers from dams. There was a plan once to dam the Fraser right down here at Lillooet and the Indians had a lot to do with stopping it. That's the big question in B.C.—who really owns the land, the federal government? the province? the developers? the railways? the hydro-companies? the Indians?"

"Or the Americans?" I venture, and Carl doesn't smile.

At Lillooet, we pick up three more cars for the busy run across the resort-strewn Coast Mountains and along Howe Sound to North Vancouver. Bobby Moleska gets off here and I have time to wander with him around the town. It's a mountain town, a regional supply center, and "Mile Zero" on the original Cariboo Road. Bobby makes a confession, "My wife and I have been thinking about getting a place in town here," and looks at me for a reaction.

"What about Thoreau and having no neighbors and watching the greatest show on earth?" I ask.

"It's not necessary anymore," he says as he waves to a man arranging a display in the window of a hardware store we pass. "Thoreau went back, too, you know. But we came to this life fleeing something—and it worked for us, our girls grew up happier and saner than they would have if we had stayed in Connecticut. But when we started, we thought it was human society we had to get away from—and it wasn't. It was just a bad society. We've found a better one."

"Is it B.C. or Canada?" I ask.

"I really don't know. I haven't spent much time anywhere else in Canada. I don't know if people are as free of social meanness elsewhere as they are here or not. You're the one doing the whole country. I suspect by the time you're through, you'll be able to answer that one yourself."

The run from Lillooet to North Vancouver is reminiscent of the *Skeena* run to Prince Rupert, though everything seems even closer to the windows here. We roll along the shores of deep-blue lakes and over passes through glaciered mountains. The train is crowded now and a spirit of conviviality prevails. At one point we cross a bridge above the top of a plummeting waterfall where the conductor has advised us to watch for nude bathers who risk more than their modesty by swimming in such a dangerous place; instead we see a pair of mating bears, standing up on two legs. That does it—from that point on, we have a train party going. Someone shouts, "Teach my husband a stroke like that!" It's the woman who got saved.

After supper (hot dogs from the takeout counter), we finally roll along Howe Sound, a true fjord. That same evening, silver light I noticed at Prince Rupert gently washes the scene here—timber barges on the waterway, plumes of a pulp mill along the dark far shore, fishermen bending over their boats at piers close along the tracks.

Around the point of West Vancouver we whip past the suburban homes whose backyards were violated by the railway. Here stretches the expanse of Burrard Inlet and the great bridges leading to the dark hump of Stanley Park and the parade of Vancouver lights on the opposite shore. A variety of ships is in the harbor, but dominating them all is the huge hulk of a U.S. Navy aircraft carrier. Passengers point it out with a curious mixture of anti-American scorn and pride that such an important ship is a regular here in British Columbia.

The train is on time into North Vancouver station and I make it to my hotel across Burrard Inlet by 9:00. It's a Saturday night and I'm not about to commemorate my arrival at the final destination of my "Out West" trip by sitting alone in the hotel room and watching TV. I have a couple of phone numbers and a rented car is waiting. By 9:30 I'm driving over the Burrard Bridge to Dunbar Street and the Cheshire Cheese Restaurant. Linda Melillo, the tour guide I met on the *Canadian* way back at the beginning of the trip, gets off work from her other job at 10:00.

At the time of confederation, there was nothing here but a coal mine and a couple of mills when the sparse population of British Columbia

147

demanded a transcontinental railway as its price for joining the confederation. The city of Vancouver, as yet unlocated and un-named, was just a vision of a great Pacific port that would rise somewhere on the island-studded and fjord-fractured west coast.

After the time of Douglas the two colonies, Vancouver Island and mainland British Columbia, eyed each other almost as warily as both eyed the republic to the south. The waves of gold fever and clashes with Indians that periodically swept the mainland meant nothing but trouble for Amor de Cosmos and his pure British is-landers. Mainlanders, sprinkled with American and other foreign influences, resented the haughty islanders, but between big gold strikes, both shared the economic depressions that beset economies stocked to the hilt with goods meant to supply boom times. During one of these painful periods in 1866 Amor de Cosmos changed his tune and sought union of the two colonies into the greater British Columbia of today.

When Canadians back east began scheming confederation, a sea change had occurred amid a substantial portion of British Colum-bians. The Americans had by now purchased Alaska, and Victoria came to be linked by sea trade with San Francisco. The Americans completed their first transcontinental railway, and another, the Northern Pacific, was headed toward the Pacific Northwest. De-spite deep emotional ties, Britain seemed increasingly remote and, with the Hudson's Bay Company gone, there was no longer any connection to eastern Canada whatsoever. Notwithstanding the decades-old struggle to hold the Yankees at the 49th parallel, a strong annexationist party arose in Victoria and actually petitioned American President Johnson for entry into the union.

It was ironically this agitation that moved Amor de Cosmos to form a party calling for British Columbia to join the Canadian confederation. With his reputation for flightiness, few of con-sequence in B.C. took him seriously at first; confederation with Canada seemed to be the most tenuous of the three options avail-able for the future of the colony. But there was a man in Ottawa who took his cause very seriously—John A. MacDonald.

The prestige of the man charged with founding a British-affiliated independent dominion on the North American continent added considerable weight to de Cosmos's fancy. In the ensuing debate, logic favored the annexationists, but with MacDonald's sup-port, the emotional vision of British Columbia as the western gate-way to a British nation extending from sea to sea won the day in the colonial parliament. When the delegation went to Ottawa with the good news, they had just one small caveat—there must be a transcontinental railway begun in two years and completed in ten.

When MacDonald was voted out of office and Mackenzie reneged on the railway, economic depression spurred the British Columbians to threaten secession if the long-promised railway were not quickly begun. MacDonald, who had lost his seat in his home riding of Kingston, stood for Victoria in 1878, where men shared his vision. In his triumphant return, MacDonald represented the province with which he had developed a symbiotic relationship of survival.

Half a dozen routes to as many sites along the Pacific coast had been surveyed, from the harbor at today's Prince Rupert, to a site on Vancouver Island, to Burrard Inlet. MacDonald finally settled on Burrard Inlet on the basis of the advice of the admiralty and set the Pacific terminus at Port Moody on its easterly end. Even before settling the contract with the syndicate that would undertake the CPR project as a whole, he gave a contract to Andrew Onderdonk in 1880 to begin construction from Port Moody up the Fraser Canyon. Vancouver Island threatened secession from British Columbia over the choice of the terminus, but with a ceremonial first blast of nitro, Onderdonk ended all thought in B.C. of secession and annexation to the United States.

By the time the project was near completion, MacDonald's later supervisor of construction, William Van Horne, had taken a second look at Burrard Inlet. Just inside the first narrows, formed by the peninsula that is today's Stanley Park, was a nearly fully landlocked harbor, miles closer to the sea than Port Moody. There was a sawmill here, and a garrulous Yorkshireman named "Gassy Jack" Deighton had earlier built a hotel. The place was known as Gastown, then Granville. Van Horne noted the vast harbor and the huge stands of tall timber for shipbuilding. He knew the syndicate had dreams of a transportation empire extending well beyond the steel rails themselves—this was to be its gateway and he would call it Vancouver. The city was incorporated, over the protests of the residents of Port Moody, in the spring of 1886. Immediately a horde of developers poured in, and in just a few months all that they had quickly built was burned down in a tremendous fire. Rebuilding began immediately, and on May 23 of the year of the Queen's Jubilee, the first transcontinental CPR train pulled into the Vancouver station.

While the railway cured British Columbia of the disease of the single-resource economy, it exacerbated the habit of overreliance on exploitation of natural resources, which is still a controversial issue today. And it never did completely triumph over the walls of the mountains and the sea, so B.C. was never fully integrated into Canadian society. The mainlander still feels closer to Americans in the Pacific Northwest, the islander still yearns for all things British, and both are tied by trade more to the Orient than to the Maritime provinces in the east. In B.C. the nationally based Conservative and Liberal parties seem currently entrenched in long-term minority opposition to the more powerful local NDP, Social Credit, and Reform parties. Though the province boasts an aggressive environmental movement in tune with the emerging national identity, it is also the province where that movement faces its strongest opposition.

British Columbia displays Canada's most variegated colors of the national cultural mosaic, and Vancouver is the only Canadian city outside of Quebec in which Anglo-Saxons make up less than half of the population. B.C. is a place where conventional labels break down. Vancouver has had a socialist mayor while the right-wing Social Credit party governed the province. Warships make the harbor a regular port of call while city officials celebrate an annual Walk for Peace. In 1971, a small fishing vessel set off from Vancouver for the Aleutian Islands to put a stop to American nuclear testing in the north Pacific. The voyage of the *Greenpeace* inaugurated a tidal wave of support in British Columbia for the fledgling organization's antiwar and pro-environment program, which soon spread worldwide.

Whatever British Columbia is, it's not quite Canada. With its roots in the fur trade and the gold rushes, it remained British without stodginess, American without barbarism.

Eight hours ago I was riding a train through pioneer country talking to a man who lives at an address you can only reach on horseback. Now I'm driving a rented car past the shops and movie theaters of Vancouver's Dunbar Street looking for the address of a neighborhood restaurant where I'll see someone I met on a train out of Toronto almost a month ago.

I find the Cheshire Cheese without any problem. It's a family restaurant with a bar in the same room with the tables. Mom and Dad have a pint while the kids order hamburgers and on the wall a

TV broadcasts summer reruns of "Hockey Night in Canada." I've seen this English pub–style arrangement in several places in Canada, but it is particularly prevalent in Vancouver. The close juxtaposition of bar and family dining might offend some, but I think it makes a positive statement about the quality of life here, of integration and civility.

Linda Melillo greets me with a plate of chicken wings to keep me occupied till she is finished with her last diners. And then, with an injunction to the bartender to catch up with us when he gets off, Linda directs me to the Railway Club in downtown Vancouver. The place is upstairs, pleasantly crowded, and humming with good live blues music. There are no ferns and no signs saying I can't smoke my pipe. Overhead an "0"-gauge electric train runs on a shelf built high along all four walls.

"So what have you learned about Canada?" Linda wants to know when we have sucked the froth off the tops of our mugs of Foster's Australian lager.

I guess I've learned that Canadians harbor a lot more animosity toward Americans than traveling Americans normally suspect. I've also learned that, by acknowledging that feeling, an American who defies the stereotype wins confidences perhaps more quickly because he is an American. I've learned that Canadians are more firmly rooted in local communities and less inspired by nationalism than Americans. I've also learned that Canadians are discovering a sense of familial nationalism just as the conflict over the Meech Lake accord threatens to tear the confederation apart. I've discovered that Canada has colorful subcultures and exotic corners that defy the stereotype of a sedate society. And I've had a hint that the conquest of the remote regions, so long touted by the national image-makers, might not be going so well. I've found that, at least on trains, women are more likely to perform the role of cultural spokesperson than they are in America, yet I've seen that men can get away with behavior that would bring quick feminine disapprobation in my country. But it's all fragments, pieces in a mosaic not yet fully patterned.

"Not bad," says Linda. "But what about yourself? Whenever you go out to explore the world, you end up finding out that you're exploring your inner world as well—previously unknown hopes and dreams, hidden limitations and strengths, unacknowledged failures and opportunities."

It's just part of her standard tour-guide repertoire, but it's a wonderful question, and one that will follow me for thousands of miles down the tracks. At this point all I can tell Linda is that I have sometimes come to feel like a person window-shopping for a different life.

When Linda's bartender arrives with his girlfriend, we get into a conversation about big city glamour and glitz. He wants to prove that Vancouver is as current as any city in North America and so takes us to "Graceland."

We have to walk down a back alley to find the place, and though there are coveys of young hipsters loitering along the way, I don't feel any of the intimidation I would in a similar setting in any American city I know. Entering you get your hand stamped the way we used to for junior high school dances, but the similarity ends quickly when we stop at a booth where a scantily clad bunny offers shooters of peppermint schnapps for a dollar.

Inside Graceland it's all strobe lights and mega-volume blandishments of house music. You don't hear any songs you recognize from the radio in a place like this. A house music artist presides in a glass booth above the dance floor. Before him glows an awesome array of keys and controls, which he manipulates to create a bone-gripping drive of dance music, punctuated with his historical quips over the microphone: "The Eagle has landed," and "President Kennedy has just been shot."

This place is big city, make no mistake. Some of the dancers are voguing poses they will strike for fashion magazines, and the blaze-eyed mannequins draped over the balconies, the tops of the speakers, and stairway railings seem wired on high-test LSD.

At first I'm offended that Linda's friend has brought me to a place I could visit in New York or Boston just to prove that Vancouver (and Canada) has stuff like those cities, and saying so leads to an awkward and embarrassing farewell in the middle of a Vancouver street after 1:00 A.M. Linda, always the conscientious tour guide, feels that she has let me down. I, having studied so hard how to avoid being an ugly American, have finally reverted to type.

In the morning, before returning my rented car I stop by Linda Melillo's house just off Dunbar, where she lives with three other young women just beginning the post-college career search. She is sleeping late, so I leave a thank-you-and-apology gift. I would never have made arrangements to begin my tour of Canada with a tour guide, and yet when Linda was the first person I met on the train out of Toronto, fate arranged it for me. She has done her job well, showing me a proper travel attitude and teaching me to ask the right kinds of questions. I'm grateful to her.

Vancouver is where the westering rail routes meet, and so it doesn't surprise me when I encounter more familiar faces at the CN station. " 'Ighya, might, sayn inny moe strippahs?" It's Australian John Smith, leaning sloppily against the ticket counter under the great brass station clock, wearing his hat and looking just as dusty as when I first met him. He's been hanging out in Vancouver, and now he's waiting for the *Super Continental* to take him to Edmonton and a ranch at Ponoka, Alberta, where he has a job waiting. I try to get him to say something trenchant about his experience of Canada, but he won't. He's more interested in checking out the girls who will be riding his train. "Gutta say ef oy kin git lighd a feeyoo moe toymes b'foe oy git beck ta wuk."

We watch the arriving passengers struggling through the doors with their baggage, and then there are two more I know, Krista Mack and her mother, Charlotte Dubois. They look tired but a lot happier than when I last saw them riding the train out of Prince Rupert. "Did you ever find your home?" I ask.

Krista breaks into a smile and shrugs, letting her mom go on and on about what a wonderful city Vancouver seems to be. They have to get back to Toronto, so they'll be riding with me back east. "But we're coming back, as soon as we get a chance. Did you know it hardly ever snows here?" They sit down with John and me for a cup of coffee in the restaurant. Something has worked a change in their moods; there was a lot of tension between them on the *Skeena* run, but today they are at ease, like two old friends back from the wars.

I began this trip to western Canada weeks ago in Toronto, boarding the *Canadian* with a thought about being born again. I've seen it happen to at least one pair of my traveling companions, and I wonder if it is happening to me. As yet I hardly know this alluring alternative North American culture, and some of the testimony I've taken holds that it's all falling apart. The first fever of new love is a good time to suspend judgment. There are thousands of miles of Canadian tracks in the east and the north still ahead of me, and winter comes down hard there only a few months from now.

PART TWO

Down East

*Better a divorce, I think, than
a marriage in name only.*

—MORDECAI RICHLER

7

Je Me Souviens

MONTREAL TO GASPÉ
ON THE *CHALEUR*

I T ' S a Sunday in late August and in the intricately carved wooden interior of Montreal's Notre Dame Basilica there are more gawking tourists than worshipers. "Most of our generation rebelled against the old French ways," says Linda Eakeley, a former college classmate of mine who has settled into the English side of life in Montreal. "They don't even go to church."

Linda is today a Canadian citizen "originally because I married a Canadian." She has since divorced but has no intention of leaving her charming French-Canadian house in Pointe Claire, near the shore of the St. Lawrence, where she is raising her two teenage daughters. She teaches French at a private school and struggles, like so many English-speaking Montrealers, to understand her French compatriots. Today Linda is giving me a resident's tour of the city during the layover between my train from the States and the departure of the *Chaleur* for Gaspé.

"It's largely a question of education and opportunity," she continues as we drive toward the high ground of Mont Royal. "It started with the 'Quiet Revolution' back in the sixties, when

Quebecers began to see that much of their religious and French tradition had held them back. But ironically that's the same time as the beginnings of the modern separatist movement and French militance."

There are no English-language traffic signs in Montreal today, the result of the infamous (in English eyes) Bill 101 making Quebec a monolingual French province. Despite a Supreme Court decision against it, Quebec continues to enforce the law. "For years the French had called for bilingualism in the other provinces. It seemed so hypocritical. They say it's necessary to preserve their culture in an English-dominated dominion, but here in Montreal, it's the English-speaking people who are under siege. And now it's becoming a question of not respecting the rule of law and the constitution."

Linda drives us through the affluent enclaves of English West-mount and French Outremont to demonstrate that in Montreal there is an equality of wealth between the two "races." It was here that the mailbox bombings briefly flared up during the agitation for separatism during the sixties. At the park on Mont Royal we see English- and French-speaking families sharing the same spectacu-lar view of their cosmopolitan city, but always in distinctly separate groups. Looking out over the metropolitan panorama below, for a moment I conjure up a horrible vision of Beirut or Belfast spread out along the tranquil St. Lawrence just a few hours away from my own home.

Linda doesn't think it will ever come to that when I tell her my thought. "The two peoples are just too intermingled in the Montreal workplace for that to happen. When we lost a lot of business to Toronto in the first reaction to Bill 101, both sides really pulled together to revive the city's economy to where it is today. If it ever did get really scary, the English would just leave. But still, even I get mad every time I drive down Boulevard René Levesque. It used to be Dorchester Street. A perfectly good English name."

At least the great CN hotel built over Gare Centrale is still called the Queen Elizabeth. Here Linda drops me off before heading to Pointe Claire to pick up her kids from dancing class. "Good luck in Gaspé," she says. And then, referring to the fact that I don't speak French very well, she advises, "At least start out by trying to speak some French to the people you meet. You'll end up talking in English when they hear your limited idiom, but they like Americans who at least make the effort."

I have one last question for her. "What will you do if Quebec separates?"

"I'd try to stay here, but if that became impossible, I'd probably move back to the States. I'd never live in Orange Ontario."

The *Chaleur* bound for Gaspé pulls out of Gare Centrale at 6:00 P.M. sharp. It is actually part of the longer train called the *Ocean*, bound for Moncton, New Brunswick. The *Chaleur* section of one coach, two sleepers, and a lounge-diner (the type with a counter and swivel stools) break off at Matapedia in the wee hours of the morning for the run on the peninsula.

As the train speeds through the flat, fertile corn-growing country of the St. Lawrence Valley, I enjoy a delicious dinner of fresh Atlantic salmon (sweeter than Pacific) while the table conversation (in English) is all about the dismal future of this run. The prospects are especially bad because CN plans to abandon the last forty miles of track between Matapedia and Gaspé, since the freight traffic from the copper mine at Murdockville has dwindled. The mine has cut production to the point where it's cheaper to move the ore by truck or barge.

With a lot of shaking of heads, it's agreed that this is a bad thing for Canadian unity. The elderly, the sick, and the young in eastern Quebec rely heavily on this connection to the big cities and without it are likely to fall prey to the separatists. I've heard that somewhere before.

There is a tendency among Americans to assume that the roots of the English-French schism in Canada go at least as far back as Montcalm and Wolfe, since their battle is one of the few episodes of Canadian history we study in our schools. But the real grievances of both parties postdate the battle on the Plains of Abraham, whose immediate upshot was one of the most enlightened and congenial of conquering regimes the world has ever seen. The Papineau upheavals of 1837 did more to bull momentum toward confederation and the amicable arrangement of inclusion of French-Canadians in governments of both parties than it did toward disunion. In those days it seemed as if conflicts over language, the touchstone issue today, could be finessed. But like two brothers of differing character who find their contentions magnified by going into business together, the Canadian French and English didn't begin uncovering irreconcilable hostility until after confederation. The closer they had to work together, the less they liked each other.

The two issues that most fed the growing animosity were the English allegiance to Britain and the French allegiance to the Catholic Church, ironically two issues that are of minimal importance today. Louis Riel was hanged as a traitor to Britain, even though he was a province-maker and, thus, in a sense a Canadian patriot. In his hanging, the French perceived a motif of British jingoism that sketched a caricature of English-Canadians as fanatically devoted to a foreign empire.

On the English side, there were equally symbolic episodes, like the incident of the Guibord corpse, that conjured up a view of the French as demoniacal papists devoid of human decency. Joseph Guibord was a French Catholic publisher of free-thinking books banned by the Church. Upon his death he was denied Catholic burial and his widow sued. When she won the case and his coffin was taken from the Protestant cemetery to the Catholic grounds, the bishops barred the gates. Under court edict, they were forced to allow him burial, but interdicted and deconsecrated the earth in which he was laid. He ended up encased in scrap iron and concrete to prevent devout Catholics from digging him up. This is the stuff that seeded the irrational bigotry that became a tumor on Canadian life that disfigured other issues—like wars.

In 1897, Canada's second great prime minister, the French-Canadian Wilfred Laurier, declared as part of his unifying policy of "the sunny way"—"Let the watch-fires be lit, and Canada will be the first to respond." When British troops were defeated at Ladysmith in the South African Boer War in 1899, Laurier backed up his word with 7,300 men sent under the command of Sam Steele, serving as a distinct Canadian regiment. Quebec exploded at this offering of French-Canadian blood so that "the English could have two countries, one here and one across the sea." Meanwhile an English women's organization in Montreal called for Canadian immigration to be restricted to persons who were "one hundred percent British in language, thought, feeling, and impulse." In the protest against participation in the war, Anglophones believed that French-Canadians were demonstrating their inability to hold loyalty to anything but the Catholic Church.

In 1909, Laurier stuck to the sunny way and declared, "When Britain is at war, Canada is at war, there is no distinction." He managed to please no one, with Tories aggravated by his insistence that the new navy would be independently Canadian and Quebecers incensed at Canadian military resources being pledged to help Britain fight its wars. The issue contributed to his Liberals' defeat in the 1911 election. Complained Laurier, "I am branded in Quebec as a traitor to the French, and in Ontario as a traitor to the English. In Quebec I am attacked as an imperialist, in Ontario as a separatist. I am neither, I am a Canadian."

With the assassination at Sarajevo in 1914, Europe plunged into the war it had been itching to fight and Laurier's conservative successor, Robert Borden, pledged Canadian troops. After the experience of the Boer War, the mere thought of war provoked the French and English in Canada to withdraw sullenly into their own communities and glower at each other. Poet Rupert Brooke, visiting Canada just before the war, expressed amazement at the division in the two communities: "A stranger is startled by the complete separateness of the two races. Intermarriage is very rare. They do not meet socially. . . . In the same city these two communities dwell side by side, with different traditions, different languages, different ideals." Borden's minister of defense believed French-Canadians were "cowards, unfit for military service" and ordered the all-French battalion to parade without guns. Newspapers in Quebec labeled the war "a cooperative crime intended to swell the profits of British arms merchants."

While the war was divisive at home, abroad the Canadian contribution brought nothing but praise. In their first action Canadian troops plugged a hole in the lines vacated by Algerians, who broke and ran under the world's first chlorine gas attack, and suffered six thousand casualties in twelve hours. Impressed, the British prime minister declared that, "Henceforth the Canadians were marked as storm troops."

Journalists were appalled at the slaughter and the battlefield conditions where men lived in trenches filled with layers of rotting bodies and human excreta and charged across fields strewn with seven thousand corpses per square mile. Yet with wartime censorship heavily enforced, little of this reality reached citizens back home. Only in Quebec were there widespread rumors of the true horror of the war and a premonition that conscription was in the air.

By 1917 Borden pushed a conscription bill through Parliament. Responding to slogans such as "If the conscription law is enforced,

Canadians have only one choice—to die in Europe or to die in Canada," French-Canadians took to the streets calling for separatism, revolution, and annexation to the United States. In elections that year, it was purely French against English, and Laurier's remaining Liberal opposition was hammered mercilessly with the theme that "A vote for Liberals is a vote for the Kaiser." They were resoundingly defeated and Quebec sprouted with banners proclaiming, *"Vive la Revolution!"* A young priest, Abbe Lionel Groulx, inspired a fanatical following of young Quebecois with his speeches combining nostalgia, Catholic mysticism, and racism—Louis Riel born again amid the university grottos of Montreal.

Meanwhile Canadian war casualties continued to soar—sixteen thousand in one segment of the line during the Marne offensive. At home the economy boomed, pumped up by the demands of war. The Intercolonial Railway, over whose route I am traveling part of the way to Gaspé, vindicated its founders, who originally had promoted it as a military railway to link the Maritimes to Canada in unity against a possible American invasion. Operating in the closed waters of the mouth of the St. Lawrence, German U-boats could wreak terrible havoc with wartime shipping coming out of Montreal or Quebec, so the bulk of the men, machines, and munitions bound for Europe rode the rails of the Intercolonial to the port of Halifax and its more defensible opening on the wide Atlantic.

When the war ended, Canada was left with a wrecked generation, an inflated economy that collapsed with the peace, and a legacy of bitterness. With a population one-tenth that of the United States, she had lost 48,121 men—slightly more than the Americans. Canadians had never reckoned the huge cost of their frenzy of transcontinental railway building during the years just before the war, and now, combined with the overnight disintegration of the munitions industry, that debt came down on their heads with massive unemployment and inflation. In Quebec, where there were nearly as many families mourning fallen sons as there were in Ontario, the memory of English accusations during the war years rang with fury. Union membership soared among masses who admired the workers' revolution in Russia. Strikes erupted and were viciously put down with bayonets and bullets. Troops sent to Murmansk in an attempt to restore the czar mutinied and were brought home, where they swelled the ranks of the new leftist unions. The pattern was ominously familiar; Borden called out the Mounties and they went to work.

I'm surprised that all the riders I encounter during dinner on the *Chaleur* are English speakers. But in the lounge, as the train approaches the south shoreline opposite Quebec City, I hear "Uhnbeeairseepleh—*Bleu*"—the unmistakable French of *"les Québecois."* The speaker is a woman about my age wearing a man's fedora with a dark band. She is seated alone and clumsily I ask, *"Bonjour. Je voudrais parler, s'il vous plait."* She laughs and says, "Sure, sit down."

Line Quirion, who works as a counselor in a shelter for battered women in Montreal, is traveling to Perce to visit her parents. "You're an American, aren't you?"

"How can you tell so quickly?"

"Your French. You Americans pronounce the words *pas mal*, but you don't know the, how do you say—idioms?—that people really use. It's how they teach you French in your schools. Europeans learn the idioms, but don't pronounce the words right. And Canadian English never make the effort at all."

I can't believe that's really true.

"Oh yes. I ride this train *toujours*. And they either speak to me in English or ignore me when they hear my language. That's why we don't like them very well."

"Is that the main problem, these days, language and not religion?"

"I think so," she says matter-of-factly. "There are many English-speaking Catholics, and many French who don't go to mass. And everyone from the generation before me can remember—'Speak white.' That's what they used to say to our parents and grand-parents in stores and restaurants. No one can ever forget that."

"So if English Canada apologized tomorrow for the sins of the past and started speaking French everything would be okay?"

Line pauses for a moment to light a cigarette. Outside we can begin to see the lights of Quebec City coming up across the river. "No. No, there is more than language. We would still know we are different."

"How?"

For an answer, she points to the brightly lit skyline of the city across the river. The view from the train is impressive with the Citadel thrust out beside the dark shadow of the Plains of Abraham, the brightly lit clifftop promenade framing the little lights of the lower town, and the soaring bulk of the Chateau Frontenac and the dome of Notre Dame Basilica rising above it all. "English Canada never built anything like that." She believes the English-Canadians harbor a deep-seated jealousy of Quebec's French culture because they don't have one of their own.

"What about merry old England, the Queen and all that?"

"That's a foreign culture, that's Britain, not Canada. French-Canadians don't care about France. We don't even like them very much. Quebec has its own North American French culture that has nothing to do with France. The English-Canadians don't have anything like that. The only truly North American English-speaking culture on this continent is in your country."

It's a novel explanation of a phenomenon that has puzzled me ever since I began looking into the mysteries of Canada. Polls have shown that a significant number of French-Canadians (as high as 23 percent in one *MacLean's* poll) advocate separation from Canada and joining the United States. For language-conscious Quebecois to want to be assimilated into monolingual America always seemed to me like jumping out of the pot into the fire. Though the prospect still seems highly improbable, Line's thesis suggests at least an affinity on the grounds of sharing the experience of indigenous North American cultures.

"Many of us like Americans better than we like English Canadians," she says with a mischievous chortle. "But I could never live in your country. It's too dangerous."

I must laugh a little too loudly because another bar patron asks me to lower my voice. Line thinks that's funny and I'm embarrassed and apologize for committing the typical American sin of being a loudmouth.

Line is sympathetic. "You live in a country with ten times the population of Canada. You have to speak louder to be heard."

I ask about her work in Montreal. The shelter is called "Multi-Femme" and is supported by the government. "We do miracles," she says. Abuse of women in Canada, especially French Canada, is more pervasive than is commonly thought. It's coming out of the closet here for the same reasons it is everywhere else. "Women are learning that beatings don't have to be a natural part of their lives. And as they become more independent, the violence of some of our men is getting worse." Line believes French-Catholic tradition makes French men especially prone to abusiveness. "Men were taught in church that their wives owed them the same obedience the men owed God."

I ask if the problem is class-related and she explains that there is evidence suggesting that battered women can be found in all social classes. Nonetheless, most of the cases that come to official attention are from the less affluent. "If you are poor, the walls are less thick."

Shelters in Quebec have been the object of some criticism by the Church for undermining the Catholic teaching against divorce. The complaint is that Catholic women wanting to get out of a troubled marriage come to the shelters and make false charges against their husbands. But Line says she can always tell whether it's just a case of a bad marriage or one of true abuse. "The key question is always, 'Are you afraid?' A liar could say yes, but you learn to recognize the signs of real fear." And many women come to the shelter with no thought of divorce, pleading that "My husband needs help. You have to help *him*."

It's an oppressive job dealing with domestic horror stories day after day. Line takes off her hat and shows me a small bare spot on her head. "It makes me so nervous that my hair falls out. I have to escape to Perce when it gets bad like this."

The train crosses the mountainous spine of the peninsula during the night and in the early morning the *Chaleur* breaks off the longer train at Matapedia and runs east along high cliffs above the shore of Chaleur Bay. The route was once actually two railways, each with names flaunting their promoters' high hopes: the Atlantic, Quebec & Western and the Atlantic & Lake Superior, later aggrandized to the Quebec Oriental. The idea was that Gaspé might become a major eastern port and terminus of a great French-Canadian railway to the west.

As we pass through little towns whose granite churches are topped with striking silver-painted spires, I meet Line for breakfast. Over sausage, eggs, and fried potatoes, we roll by New Carlisle, where separatist and Parti Quebecois leader René Levesque was regularly beaten up by English bullies during his boyhood. Across the bay we can just barely see the coastline of New Brunswick. Line wants me to understand that though she and her family are separatists, she was speaking more for French people in general than for herself last night. "In Perce the French and English get along better than they do in most of the country because we share the same poverty. You should get off with me and see Perce and meet my father." He is an artist—a painter—and is old enough to have witnessed much of the modern history of Quebec.

It's a tempting invitation. I had planned to ride the train to the end of the line at the little port of Gaspé, thirty-nine miles around the cape from Perce. But Line insists that there is nothing much at Gaspé while Perce has Bonaventure Island, Perce Rock, and the home of a French family where I am welcome. That settles it, and for the remainder of the morning after breakfast, I concentrate on watching the passing seascape rather than feeling the compulsion to talk to people. As a guest in Perce, I'll have plenty of opportunity for that.

The run of the *Chaleur* along the Gaspé Peninsula fascinates. The coastline is just as rocky but otherwise very different from that of Maine. Instead of narrow fjords and fingers of land, it is dominated by large bights providing sweeping views of gracefully curving shoreline. Sometimes the tracks run along the top of coastal cliffs, elsewhere they run along the verge of sandy beaches only a few feet from the water's edge. Old-fashioned wooden drying racks for codfish appear along the shoreline even in places seemingly remote from any of the little towns.

The bay presents a benign aspect this sunny July morning, but the rusting hulk of a freighter grounded a few hundred yards offshore testifies that it is not always so. A conductor explains that the ship was safely in port when the storm blew up, but harbor officials feared it might crush smaller boats lying nearby, so they ordered it out to sea to weather the storm. The captain wasn't too pleased about having to hove to on a lee shore during a storm but obeyed and fought the winds till the ship was finally grounded. He and his crew were all safely rescued and had the last laugh when the ship's owners found it would cost more to get the aging ship loose and repaired than it was worth.

Concerned with the Depression and the Communist menace in union activity, few Canadians noted how far Quebec had drifted from its moorings in the confederation during the years between the wars. A few far-sighted Quebecois leaders, like Louis Alexandre Taschereau, wondered, "Since Quebec is so necessary to confederation, is it not deplorable to note its isolation?" More commonly the Church and certain racist leaders like Groulx were quite content to let *"les habitants"* live a provincial life with little interaction with the rest of Canada. Visitors to Quebec during those years came away bewildered by the observance of holidays that riotously celebrated a host of parochial and Catholic events but none of the national dates. Quebec was out of step with Canada and the rest of the world in other ways. The hardening of loyalty to their own engendered an aversion to non-French, particularly Protestants and Jews. Even before Hitler's *Kristallnacht*, French-Canadians in Montreal were trashing Jewish establishments on St. Urbain Street.

Inflammatory new leaders emerged who were insulated enough from the rest of the world that they were honestly innocent about the overtones of their calls for "racial purity." One such was Maurice Duplessis, who urged that *Canadiens* should "become masters in our own house." On a platform opposing the exploitation of Quebec's resources and workers by foreign interests, he founded the Union Nationale and, after winning power in the 1936 election, ruled Quebec with an iron hand reminiscent to Americans of Huey Long in Louisiana. With the Communist threat as his whipping boy, he curtailed civil liberties and beefed up police powers over dissenters. When English civil libertarians complained that he was trampling the Magna Carta, he was unmoved. The Magna Carta was a foreign document.

At the same time, the bishops began issuing statements admiring the Catholic fascists Mussolini, Franco, and Salazar. When a Canadian delegate to the League of Nations introduced a resolution condemning Italy for its invasion of Ethiopia, the reaction from Quebec was so angry that Liberal Prime Minister Mackenzie King was forced to repudiate the sanctions offered by his own minister. Thus it was that when Hitler invaded Poland, Quebecers found that they had been reading a different page of history than the rest of Canada and the Atlantic world.

Due to exposure of widespread corruption in his government, Duplessis was defeated in 1939 and replaced as premier of Quebec by Liberal Adelard Godbout. With his election, Quebec was back within the Canadian fold as long as the federal government refrained from committing the sin of conscription.

More disturbing to the Liberal federal government than Duplessis was Camellien Houde, mayor of Montreal, who had been elected and then thrown out by the voters half a dozen times because of rumored connections to the underworld. Ugly as a stump and prone to losing his false teeth during particularly vituperative speeches, he nonetheless could turn out huge followings—

especially from the neglected underclass of Montreal—with his powerful demogogic appeals to French pride. Educated on the slum streets himself, Houde could work his will with a crowd, or a mob, better than anyone in Canadian politics. In 1938, Houde began his crusade against the government's preparations for war, threatening that if the government tried to drag Quebec into this war, it would force Quebec into complete independence.

After the fall of France, the government had no trouble getting a bill for national mobilization. Houde stood nearly alone against the tide, declaring unequivocal opposition and going further to insist that he had no intention of conforming to the law: " . . . and I ask that the population not conform, knowing full well what I am doing and to what I expose myself." At first the government tried to censor Houde's speech, but it got out and stimulated rumblings in Montreal's slums. An arrest warrant was sworn out under Defense of Canada regulations, and the French-Canadian mayor of Montreal was thrown in jail.

The reaction in Quebec was deceptively mild when the Mackenzie King government won a national plebiscite that asked voters to release it from its pledge not to enact conscription. It was the isolation of ordinary Quebecers from the national limelight combined with the din of war that created the illusion of placidity in Quebec. But on the working-class streets of Montreal and in the insular villages in the countryside, Houde had become a martyr. Inspired by his sacrifice, fiery radicals in small towns declaimed, "The RCMP will have a hard time persuading us, at pistol point, that England is fighting *pour la civilisation Catholique*." Others argued that the only Englishman who could understand would be one who lived in a land conquered by the German empire years ago and was now forced to put on a German uniform. When Hitler invaded Russia and Canada became an ally of the Communists, the Catholic press wondered aloud if the country were not fighting on the wrong side of the war.

As in the past, Britain was none too delicate about how it used the troops Canada sent to the war. The first Canadians in Europe landed at Dunkirk just as the British began evacuating and were almost trapped there. In Hong Kong they weren't so lucky. In 1940, Winston Churchill said, "There is not the slightest chance of holding Hong Kong or of relieving it. It is most unwise to increase the loss we shall suffer there." Nonetheless, the following year he sent two hastily trained and poorly armed battalions of Canadians, one the

Royal Rifles of Quebec, in a symbolic gesture to ensure that the Japanese conquest of a crown colony did not go unopposed. On Christmas Day of 1941, the survivors of the Japanese onslaught were sent to a grisly four-year ordeal of forced labor in prison camps. Three hundred died before the end of the war; most who survived returned permanently damaged.

In 1942, when the allies made a tentative landing at Dieppe in response to Stalin's pleas for a second front, the first three waves were slaughtered in broad daylight. They were Canadians. When conscription finally came and seven thousand of the first ten thousand drafted deserted, many of them French, Ontarians were convinced that Frenchmen were an inferior cowardly breed unfit to enjoy the same advantages of Canadian life as Englishmen. Yet thousands of Quebecers had volunteered without conscription and served just as nobly as English-Canadians.

As in the First World War, Canadians earned a reputation as particularly fearless soldiers, especially in the Italian campaign and the invasion of Normandy, where they absorbed the highest casualty rate of any of the allies. Earlier, at the darkest hour of the war, Britain had made plans for a government in exile in Canada, should Hitler overrun the British Isles. In preparation the Bank of England gold reserves, some $7.5 billion, were brought to Halifax on a cruiser. From there the Intercolonial Railway carried the shipments in top secret on special trains with no windows to vaults in Montreal and Ottawa.

As a partner in the alliance of powerful nations, Canada's time had come. Mackenzie King was consulted by Churchill and Roosevelt and a high-profile role for Canada in the post-hostilities order was envisioned. But in the mourning working-class homes of *les habitants* of Quebec, it all looked like the realization of their age-old fear. English Canada was intoxicated by service to Britain. French-Canadians found themselves despised as an inferior race due to an alleged lack of enthusiasm for Britain's war. Their resources were owned by outsiders and their workers were employed at the worst jobs for the lowest pay. More than a few began to see a parallel between their situation and that of another oppressed race in the States. But there was one great difference: this land belonged to them; they had founded it.

Approaching Perce, the train veers away from the shore and climbs the cliffs. The station, a quaint French-Canadian clapboard building with curved eaves, is located on a lonely hilltop a mile or two from the village. Line's mother is waiting with her car and, after whispered explanations, we drive into town. Perce looks, on first approach, like a thriving tourist town. Out in the water I can see the hulk of Bonaventure Island, a sanctuary for half a dozen endangered species of birds, and the spectacular, split trapezoid of three-hundred-feet-high Perce Rock with the famous hole right through it. The main road through town is lined with little shops freshly and brightly painted in yellow, green, pink, and blue as well as the traditional white. The people out walking are dressed like tourists, but Line says that many are locals who have adopted the tourist style of dress since tourism became the town's leading industry.

Line and her mom drop me off at her father's gallery and head home after making arrangements to meet me later on. Raymond Quirion is a tall, white-haired, gentle, almost fragile-looking man. He greets me with dignity and speaks in flawless English so we quickly dispense with my attempts at French. Displayed on the walls of the glassed front gallery, his paintings are small, almost miniatures, which he painstakingly creates with a knife and thick paint. He calls his style figurative and his subject is always Gaspé.

He agrees with his daughter that the French and English of Perce get along better than elsewhere in Canada because of the hard times and isolation they share. With a year-round population today of about seven hundred, and two hundred more like Raymond who depart for the winter, Perce was a larger, thriving fishing town in the thirties and forties, when Raymond's father was a fisherman. "The average codfish was then five to ten pounds, today it's two to four. Fishing has gone to the rocks in Perce." The big trawlers with bottom-scraping dragnets have done it.

"Then someone discovered what a wonderful postcard the rock made, and tourism began." They come from as far away as California, flying to New York and taking bus tours up through New England and New Brunswick to Perce. Tourism has brought a touch of prosperity to the dwindled population, and most of the old fishermen now make their living taking people out on charters. Raymond thinks that the same qualities that drive him and others to paint bring the tourists here. "There's so much open sky and water framing the green land and the red and gray rock. It truly inspires."

Raymond's ancestors have fished the waters off Perce for two centuries. Raymond was born in 1919 in his family's ancestral house located near the high cliffs of Mont Joli above the sandbar that leads, at low tide, to Perce Rock. As a child he began painting watercolors on seashells and later graduated to oil and canvas under the tutelege of Frederick Rothermel and Boris Chezar. But in 1940 the world went to war and Raymond didn't wait to see what would happen with the old issue of conscription. Having never traveled outside of Gaspé, he wanted to see the world, so he enlisted.

"They put us on a train and we rode all the way across the country in cars with no windows. Then we boarded a ship at Vancouver. I saw the Orient before I ever saw Montreal."

Raymond won't talk about his war experiences except to say that he's sorry he went and today wouldn't support conscription. After the war, he married, had two children, and pursued a business career in Montreal but never got far from his love of painting. "And thanks to the train, I kept my roots here. We brought the children here every summer." He retired from business in 1963, established the routine of staying in Perce for three seasons of each year and pursued painting full-time. Today he has the good life. "I'm not rich, but I have my family and my work and I can live in my hometown," he says with a shrug that intimates he has more than a person has a right to expect.

I ask what is the most troubling issue to French residents of Perce.

"If you mean something about trouble with the English or separatism, here that all just seems so far away. But if they tear up the railway, that will be a bad thing. We have no major medical facilities and we elderly depend on the train to get to Quebec City or Montreal for care. You know the sleeping car is called the traveling hospital. Losing that train could make it hard for some of us to stay here."

Just behind Raymond's gallery, the ocean pounds the pebbly shore. Here it's *au revoir* to Raymond, and I hike toward the center of town to meet Line for a tour. I had noticed in Raymond's paintings that, though he says his subject is nature, there is often some brightly colored object of human works. Hiking along the shore behind the buildings lining the main drag of Perce, I discover that, despite the striking natural panoramas, the eye is drawn to the kinds of manmade images that pop up in Raymond's paintings—a row of freshly painted red, blue, and yellow skiffs pulled up on shore; a fisherman's shanty painted bright purple; a pile of electric-orange lobster buoys; a wooden barrel bursting with magenta flowers; and the people, clad in those vivid tourist colors.

171

At the town pier I spot Line in the crowd of tourists and we begin the hike up Mont Joli, which is itself a huge rock, but attached to the mainland. We pass several tiny houses surrounded by tall sprays of flowers and painted the most outrageously bright colors. "That's French," says Line. "Everything in English Canada is in black and white."

She shows me the site of the ancestral Quirion home—a grassy field perched high up the *mont*, just a stone's throw from sheer drops of hundreds of feet to the shore below. The original house was torn down in 1959 and Raymond built his studio, a small cabin, on the site shortly thereafter. Then the government expropriated the land as part of a national park in 1974 and Raymond moved the cabin to the backyard of the house in town where the family resides today. Line points to a large wooden cross atop the *mont* and recites the tale of her father's youth told by him to her so many times.

"He lived here with my *grandpère* Antoine, and my Irish *grand-mère*, Aurelia Dunn, who came over during the potato famine. Every morning, even in the snows of winter, he would race his sisters and brothers barefoot from the house up to the cross. Grand-mère always worried about the cliffs, but as long as they went for the cross, she knew they were safe."

Beyond the cross a narrow path winds along a narrow rocky spine with dizzying drops on both sides to the beaches below. From the point, one looks out over a gulf, empty except for wheeling sea birds, toward Perce Rock. Three hundred feet below tiny figures crawl along the sandbar between the point and the rock. Perce Rock, looming so large before us that it seems we can reach out and touch it, is limestone and contains fossils, unlike the rock on the shore. It carries an aura of mystery since geologists have a difficult time explaining how it came to be there. It looks as if it broke off from the mainland, but its composition is different.

The rock has also been the site of human drama. Line remembers the whole town watching a strange group of men climb its sheer cliffs when she was twelve. When they got to the top they unfurled a huge German flag that upset people up and down the coast. There have also been stories of lovers' leaps. An old Indian legend tells of the Gou-Gou, a huge female monster who lives on Ile Bonaventure and uses the rock as a stepping-stone to come ashore and gather humans whom she eats alive and screaming back at her table on Bonaventure. Occasionally someone mysteriously disappears and people assume that the individual jumped from the cliffs and was washed out to sea.

Children still have nightmares about the Gou-Gou, and there are dark adult rumors that the cliffs have provided a handy solution to the problem of a nagging wife or an inconvenient birth.

Line leads me down the winding path to the base of Mont Joli and the sandbar that extends to the rock. The tide is coming in so we can't cross the bar, but a cheerful gathering of fellow explorers sits here on the rocks and watches the waters roll in. Huge birds with six-foot wingspans pass overhead and Line explains that they are the Fou de Baissan. They come back to Ile Bonaventure every year to the same mates and lay one egg. "They recognize each other by their nests."

As the afternoon wanes toward the time when I have to catch my outbound train, I follow Line back to her family's house. Her mother has made tea for us and we sit in the backyard near Raymond's old studio and talk about the war. Mother is more radical in her talk than is the rest of the family. "When Mayor Camellien Houde was released from jail after urging us to resist the draft, there was dancing in the streets," she says. "We don't like the English very much anyway, but people of my generation will never forget what they did with the French boys they drafted for their war."

Suddenly I almost understand. "But Raymond enlisted," I say.

"Yes, he did. He wanted to see the world. And they sent him and the rest of the French contingent to Hong Kong, which they already knew the Japanese were going to overwhelm. Our boys were expendable. Could you ever forgive that?"

Raymond was captured along with the entire Canadian force when the Japanese took Hong Kong in 1939. Those who survived the invasion spent two years in Hong Kong and then two more in Japan doing slave labor. "He has never talked about the horrors of those years, but at reunions of the regiment he was imprisoned with, his old war buddies do. That's how we know the story, of the beatings and the men dropping dead from physical exhaustion. They never expected to live beyond those years of agony. And then it was the American atomic bomb that finally got them released."

"Has Raymond somehow blanked it all from memory?"

"No, he remembers. He cries a lot and to this day he wakes up screaming at night, reliving it in dreams."

The history of the French-Canadian separatist movement since World War II is marked by the striking evaporation of the issues of religion and empire and the movement's final surge into the national forefront fueled by economics and language.

Mackenzie King had presciently observed during the war the potential for disunity in the economic disparity between various regions of Canada. In response, he instituted programs for redistribution of wealth and a family allowance scheme that became the basis for the welfare state that prevails in Canada to this day. After the war the nation turned in the opposite ideological direction from its American neighbor.

Quebec nonetheless became a labor battleground. At Arvida, Montreal, Valleyfield, and finally at the American-owned Johns-Manville mines at Asbestos, violent strikes broke out. Duplessis, back in power, sent in the police to bust heads. A brilliant young journalist named René Levesque covered the story. An equally brilliant young lawyer named Pierre Trudeau was among the activist intellectuals allied with the workers.

After years of stagnation under the repressive hand of Duplessis's Union Nationale, Quebec flowered with its defeat and the election of Jean Lesage's provincial Liberals in 1960. Lesage brought talented young men like René Levesque to the task of governing Quebec and they initiated long-overdue initiatives that collectively came to be known as the "Quiet Revolution." American- and British-owned hydropower plants were nationalized. Education, traditionally run by the Church, was reformed with the introduction of practical math, science, and technology into the classical regime that had limited the opportunities of even educated Quebecois for so long. Encouraged by government grants, writers, dramatists, artists, and musicians flourished in a mini-renaissance whose continuing theme was the resurrection of French confidence—enough that Quebec would dare to say to the world that had once ordered it to "speak white": "In Quebec you will speak French."

In contrast to the years before World War II, suddenly Quebec was more in step with the world at large than the rest of Canada. For a moment in the early sixties, even English Canada looked toward Quebec with admiration and pride. Here the elusive, long-sought Canadian culture and identity were being born.

The era of good feeling didn't last long. A terrorist underground, heavily infiltrated by agents provocateurs of the RCMP, the Front de Liberation du Quebec (the FLQ), stole dynamite, blew up Westmount mailboxes, and threatened worse if independence didn't happen soon. Queen Elizabeth visited Quebec City and was abused and heckled by separatist protesters. By the middle of the decade, the mood in English Canada had reverted to sullen resentment, touched with a little envy, at the incomprehensible happenings in Quebec.

Disdaining the English backlash, Liberal Prime Minister Lester Pearson responded to the challenge of the "Quiet Revolution" by courageously broaching the issue of a national flag. Canada had always flown the Union Jack or a red ensign including the Union Jack, and Orange Tories were not pleased when he selected a design from a national contest with a red maple leaf to replace it. The act removed the last symbolic vestige of the French-Canadians' old Anglophobia.

In a more material move, Pearson proposed the Official Languages Act, which would make bilingualism mandatory for federal services in regions where more than 10 percent spoke the minority language. As his final act before retiring in favor of Pierre Trudeau, Pearson doggedly pushed through legislation that put French on the signs, documents, and labels of nearly everything Canadians handle in their daily lives. "What is at stake is no less than the survival of a nation," he said. English Canada groaned like someone suddenly inflicted with an upset stomach caused by the aspirin taken for a headache.

With the election of the anti-separatist French-Canadian Pierre Trudeau as the national prime minister, Quebec was split no less than the nation as a whole. René Levesque founded the party of nonviolent separatists, the Parti Quebecois, and promised that when it came to power in the province, it would take Quebec out of confederation. In the extreme left wing beyond Levesque, the FLQ continued its program of tentative terrorism. But Trudeau's Liberals kept alive the hope that Quebec could thrive within confederation. Under his government, French-Canadians swarmed into the federal government and exercised power as never before.

English-Canadians, alarmed by the renewed advance of American economic and cultural influence, tended during these years to assume the necessity of keeping Quebec in confederation, an assumption many would soon begin to question. With his staunch anti-separatist sentiments, Trudeau was their last best hope, but just how far did the nation have to go in making concessions to this militant province? English-Canadians' anguished question in the Trudeau years was, "Just what does Quebec want?"

They didn't like the answer they got from the leader of the

revived Union Nationale, Quebec's Premier Daniel Johnson, who proposed a language bill that required that children of immigrants to Quebec attend French-language schools. Despite the energy of the "Quiet Revolution," surveys showed that spoken French was in decline. The *revanche à baissans* (revenge of the cradles) dematerialized as French-Canadians, increasingly liberated from the strictures of the Church, came to have the lowest birth rate in the nation.

With the charismatic excitement of the Trudeau government, a new Liberal provincial government under Robert Bourassa promising prosperity through a great James Bay hydropower project, and Levesque's nonviolent separatists dominating the headlines, the FLQ by 1970 was gnashing its teeth and beginning its clumsy campaign of kidnappings and violence. Trudeau invoked the War Powers Act and in one night of police-state action like nothing the United States has ever seen, the RCMP rounded up hundreds of people (almost entirely French-Canadians) on the flimsiest of suspicions. Besieged English Canada applauded the arrests. French-Canadians were appalled. Young Americans fleeing the Vietnam War draft were sobered to realize that Canadians enjoy less protection of civil liberties than they had had in the country they had just renounced.

By 1976, the luster had begun to fade from the Trudeau regime. The RCMP had gone berserk in its pursuit of the FLQ and the economy was turning sour. In Quebec, Bourassa instituted Daniel Johnson's plan mandating French education for immigrants. It was English-Canadians who now felt their language threatened and the first English exodus from Montreal to Toronto began. Then in November, René Levesque led his Parti Quebecois to a landslide victory in Quebec on a platform promising to take the province out of confederation.

Canada was stunned when the unthinkable finally happened. Newspaper editors in the Maritimes said that if Quebec left confederation, so should they. Voices in Alberta and British Columbia said the same thing. But the national consensus, though weakening, was still that a way should be found to keep the confederation together.

Quebec forged ahead with Bill 101. As a final solution to the erosion of the French language in Quebec, the bill required that all signs be in French only and that businesses of more than fifty employees conduct their affairs in French.

Finally, in preparation for the referendum on independence that

Levesque had promised, he described his concept of "sovereignty association," which he envisioned as the future of Canada after separation. Quebec would be independent in all ways except for the sharing of currency, open inland navigation, and free trade with the rest of Canada.

On May 20, 1980, Quebec held its referendum on separation. Confusion reigned. Ambiguous wording prompted speculation about what Levesque really wanted from the vote. Perhaps a large but less than majority "yes" vote would force Ottawa into granting further concessions that might make separation unnecessary. On the other hand, a "no" vote might provoke English Canada into an overconfident obnoxiousness that would guarantee a true separatist vote in the future.

Thus the 60 percent vote against the question settled nothing, despite the fact that Levesque gracefully conceded that the people of Quebec had "clearly given federalism another chance." English Canada, committed to bilingualism in nine of its provinces, was still confronted with Bill 101 and the special exception it created for the "distinct society" of the tenth.

In an attempt to break the deadlock, Trudeau patriated the constitution but failed to get the provincial premiers to agree on a formula delineating federal and provincial rights. The Supreme Court disallowed Bill 101, but Quebec enforced it anyway. Canada has existed under a constitutional crisis ever since.

A conservative government under Brian Mulroney would come to power and the change in leadership would distract Canada for a time from its fundamental issue. But sooner or later the constitution would have to be dealt with. It is Canada's misfortune that the issue has come to the fore in the context of the end of passenger service on the rail route that unified the nation; the opening of free trade with America amid a continental economic recession; and the precedent-setting breakup of another large federal empire—the U.S.S.R. The run of good luck that had assisted the cause of confederation since the days of Louis Riel and Donald Smith is over.

In the late afternoon I catch the return *Chaleur* headed west to the big cities. But I'm not going that far. I'm getting off for an overnight at Matapedia before catching the *Ocean* for Nova Scotia. At the Perce station there are only two others waiting for the train, a voyageur from Germany traveling à la backpack through Canada named Nicole and a fellow from British Columbia named Kenny who is doing the same. In previous encounters with backpacking young voyageurs I have thought that, with their spontaneity and freedom, they see more of the true life of the country than I do. But Kenny and Nicole came in on the same train I did this morning. They didn't have the money for a taxi and they thought it would be too far to walk to town. After a tentative climb down the slope to the ocean, they have spent the day just hanging out here at the station. They didn't even see Perce Rock.

Traveling west in the late afternoon and early evening, the *Chaleur* traverses ocean beaches, blue mountains, the broad bay shoreline, and finally the narrowing of the bay that becomes the Restigouche River. For years I had heard of the river from fellow fly-fishing buddies back in New England. Those with the time, money, and/or will talked of fishing a river in the Gaspé Peninsula where the Atlantic salmon still run as big and as numerous as they did in our New England rivers before we ruined them. In the bar car during the evening, instead of French politics, I talk fishing in hopes of landing a knowledgeable local who might take me out on the river tomorrow.

About a half-hour before arrival in Matapedia, I get a bite. "Are you the *Américain* who want to fish the Restigouche?" asks a burly fellow with a strong French accent who has been talking to the bartender at the other end of the car. The man is Jacques Boucher, a resident of Matapedia and—luck is with me—a fishing guide. He promises to take me out for free in the morning if I will write nice things about the Restigouche in my "fishing book." Apparently he feels a sense of competition with the salmon rivers in Cape Breton, Nova Scotia, which have been getting a lot of attention in fishing magazines. "Orange rivers," he calls them with a wink. The best salmon run in "good, Catholic rivers."

At 5:30 the next morning Jacques is waiting in a pickup truck as I trudge sleepily to the station across the tracks from the Restigouche Hotel. He has brought fly-casting equipment for me, an Orvis rod "because that's what *les Américains de New England* always want." We drive less than ten miles to a bend in the river that is down a dirt road just off the highway. Jacques is deliberately vague about where we are; he wants me to praise the fishing experience he is going to provide, but he doesn't want me to be able to write about how to get to the spot.

It's been a few years since I did any serious fly fishing for the little state-stocked brook trout that we call fish in New Hampshire. Jacques pulls out a wallet of exquisitely tied flies and advises that a wet fly would be my best bet. But I've never had much luck guessing when to strike on a submerged fly I can't see, so I pick a dry fly that looks like an oversized mosquito with red and gold wings and fumble to tie it on to the tiny end of the nylon tippet. Then we creep down a bank from the parked truck and Jacques shows me where to stand. The water moves pretty fast through the constriction of the bend, but there are relatively still pools in the lee of large submerged rocks. He points to one where even I can see surface disturbances that aren't caused by the current.

I pull off what I think is enough line from the reel and begin whipping the long salmon rod back and forth overhead—and snag, I've caught a weed on the slope behind us. Jacques mutters in French as he untangles me and I begin again. This time the fly sails toward the ripples and lands—about twenty feet short. Jacques grumbles, "I show you where to fish, I don't teach you how to fish."

But on the fifth cast the fly lands within a few feet of the spot I'm aiming for and instantly the water froths—wham—snap—I've overstruck and broken the leader. Jacques shakes his head and says, "Easy, easy, you don't try to break his jaw." And then he leads me along the shore to another pool. For the remainder of the morning I never get another strike and Jacques finally resigns himself to my ineptitude and we talk while I fish.

Jacques is a fatalistic separatist. "They don't want us and we don't want them. We never belong to Canada." He wonders what all the fuss is about. Independence for Quebec seems like normalcy, the confederation like a weird arrangement to be borne only for a time. He thinks the controversy is something invented by the media. "They make big talk about it to sell newspapers. I don't believe *les Anglais* are really against it. To them, we are just—*le mal à tête*—they want to be finished with us."

And politicians, even French ones, are not to be believed. "*Ils sont tout* what you call—power crazy. Bourassa, Mulroney, Bouchard, it does not matter. They all play games."

I challenge him with the results of the referendum and he is not fazed. "Some think the referendum was, how you say, patched?"

"Fixed?"

"*Oui*, fixed, not the truth. I don't know, but it does not matter. The newspapers and politicians made people so confused—no one knew what to do."

Despite polls that fail to show a clear majority for independence, Jacques believes a new referendum that wasn't fixed would speak loud and strong. "Many people say they are undecided. But you don't have that choice in a referendum."

I try to take him back for a deeper response to the basic question of—why separation? Exasperated, he reiterates, "Quebec is a separate country—we have a different language, a different religion, our ancestors come from a different part of the world, we think different, we live different, we look different—what is the big surprise?"

We finally get a fish. Just before giving up for the day, Jacques takes over and casts a perfect fly right on the nose of a salmon finning at the bottom of a small rapids. Instantly the fish sucks in the fly and Jacques expertly sets the hook and hands the rod to me. The fish runs hard downstream pulling line and then everything goes slack as he turns and rushes back toward me. Furiously I take in line and get tension just in time as the fish leaps less than ten yards from the shoreline where I am standing. "Ohn, hohn-hohn," approves Jacques, who had given up any hope of my doing anything right. The fish makes one more run and returns with something more like a wallow than a jump at the end this time and Jacques plunges into the water with the net and we have him. Two and a half pounds—not big but still a real Atlantic salmon.

Back at the hotel, Jacques refuses to take anything except the fish in pay for his services. I ask him what he thinks about French-Canadians who get along with the English in their communities and don't support separatism.

He concedes that there are a lot of people like that, and that they may be good people but they suffer from a lack of memory. "If one could stop the memory, maybe one wouldn't be separatist. But those people with the little memories. They will be with us. They already are—in their dreams."

8

Lifeline

MATAPEDIA TO HALIFAX ON THE *OCEAN*

F OR the second morning in a row, I struggle out of bed at the Restigouche Hotel before 5:00. This time it's not a fish but a train I have to catch. I'm at the station in time for what should be the 5:10 departure of the *Ocean* for Moncton, but there's no train, and nobody at the station either. I check my watch, the clock inside the station, my ticket, and the timetable.

A pickup truck with the CN logo painted on the side pulls in beside the station and a man wearing a VIA cap gets out. He is the stationmaster, and he has bad news. The *Ocean* is delayed at least three hours because of a collision with a truck at a level crossing.

After a desultory attempt to retrieve some of my lost sleep back in my hotel room, I finally board the *Ocean* at 9:00 and head for the diner for breakfast. As we rumble along the south shore of the Chaleur Bay past extensive stands of white birch, the talk in the diner is of the accident and its effect on our schedule. The truck was carrying a full load of bricks and the driver was stupidly racing the train to the crossing. The crew are still a little shaken. Usually level crossing accidents are not life-threatening to anyone but the occupants of the auto involved, but that truck had the kind of mass that could have derailed the whole train.

Steward Winston Grosse, a jovial, outspoken black man, supervises cook Carlos Lopez and waitresses Leona Belliveau and Stella Madora, who keep burning the toast because they are so busy entertaining us diners with their chatter. There isn't a trace of Anglo-Saxon blood in the entire group, but when the subject of Quebec separatism comes up, everybody agrees that the separatists are like a bunch of spoiled children. As an afterthought, Leona jokes that, present company excepted, nobody likes Americans very much either. So it goes in Canada—board a different train and cross over to another regime.

Winston pursues the allusion to Americans and hopes I understand that what he has to say is offered as constructive criticism. "When you see bad things happen to the Americans on the news, like their hostages taken in the Middle East, or a Panamanian dictator thumbing his nose at them, or a nuclear reactor melting down, you want to feel sympathy for them, but you can't. You just don't feel sorry for them getting the natural consequences of their ways."

A few questions reveal that Winston's image of benighted Americans is based on encounters with Southerners in particular. He sees a lot of them in Halifax, increasingly a popular summer escape from the heat of the southland. Once a Virginia couple asked to hold his baby. They were fascinated by the little bundle of wiggling black toes and fingers and explained that, "Back home we can't do this, you know." I protest that his story is very uncharacteristic of America these days and he asks what part of the country I'm from. When I say, New England, he harrumphs, "Hell, what do New Englanders know? You're not much more American than us Maritimers. You haven't been able to elect a president since Kennedy."

"What about George Bush, he's from Maine."

"That's not what I heard the man say. He's from Texas. 'Read my lips,' and don't you forget it," says Winston with a mischievous giggle. He is taking this conversation only semi-seriously, but I am intrigued by this southern influence on the Canadian image of America. During the boom years of the Sun Belt, it was Southerners who had the disposable income for lengthy summer vacations to the coolness of Canada. And Canadians, who follow our politics much more closely than we do theirs, can't miss the implications of successful national campaigns stressing themes aimed at the South.

"Face it," laughs Winston. "You Yankees don't run your country anymore. The South has avenged the Civil War."

Now in the spirit, I retort, "And the last time Canada listened to you Maritimers was when you conned them into building this railway about a hundred and thirty years ago."

The group laughs and Winston whistles with delight. "Zing. But you watch, we're about to have our day. New Brunswick and Newfoundland haven't signed Meech Lake yet."

The Meech Lake accord is the historic agreement proposed by the Mulroney government and provincial representatives as a resolution to the constitutional crisis in Canada, recognizing Quebec's special status as a "unique society" with particular provincial rights that transcend those granted to the provinces collectively. As the ratification deadline of June 28, 1990, approached, the Maritime holdouts, along with Manitoba, were in a position to scuttle the deal and seemed to relish the reemergence of their ancient role. Newfoundland signed and later New Brunswick would too, but the accord failed because Newfoundland rescinded its approval and Manitoba held out in deference to concerns of its native people about their status.

Despite the reputations of Quebec and British Columbia, the Maritimes were Canada's first separatists. Betrayed twice by the colony of Canada in the years before confederation, the British Maritime colonies despised the bicultural monstrosity that coddled "the papists" and allowed the language of the ancient adversary in the halls of government. It would take an offering that promised opportunities for enormous profit to make these cantankerous traders join and stay in confederation. It would take a railway.

In 1842, the dream of a continental Canada wasn't yet even a glint in anybody's eye. Upper and Lower Canada (Ontario and Quebec) had only recently been united and the four separate provinces in the Maritimes were more interested in their sea trade with New England than in anything Montreal or Quebec had to offer. Halifax was effectively closer to London.

Maritimers were late to catch the fever of "progress" that was sweeping the rest of the British and American world. Men tilled their farms in conformity with the methods of their grandfathers and cultivated the same thoughts. Life was meant to be grim and colorless as preparation for Judgment Day; education was suspect; travel for any purpose besides the exchange of goods was queer.

But in 1842 Britain ceded large chunks of territory to Maine in the Ashburton treaty and belatedly realized that it had almost cut its Maritime provinces off from the province of Canada. Suddenly some kind of connection for purposes of military defense of the colonies against American designs seemed prudent.

The decade saw the eruption of railway mania almost everywhere, even in Nova Scotia, where tenuous little lines began radiating out from Halifax to help farmers bring their goods to market. By its end the American promoter John Poor was proposing a fantastic scheme of linking the Maritimes and their shipping lanes to Canada with a rail route running through Portland and Maine. A rambunctious young newspaper publisher named Joseph Howe had established himself and his paper as the voice of Nova Scotia and, as colonial secretary, he saw in Poor's scheme the means to shake the Maritimes awake. With a vocabulary that stirred Maritimers out of their torpor, he railed against the stifling policies of British colonial administration and dazzled men with the possibilities inherent in Poor's scheme.

Then Howe took ship for Britain, where he painted a vision of the Canadian colonies united by a publicly owned railway that would make them the economic jewel of the empire. British business and government leaders responded with a guarantee of financing for such a line. But it wouldn't be built according to Poor's plan—with the continuing threat of American expansionism, any intercolonial mainline would have to follow an all-Canadian route as far from the American boundary as possible. Howe returned to Halifax triumphant, believing that he had an imperial mandate to "Construct your railways, people your wastelands; organize and improve the boundless territory beneath your feet; learn to rely upon and defend yourselves; and God speed you in the formation of national character and national institutions."

In Canada, a rival scheme was brewing. In machinations that would lead to the founding of the Grand Trunk on the western leg of Poor's plan (from Portland to Montreal and westward), the province of Canada was planning its own main line. Promoter and politician Francis Hincks sailed to London in 1852 and announced that Canada was no longer interested in Howe's route to the Maritimes and effectively scotched it. It wasn't Halifax that mattered, it was Chicago. Thus the Maritimes' first impulse toward colonial unity was betrayed in favor of the American mammon. The Maritimes wouldn't forget it.

Ten years later, with the Grand Trunk project established, the American Civil War set the intercolonial project on the agenda once more. It was feared that once finished with the South, the Union army would turn north and mop up the British North American provinces in return for Britain's kindness in tilting toward the South. Seven American railheads sat at the borders of the colonies that had no continuous internal communication of their own.

Howe and Leonard Tilley of New Brunswick again went to London and negotiations proceeded smoothly. They returned home thinking that this time they had the thing in the bag.

Inexplicably the Canadian delegation to London wrangled over every conceivable detail of the deal. With British troops now accumulating in Canada and southern victories threatening to tie up the Union forces indefinitely, the urgency of the threat from America seemed diminished. Finally they declared the negotiations at an impasse and sailed home. When Howe learned of this second betrayal, he turned and became from that day on one of the most rabid anti-confederationists on the continent. An angry Nova Scotia was prepared to follow him. In New Brunswick, Leonard Tilley was thrown out of office and replaced by a government pledged against confederation. "No more truck or trade with Canada" was its slogan.

New Brunswick went on to build its own rail connection from Saint John to Portland along the lines of the old Poor plan; Nova Scotia continued its little lines hither and thither. Never again would the Maritimes have the same fervor for confederation that Howe generated in those first years of awakening.

As the end of the American Civil War came into view, Canadians began to realize to their horror what they had done. The issue had been money and a surly assumption that the project was a way for the perennially poor Maritimes to feed simultaneously at the British and Canadian troughs. Now American politicians were making ominous noises about the uses to which the Grand Army of the Republic could be put after the war. Fenians in America openly called for an invasion of Canada.

Suddenly the Canadians became the supplicants, begging the Maritimes to help them revive the project. They claimed they had been duped by British money men. They stood penitent while Maritimers heaped scorn on their heads and listened, chastened, to diatribes on the behavior of gentlemen in matters of ratified agreements.

It took a promise to pay for the entire survey cost, the establishment of a railway commission on which the Canadas were guaranteed to have minority status, and the appointment of British North America's greatest railway engineer, Sanford Fleming, to convince the Maritimes that this time their cousins were serious.

With the railway now an imminent reality, the four Maritime provinces suddenly experienced a spasm of mutual attraction. It was partly the practical political need to present a common front to discourage any further betrayals by Canada and partly a genuine discovery that these sea-bound provinces—two of them islands and two that may as well have been—had a lot in common. In 1864, the provinces arranged a meeting in Charlottetown to discuss the railway and ways they could cooperate. Alarmed Canadian officials quickly huddled and managed an invitation as observers. They descended on Charlottetown, where they weren't particularly welcome, with an entourage that outnumbered their hosts and with a greater sense of purpose. By now they knew what they wanted, and thus the Charlottetown conference got down to business discussing nothing less than dominion and confederation of all Canada. Reluctant Maritimers were sufficiently impressed by the advances of the greatest of the British North American colonies that they consented to a second conference in Quebec and the confederation bandwagon began to roll—though not without loud squeaking from Maritime wheels with a long memory, like Joseph Howe.

We have left the wide watery vistas of the Chaleur Bay, and in the late morning the *Ocean* plunges through miles and miles of dense New Brunswick forest. I'm sitting with the waitress, Leona, and the cook, Carlos, at one of the little diner tables now that the breakfast sitting is finished and the galley is closed except for takeout orders. "That's New Brunswick," Leona says. "That's all there is, nothing but trees."

"And rocks," adds Carlos as he lights up a cigarette. The tobacco smells good, and I haven't smoked my pipe all morning because the diner is a no-smoking area. He says it's okay, so out comes the pipe and soon the car is perfumed with coils of my tobacco smoke.

Leona teases, "Your tobacco smells great. Is it true that men smoke pipes just to attract women?"

In mock anger Carlos answers for me, "No, dammit. People smoke because it's a pleasure." He is aggravated by the anti-smoking offensive, just beginning to be felt in Canada where a far larger percentage of the population still smokes than in the U.S. He has a sign in his house that says, THANK YOU FOR SMOKING. With condescension mocking the conventional voices of the health conscious, he declares, "Smoking is the right thing to do. If you don't smoke, you might live to be ninety and become a pain in the ass."

Now that they're off duty, I want to know how Leona and Carlos feel about the government's plans to cut passenger service. Carlos rolls his eyes in persecuted exasperation. "It's the same people who don't want us to smoke. They know what's good for us. Everything that's fun is either unhealthy or too costly."

Leona answers my question more directly. "You've seen who rides these trains. Old people, young people, and people who live in isolated places. If you're not rich enough to fly, not interested in taking amphetamines so you can drive all night, or not desperate enough to ride a bus, you take the train. It's a lifeline, especially to people who live in the little towns far from the big cities."

Outside, the wall of trees opens and the train slows and pulls into the charming little station at Newcastle. Confirming Leona's statement, two girls with backpacks and several elderly couples detrain and are replaced by some more elderly, a young workingman, and two very young mothers carrying small children. After Newcastle we cross the two branches of the Miramachi River on two quarter-mile-long bridges and then the forest closes in again.

During the last hour to Moncton, the little diner is invaded by four officials of a group called Transport-2000, a national organization promoting environmentally sound transportation planning for the future. They are particularly active in the campaign to save and extend the VIA Rail passenger system. Dressed in suits and carrying stuffed briefcases, they look and talk like a high-powered sales or promotional outfit.

They sit at the table across the aisle and spread out copies of speeches and tables of statistics they will present at an upcoming conference. When they find me a willing audience, they drop their work and swing into their pitch.

"Government was not elected to trash the most energy-efficient, environmentally benign, land-efficient, weather-immune, and accessible form of transportation we have," declares John McCullum, president of the Ontario chapter. He then proceeds to catalogue the causes of VIA's dire straits in terms of comparison to America's Amtrak.

When the government took over the responsibility for passenger rail service and formed VIA in 1978, it did so in an atmosphere of attitudes and assumptions quite different from those prevailing in America in 1971, when Amtrak was formed. Americans knew their passenger railroad service was in deep trouble so they took what would turn out to be some rather radical steps in setting up Amtrak as an independent corporation with a national legislative mandate. Thus, at least in theory, Amtrak trains have the right-of-way over freights, and if a railroad refuses to keep its tracks up to passenger train specifications, Amtrak can seize the line, as recently happened with the *Montrealer* route through New England. Congress voted a large capital investment in new and rebuilt equipment. And because Amtrak is not an office of the federal government, its officials are free to lobby actively and promote their cause when the politics of the executive branch are hostile, as they were during the Reagan years. Finally, Amtrak recruited one of the most successful of the presidents of private railroads, Graham Claytor of the Southern, to run the operation.

When VIA was formed, the CN and CPR had not let their service slide as far as had the American railroads, so Canadians didn't see a need for the drastic remedies incorporated in Amtrak. The horror stories of Amtrak's first five years offered Canadians no incentive to emulate what looked at the time like a disastrous experiment that would merely preside over the demise of passenger railroading in America.

Thus VIA is a crown corporation, subject to the politics of the government in power, with no national mandate of its own and no opportunity for its executives to promote their cause in opposition to the whims of the prime minister's party. It was never given the necessary capital to replace or rebuild its equipment, and its schedules and the rates paid to the contracting railways are subject to their priorities. VIA's officers have all too often been political appointees of the party in power.

Today, according to John McCullum, VIA is burdened with a massively top-heavy administration, which is characteristic of operations with strong political entanglements. Its aging equipment must be repaired at monstrous cost after nearly every run, and the contracting railways extort fees anywhere from three to six times what Amtrak pays American railroads. Political considerations prevent VIA from discontinuing costly but little-used runs and from adjusting its schedules to attract greater ridership. The result is that VIA, with about half the track mileage of Amtrak and financed from a federal budget less than one-tenth the size, has required a federal subsidy in recent years over twice that of Amtrak. The one point upon which nearly everyone agrees is that this horrendous state of affairs cannot continue.

Though Mulroney's government claims it intends to save passenger rail service in Canada, nearly everyone (89 percent nationally, according to a *MacLean's* poll) believes the policy is to wreck VIA so that it can be scrubbed from the budget entirely. With Transportation Minister Benoit Bouchard and VIA and CN President Ron Lawless leading the charge, the government has fired broadsides at rail passengers for three years. Bouchard has promoted bus service as an alternative to such an extent that rail-riding Canadians refer to buses as "Benny Buggies" and has declared that the future of Canadian travel is in the air.

For the sake of argument, I ask about the figures showing that only 5 percent of Canadians actually use the railway.

"That's because it's run so badly. That's what happens when you let the politicians try to run a railway," John McCullum insists.

And so it goes—the new-old discussion of the problem of government and transportation. Despite the North American myth of the great transportation barons of private enterprise, the fact is that few transportation systems of any type have ever thrived without government subsidy, direct or indirect, honest or dishonest, and today's massive and complex transportation needs have made a government role even more inevitable. No transportation enterprise ever better illustrated the perils of total government operation than the original railway, whose tracks I am riding now—the old Intercolonial.

Sanford Fleming must have had his first inkling of what he had gotten himself into when he surveyed the line linking the little Nova Scotia routes terminating at Truro with the fledgling New Brunswick routes at Moncton. He laid a good straight line over flat low ground, but when the contractors began work, he found that the line had two huge semicircular detours appended to it. One of the political backers of the contracting company was James Livesay, an iron-monger whose property lay on the southern slope of the Cobequid Mountains, miles away from Fleming's tangent. To this day the route carves a great half-circle to run by the site of Livesay's old ironworks.

Across the border in New Brunswick, Fleming encountered the same thing where his straight line route missed the town of Dorchester, ancestral home of provincial legislator Edward Barron Chandler. Chandler didn't even have an ironworks, he just wanted a railway station in his village. When Fleming demurred, the New Brunswick legislature exploded with protests that they had been sold into confederation at eighty cents a head and would at least have their railway where they wanted it. Still sensitive to the twice-betrayed New Brunswickers, the federal cabinet let them have their way, over Fleming's strenuous protests, and the route today runs out of its way to Dorchester and past its penitentiary.

When the British North America Act was signed in 1867 and confederation achieved, New Brunswick's Tilley informed Mac-Donald in no uncertain terms that the Maritimes' participation was conditional on the satisfactory prosecution of the Intercolonial project. With this gun at its head, the MacDonald government countenanced political shenanigans that whitened Sanford Fleming's hair before its time. The public commissioners under whom Fleming worked had no understanding whatever of railway building but a great deal of worldliness concerning patronage, which, according to one historian, "was the breath of life to them, and one and all they were determined to breathe deeply."

When MacDonald fell in 1873 and was replaced by Mackenzie, the new government cleaned house and Fleming enjoyed relative peace during the last few years of construction. The line reached Quebec and trains began running in July 1876.

Not historically averse to government involvement in great enter-prises, Canadians nonetheless to this day point to the Intercolonial as the model of how not to let government get things done. Still prickly over the betrayals of earlier years, Maritimers were less enamored of the Intercolonial as an agent of national unity than as a machine for generating local wealth. Their loyalties coalesced close to home and hearth; this railway running through their backyards, financed and run by anonymous alien powers far away, was nothing to them if not an artery through which might flow the sustenance their anemic economies so badly needed—money. When the "clean-hands" regime of Mackenzie fell and MacDonald returned to power, the Maritime politicians went to work to make up for lost time.

There was the matter of fuel and supplies. Purchasing agents were required to inform the leaders of the eighteen constituencies through which the railway passed of material needs and were directed to the politically correct suppliers. There was never even the pretense of selecting low bids, and no one complained because the right folks at home were properly remunerated and the party's representatives in Ottawa squelched queries from the federal end. Cylinder packings that should have cost about $12 ran to over $200; one consignment of sand valued at less than $10 ultimately cost $16,000.

Employment was even more of a scandal. Local politicians expected railway superintendents to appoint those they recommended, regardless of qualifications or inclination to actually perform assigned tasks. What mattered was service to the party during elections. Superintendents often had to hire two men for the same job—one for political purposes and one to do the work of keeping the railway running. Those hired for the latter purpose had tenuous employment at best. Egged on by the slanders of political appointees, politicians continually intervened to urge the firing of good men not placed through the political pipeline.

Nineteenth-century railways everywhere were plagued with the problem of free passes, but in the case of a publicly operated railway, it was the taxpayers whose pockets were picked for these perks. It was assumed that activists of the party in power had unlimited access to free passes. Sometimes the nicety of passes was dispensed with and invitations to political events, rallies, and picnics were treated as valid tickets.

But the worst offenses of the Intercolonial that the public came to know firsthand involved conduct of train crews, many of whom, as political appointees, were immune to disciplinary action. They were often plain, rough men from the hustings who had no previous experience of the world at large. Railway employment conferred on these bumpkins status and an intoxicating sense of freedom. Railway rules were routinely broken with swagger and zest.

First there was the matter of imposing uniforms on free men. Some refused to wear them, showing up for work as conductors or stewards in their farm clothes. Others wore them continuously, on and off duty with little regard for their care or cleanliness. The code regarding mannerly behavior was equally noxious to adult men, who regarded it as a throwback to their days in the schoolhouse. Lewd comments to female passengers, insolence to superiors, fistfights and roughhousing, smoking and spitting in the aisles, and all forms of profanity and blasphemy were considered the employees' personal business and not that of their superiors.

Drunkenness was common, especially as work on the railway freed Maritimers of the Calvinist watchfulness of their home parishes. Such men had little physical tolerance for alcohol and so their binges on homemade whiskey available at twenty-five cents a gallon were devastating. With the backing of local ministers and frightened passengers, railway officials had better luck disciplining men for intemperance than for other breaches of conduct, but still the ethic among many crewmen was to drink as much as they could get away with.

Other miscellaneous irregularities were common. Engineers took fiendish delight in long, fearsome blasts of the whistle, which often sent horsemen riding parallel to the tracks into the ditch. Schedules were meaningless and trains often halted in the middle of nowhere so that a crewman could hike up to visit with the engineer or borrow a chaw of tobacco. Train supplies were dropped off along the property of friends of employees. Section men worked on their foreman's personal projects, such as raising his local church, cutting his firewood, clearing brush from his farm, digging his wells, or moving railway fences from the right-of-way to more suitable locations around his fields.

It all came to a sudden end when Wilfred Laurier was elected prime minister in 1896. Other railways throughout North America had long since cleaned up similar forms of abuse, and Laurier saw no reason why it wasn't time for the Maritimes to grow up. He found the right man in A.G. Blair, who just happened to be the outgoing premier of New Brunswick. Laurier gave Blair a firm mandate to clean house, and Blair, a good man embarrassed by the antics of his compatriots, went to work firing men in droves. Politicians in Parliament screamed, but Blair and Laurier ignored them. It was nearly fifty years after Canada's betrayal of the Maritimes, and the memory no longer held its former power of intimidation. The Intercolonial, which so long stood as a lesson in how not to run a railway, would carry on in the twentieth century as part of the Canadian National system as a model of how it ought to be done.

As we pull into Moncton, it becomes apparent that the run isn't doing so well today. We are still two and a half hours late and our connecting train to Halifax has already departed. The service chief comes through the diner explaining that VIA will provide a bus to get us to Halifax this afternoon—a three-and-a-half-hour ride. John

McCullum, who is not headed for Halifax, teases, "Well, you get a chance to ride Benny Bouchard's transportation of the future today. Enjoy." Carlos, Leona, and Winston, who have been part of the audience for the T-2000 dissertation on transportation, are sympathetic and suggest survival strategies. "Take a pillow and stuff it in your carry-on bag," says Leona.

"Get something really trashy to read," adds Carlos.

"If we had known, we could've gotten you plastered in our bar so you could pass out on the bus," apologizes Winston.

With their good wishes as consolation, I detrain and, along with several dozen other hangdog-looking passengers, follow the VIA agent who leads us to a bus parked and idling by the tracks. As we line up for the bus, we are handed little brown bag lunches and advised to dash quickly for the restrooms if we have the need; the bus will not be stopping.

Boarding just behind me is a familiar face beneath a huge backpack. It's Nicole, the young German voyageur I met at the Perce station. "Where's Kenny from B.C.?" I ask after we recognize each other.

"We parted company," she explains in excellent, educated English. "A case of irreconcilable differences of itinerary. I tired of never seeing anything but the stations of the places we got off at."

Nicole rode with Kenny to the Levis station across the river from Quebec City, but when he showed no interest in taking the ferry to the city, she determined she would see more of "beautiful Canada" on her own. She spent the day in Quebec City and then decided to train back this way to see Nova Scotia before heading west. With her open-ended Canrail pass, she can make that kind of spontaneous change in travel direction.

When the bus pulls out of the station, Nicole, who is relatively new at this voyageur thing, explains that she doesn't like traveling alone. "You're supposed to be able to just strap on your backpack and head for the sunset. But I won't hitchhike. I won't get off alone at an isolated stop, no matter how much I want to see something there. And I won't travel in the U.S.A. at all."

Nicole is another of those young European university students whose education is not complete until she has seen the world with a pack on her back. But because of her timidity and the lack of airfare, Canada and its trains are just about the only travel option that works for her. Thus she feels a bit out of step with many of the really footloose fellow voyageurs she has met. Plus she has a destination.

"I'm going to raise children in British Columbia." Later this summer she begins work as a nanny for a Vancouver family.

By then I will not be surprised at all to meet young European girls coming to America for work as nannies, eventually meeting more of them on the trains than even Canadian nude dancers, but Nicole is my first nanny and she explains that the phenomenon is sweeping her generation. "There are a lot of young people who can just go and travel the world, either because they have the money or because they just don't care what happens to them. But the nanny option opens the door for more conservative, bourgeois girls like me. The journey has a goal where I'll make some money and learn about a foreign country by living with a respectable family." Nicole explains that European university employment bulletin boards are full of notices for nannies in Canada and the United States. Several of her friends had just returned from working as nannies in Canada when she graduated in May, and they raved about the experience. Nicole wrote to the Vancouver family whose notice was one of the last still on the board at the University of Bonn the day after matriculation. Employment counselors at the university helped her put together the necessary package of references, and by July she was flying to Montreal with the scheme of touring eastern Canada before making her way across the country on trains to her August date with five Vancouver children.

She is bemused by the fact that people like me are intrigued by the trend. "With all of the women in North America pursuing careers, who did you think was going to take care of your children? Why is everyone in North America always so surprised to hear about European nannies?"

Despite Nicole's pleasant company, the bus ride quickly tyrannizes the senses. The brown bag lunch of thin ham and cheese sandwiches, onion-flavored chips, stale cookies, and Coke gives me indigestion. The seats don't recline. The bus lurches around corners and the vibrations of the engine get into the bones and highway exhaust fumes into the head. Two hours out of Moncton, Nicole (who has a VIA pillow in her satchel) tries to sleep with her head against the window, and I am well past the time that I would be enjoying a pleasant train-walk through the cars on a train. Two babies are crying nearby and somewhere someone is sneaking a smoke, further fouling the laden air. If this is Transportation Minister Bouchard's idea of how Canadians will travel in the future, may he be condemned to ride this way to Patagonia.

But the bus ride isn't a total loss. It highlights the contrast between what the highway traveler sees of his country and what the rail traveler does, and it provides some perspective for a foreign visitor to Canada. Canada looks much more like America from the turnpike. Instead of railway stations, grain elevators, and country cottages, you see gas stations, fast-food joints, and shopping malls. Trees appear at a greater distance from the traveler's eye and there is a lot of grass on the highway medians and verges.

Now there's a question. Why have we decided that grass is needed along the routes traveled by autos? Nobody ever planted grass along railway tracks. And why do the trees have to be cut back so far from the roadway? In fact, everything real is far from the road so that the highway traveler squints at the world from a distance. And while I'm at it, what does it say about the future of highway travel that everything built along highways looks temporary? In light of the devastating figures concerning auto pollution, perhaps we have been instinctively more farsighted than we know. Perhaps we've always apprehended subliminally that highway travel is a regime that cannot last.

From the highway, you see the front of everything rather than back doors as you do on the railway. And yet, as I look at the lumberyards and warehouses with their cheery signs and neatly striped parking lots, I can't help but prefer the gritty reality of their business ends, back by the tracks where the stuff of commerce gets loaded and unloaded and the trash of commerce piles up and is often strewn by the breeze of passing trains half a mile down the right-of-way. Make no mistake, how one travels shapes different visions of the same world.

Eventually we get off the turnpike and work our way through the suburbs into downtown Halifax. Here the bus comes into its own, and I have to admit that I get a better introduction to the city than I would on a train rolling through remote rail yards. As in New England cities, there is a progression as one approaches center city—from outlying suburbia, to a zone of "clean" industry, then gentrified neighborhoods, then run-down inner city neighborhoods and "dirty" industry, and finally the bustling, rejuvenated and reno-vated old town at the center. The railway station and the refurbished Hotel Nova Scotia lie on the boundary of these last two zones.

Nicole asks if I want to hike to the center of the city. This time I'm the one who isn't going to see anything beyond the station, though I plan to spend some time here a couple of days from now.

Today I have to catch a train that will get me to the land of the Acadians at Port Royal on the Bay of Fundy before midnight.

"Well, this seems like a nice city so I'll be all right," says Nicole. "But if it was a remote stop or a city like New York and you wouldn't come with me, I'd get back on a train going anywhere."

After farewells to Nicole, I make my way to the station platform where signs announce the imminent departure of the *Evangeline* for southern Nova Scotia. There stands a two-car lash-up of RDCs, like those I rode in British Columbia, but these have a very different appearance. They look as though they'd derailed from the Fraser Canyon cliffs and rolled all the way to the bottom.

9

Sweet Apples and Sour Grapes

HALIFAX TO ANNAPOLIS ROYAL
ON THE *EVANGELINE*—
HALIFAX TO SYDNEY
ON THE *CABOT*

E VEN the sound of the idling engines on the *Evangeline* is unhealthy with more than the usual rattle and clatter. The body of the lead car is dingy and dented, its horn bent at a decrepit angle and one window cracked and taped. The usually immaculate VIA paint scheme is scraped and faded.

But inside the train is clean, though threadbare. The lead car has a takeout bar and a couple of booths at the front end. A friendly fellow with a scraggly beard who looks like Pete Seeger gestures for me to join him, and we soon have a couple of Blues open while the train is still creeping out of the Halifax yards in the late afternoon. Despite the battle-scarred exterior, the *Evangeline*'s air conditioning works much better than that aboard the bus on this sultry summer day, and soon it combines with the soothing clickety-clack, the beer, and the passing countryside to put me into a mood of ease. Crossing the spine of Nova Scotia heading northwest toward the Bay of Fundy, I am surprised at such wilderness so close to Halifax. There are forested mountains and lakes, but few villages or people;

Nova Scotia's population still clings to the shores and the coastal valleys, just as they have for centuries.

After Windsor and the crossing of the Avon River, we follow the curving sweep of Minas Basin, which is an arm of the Bay of Fundy, and the haunts of men begin to multiply. Here the route is the line of the old Dominion Atlantic Railway; this segment was completed in 1869. The DAR for years carried on as a strictly local line, serving the communities along the shore of the Bay of Fundy, without its own entry into the rail nexus of Halifax. As such it developed its famous disregard for the formalities of timetables and established stops. DAR trains would stop anywhere for anyone standing by the tracks with a hand in the air. Passengers were treated to unscheduled pleasantries such as the frequent stop near the park at Grand Pré where the park's gardener would hand the porter armloads of freshly cut flowers that were then distributed throughout the train. The CPR bought the DAR in 1912 and connected it with its "short line" from Montreal across Maine to Saint John by way of ferry steamer service, but the "by the books" management of the CPR never quite succeeded in snuffing out the DAR tradition. Even today under VIA, legend has it that the train will still stop at spots far from any station.

My companion points out a huge black-iron cross near the tracks and explains that it marks the spot where the French Acadians, heroes of the Longfellow poem which is the train's namesake, were ordered by British soldiers into boats for the expulsion from the colony in 1755. Beyond this I can see unmistakable manmade ridges in the marshy fields, remnants of the dikes those ancient Frenchmen built to reclaim farmland from the voracious tides.

Matthew Cupido lives in Canning at the northerly end of old Acadia. He has been an artist, a teacher, an architect, and is today a public relations consultant for communities in the *Evangeline* region. Though he doesn't directly say so, his life story is of the search for a good place to live. It has brought him finally to the land of the Acadians in Nova Scotia, and he thinks this might be the place, though he is too circumspect to swear to it.

Born in the city of Dordrecht, Holland, in 1939, Matth moved to Edmonton with his family as a small boy. Wandering along the North Saskatchewan River with his sketchbook, he decided that art would be his calling and he would dedicate it to his religious faith and his adopted country. In search of an ideal setting for his work, he moved to Jasper with his bride and opened his first studio in

1965. Then it was Victoria, Vancouver, and finally Toronto. "Each move followed an exhibition or some sort of commission to do a project in the new place. I guess I never saw a new place I didn't like, so I always moved there shortly after my first contact with it."

But each place he lived after Jasper was busier, more urban, and more expensive. "After Toronto I needed a change, this time not just of place but of direction." He first saw the Acadia region of Nova Scotia during an exhibition in Wolfeboro and was delighted by the slow pace of life, the quiet, the tradition, and the regional respect for art. "It also helped that there are lots of other new people here like me, fleeing a more complex and problematical life somewhere else."

Matth is saddened that the government is considering canceling this rail route. As part of his striving for simplicity, he does not drive and the train is his connection to Halifax and "all those other places I've lived in." He believes people would pay $50 instead of the $18 his ticket costs if that's what it would take to save the line. He fears that in the intraprovincial scramble for the lines that will survive the government's cuts, Nova Scotia's interests will be sacrificed to the requirements of the influential premier of Quebec, Robert Bourassa.

Matth is pleased to prep me for my visit to Annapolis Royal, site of the first settlement in Canada in 1605, two years before Jamestown. After its tumultuous history, it is today, he says, "a quiet retirement kind of place, with lots of professionals retreating from places like Toronto." He gives me a list of sites to check out before he detrains at Kentville. He doesn't think I will meet any real Acadians, but I will find their trees in Annapolis Royal. They planted the apple orchards that sweep up the hillsides and the willows that line the roads throughout the Annapolis Valley.

I'm going to Annapolis Royal because this is where Canadian history began, in a chapter left out of most of our American history books. If we know it at all, we know it through the poem of the New England bard, Henry Wadsworth Longfellow, who never even visited Acadia and told only the ending of the tale. First of all, Canadian historical consciousness puts a different spin on the movements that led to the exploration of a New World. In America we learn that the voyages of discovery by Columbus, Cabot, Champlain, and others were part and parcel of the explosion of human curiosity manifest in the Renaissance. Thus we tend to see these discoveries in idealistic terms of humanity extending its reach—a vision that projects neatly onto our American myth of the New World as a land of limitless possibility. But Canada still encompasses two (or three) contending races and a historical memory of how they came to compete here in the first place.

To the sitting monarchs of Europe, the world of what we call the Renaissance was a very dangerous place. Europe had barely survived the onslaught of plague, of the khans and the Moors, and now the edifice of Christendom itself was being sundered by the Reformation. Besides the spiritual upheavals involved, the Reformation unleashed ideas about the relationship between men and their masters—ideas vaguely resembling the Communism of modern times. What the sitting monarchs of Europe needed to forestall revolution was some new source of wealth with which to lighten the burden that their expensive regimes laid on their subjects' backs. This is what the kings of Spain, England, and France were seeking when they sent explorers sailing west, and once the New World opened up, it performed additional roles in giving a new life to the ancient European regimes. To a great extent, the impetus toward revolution was exported to this continent, where it wouldn't touch the thrones of Europe so closely. North America provided a conveniently remote battlefield for the opposed forces of the Reformation to have it out.

When Sieur de Monts, Baron Poutrincourt, and Samuel de Champlain sailed up the Bay of Fundy and discovered the huge harbor through the Digby Gut in 1604, they understood only that their king had ordered them to plant his flag and claim everything in sight. They were surely aware that English explorers were doing the same thing along other coasts in this New World, but the continent must have seemed so vast that little thought was given to the possibility of conflict. Only a year later they returned with settlers and founded a place called Granville, just inside the Gut. Champlain established his headquarters here and soon enough settlers, including women, had poured into this surprisingly agreeable region that a second settlement was laid out farther up the estuary—Port Royal. With its plentitude of game, fertile soil, and the mildest weather to be found along any of these coasts, the larger region was given the paradisiacal name Acadie, a French corruption of an Indian word meaning "the place."

Champlain went on to explore the St. Lawrence and establish Quebec. The communities he left behind in Acadie flourished, and in

1610, still a decade before Plymouth Rock and all that, a young man named Charles de Saint-Etienne de la Tour came over with his father to settle. In the archetypal pattern of most early Frenchmen in North America, de la Tour learned the language and lore of the natives and became expert at thriving in the wilderness and trapping the valuable furs wanted by his king. With his father away looking for new sites for trading posts, young de la Tour and the governor's son, Biencourt, were in the woods checking trap lines when the British warship from Virginia paid a call and leveled Port Royal with her guns in 1614. De la Tour and Biencourt spent the next seven years living with the Indians till a French fishing vessel happened by and took Biencourt back to France. De la Tour stayed behind.

Meanwhile de la Tour's father reached France seeking relief for the devastated communities of Acadie. Returning to North America, he was captured by the English and taken to London, where, in the curious manner of the times, he flourished as a Frenchman in the English court of King James. James thought that along with New England and New France, the New World ought to have a New Scotland, so he commissioned his fellow Scot, William Alexander, to establish the colony of Nova Scotia. De la Tour *père* managed to wrangle an English baronetcy for himself and his son, and with Alexander set sail for Acadie under an English flag.

Back at Port Royal, the younger de la Tour had set himself up as leader of a French colony on the rebound, and when his father arrived, had no interest in changing allegiance to England. The two men quarreled while King James died and his successor gave the entire region back to France (though the name Nova Scotia and the coat of arms stuck).

When Louis XIII heard of young de la Tour's loyalty, he granted him the lieutenant governorship under Governor Rasily. De la Tour set up residence across the bay at Saint John while Rasily sat at Port Royal. When Rasily died, de la Tour naturally assumed that by king's appointment, he was now governor of the whole province. But a nasty feud developed between him and one de Charnissey, a cousin of Rasily, who ruled Port Royal with an autocrat's hand.

With de la Tour absent on a trading expedition, de Charnissey sent a force across the bay to destroy the settlement at Saint John— every man, woman, and child. With his foothold in Acadie razed, de la Tour headed north to Quebec and eventually Hudson Bay, trading furs with Indians. But somehow he got word of de Charnissey's death in a canoe accident on the Annapolis River; he set off for France to get the king's personal imprimatur on his right to govern Acadie.

In 1653, at the age of fifty-eight, de la Tour was back as governor of Acadie and, in a final gesture of triumph, married the widow of de Charnissey. When just a year later the British recaptured Acadie, Cromwell, impressed by de la Tour's story, allowed him to continue as governor under an English flag. He ruled for another eleven years until his death in 1666, and his legend engendered a sense that despite the ebb and flow of colonial rivalry in the peninsula, the French of Acadie would somehow always be able to persevere.

Right on time at 9:10 in the evening, the *Evangeline* slows for the stop at Annapolis Royal. I'm the only passenger off here this evening and when the train pulls out there's not a soul in sight except a small boy on a bike. I ask him how to get to the Poplars Inn and he points to a large, well-lit old house just a few doors down the empty tree-lined street before me.

Sid and Iris Williams run the place and welcome me with an admonition not to smoke in the room and the story of how they came to be here. They hail from Moose Jaw, Saskatchewan, where her father was a CPR man. Like my rancher friend, John Solaris, they yearned for big trees. Here at the Poplars, they found what they were looking for, a sprawling Victorian guesthouse on a tree-lined street, under the towering branches of two of the biggest poplars I have ever seen, one fourteen feet around the trunk. Guests at their house are treated like family, joining them for Iris's home-cooked meals and gathering around the TV in the family room in the evening.

Having fasted on buses and trains since breakfast, I wolf down the meal but pass up the TV because I want to see what happens in the town after dark. Sid offers to drive me, but I need the walk.

Down Victoria Street, past the beflowered Bread and Roses Bed and Breakfast, and then Saint George Street along the waterfront, past darkened shops in ancient buildings and a deli, still open at this late hour, and specializing in whole fresh trout, salmon, cod, and halibut, I make my way to the Towne Pub on Church Street. In the darkness behind the row houses on the north side of the street, the estuary of the Annapolis River flows uphill with the incoming tide.

The air is rich with the freshest sea smell I can recall since visits to Chesapeake Bay as a child thirty years ago.

The Towne Pub is a smallish room with board floors and dark green colonial wallpaper. There are benches along the walls under old orchid glass lamps and captain's chairs at the small wooden tables. The patrons divide themselves into two groups who know each other but don't really mix. Near the bar at the back sits the proprietor, Kent Durling, and a handful of year-round locals. At the tables near the front, a group of summer performers for the local theme park rehearse lines and share laughs over pitchers of beer.

I sit in the middle and, following Sid's advice, order a house beer and a platter of steamed mussels. The beer is brewed in the back room and the mussels are cultivated in the bay. They are small and tight, not like the gloppy things I've had in Cape Cod. Even to the eye they're more attractive than clams, a dark tan with a darker stripe running down a firm ridge on each mussel inside their deep blue-black shells. Dipped in melted butter and lemon and washed down with drafts of the rich local brew, they make a second meal whose satisfaction lingers during the walk back to the Poplars.

In the morning I rouse myself at first light to see what I can of the town before catching the northbound *Evangeline* back to Halifax. The air is foggy—the dense kind that provokes clichés about what you can cut it with. As I head down Victoria Street toward the waterfront, the few other figures up at this hour loom out of the murk at the last moment and utter startled greetings. Down at the government wharf and along the river boardwalk, I can't see across the river, but I can see what looks like large hunks of snow or ice floating past on the current. I try to resolve the mystery by throwing rocks at the little white icebergs, but when I manage to hit one, it just swallows the rock with no sound.

I head down St. George Street toward Fort Anne looking for someone to explain the mystery to me. The fort is typical of eighteenth-century sites, with cannons, stone walls, and vast stretches of mown grass. I'm surprised at this early hour to find a group of young people carefully excavating an archeological site right behind the main building. One of them, a red-haired young woman with masses of freckles, explains that they made a find yesterday and none of them slept all night anticipating further discoveries this morning. I ask about the snow in the river and the whole group laughs. "It's foam," the spokeswoman says. "From the tidal power station. The sea water foams like that when it runs through the turbines." As if Canadians didn't have enough hydro capacity, here they harness the huge tides of the Bay of Fundy.

Down the street from the fort, past the cemetery and courthouse and over the railway bridge, one finds the Historic Gardens. Matth Cupido had told me this was a sight I didn't want to miss, but not being an avid flower gardener, I couldn't imagine what would be the great attraction. Under dripping linden and willow trees, I can see attendants moving about amid what looks like a maze of roses. The place isn't open yet, but one of the gardeners lets me in for a look around. The maze of roses turns out to be exactly that, and, at least in today's misty air, the whole place is pure enchantment. As I walk along the paths, ghostly specters of color materialize out of the damp gloom and crystallize as tableaux of roses, tulips, hyacinths, or phlox. The effect reminds me of late-Renaissance poems extolling the power of the garden's joining of the hand of man with the hand of God to transfigure earthly life.

By the time I am back at the station waiting for my train, I haven't met any French Acadians—the gestalt of this town has been pure English—but I am touched by Annapolis Royal. For less than twenty-four hours, I have been a tourist here, plain and simple, stroked by the escapist sensations that tourists travel for and satisfied with surface impressions—of tasty food, novel sights, and a feeling of removal from real concerns that lingers long afterward.

This morning the station is open and a half-dozen other passengers wait with me in the fog for the arrival of the northbound *Evangeline* from Yarmouth. Several came down from Halifax two nights ago for a performance at the King's Theatre on Saint George Street. They appreciate how easy it is just to hop on the train and get away from the bustle of the big city to a quiet place like this.

With two toots, the trio of headlights on the battered *Evangeline* gleam out of the murk under the bridge right on time. On board, the smell of freshly brewed coffee kicks me wide awake and I sit down at a bar booth to order a mug beside a very large stuffed bear. Its owner is a plump, cheery teenage girl sitting across the table. She is Rhonda Clark, returning from a visit to her mom in Digby to school and her job at Tim Horton's (a Canadian equivalent of Dunkin' Donuts) in Moncton. "My mom says I'm still just a little girl at heart. I don't go anywhere without my bear," she confesses. "They tried to make him pay a fare once."

The coffee is good and strong—it evaporates the morning's moisture from the bones. By Bridgetown, we are away from the tidal region and into the Upper Annapolis Valley of apple orchards and dairy farms. Most of the stops listed on the schedule are flag stops, where the train doesn't halt unless someone needs to get on or off, but near Lakeville the train slows as we approach a dirt road crossing not listed as any kind of stop on the schedule. Out the window I can see a boy, maybe thirteen or fourteen, wearing a Guns n' Roses tee-shirt and carrying an old-fashioned hard suitcase and a fishing pole, his hand held up as if he were responding to a teacher's question in school. The train brakes to a halt and the boy clambers aboard and sits down at the booth with Rhonda and me.

So the legend of the DAR lives. "I don't know about that," says the boy when I ask him about it. "But they always stop for me. I ride the train to go fishing with my uncle in Lakeville. My name's Mike Marchand," and he holds out his hand for a firm handshake just like any adult.

I'm intrigued by the French name—Acadian?

"No, my father's family is from New Brunswick and Quebec. But my mother is Acadian. Her maiden name is Pothier [pronounced Po-tchee-eh]." He doesn't know how many generations back his mother's family goes, but he knows that his grandfather, who lives today in Yarmouth, always makes a big deal of their being real Acadians. Together they recently attended the Apple Blossom weekend, where Pothiers from as far away as Louisiana gather every year.

Mike is dying to show off something in his suitcase. When Rhonda and her bear object, sensing that it's a fish, he insists it's okay because it's frozen. Out comes a three-pound bass wrapped in newspaper, and he unveils it for the approval of the whole car.

With the typical enthusiasm of a young boy who has an attentive adult audience, Mike never stops talking for the rest of the ride. He asks if I believe in paranormal communication. His parents are divorcing and since he has been living apart from his father, he still hears his stern voice every time he is about to do something he shouldn't. It reminds him of an incident that happened when he lived in Labrador as a small child. There was a good sledding slope that had a pond near its bottom. When he defied his father's orders not to slide down the hill he got spanked. The next time he and a friend stood at the top of the interdictory hill, he heard his father's voice "like it was coming out of a radio or something" warning him not to do it. He didn't but his friend went ahead and broke through the ice on the pond and drowned.

"That's forerunner," says Rhonda, suddenly interested.

"That's what I think," says Mike. I want to know what "forerunner" means.

"You probably don't believe in ghosts, do you?" asks Rhonda, and then I remember a book called *Bluenose Ghosts* and the legends of Nova Scotians' belief in the supernatural and the appearance of apparitions foretelling disaster.

"Here's another one," says Mike, and from here on I can't tell whether they're telling stories from personal experience or passed on as oral tradition. "My grandmother Pothier dreams of chasing black horses. She almost always catches them in her dream, but once when she didn't, my cousin got hit by a car and was killed the next day. Now whenever she has the dream and doesn't catch the horses, she calls everyone in the family and tells them to stay home. One time she made my father stay home and skip a day of checking his lobster traps. A storm came up and two boats were lost at sea."

"I know that one," says Rhonda, furthering my suspicion that the personal dimension of these tales is in the nature of a rhetorical device. "I know a woman whose son was a miner in Springhill. One night they were sitting by the hearth when they heard a knock at the door. When she answered it, there was no one there. Then it came again, but still no one there. Finally there was a third knock, and again no one was at the door. But she knew it was forerunner and kept her son home from the mine the next day. There was a mine accident and three of his friends were killed."

"Yeah, that one's good," says Mike.

I decide to try a little experiment. This last story of Rhonda's has reminded me of W. W. Jacobs's story, "The Monkey's Paw," the one in which stroking the dismembered paw gives its owner three wishes that always have a tragic side effect. For his first wish, the old man asks for money and gets it in a mortality payment when his son is pulverized by machinery at his job. For the second wish, his wife asks for the son to come back home. When there's a knocking at the door in the middle of the night the father makes an unspoken third wish before the mother can open the door and the knocking stops and there is no one there. I tell the story in the same personalized manner as my companions. Their eyes widen and they lean forward intently.

"What was the third wish?" asks Mike.

"Don't you see?" says Rhonda. "It was the son at the door. All mangled and horrible. Something terrible happened with every wish. The last wish was to send him back to the grave."

"Wow," gasps Mike. "I never heard that one before."

"Me neither," says Rhonda. "The forerunner must have been the man who delivered the check after the first wish." And both urge me to tell it again so they can remember the details. Mike even writes down a few notes. Thus, with a little help from W. W. Jacobs, I make a contribution to the Nova Scotian lore of forerunner.

Mike and Rhonda carry on with more stories in the same vein. One that I mean to confirm in Halifax involves the famous explosion during World War II when munitions ships caught fire and the blast leveled most of the city. A man was blown through a window, and when the window was replaced, the man's face appeared etched in the glass. The window has been replaced several more times, but Mike insists you can see the face in the glass today.

I wonder how these sessions are brought to conclusion and Rhonda answers my unspoken question by telling about the time her grandfather got drunk and saw a white apparition in a field. "He said, 'That's a ghost—I can run right through it.' When he tried, he buried his face in the ass-end of a cow." Humor appears to be the only way to break the spell.

Is the Bluenose penchant for ghost stories the result of the peninsula's fogs and eerie climate or the remains of a vanished people? The story of the Acadians after de la Tour is one likely to leave troubled ghosts prowling the fog-bound rocks of Nova Scotia. The colony changed hands again and again in the latter seventeenth and early eighteenth centuries, but the Acadians always came through unscathed in their role as provisioners of the military garrisons of both sides. They farmed the entire Annapolis Valley, and at Port Royal and Minas Basin performed feats rivaling the Dutch in reclaiming good farmland from the ravenous Fundy tides. Out of the wilderness they forged one of North America's most prosperous kingdoms, and they cared little who claimed the region as long as they could build their steep-roofed homes and churches and raise their crops.

Meanwhile the French built the great fortress Louisbourg on the coast of Isle Royale to protect Quebec and the British built Fort Anne at Port Royal and renamed the town Annapolis Royal in honor of their queen. With the stakes getting higher, a British commander at Fort Anne in 1713 announced that under new policy, Acadians could choose between selling their estates and moving to uncontested French territory or staying and swearing allegiance to the throne of England. Acadians, aware that there were not enough English settlers to serve as buyers and really no such thing as uncontested French territory in the New World, and disinclined to dishonor the memory of de la Tour by kowtowing to the English monarch, ignored the declaration and carried on, confident that they would continue to thrive as they always had.

But times had changed by the mid-century. The Seven Years' War was fought to settle once and for all which power would dominate North America. New officers were sent to Fort Anne, and though official British policy attempted to protect the Acadians from unjust treatment that might give them incentive to take a more active role on the French side, these new governors were horrified to find a French population of ten thousand ensconced in the heart of Nova Scotia. They ignored the voice of reason from across the sea and persecuted the Acadians for their time-honored practice of supplying French bastions as well as the English. In response, the Acadians became more militant, with some now acting as a fifth column to undermine English rule in the region.

Still, the increasingly uneasy relationship might have held and a benevolent English rule of native French worked out—as in Quebec following the conclusion of the Seven Years' War—were it not for events unfolding in Massachusetts. There revolution was in the air and patriot and Tory alike regarded the French presence in Nova Scotia as a problem. The patriot, hoping to lure Nova Scotia into the rebellion, had no use for a large French-speaking population in his new nation; the Tory saw the restive Acadians as possible allies of the patriots. In one of the few moves upon which both sides could agree, Massachusetts Governor Shirley urged the British governor of Nova Scotia to remove the Acadians before hostilities in the southern colonies commenced.

Thus, on his own authority, and despite an order from England forbidding the action that arrived a day after it was carried out, the governor of Nova Scotia ordered the unprecedented deportation of the Acadians in 1755. Troops swooped through the Annapolis Valley, rounding up every Acadian family in sight. They were herded to Grand Pré and forcibly put aboard ships whose destinations were withheld. Some of the more zealous officers deliberately separated families and sent them on ships bound for different ports. In the end, six thousand Acadians were dispatched to sites throughout the American colonies. Thousands died in transit; others were not allowed to land and spent months in an odyssey in search of a place that would take them.

The largest single group landed at New Orleans, where they glumly settled in the muggy and agriculturally forbidding bayous to await an apocalyptic end. But they still had their faith, and the Acadians of Louisiana were visited with a miracle. In the waters of the bayous they found tiny creatures they recognized as their beloved Nova Scotia lobster. The saints had sent the creatures swimming the long voyage alongside the Acadians' ships and could hardly be faulted if the ordeal of the journey had shrunk them considerably in size. With the sustenance of the crayfish miracle, the Louisiana Cajuns took root and thrive there still.

Others didn't fare so well. Desperate bands deposited in New England and New York walked back to Nova Scotia in the late 1760s only to find their homes and churches burned, their livestock slaughtered, and their lands taken over by New Englanders brought here to provision the garrison at Fort Anne. Those Acadians who had managed initially to elude the British troops had removed themselves to new communities farther south along St. Mary's Bay and at Pubnico Harbor. Here the returning Acadians resettled, among them families with the name of Pothier. Though they eventually numbered several thousand in those places, they never flourished again as they had in Acadie, the trials of their journeys making them somehow smaller in cultural stature, like the lobsters that followed their cousins to Louisiana. In the entire Annapolis Valley, today nothing remains of the Acadians but one church, the mounded ridges of some dikes, apple orchards, and ghosts.

At Kentville, a flashy young woman with strawberry-blond hair, dressed in pink sneakers and purple socks, white shorts and an artsy pink tee-shirt, gets on and sits in the empty booth across the aisle. It isn't only her colors that catch the eye. There is something about the way she wears her makeup that is curious—almost as though a playful little sister had decorated her face with crayon earlier and now she can't get it all off. I have been asking Rhonda and Mike how it would affect them if the government cancels this train when the girl overhears me and shouts across the aisle, "John MacDonald would roll over in his grave if he saw what the government is doing to the railways."

I move over to join her and ask her to elaborate. "Well, if you know your history, you know that railways hold this country together, always have since MacDonald built them to lure provinces into confederation. You must be an American."

Her name is Jenny Fulton and she is another immigrant from abroad. Her family left Yorkshire, England, thirteen years ago when they decided at a "family meeting" that England no longer held anything for them. "Our family has a lot of pride, my dad even once played guitar with the Rolling Stones, and we expected better opportunities than that from the country we lived in, so we came to Canada. We called ourselves the 'Fightin' Fultons'—we can make a living doing anything, if there's anything to do." They settled first in Toronto with nothing but a couple of blankets, a teapot, and three kids. But the city was too complex and too expensive and they soon moved to Nova Scotia where they finally got a home by building it themselves on a rented piece of rural land.

Her father found work with the Michelin tire company and her mother walked into a newspaper office and asked for a job. "She had no education beyond secondary school and didn't know the difference between a Kawasaki and a Pentax, but they needed a photographer, so Mom was a photographer." A fast learner, she began by handing the camera to spectators at events she covered and asking them to take the picture. Today she is an editor.

Jenny is a student in liberal arts at Mount St. Vincent College in Halifax and a performer—Lolly the Clown—in the Summer Festival Showcase in the Annapolis Valley. She had no training for stage work, but following her mom's example, she walked into the student summer employment office and asked for the highest paying job they had. At $25 an hour the clown won out. She is returning today to her classes from a performance.

Nova Scotia is a good place for students, according to Jenny. The whole province is experiencing a bit of a renaissance as a result of the government's expansion of vocational schools into community colleges and the availability of money for cultural events. This puzzles me, because across the country I've heard talk of Nova Scotia being one of the "basket cases" of the nation economically. I know that the fishing industry is experiencing the same problems as Perce, and the mining industry is a blot on the province. Jenny, who is surprisingly knowledgeable about the kinds of things I paid no attention to when I was in college, explains.

"The schools are where the province chooses to invest some of the resources it gets from the federal government. The long-term idea is that a better-educated populace will generate a healthier economy. The money for cultural events comes from a trend that doesn't show up in the government's measures of prosperity. It's retirement money—dollars donated by the wealthy retirees who are choosing Nova Scotia for their golden years."

Click. That's exactly what Annapolis Royal was all about. It's the missing variable in the equation that makes Nova Scotia one of Canada's biggest net recipients of federal dollars while presenting an image to American tourists of gentrified prosperity in postcard towns like Annapolis Royal.

As the train runs down the wilderness slopes of Mount Uniacke past unspoiled lakes toward the Dartmouth-Halifax metropolis, Jenny watches the passing landscape and wistfully says that riding this train always makes her want to take off on a cross-continent ride. I tell her about John, the fellow from England I met on the *Skeena*, and other young international travelers whose odysseys have been inspired more by alienation than lust for adventure.

"Oh, I'd fit right into that," she muses cheerlessly. And then, shifting into that level of confidence that emerges out of nothing in so many conversations on trains, Jenny tells me of her plans to chuck everything and join Canada World Youth, an organization like the American Peace Corps. "I need a radical change of environment. It's the problem of the English-speaking world everywhere— England, America, and now Canada—the deconstruction of morals and values."

I ask why she calls it "deconstruction."

"Because it's orderly and deliberate. We're taking the progressive Anglo-Saxon values of justice, fair play, and commitment to something greater than oneself and consciously dismantling them, a log at a time. Selfish people dare to proclaim as matters of principle their worst instincts. Take the outcry against paying taxes to help poor people, for instance. Take the advertising that appeals to the male urge to violently subdue women. Take the fundamentalists who cloak their bigotry and violence and greed for power and money in the mantle of Jesus."

"What makes it happen?"

"Oh, God, so many things. Partly that people are freer to speak their minds, even if what's on them is obscene. Your generation caused that with your sixties' liberation. And partly that people have higher expectations of what they can personally get out of life, and if a moral scruple stands in the way, then trash it. And partly that those who traditionally filled the role of moral authority are themselves corrupt."

This last issue was the crisis for Jenny. There was a priest in Halifax who preached fire and brimstone to those who strayed from the Church's teaching concerning birth control and abortion. He was arrested for having sex with altar boys. In court, he didn't even deny it. " 'It's a common problem in the celibate clergy these days,' the lawyers said. They assumed that his hypocrisy as well as his crime would be tolerated."

Then there was a well-known traditionalist family patriarch in the Annapolis Valley who was convicted of molesting an eleven-year-old girl. In court he pointed to the victim and, appealing to the worldliness of the all-male jury, declared, "What's a man to do when an eleven-year-old like that crawls up into your lap?"

"If our moral systems were working, guys like these would never have expected society to excuse their crimes. When I heard these stories I realized that amorality had become the norm and I wanted out."

As the train wends into the outskirts of the Halifax region, Jenny stares out the window and occasionally adds postscripts to the spirited ethical treatise she has shared with me. She doesn't blame Americans for the trend, as some do. "Sure, we see a lot of corrupt values in the TV shows you send us, but they merely appeal to instincts that are in people already." And she doesn't blame government, though the impending cuts to VIA, another example of crassness triumphing over something that embodies decent, traditional values, "will pull the rug out from under students everywhere and set them hitchhiking out on the highways where they'll learn all the wrong things." As for Nova Scotia, with its tradition of moral staunchness combining with the influx of progressive-minded retirees, it's probably as good as it gets, but the evil is here, too.

"People everywhere in the English-speaking world are just more rotten than I thought and now they're demanding the right to be that way. My dad used to tell me how mean and rotten people were and my mom would shut him up. I wish she had let him talk."

I want to know why she tags the English-speaking world.

"It's the only world I know and I want to leave open the possibility that people elsewhere might be different."

Jenny once spent some time with Ukrainian Hutterites and Mennonites out near Edmonton. She helped them raise organic food and sell it at farmer's markets. "Those people were different. I'm not sure I could live with their restrictive traditions, but if they could remain true to such limiting ones, why can't we hold to our more liberal ones?"

At Armsdale, where Jenny shares an apartment with two other students, she gathers up her stuff and is gone. As I watch Jenny cross the platform to meet her waiting friends, I marvel that this young figure is hardly the image in which I expected to encounter the legendary Nova Scotian moral scruple.

After the Acadians, the Nova Scotian demography and character that prevail today were shaped by two dominant groups: American New Englanders and Scots. The two groups had one thing in common—an abiding sense of moral and intellectual superiority. Here spiritual descendants of John Calvin rediscovered one another after a century of separation by the Atlantic. Here they would stand fast and resist the corruption of the wheeler-dealer Americans and the compromises of the York (Toronto) and Montreal Canadians.

Halifax was founded in 1749 specifically to help protect New England from French adventurers. Thus the first New Englanders in Nova Scotia came here as part of a military operation and brought with them the conservative certainties of the military frame of mind.

They were followed by a wave of pioneer Puritan farmers attracted to the lands abandoned by the Acadians. They, too, brought a mentality of stark certitude and found the harsh Nova Scotian climate just as true to the belief that life on this earth was meant to be merely a time of trial for something better beyond, as they had in New England. But somehow they lost some of the counterbalancing habit of Yankee initiative, and when Nova Scotian property values plunged after the opening of Ohio, they settled into a pattern of perennial helplessness before forces they no longer believed they could control.

The final wave of New Englanders to settle in Nova Scotia were the Loyalists, the wealthy, privileged Tories who lost their standing with the American victory in 1783. When they appealed to George Washington, a man of their own class who fought on the other side, he is said to have responded that perhaps they ought to consider mass suicide. Instead they were allowed to board ship for Saint John and Halifax without property. These men and women were not Calvinists, and they weren't particularly welcomed by those already established, but the sufferings they endured in their first winter of working with their own hands must have darkened their Anglican brows with a gloom that brought them closer to their common Puritan neighbors than they would have ever imagined possible back in New England.

The final force in the demography of Nova Scotia is the Scots. Ironically, it was at about the same time as the deportation of the Acadians that something similar occurred in Scotland. With the defeat of Bonnie Prince Charlie and the end of the Jacobite rebellions, the English embarked on a campaign to destroy the power of the clans in their homeland by outlawing their customs, taking their lands, and deporting them to new homes.

The thirteen southern colonies in North America let it be known that they would not welcome whole clans of highly organized Scots. But Philadelphia land speculators, who were in danger of losing their shirts in Nova Scotia after Ohio opened up, offered a farm lot and a year's worth of provisions to every Scottish settler who would attempt to sink a plow into the harsh earth of their holdings in the region around Pictou. Despite King James's earlier scheme that gave the colony its name, those who immigrated in 1773 were the first successful Scottish settlers in Nova Scotia.

At the beginning of the nineteenth century, much of Scotland was still heavily settled by crofters who stood in the way of wealthy English landlords' plans to turn the estates into parks for shooting game. Under the pressure of this process of gentrification, the crofters now became a second wave of Scottish immigration to Nova Scotia. The only land left for the taking was in the forbidding highlands of Cape Breton. Despite their superficial resemblance to the lands back in Scotland, these highlands had not experienced centuries of cultivation and the crofters became one more Nova Scotian contingent struggling to survive in diminished circumstances. That's the story of Nova Scotia and why some Canadian writers argue that Nova Scotians don't celebrate holidays, they mourn them. The racial memory of a better life in lost homes makes times of tradition into times of bitterness.

Even more than the New Englanders, the Scottish brought with them their profound faith in the rightness of their own thinking. To this they added a disdain for class consciousness based on anything except intelligence. They believed themselves to constitute an aristocracy of the intellect, and when economic necessity eventually forced them to leave their clans and go into the larger Canadian world, they came to dominate the country as no other piece of the mosaic ever has, including the founding French and English. From MacDonald to Mackenzie King, Canadian history is peppered with the names of Scottish families, tempered in Nova Scotia, who left their mark on the national character.

Not all Nova Scotians have tolerated the passive fatalism, moral rigidity, and resistance to change that is the province's inheritance from its unique demographic makeup. Two, in particular, stand out. Thomas Chandler Haliburton, son of a Scottish wigmaker and married to a New World blue blood, became a writer whose theme emerged as a satirical attack on both American vulgarity and Nova Scotian pridefulness, moral narrow-mindedness, backwardness, and lack of initiative. His character, the sardonic Yankee wit Sam Slick, could make devastating sallies against the Nova Scotian character while unintentionally satirizing himself and his Yankee brethren. It was quite a trick and caught the eye of later authors like Mark Twain and Charles Dickens who modeled some of their most famous characters on Haliburton's knave.

Haliburton may have cracked the hidebound character of Nova Scotians in the nineteenth century, but another man set out to do nothing less than to provoke a great awakening. I related earlier how Joseph Howe fought to jolt Nova Scotia out of its slumbers and link it to the Canadian world by way of railways such as the Intercolonial. He used his newspaper pulpit first to break the power of the Family Compact, a cozy little arrangement of local aristocrats and the British governors, then he traveled to virtually every village in the peninsula with his message about railways and his belief that isolation was the stuff upon which backwardness fed.

But Howe's transformation of his home province was only partly successful. The short-lived boom in ship construction during the latter third of the nineteenth century created an illusion that Nova Scotia's endemic limitations had been surmounted. The province's best minds continued to leave home for the excitement of Montreal, Toronto, or America. Fishing continued to occupy much too large a role for a province approaching the twentieth century and the one economic alternative, after the bust in the shipbuilding industry, was the man-eating enterprise of mining.

It is perhaps symbolic that the key link in the railway route I will take to Cape Breton, the causeway across the Strait of Canso, wasn't completed until the mid-1950s. Nova Scotia has never been accused of moving too quickly forward. Perhaps that's why today prosperous folks are moving into and gentrifying a province that appears on the federal financial ledgers to be a neighborhood in distress. On the train to Cape Breton, I will meet a man whose story suggests that, as a result, the province's archetypal racial nightmare is happening all over again.

Halifax is too much like New England seaport cities to feel very much like Canada, and though it has long been the focal point of the little railways of Nova Scotia and is today the eastern terminus of the transcontinental route, it has never been a railway town. During my stay, the place is overrun with British sailors off a ship making a call. Evening visits to the Peddler's Pub, the Silver Bullet, and the Middle and Lower Decks remind me of spring weekends in Boston's crowded college bars. The drunken sailors don't make good conversation and the besieged locals aren't talking to anybody.

In the morning I find St. Paul's Church with the face in the glass. The glass is a bit wavy, and at certain angles with the light reflecting off it just right, I can imagine that I see something—like looking for faces in clouds.

The renovated area of the old town is pleasing to the eye and bustles with tourists and shoppers. But again it feels like Boston or Portland—fine cities, among the best America has to offer, but not foreign, not Canada.

So it's with the same anticipation I feel when I board the *Montrealer* headed out of New England for Quebec that I board the *Cabot* in the early afternoon, bound for Sydney and Cape Breton.

The train is another RDC, this one with three cars and in a little better shape than the *Evangeline*. As far as Truro, the train is crowded, not a seat to spare. The passengers on this early afternoon run are a mixed lot—well-dressed women with full shopping bags, middle-aged workingmen, suited men with briefcases, the usual young mothers of modest means with crying children, students, and the elderly. At Truro there is a big scramble of people detraining (including almost all of the briefcase and shopping bag sets) and not quite as many getting on. Beyond Truro the crowd thins out; at Sydney, only a handful remain.

At Antigonish I ask the conductor about it and he says this is the way it is on weekdays. Though the greater Sydney area at the end of the line is a large population center, it's a workingman's town, so he gets most of his through passengers on the weekend runs. Then he has an extra car or two and still has to turn people away. "But of course, the government says all those bodies exist only in my imagination. They want people to think nobody rides these trains so they can discontinue them. They don't care about Nova Scotia or trains so we get screwed on two counts. Mark my words, a year from now this train will be gone."*

A huge, burly fellow sitting at the bar table with a guitar case beside him has leaned into the aisle to overhear what the conductor has been telling me and growls, "The bigshots in Ontario don't give a shit about the Maritimes—they can't make as much money off us as they can off of Quebec or Alberta. But they got a fight on their hands; they're not gonna cut us off without getting their three-piece suits a little mussed up." Then he invites me to join him, and as I accept his invitation, the conductor gives me a funny look, possibly a warning of some sort, before heading down the aisle to take tickets.

Ron McCrea is an out-of-work fisherman, roustabout, and some-time folksinger from Sydney. He wears a ring in one ear and sports a heavy stubble of new beard on his face. "I tried shaving my beard to see if I'd have better luck finding a job, but it made no difference, so what the fuck."

Ron pounds down the beer at a prodigious rate and after each one crushes the can into something that looks like a metal paper wad. By the Canso causeway, he has a little pile of these wads, which he arranges in various shapes on the table in front of him during the long silent respites that follow brief profane mumbles about boarding passengers or sights passing outside and occasional gales of conversation. For a while I think he's the kind of alcoholic who needs a warm body nearby while he nurses his habit, but as the car becomes less crowded and the sky darkens after Grand Narrows, the conversation becomes more connected and I begin to believe the man has an obsession on his mind.

His little snatches of talk have centered around abandonment, beginning with the business of the government wanting to abandon

* A year later this train and the *Evangeline* were canceled.

the Nova Scotia trains, then moving on to obscure references to his own father ditching him and his mother when he was a child, and anecdotes about various jobs he has lost when the company folded or closed a plant. There's a villain lurking at the back of most of his stories, the "Ontario money-men in their three-piece suits who suck the workingman dry and then toss him aside like a piece of trash." They ruined the fishing industry by making it into a big business that overharvested the Grand Banks, they ruined the youth of coal miners and then left them in the lurch when they found other more profitable sources of energy, and they let the Americans take over too many industries so that decisions made in New York throw men in Nova Scotia out of work.

"But you know the worst thing? Now that they've ruined us, they want our homes. They decide that Nova Scotia is a cute place to retire or own a second house, so they're moving into the province in bunches. They force the price of land or a house up so high that a fellow who's worked here all of his life can't afford shit."

He thinks the province is ripe for nasty strikes, and if the gentrification of Nova Scotia continues, perhaps even something worse—some kind of class war. "You get a hundred guys like me together and go into one of those cute little fixed-up towns like the place you just visited and trash things a bit. Show them that they gotta pay a price for ruining lives. They'd get you for it in the end, they'd get you good, but who gives a shit. They get you anyway."

The conductor has kept a wary eye on us and huddles with the bartender. "We better talk about something else. I got a ladyfriend getting on pretty soon and I don't want them to cut me off. You like music?" he asks, and opens his case and takes out his guitar. It's a fine old Harmony twelve-string that looks as though he's used it as a weapon in brawls. But he handles it with a gentleness that hasn't showed till now and lightly picks out a bluegrass melody with a deftness that belies the size and toughness of his scarred, callused fingers.

When I compliment him on his playing he reacts with the first smile untouched by malevolence since I met him. "A man's gotta have one thing that they can't take away." Then the tough-guy tone returns. "You don't want to know what I did to the last guy who did try to take it away."

The car is nearly empty now, just a dozen other riders as the train speeds along the shore of the Bras d'Or, the little inland sea of Cape Breton. Outside the moonglow sweeps across the water and inside Ron's soft guitar playing combines with the clickety-clack to cast a romantic spell.

Now he's more interested in singing blues. "Freedom's just another word for nothing left to lose," he sings, and shortly the bartender speaks up. "There's no singing allowed in the car. Disturbs passengers."

Ron stops playing, looks at me and says, "You don't mind, do you?" I don't.

But the bartender perseveres. "I don't mind either, but other passengers might. I can't let you break the rules."

Ron's eyes narrow, though he keeps just a touch of good humor in his voice as he answers, "Then how about if I just challenge every man in the car to a fight. Would you like that better?"

"Okay, fella, you're cut off." And the bartender calls the conductor to back him up.

Hearing this, I expect trouble, but surprisingly Ron mildly turns to me and mumbles, "Now I've done it," and puts his guitar away. At Boisdale, a tough-looking woman wearing a very pilled sweater and well-worn jeans gets on.

"Oh, Annie," whispers Ron, and then to me, "I hope you understand if I soon don't need your company any longer."

Annie gives Ron a wave but sits facing away from us without offering any further signs of encouragement. "That woman kept me from killing a man once."

Finally Ron lets go of the story that has been so obviously looming behind his conversation so far. He had a wife, "a pretty young thing," who was mild-mannered and innocent and just what this bad boy needed to give him a good reason to stay out of jail. But she got a clerical job in an office in Sydney. At first he was proud of her having a good-paying job that didn't get her hands dirty, but soon she was spending more time at work and bringing home "an attitude." One day she didn't come home. "Took off with one of the clients—a guy from Ontario. I haven't heard from her since. It was two years ago."

Ron found out the guy's name by making inquiries at the office and set out to find him. "To this day, I have no doubt that if I'd found him, I woulda killed him. But that's when I met Annie, on the train. She's always on it, commutes back and forth to Sydney. I still don't know whether she really liked me or just wanted to keep somebody from getting killed. But she took me to a motel and showed me that there were still good reasons not to go to jail, even after losing my wife. I meet up with her on this ride every once in a while and we have a few beers and she just makes me into a gentle pussycat."

By the time we are rolling around the harbor toward Sydney, Ron has cajoled Annie into joining us. "I'll hev a brewski with yeh, Ron McCrea, and then at the station I'm hist'ry."

Ron winks at me and loudly orders a round. The bartender relents, possibly seeing Annie as a moderating influence, and brings us our suds with the proviso that this is the last before Sydney station.

Suddenly I'm a third wheel. Annie and Ron reminisce about other train rides and mutual acquaintances in Sydney. As they talk they lapse into a deeper version of the Cape Breton accent that was only mildly apparent in his talk earlier. Clipped long *e*'s are appended to words ending in vowels and sentences accelerate with the final words blurred together into a single multisyllabic phrase that tails upward like a question. I know that this Breton accent is considered a Scottish influence, but it strikes me that it's an exaggeration, almost a caricature, of the distinct Canadian English that has charmed me coast to coast and that I have found myself consciously emulating, occasionally successfully enough that some fellow passengers have not taken me for an American. Of course, the Scottish influx has been a major demographic factor in Canada's history, but this is one of those little hidden gems that only travel reveals. You can hear it in the way Canada talks.

When we pull into Sydney station around eleven, Ron has had more than enough to drink. I marvel at how Annie handles him, firmly but with humor enough to keep him civil. No, she won't go to a motel with him. No, he's not going to pick a fight with anybody because if he does, she'll be just a memory. No, there won't be any bars open this late, but she'll treat him to a cup of coffee if he behaves himself.

Next morning in Sydney, I rent a car and drive across the empty windy spine of Isle Royale to visit the fortress of Louisbourg. At Fort Edmonton the booming metropolis of the city lies nearby, and at Fort Anne the gentrified little town of Annapolis Royal anchors the prosperous Annapolis Valley.

But around Louisbourg there is nothing but a fogbound granite shore blasted by breakers and separated from the nearest contemporary haunts of men by miles of the coldest, most desolate upland terrain in a desolate province. Louisbourg, which changed hands several times without a true fight and was finally leveled stone by stone by the conquering English, is currently under restoration as a national monument. Standing on its ramparts, shivering under the wind-whipped North Atlantic spray, I wonder—a monument to what? A tour guide says it represents an early effort at global strategy. But the Acadians were deported and Quebec fell. What is Louisbourg? A fort in eastern Canada that Americans can identify because it is one of the few Canadian sites referred to in their history books. It's also a fine place to contemplate Shelley's poem, "Look on my works ye mighty, and despair. Nothing else remains. . . ."

After spending several days driving the Cabot Trail, I take the train back to Halifax. I hear a few more stories from proprietors of roadside diners confirming Ron's revelations of a local common man's backlash against the gentrification of the province, but Nova Scotia has hexed me whenever I've gotten off the train. I can't get past the conventional forms that stand between tourist and host. Maybe it's the car. Maybe it's my American accent (in Cape Breton even my best attempts at speaking Canadian won't pass muster). Maybe it's the same reticence toward strangers that Nova Scotia shares with my own home region of New England.

I spent more time in Nova Scotia than I spent in Alberta or British Columbia, yet I came away with less confidence that I had come to know anything about the place. Out west the character of the country is wide open, easily accessible. In Nova Scotia I never felt that way. Even when I did break through the down east reticence, the contacts I made seemed so quirky, from ghost stories to class warfare, that I didn't quite trust them. The voice that seemed most reliable was that of a transplanted English college student.

But as soon as I board the *Atlantic* out of Halifax bound for Montreal by way of Saint John, New Brunswick, and Maine, the walls come tumbling down and I'm a citizen of the world again. Maybe it's not Nova Scotia. Maybe it's me. Maybe it's trains.

10

Boys or Men?

THE *ATLANTIC* FROM HALIFAX
TO MONTREAL

IT was hot in Halifax; the air conditioning in my sleeping car is the first of many good things about this ride on the *Atlantic*. The Nova Scotia RDCs had their own charm, but you don't settle in and take up residence on short-run trains. Here I have a bed, a sink, and a toilet; a short walk to a full-service dining car or several choices of lounge; and the anticipation of an extended stay in the hermetic train world of changing faces, places, and phases of the day. Since the *Atlantic* is the CPR's eastern extension of the *Canadian* in the transcontinental scheme, this train has the same delightful equipment and consist pattern—coaches in front, a Skyline car, a full-sized diner, sleepers, and a trailing Park car.

As the train skirts Bedford Basin with its broad vistas of blue water and sailboats, it's lunchtime—clam chowder and hot open-face pork sandwiches. I am seated with two college women from a province I will miss because it no longer has any passenger trains: Newfoundland.

I have heard Newfoundlanders derided across the continent as the low men on the provincial totem pole, and I assume that part of this stereotype is due to the fact that it took Newfoundland until 1949 to decide to join the dominion. Kim Roache and Penny Kean are fourth-year students in general studies at the University of St. John's (not to be confused with New Brunswick's Saint John, through which we will shortly travel). At first, with their fashionable clothes and collegiate talk, they defy the stereotype of interprovincial jokes, but there is something about them—a kind of "gee-whiz" innocence that reminds me of the American Midwest.

"Sure we know what they say about us," says Kim. "Newfies are stupid. Everybody knows that."

I ask if they have any idea where the stereotype comes from. Again it's Kim who responds. "Newfoundlanders don't travel much. They say it's held back our development. And when we do go out into the rest of Canada, like us now, we seem like country bumpkins."

Kim and Penny are traveling to visit relatives in Ottawa who moved off-island three years ago. It's the first time either of them has traveled beyond Nova Scotia in their lives.

"We're scared, actually," Kim admits, and Penny adds a nervous giggle. They have to spend seven hours in Montreal tomorrow between trains and have questions for me about what to do and where to go during that time. They're also not quite sure what to do with themselves on the train ride. They have a section, one of those inexpensive overnight accommodations which convert from daytime couches to berths that open on the corridor during the night. They wonder if they are allowed into the first-class Park car at the rear (yes), if it's disreputable for girls to order themselves drinks in the bar car (no), if they will have to be on guard for train-riding Casanovas who will try to hit on them (maybe), and where they can find working toilets, since the one in their car has some terrible malfunction that causes it to blast its contents upward when flushed.

After lunch I head back to the dome of the Park car for a little sight-seeing. It's a sunny August day that invites panoramic viewing. Until Moncton, this train follows the portion of the Intercolonial route I missed before during my bus ride, and after Truro, we cross the gentle valley of the Debert River that was bypassed with the semicircular detour past Livesay's ironworks near Londonderry. At Springhill, the rolling green hills belie the string of tragic accidents that have struck this coal-mining town since its founding. I recall a song recorded by Peter, Paul and Mary in the sixties: "In the town of Springhill, Nova Scotia, Often the earth will tremble and groan. When the earth is restless miners die, Bone and blood is the price of coal." It's a song and a sentiment that I'm sure my Breton friend Ron knows well.

Today the ground holds firm under the tracks and soon we are skirting the immense tidal flats of the Cumberland Basin. Another wide curve to the west turns out to be the infamous Dorchester diversion.

After a long stop at Moncton, where I boarded the bus nearly a week ago, the train turns southwest over tracks laid on one of the oldest routes in Canada. Though it was eventually incorporated into the Intercolonial system, the line at one time was part of New Brunswick's response to the Canadian betrayal—a route following John Poor's scheme of a European–North American connection via Portland, Maine. It was the perceived threat to Canadian economic independence of international lines like this that was a factor in getting the Intercolonial built. Though today's *Atlantic* route through Main does not follow Poor's route over its entirety, it incorporates the basic principle of an international line, making the best use of geography in defiance of national boundaries. And Poor's story is the opening chapter of Canadian railway history.

Though Canada had a few short portage railways before John Poor, most notably one running from Lake Champlain to Montreal, Canada's first major railway began partly as a side effect of the competition between the Atlantic cities of America. One by one each of the great American seaports began building railroads westward seeking economic empires. Baltimore had the Baltimore & Ohio, Philadelphia had the Pennsylvania, New York had the Erie and the New York Central, and Boston had the Boston & Albany. In Portland, John Poor saw the implications of westward railroads for seaport cities and saw further that Portland was in danger of getting cut out of the action because Boston and New York lines were staking out the northernmost routes across American territory. But in Portland's advantages as a seaport, he spied the key to its future success. Portland is the closest of all American ports to Europe and is much closer to Montreal and the heart of Canada than Saint John or Halifax. Poor concluded that Portland's westering railroad should run to Canada and through it to the American Midwest by way of Montreal, Toronto, and Detroit. Portland would become a great American outlet for Midwest trade as well as the premier Canadian warm-water port.

In 1843, after years of personally surveying the "Big Woods" between Portland and Montreal, Poor made his proposal to the state legislature. With Portland desperate for an economic miracle after the decline of its once great shipbuilding industry, Poor's proposal electrified the city. In Montreal, he found a powerful ally in Alexander Tillich Galt, who happened to own huge tracts of land in the Eastern Townships through which the railway would pass. Impressed by the combination of the eloquent American and the shrewd Canadian Scot, Montrealers jumped at the chance to have an ice-free port at the end of an American rail link.

Quickly, rival interests in Boston moved to preempt Poor with their own offer of a railroad linking Montreal to Boston. In 1845, emissaries of Boston were in Montreal meeting with bankers and civic leaders to close the deal for Boston. When Poor, stranded by a Maine blizzard in Portland, learned of the impending decision, he defied the advice of family and friends and set out with a Mr. Cheney on a journey through the "Big Woods" that nearly killed him.

It took six hours for his horse to pull the sleigh the first seven miles of the trip, but Poor pressed on. Badly frost-bitten and exhausted, he reached Andover twenty-four hours later. Ahead lay the real wilderness, trackless and empty through the Dixville Notch in the New Hampshire White Mountains, where ice-laden winds howled at near hurricane strength.

He recruited rugged mountain men he met along the way to help drag his sleigh through the ten-foot drifts. His journal records the temperature in the Notch at eighteen degrees below zero and the difficulty of breathing as icicles formed inside his nostrils. He crossed the Canadian border five days after leaving Portland and finally reached the St. Lawrence where dangerous ice made the crossing a feat that only a few French boatmen would attempt. Poor recruited one of them and got to Montreal two hours before the meeting that was to seal the pact with Boston. He slept for an hour and then strode into the Board of Trade. Stressing the fact that his route was one hundred miles shorter than the Bostonians' and aided by the fortunate arrival of Portland's Judge Preble bearing a formal charter, he persuaded the Montrealers to choose the Portland line. Perhaps it also helped that this American had come to make his proposal after one of those harrowing journeys that Canadians so revere.

Ground was broken in 1845, and the world's first international railway and the first major route of any sort in Canada was begun. The Canadian portion was named the St. Lawrence & Atlantic. The American section was the Atlantic & St. Lawrence.

With his initial scheme becoming a reality, Poor began to dream something bigger—a line from Portland through Saint John to Halifax joining a transatlantic link of relatively short steamship connections to a port on the west coast of Ireland, a rail connection across that country, a ferry to Liverpool, and another rail link to London. He would call it the European & North American Railway and it would forever subordinate the rival Bostonians to a Portland transportation colossus.

The idea took hold in New Brunswick, which immediately saw the advantage of a railway running westward from Saint John. Halifax was less enthusiastic, until Poor combined with Joseph Howe. It was Poor's scheme that Howe was pushing when he went to England and thought he got the imperial guarantee for some kind of railway linking Halifax to Montreal. Poor was left stranded when the strategic decision was made favoring the Intercolonial route described earlier. Yet then so was Howe when the Canadians reneged on the entire deal.

During the time of the Maritimes' most profound disenchantment with the rest of Canada, New Brunswick built a piece of Poor's second dream, the section of the route over which I am riding now, connecting Shediac at the upper reaches of the Bay of Fundy to Saint John and, beyond, to Maine. Poor's intercontinental scheme never came to fruition, but the international pieces of it that were built marked the beginnings of serious railways in Canada.

At dinner I meet Kim and Penny in the diner and we are joined at our table by Mike Wallace, a professor of political science and environmentalism at the University of British Columbia.

Kim and Penny have spent much of the afternoon hanging out an open vestibule window taking pictures of "trees, rocks, marshes, water, and train stations." I point out that it's against the rules and ask how they managed to avoid the conductor.

"Oh, he came by and opened the window for us. He was really nice, told us stories about places we passed and helped us take pictures." It looks as though Kim and Penny might be able to get by without my help.

Mike Wallace is pleased to see college students traveling by train during their summer vacation. To him it's more than a pleasant alternative mode of travel, it's an environmental obligation. "We're headed for environmental catastrophe," he maintains. "When the advanced nations of the world finally take the drastic measures necessary to save the planet, trains will be one of the few travel options left.

"You know that the Mulroney government wants to get rid of trains as a travel option entirely and we're still struggling with the question of whether or not we will remain a united confederation. It's a question of political maturity, and in many ways you Americans are way ahead of us, despite your fling with the movie actor. But you've got your hang-ups and we've got ours. We've all got to do a lot of growing up fast. We're like the young man who hangs on to his fast car a little too long; what it's going to take is crisis, disaster, some pain and suffering to make us all mature."

I ask Mike more about the Canadian hang-ups regarding national maturity. Of course, there's Quebec and whether or not the Meech Lake accord will be signed and whether it will provide a permanent solution to the problem. Mike is pessimistic. He thinks that one or two provinces will hold out because of issues related to their own sense of distinct identity. "In most of the world, the problem is nationalism hampering globalism. Here it's provincialism hampering nationalism. We still have an extra step to go."

Mike sees the Mulroney government as a sophisticated version of Reaganism. "He has that same urge to roll back the clock when we need to set it forward in a hurry."

And then there's the free trade wrangle. Despite occasional experiments with free trade, one of the cornerstones of Canadian "national policy" (since John MacDonald coined the phrase) has been the maintenance of tariffs to protect Canadian industry from the overwhelming economic power of America. Mike argues that the policy represents something more than simply a way of dealing with a powerful neighbor. "It's a different economic system, not socialist, not capitalist, but mercantile—a system in which government works hand in hand with national private enterprise for the benefit of the country as a whole. The Japanese are conquering the world with something like it. We've had it all along and now Mulroney wants to scrap it."

"Why?"

"I guess he has his own ideas about what it takes for Canada to mature. He wants to make us more like you Americans. He wants pure capitalism. And the powers in Toronto and Ontario are all for it. You visit that part of the country and you feel like you're in America, right down to the street crime and the fact that there are places you can't walk at night."

For the sake of argument, I suggest that mercantilism is hardly a step toward the future. It's the Hudson's Bay Company and the system that the American colonies rebelled against two hundred years ago.

"Good point, on the surface. But remember that mercantilism was the system of empires—the closest thing we've ever had to the globalism that is necessary in the future." Mike maintains that free trade creates a competition in which somebody has to lose. A globally adjusted system of mercantilism could guarantee that there were no big winners and no big losers. Third world countries would have the biggest tariffs, and economic powerhouses like Japan, Germany, and the United States would have the lowest. In a global economy, governments have an economic role, not just to regulate the excesses of capitalism, but also to nurture it in areas of human benefit.

"The best model for this is the construction of the first transcontinental railways in both our countries. It was accomplished by private enterprise, but government had a major role in funding it so that the mammoth investment could eventually be profitable. The same thing needs to be done today with the recycling, pollution-cleanup industries, and the search for non-polluting sources of energy."

Kim and Penny have listened wide-eyed to Mike's dissertation but have managed to finish their meal. As Mike pauses for air, we realize that while he has talked and I have frantically scribbled in my notebook, neither of us has touched our food. Now Kim speaks while Mike and I down a few bites of our chilled dinner. "People in Newfoundland don't like the idea of free trade. They're afraid it will put people out of work."

Mike nods and concedes that there is a deep instinctive opposition to it in many parts of Canada. Unfortunately the opposition is based on the wrong grounds. He thinks free trade will produce just the kind of short-term economic bonuses that Mulroney expects— lots of economic activity because of increased trade with the United States. Canada has already begun to turn the tables on the traditional pattern of North American investment, with Canadian interests owning increasingly large hunks of American business.

"Mulroney wants to get into the arena on American capitalist terms and slug it out, confident that today we can hold our own. But it's a capitulation to the American system, and I don't want that for Canada. I don't want a system that gives us styrofoam packaging and aerosol cans. I want a system that gives us what is good for the planet."

As we get up to pay our checks, Mike shows me something that he says illustrates the continuing Canadian obsession with American influence. He takes a five-dollar bill from his wallet and points out the flag in the illustration of the capitol. The graven image is tiny, but an unmistakable dark spot in the upper left-hand corner makes it look like an American flag. He shows me the same illustration on other denominations and I can clearly see two dark bars along either side that suggest the Canadian flag. "You wouldn't believe how worked up people got over this. I don't know if somebody at the government printing office was really playing a prank or not, but the symbolism is so trenchant—the American flag on Canadian money."

During dinner the train has followed the southeast shore of the Kennebecasis River. At some points a mile wide and looking more like a bay, the river is the site of numerous large summer homes and is plied by pleasure craft of all sorts. We are approaching Saint John, originally populated largely by American loyalist Tories fleeing the new republic in 1783. Today there is still a very Tory look to the city from the perspective of the train—well-founded, genteel, with huge granite churches that must be Anglican.

Thus it's surprising that at the station the largest contingent of boarding travelers seems to be American tourists. Though I've encountered a few American tour groups in my travels, especially on the *Canadian*, this is the first train where Americans have been a significant presence. Having been immersed in the Canadian milieu for some time now, I am struck by how their presence changes the atmosphere of the train to something like a high school corridor with teenagers passing to classes.

Besides physical restlessness, the voices of Americans mark their presence more than anything else. Compared to the lower tone of Canadians, their voices stride above everything. It isn't really that Americans are boastful, domineering, or deliberately loud as some think. It's more a blitheness that assumes that, just as they want to be part of everything going on around them, surely everyone else wants to be part of the excitement they're feeling. And it's also simply a difference in speech. Americans, especially those from the South or the Midwest, speak with their mouths wide open. You can see a lot of teeth when they talk and the sound is correspondingly broad and strong. Canadians do the opposite. I've put some effort into learning to mimic Canadian speech, and when it works for me I realize that in addition to accelerating through sentences and tailing them upward in tone, I'm keeping the inside of my mouth tight and round and my lips barely open. It's hard to talk loud that way.

As the train pulls out of the station, I head for the dome along with a rush of the newly boarded Americans to view one of the most unusual sights to be seen from a train anywhere, the reversing falls on the Saint John River. The train slowly crosses a bridge over the falls and offers a better view than can be had from any place on the ground. The phenomenon of the falls is caused by the fact that, directly beneath the bridge, the river is constricted sharply by granite shoulders on either side. At low tide the river pours over a typical waterfall precipice into the Bay of Fundy. But with the extreme tidal fluctuations of the bay, at high tide the water in the bay rises well above the precipice ledge and up near the tops of the granite shoulders so that it pours in between them, cascading down to the level of the upstream water in the river and creating a waterfall falling upstream. At a certain point between the tides, the water in the passageway between the shoulders is still as a millpond.

Today as we cross it's high tide and the waters of the ocean foam upstream. It looks like what would happen if a great breach occurred in one of Holland's dikes.

Beyond Saint John the train soon plunges into more of that numbing New Brunswick forest I saw on the *Ocean*, and then it gets dark as we approach the Maine border. In the Skyline bar downstairs, one of those rowdy sessions I enjoyed on the trains out west develops.

A spirited argument centers around a flirtatious young woman named Denise, who teases the four men present with the contention that men are immature compared to the women they try to dominate. Her ex-boyfriend in Halifax has just ditched her because she insisted on taking this trip alone to visit a friend having a baby in Montreal. She says she's had it with boys and from now on wants to know only men. She is backed by an older woman from Cape Breton named Maggie who recently divorced her husband, who wouldn't let her go anywhere "while it's his goddamn right to go out and carry on however he wants." Three of the four men, young working guys, argue that women are either naive about the ways of the world or secretly looking for opportunities to stray and need the guidance of the worldly male hand. The fourth, a preppily dressed "thirty-something" fellow, initially keeps quiet but eventually begins to make occasional comments taking the women's side. But it's all a game. What is really going on is a competition of flirtation and seduction. Denise makes it clear that in response to her boyfriend's tantrum, she is available.

When I sit down, there is the usual round of introductions and offers to buy me a beer. You just can't be a fly on the wall in the Skyline bar, whose seats all face one another and where any newcomer sitting down is automatically joining the drinkers' circle. "You're the guy with the two pretty girlfriends. How about sharing one of them?" blurts out one of the irrepressible young fellows. I explain that they're not my girlfriends, that they are shy and probably won't be seen in the bar car tonight, and that I am a married American. At this last there is genuine surprise, which I take as a compliment to my efforts to adopt Canadian speech and behavior. "Goddamn Americans," says Maggie to an applause of laughter around the bar. "They're getting so clever you can't even spot 'em anymore."

The debate over men and women is suspended for a while as the competition shifts to enlightening me with nifty little insights about Canada. "Have you noticed that there are very few freight trains in the east?" asks one. "It's because the government is preparing for Quebec's separation by keeping economic activity west of Montreal."

"Bullshit," says another. "It's because nothing but lumber, wheat, and minerals is shipped by train and those things aren't produced in the Maritimes."

"What do you think of seeing so few blacks in Canada?" another wants to know. His lasting impression of Americans is the encounter he had with one in Ottawa who asked him, "Where do you hide all your blacks?"

The first guy jokes, "Well, we got our own, you know." And then he whispers conspiratorially, "The ones that speak Fransay." A mean giggle passes round the bar. It's intrigued me throughout these travels that in groups like this, English-speaking Francophobes always seem to know when it's safe to make disparaging comments about the French. One of the fellows explains, "They're easier to spot than foreigners, even if they're not talking." He can't articulate how it's done; it just seems to be like some kind of radar.

231

The thirtysomething man speaks up and says it's because of the Canadian mosaic. "Without the pressure to conform to the melting pot, people reveal their ethnic identity in their dress, their mannerisms, and a host of subtle signals, so that Canadians always know whom they are dealing with."

Obviously better educated than the rest of the group, his idiom sets him apart almost as if he were one of the ethnic minorities he refers to. The other fellows nod in agreement while Denise's flirtatious eye twinkles at him. I'd guess that so far, with his enlightened stance on the male-female issue, his age, and his uniqueness in this group, he's winning the competition for her company later on.

Maggie wants to pick on the French some more. Her bête noire is Pierre Trudeau. It was during his government that the steel plant in Sydney cut production and jobs, the Sydney Mines closed, and "the fishing went south. Then he had the gall to say that the people of Cape Breton were lazy. We've never forgiven him for that." She left to find work in Ontario, where she lives today, but her home is Cape Breton and she returns by train to visit often. "So don't ask me to be sympathetic to the Frenchman, not after what he's done for me."

"Nova Scotia's not so great, though," argues Denise. "You know that couple we met who needed an abortion of the fetus that had Down's syndrome? They were going to Montreal to get it done because they couldn't do it in Nova Scotia. Now that's bullshit."

After the train stops at Vanceboro, Maine, for customs officials to board, the group begins to break up, as Thirtysomething huddles privately with Denise in the corner and the younger fellows begin a game of cards. Maggie heads back to her seat and I begin to review the notes I've collected during the trip.

As I'm about to head for my compartment myself, I notice that during one of TS's trips to the bathroom, Denise moves over to the table where the younger fellows are playing cards and squeezes in among them. When TS returns he is suddenly on the outside of a circle that no longer admits him as Denise joins the younger fellows in their game. TS makes several attempts to lure her away, but eventually it's clear that she is really shutting him down. Finally he stands up, slams his beer can down on the table, and hisses between his teeth, "Boys or men?" and stalks out of the car.

The three young fellows are on their feet in an instant and charge through the door after him shouting, "What's that you say? You come back here." But he's gone and the conductor happens along in time to herd them back to their seats with a warning about fighting on the train.

When they're settled down, one of them asks Denise, "What was that all about?"

"A matter of sexual preference," she says. "Buy me another beer, boys."

It's a curious fact of North American railway history that Canada has operated far more miles of railways in America than Americans ever did in Canada. With the exception of some Great Northern trackage (today Burlington Northern) in southern British Columbia and a period of indirect ownership by the Vanderbilts of a route across lower Ontario that connected Buffalo to Detroit, no American corporation ever owned a Canadian railway outright. But Canadian enterprise has owned huge networks of American railroads and the character of their operation has cast a very tall profile across the American rail landscape.

The first was the Grand Trunk, arguably a British rather than a purely Canadian creation, but nonetheless based and managed in Canada. The main line, completed in the 1850s, connected Quebec with Montreal, Toronto and Windsor, Ontario, opposite Detroit. But the vision that led Francis Hincks to betray the Maritimes scanned more distant horizons across American territory. Backed by the muscle of its British financiers, the Grand Trunk acquired John Poor's Atlantic & St. Lawrence, connecting the excellent ice-free harbor of Portland with Montreal by way of Maine and New Hampshire.

The original Atlantic & St. Lawrence had not been one of the best built and operated railroads. The radical improvements wrought by the new regime generated a loyalty throughout New England toward this foreign corporation, which foreshadowed the loyalty of latter twentieth-century Americans toward Japanese automakers—the foreigners simply did a better job.

At the western terminus of the Grand Trunk, another opportunity opened up for the Canadian white knight. Chicago was the object of intense competition among American railroads, and the Vanderbilts were determined to make of it a monopoly for themselves. Thus they bought up competing lines, and when others did manage to get a toehold in Chicago, the Vanderbilts were quick to make friends and rate-setting agreements that infuriated Americans along the routes, particularly in Michigan.

Grand Trunk President Henry Tyler watched all of this and made no secret of his intentions. A connection across Michigan to Chicago was the "grand" in the Grand Trunk by which Tyler intended to offset the huge costs resulting from the acquisition and upgrading of the Portland extension. He promised that the Canadian route to an American Atlantic port would never participate in rate-setting agreements.

The Vanderbilts went for Tyler's bait and began buying up everything in Michigan in an attempt to block the Grand Trunk from entering Chicago. They adjusted terminal charges where the Grand Trunk connected with their lines to make through shipping exorbitantly expensive. Their moves had just the effect Tyler had hoped. Chicago and Michigan were ready to assist any enterprise that might break the Vanderbilts' power.

Though Tyler had no hope of finding the kind of capital from his British backers or the Canadian government that he would need to take on the Vanderbilts, he had an ace up his sleeve. The Grand Trunk owned 125 miles of rusting line running from Quebec City eastward to a junction with the proposed Intercolonial. Upon completion of the publicly financed railway to the Maritimes in 1876, Tyler sold this track for $1.7 million to the Canadian government.

With anger at the Vanderbilts in Michigan peaking, Tyler hosted a series of Grand Trunk parties in Detroit and Chicago in 1879. Railroadmen and politicians from all over Michigan were feted, toasted, and promised a better deal under the Grand Trunk. Tyler modestly ventured that the Vanderbilts' methods seemed sometimes unconcerned with the good of the public and that they might have trouble getting away with such practices in Canada or England.

The key route across Michigan included a couple of short railroads at each end, which the Vanderbilts ignored, confident that their large holdings in the middle would make them useless to Tyler. That strategy made them useless to anyone but Tyler as long as the artificial gap between them stood. Thus Tyler was able to buy both ends of the route at fire-sale prices, and it didn't hurt that the interests involved knew that they were aiding in an assault against the hated monopolists. When Tyler began building a dogleg bypass of the Vanderbilt section, the Vanderbilts capitulated and sold the central section to Tyler for half a million dollars. With a continuous line all the way from Portland to Chicago, Tyler gave credit where it was due: "We are not indebted to anyone so much as to Mr. Vanderbilt for the cheap rate at which we have acquired this valuable property."

Midwestern Americans hailed the defeat of Goliath, and Tyler hastened to emphasize that this wasn't a defeat of Americans by Canadians and British but a defeat of New York by Michigan and Chicago. He held to his pledge not to enter into rate-setting agreements (for which the Vanderbilts were now in a lather) and granted a variety of other concessions to shippers that American railroads had always denied.

Today the Grand Trunk name commands greater respect in America than it ever has in Canada, where its contention with the CPR has been far less successful. When the government took over the Grand Trunk in 1923 as part of the Canadian National system, it recognized this fact by organizing its midwestern American lines as a separate subsidiary under the name Grand Trunk Western, which continues to the present.

Meanwhile in Vermont, one John Smith attempted to build and operate a railway in the manner of Jay Gould. He and his Vermont & Canada persevered through receiverships and bankruptcies, corrupt financing, blackmail, bribery, and financial compromising of judges. After amalgamation with the Rutland and old Vermont Central, the now-named Central Vermont established a route that ran all the way from the Canadian border to the port of New London in Connecticut.

During all of this the railroad was an important New England connection to the Midwest via the Grand Trunk. When the Vermonters fell behind in their payments, the Grand Trunk began to collect in stocks and bonds instead of cash. By 1898, the Grand Trunk had taken full control of the Central Vermont and began to tangle with another bare knuckles American outfit, the Mellons and their Boston & Maine.

Under Canadian National operation in the twentieth century, the Central Vermont line has competed with the Boston & Maine in a manner reminiscent of Tyler's contest with Vanderbilt in Michigan. The Boston & Maine is derided throughout New England as a rapacious outfit, while the Canadian-owned Central Vermont is seen as a foreign white knight. When in 1987 the Mellons' holding company, Guilford Industries, allowed track conditions on Amtrak's *Montrealer* line over the Boston & Maine tracks south of White

River Junction, Vermont, to deteriorate below passenger train standards, Amtrak used its legislative mandate to seize the line and sell it to the Canadian owners of the Central Vermont, who today run the *Montrealer* over much of its route. The Mellons were flabbergasted that the U.S. government would seize an American-owned property and sell it to foreigners. Again, the Canadian way of doing business triumphed over the brutal methods of perhaps the last of America's rail barons and has generated appreciative American friends all along the route.

Not to be outdone in this business of acquiring American properties, by 1890 the CPR had cobbled together its "short line" across Maine to the Maritimes, over which the *Atlantic* travels today. With no American ports or trade centers at either end of the route, some Canadians have expressed concern over the use of American soil merely as a shortcut, seeing a dangerous precedent that they don't want America to reciprocate. (Others see a point of pride in owning this strip of American soil.)

The CPR also took over a network of bankrupt railroads west of Lake Michigan in 1961 to form the Soo Lines, over which Amtrak's *Empire Builder* runs from Chicago to Minneapolis. Thus the CPR's ancient fear of American railroads' striking into the soft underbelly of Manitoba has been reversed. The international connection of Winnipeg to Chicago across that region is now firmly established— but it is the CPR who owns it.

Looking at North American railway history, one might have a hard time conceiving that Canadians ever approached American economic competition with fear and trembling. Perhaps it's instructive to consider the historical exception of the railways. It doesn't take too much oversimplification to see their triumph as an illustration of what Professor Mike Wallace wants to preserve in the Canadian system—a tendency to deliver what is good for the public rather than what will generate the greatest profits.

Is the benevolent nature of Canadian private enterprise a myth? Most of the Canadians I met would say no. It is one of the few points of universal agreement concerning a national identity distinct from America. As it emerges under free trade, it will be pressured by the American market toward compromise. But if it stands fast and makes a contribution toward an economically saner world, perhaps it will mark a rite of passage for Canadians toward a manhood that Americans still have not achieved.

In the morning, the train has crossed Maine and we are back in Quebec approaching Montreal. I find Kim and Penny at an open vestibule window with a young conductor, and they introduce me as the American who's going to show them around Montreal. Soon the train pulls into Gare Centrale under the Queen Elizabeth Hotel.

Like New York's Penn Station, Gare Centrale has had its once grand waiting rooms lobotomized. Today the station connects with Montreal Underground and Place Ville Marie, two ambitious underground shopping malls. But staying underground is the last thing Kim and Penny want to do in the big city, so after checking our bags, we emerge into the hot sun on Rue Mansfield. It's humid, stifling.

They want to see if we can hike to the top of Mont Royal, so we set out across the McGill University campus and begin climbing steep streets. Before long the heat and the fact that none of us knows where we are going combine to quench even their enthusiasm for this much exercise and I suggest lunch in someplace that is air-conditioned.

Two blocks beyond Dorchester Square on the corner of Metcalf and Ste. Catherine is Ben's—the restaurant that makes the long Montreal connections worthwhile. It doesn't look like much, with its neon and stainless steel sign and cafeteria-style interior, but it claims to be the home and birthplace of the Canadian smoked meat sandwich (though a Mennonite nude dancer I know in Manitoba insists that her people claim this, too). I always thought New York was the capital of the deli, but in Vancouver and Montreal I have found delis that rival anything in Manhattan.

Ben Kravitz came to Canada from Latvia in 1910, bringing with him his family's recipe for pickled (not really smoked) meat. He adapted the recipe to good Canadian brisket and began selling the stuff on Ste. Catherine. Canada was experiencing a wave of East European immigration at the time and the new arrivals in Montreal quickly made their way to Ben's shop and took word of his food with them throughout Canada. Soon other East European entrepreneurs picked up on Ben's recipe for success and the smoked meat sandwich became the foundation for the considerable Canadian deli industry, which still flourishes. Ben's sons carried on the tradition, and their sons still do today.

A Ben's sandwich is a huge mound of thinly sliced, delicately pickled beef brisket, always served warm, never cold or hot, garnished with slices of rye that are dwarfed by the mass of meat within. The bread serves merely as a pair of fragile handles with which to artfully manage the pile of meat.

There is also matzo ball chicken soup, corned beef and cabbage, jalupkes, and spiced french fries. The place swarms with waiters so that one can eat and dash or, as is encouraged, eat and eat again. During lunch we sit next to a group of French-speaking college kids who have just finished their sandwiches. When the waiter asks if they want anything else, instead of ordering dessert, they order corned beef and cabbage and cups of bean soup to go. They leave sipping their bean soup like coffee as they walk down Ste. Catherine Street.

In traditionally French Montreal, one of the favorite eateries is a place with East European Jewish ancestry. Back in the hot, smoky railway station, Kim and Penny queue up for their train to Ottawa. I ask them what they liked best about the little they saw of Montreal. "Ben's," answers Penny, who usually is the silent partner. "And the feeling of being a citizen of the world."

"Yeah," agrees Kim. "You always hear about Canada being a great international country, but in Newfoundland you don't see it much. Being here makes me kind of proud."

Even in the quirky east, Canadians do have a very distinct national identity—I could be plunked down in almost any of the places I've been, even Halifax, and know almost instantly that I was in Canada and not the United States. But, besides the cultural mosaic and the belief that their enterprises are more benevolent for humanity than America's, the Canadians I've met have a difficult time articulating that character.

Many of the Canadian writers who tackle the problem eventually focus on a vague inspiration of the north, the vast tracts of wilderness that stretch from the northerly fringes of populated regions to the Pole. This inheritance is said to be the shaping facet of Canadian experience, just as was the West for Americans. Surprisingly, I have heard few references to this as a key to Canadian identity in my conversations—but I haven't ridden any trains headed that way yet.

PART THREE

Up North

There is a town in north Ontario . . .
In my mind I still need a place to go,
All my changes were there.

—NEIL YOUNG

11

The Train Nobody Rides

TRAIN 141–144 FROM MONTREAL TO COCHRANE, ONTARIO

*U*P *north*. In Canada the phrase resonates deeper than it does elsewhere. In America, up north there are big cities, and farther north there are lakes and mountains full of vacationers who think nothing of motoring even a little farther north across a border and into the comfortably familiar milieu of another country that they imagine is not much different from their own.

But in Canada, up north is true north, ultimate north, magnetic north, snow, ice, and the North Pole. Americans, if they think of the Canadian north at all, think of perfect lakes for fish that grow bigger than they do in places where people live, game you can't shoot anymore at home because it is endangered or extinct, and *National Geographic* photo-essays on polar expeditions to find things you see only in zoos or museums.

Canadians have even stranger ideas about their north. At first blush, they seem to share a myth with America in which north is substituted for west. North is the frontier. North is the place where men have tested their abilities to be self-reliant and forged an ethic that partially shapes the nation's identity. North is the repository of

241

a great national wealth of natural resources and open space, the symbol of the prosperous future. But there is one great difference. Canadians have never conquered and subdued their north, and maybe never will—not only because they haven't been able to, but perhaps also because they don't really want to.

Thus the Canadian north and the reasons Canadians dream of it and venture into it are different from anything Americans feel about their west. There are still aboriginal people living in the Canadian north—lots of them—and not all of them confined to a life of dependency on culturally isolated reservations. Indian spirits have crossed the cultural divide in reverse osmosis, so that white sojourners in the north not only are familiar with them but, in primordial wilderness dramas of survival and epiphany, have been touched by them. It is a land where men swear they have seen three suns by day and have heard the ringing of the northern lights at night.

As the American relationship with its west is fundamentally masculine, the Canadian relationship with its north has been profoundly feminine. Many of Canada's best writers on the subject are women, and the men who have penetrated it have not done so in conquest, but under seduction. If earth anywhere is still a woman, a primal lover, a mother, who calls, enchants, nurtures, and chastens, it is so in Canada's far north.

Traveling by train rather than by canoe or snowshoe, I realize that my participation in the northland experience will be limited. But I will be granted enough of a glimpse to see that the north is fundamental and rich—like the hidden sex life that flourishes behind the conventional public image of a couple who defy the odds and stay married till death.

All overnight trains in Canada have names but one; all but two are described in Bill Coo's essential *Scenic Rail Guides*. But the train that meanders from Montreal up through the central interior of Quebec and then westward across the border to terminate at Cochrane, Ontario, is not described by Coo and has no official name (though rail people call it the *Abitibi* for the region it serves). A piece of it that splits off and heads for Jonquiere on Lake Saguenay is called the *Saguenay* route and is given a chapter in Coo. But the longest segment of the route remains undiscovered unless one carefully scrutinizes a Quebec road map, which shows a great circle of roads marking the circumference of a vast trackless wilderness in the Laurentian Shield (an eastern extension of the Great Shield). Across the center of this megacircle, one spies a thin meandering black line; this is the route of the eastern extension of the old National Transcontinental Railway, today run by CN. A close look at a VIA timetable confirms that an overnight passenger train makes this run. You can also find it on the government's list of "essential routes."

Innocently, I board assuming that the run must serve places of economic significance along the way—perhaps hydropower or mining or forestry centers. This is my first ride on a Canadian train whose general direction is north, rather than east or west. Surely the story of these lines will focus more on exploitation of a frontier than on unification of a reluctant nation.

The train leaves Montreal at 8:30 P.M. on a Friday (another version leaves at 6:30 P.M. on Monday and Wednesday). Thus there is no chance to make acquaintances at dinner, and as the train rolls out of Montreal and I wander through the consist checking out who's on board, I can see I'm going to have my hands full here. Despite the fact that our ultimate destination is in English Ontario, there isn't a single English-Canadian aboard and certainly no American besides myself. Everyone is French, even the conductor, who must have just barely passed the exam requiring bilingualism for VIA jobs. And the French everyone speaks in the bar car is that most staccato Quebec form, which I can't understand at all.

The bar car on this train is a configuration I haven't seen before. There are coach seats at one end, the usual partitioned bar in the middle, and a nifty lounge with soft padded seats and tables at the other end. Many of the patrons are college students heading to homes in the Senneterre region, a settled area beyond the wilderness that we will pass through tomorrow. One exception is an old Indian guide wearing a Montreal Expos baseball cap and whose hands and face are like gnarly tree joints. His name is Isaac Itapp, and somehow he spots me for an American as soon as I sit down and order a beer in my best Canadian inflection. "Hey, Joe," he says. "You want fish, hunt?" But that's all I can understand. I can't even tell what language he is speaking; I think I recognize bits of English and French in it.

The bartender helps out. He explains that Isaac and his brother run a thriving business in Senneterre where they are well known and respected as guides and as gourmet camp chefs. The brother speaks fluent English and Isaac is the master woodsman and cook. Their clientele is mainly well-connected Americans or Toronto or Montreal Canadians with the money, time, and hardiness for trophy hunting in the deep Quebec wilderness. He says I should be flattered that Isaac called me Joe, his generic name for the Americans he guides. It means that just by my looks I appear to be one of the rare breed he caters to. I shouldn't be disturbed at not understanding Isaac's speech. Since it's his own blend of Cree, French, and English, none of which he speaks well, nobody understands him except his brother. When he's not guiding sportsmen, he makes mittens and snowshoes that are prized throughout the north woods.

I've been asking the bartender some questions about Meech Lake and the issue of Quebec separatism and Isaac has leaned toward us, listening intently to my words. Suddenly he starts shaking his head, gesticulating vehemently and muttering in that strange language no one can comprehend. No one but the bartender, anyway, because he explains that Isaac is insisting that I am pursuing the wrong story. It isn't the French who will dominate Canadian headlines in the coming years, it's the native peoples.

If I could engage in any kind of two-way communication with Isaac, I would love to. But as it is I am drawn to the conversations of a tableful of French young people all sporting the ripped-denim-and-commercial-logo-tee-shirt look. One of the guys, a little older looking than the others and sporting a spectacular walrus moustache, has been listening with amusement to my attempts to talk to Isaac. He invites me to join the group, and when I do, Isaac Itapp looks at the two women, grunts, shakes his head, makes a circle with the thumb and forefinger of one hand, slides the middle finger of the other in and out of the oval, and murmurs, "No more [unintelligible mumble] women [more unintelligible mumble] trouble."

When I try French the fellow of the walrus moustache compliments me on my pronunciation. When I insist, in French, that I know that my French is bad, he explains in halting but serviceable English that it's unusual in Quebec to hear English speakers even attempting to pronounce French correctly. If they deign to speak it at all, they do so with a deliberate English pronunciation that grates on French sensibilities.

His name is Elphage Lauzon, a married workingman. Annie and Any (both pronounced exactly the same) are college students returning to their families for visits. Jocelyn is a deadheading CN employee.

During my previous foray into Quebec on the train to Perce, language was not such an issue. The French-Canadians I spent time with spoke reasonably strong English. But the English of the group in the bar car of train 141 is little better than my French. Elphage does the best; he has little trouble framing sentences and understands me as long as I speak slowly. Annie and Any don't frame sentences at all; instead they seem to draw upon a storehouse of standard phrases and idioms, which they can rattle off fluently. They only understand me when what I say fits one of the linguistic sound bites they have learned in school. Thus conversation with them is limited initially to rather conventional concerns—weather, food, clothes, destinations, and so on.

Jocelyn makes little effort to talk to me at all and even seems to resent this whole business of bridging language barriers. Finally it is French and nothing but French for the rest of the evening. Buried vocabulary I haven't remembered in years is unearthed as the trains rolls deeper into northern Quebec. It's not quite like riding a bicycle, but for the first time in my life, the years I spent suffering Cs in French courses seem worthwhile.

The first thing I want to know from my new French friends is what they think will happen if Meech Lake is somehow derailed. When Jocelyn finally understands what I am asking, he rolls his eyes in disgust and says, "*Ça ne fait rien.*" He professes not to care, and the others also seem bored by the question. Apparently it's a standard query from traveling English-speakers. Any explains that, first of all, the whole issue of separatism and contentions with English Canada is a generational thing; people my age are the ones who get lathered up about it, especially in the cities. But for young working people from the countryside, like my companions here, it ranks low on their list of concerns—well below learning a profession and getting a job.

Annie adds that what Meech Lake attempts to confirm is already a reality. Quebec is a distinct society and no piece of paper will influence that fact no matter how many provinces do or don't sign it. "*C'est vrai,*" confirms Jocelyn, who now reveals why the question bothers him. The Meech Lake accord and its attendant controversy are an insult to French-Canadians, who don't need the approval of the rest of Canada to know who they are.

But they have all dodged an answer to my question. Now that it is on the table, how will Quebecois feel if it is actually turned down?

When I push, everyone seems to squirm a bit, and it dawns on me

that they don't want to consider the possibility. That's why broaching
the issue makes them so uncomfortable in the first place. They already tacitly have what Meech Lake proposes to give them. Now,
thanks to the effort to enshrine it, they feel in danger of losing it.

Elphage explains for me in English, "We know the federal government treats Quebec well. We have a good life—our own culture,
and good things from Canada, like this train. Not everybody wants
separatism. But if they don't pass Meech Lake—everything will
change. *Tout sera fini.*"

I have described former Prime Minister Pierre Trudeau's efforts to
keep his fellow Quebecois in the federation by aggressively pursuing a policy of national biculturalism. Trudeau, who emerged during
my travels as one of the most eloquent opponents of the Meech Lake
accord, believes that any society's identity and its potential greatness transcends language, religion, and ethnicism. So he has been
an ardent opponent of granting concessions to his home province of
Quebec or anyone else on the basis of uniqueness of language or any
other human characteristic. He has been accused of wanting to
replace the Canadian mosaic with the American melting pot.

For Trudeau the issue is a question of expanding human character or limiting it. Adapting to multilingualism ennobles people.
Succumbing to the retrogressive desire to cling exclusively to a
language or any other ethnic characteristic degrades them. In this
sense, Trudeau is a classic liberal, insisting on the perfectability
of man.

But his arguments also have a hard-nosed practical side. If
Quebec is encouraged to promote exclusive ethnic characteristics,
what about other provinces, or even communities, with unique
characteristics—say those with substantial aboriginal populations
or East Europeans or Asians?

In this Trudeau anticipates a crisis that may soon be sweeping
the world—the balkanization of great societies, the tendency of
large pluralistic nations to break up under a maladaptive return to
ancient tribalism. Americans might at first cheer the process when
we see it in the Soviet Union; we might be mildly disturbed seeing it
in Canada. But where will we stand if we see Washington, D.C.,
declare itself a distinct black society, New York or Miami establish
Spanish as the official language, or Alabama make the Southern
Baptist Church the official state religion?

Thus Trudeau gives separatism and concessions to it, such as the Meech Lake accord, no quarter. When he patriated the constitution in 1982, he affixed a set of amendments, a bill of rights, intended to guarantee true pluralism and national equality to all races. The secessionist provincial government in power in Quebec at the time was less impressed by the power of Trudeau's bill of rights to protect French-Canadians in English Canada than it was with the amendments' potential for thwarting exclusively French initiatives in Quebec. The constitution was adopted without Quebec's imprimatur, and Quebec passed laws such as the infamous Bill 101. Thus ensued the constitutional crisis that Prime Minister Brian Mulroney promised to resolve when he came to power in 1984.

Mulroney, while known for certain initiatives that depart radically from Canadian tradition, such as promoting free trade with the United States and retrenching the national commitment to passenger railway transportation, attempted to solve the problem with the time-honored Canadian tradition of compromise. No stranger to the life of a minority population himself, Mulroney grew up an English speaker in Quebec. For him it was a simple (though delicate) matter of asking Quebecois what they wanted and then drafting a series of amendments to the constitution, carefully formulated to avoid objections by Canada's English-speaking majority. In his mind, it was not so much a matter of philosophical vision (beyond the firm belief in a united Canada supported by the hearts and minds of Quebec), as it was a matter of crafting something that everyone could accept—a bridge to the "island" of Quebec.

The non-secessionist Quebec provincial government of Robert Bourassa that came to power in 1986 gave Mulroney what he wanted, a precise list of conditions under which Quebec would sign the constitution. Foremost among these was that Quebec be recognized as a "distinct society" with the right to enact laws such as Bill 101, intended to advance the use of the French language in the province's social and economic life.

In the spring of 1987, Mulroney convened a meeting of the ten provincial premiers at a guesthouse on a little lake just north of Ottawa. The house had been built by an American minister, who is buried there under a tombstone that reads: "I ask not to stay where storm after storm rises o'er the way."

The national leaders emerged with an accord that all supported—including Quebec. Besides granting Quebec exactly what it said it wanted, the agreement gave to all the provinces increased authority over federal appointments, the makeup of Parliament, and the local application of national social programs. In effect, the prime minister said, "If you give this special gift to Quebec, I will give you all something you've always wanted."

Three years were allotted for provincial parliaments to ratify the amendments to the constitution. Eight provincial parliaments quickly signed on, including Quebec; only Manitoba and New Brunswick delayed, and in their deliberations were seen the seeds of possible defeat. In Manitoba, the issue is native people who refuse to grant Quebec concessions they believe they should have received themselves long ago. In New Brunswick, it is the issue of civil rights and the fear that Quebec, residence to many English families with relatives in New Brunswick, may become a repressive regime for those who do not speak French. And in Newfoundland, a new premier was elected who pledged to rescind his province's approval.

During my travels in Canada, the papers are filled with stories of Mulroney's frantic, sometimes shrill attempts to overcome this opposition. He has warned of doom in the form of everything from Americans to Russians to civil chaos in the streets. Many resent his strong-arm tactics. A growing number of respected voices are finding problems in the accord. Writer Mordecai Richler has said, "Better a divorce, I think, than a marriage in name only." Trudeau has reemerged as a critic, with a book attacking the accord as the destruction of a vision of a greater Canada. Since my travels, the deadline has passed and the Meech Lake accord has failed. Manitoba held out. Newfoundland rescinded its approval. A new referendum on Quebec's independence has been set for June 1992. While federalists scramble to patch together a new amendment process that will keep Quebec in, separatists are increasingly confident that, this time, they will have their way.

Meanwhile, the results of Mulroney's other grand initiative have made Quebec stronger and more confident of going its own way in the post–Meech Lake world. For several years, its vigorous young business community has competed in the marketplace under free trade and thrived. Gone are the days when Montreal lamented the departure of English business for Toronto. National economists on both sides of the border agree that Quebec has shown that it just might be able to make it on its own.

During the night we run through sportsman's country, the great Quebec backwoods, where most of the stops have names like Club Wigwam, Oskalaneo Lodge, and Maniwawa Club. Though I don't get to see any of the backwoods camps, the conductor tells me in the morning that they span quite a spectrum of clientele, ranging from a camp for Montreal electricians, plumbers, and cops to places where the prime minister might retreat with visiting heads of state, as the American president does at Camp David. The camps' presence here is one of the reasons that this is a protected essential route. Many of these establishments were built because of the railway connection to Montreal and have no other access, not even air for some not located on a lake. There are also stops for native villages, another constituency that would be sensitive to the loss of their railway connection to the rest of the world.

As the conductor is telling me this over coffee, a curious transformation happens to the landscape outside. The forest opens here and there for green fields and cows; occasionally we pass farms with cultivated crops. The conductor explains that we are approaching Senneterre, the eastern edge of the "clay belt," a relatively fertile area of glacial deposits on the ancient Laurentian Shield.

As we slow for the stop, Isaac Itapp comes into the lounge and sits down with us. He commences to berate me in his gruff lingo and the conductor translates. I won't learn anything about Canada unless I start talking to native people instead of French-Canadians. I should stay away from young people, especially the women, who are full of nothing but trouble. And I should give up my intention of riding beyond Senneterre. It's the end of the world—there is nothing west of there.

In the late morning we pull into Senneterre, a surprisingly big town, considering the wilderness we have just crossed. Isaac Itapp, Elphage Lauzon, Annie and Any, Jocelyn, the bartender, and the conductor are all getting off here. In fact, the VIA schedule shows this as the end of the line. But if you turn the page, you see a train listed that runs from Senneterre to Cochrane in Ontario. It is really this train, continuing on after a half-hour stop and the removal of most of its cars, including the bar car, two of the coaches, and the sleeper. From here to Cochrane, two hundred miles and five and a half hours away, it's just two bare coaches, not even a takeout counter.

And no passengers either—not many, anyway. Everyone, every last man, woman, and child, detrains at Senneterre. One old woman and a middle-aged Cree man board, and neither of them will talk to me for the entire ride. I end up moving into the empty coach where the skeleton crew hangs out, a young male conductor and his younger female assistant, who can't be more than twenty-one. He wears the traditional uniform, but she is dressed for work in boots, dungarees, and a sleeveless tee-shirt. He speaks a tiny bit of English; she speaks none at all.

They have a radio-tape player set up on the windowsill, connected with wires and alligator clips to a large nine-volt battery. It saves money on replacing the small internal batteries, explains the conductor, when I express my curiosity about the hookup. A lot of people who work on the railway run their music machines this way.

The station the radio is tuned to plays an eclectic mix of well-known sixties stuff and a handful of tunes current on the American top forty, interspersed with French-Canadian pop music. Music is one of the ways Quebec is a distinct society. Though Quebecois listen to English acts from the Beatles to Phil Collins, they have their own pop musicians, who somehow make a living with totally original French-Canadian material and virtually no play outside Quebec. The sound of this music ranges from something like sixties hootenanny to Euro-pop to heavy metal. The one commonality running through all of it is a tunefulness and sentimentalism (sometimes downright drippy) that is a bit refreshing to ears affrighted by 2-Live Crew and Guns n' Roses.

To pass the time, the conductor and his assistant share a copy of Quebec's *Croc* magazine, showing me things in it that they find particularly funny. *Croc* is a French-Canadian satirical humor magazine with a look superficially similar to America's *Mad* magazine, though the content is somewhat weightier and sexier—I'm sure that *Croc* fans would be insulted by my comparison. One particularly memorable cartoon illustrates a beleaguered survivor of the eighties swimming in a place labeled LAC MEECH where figures resembling Prime Minister Mulroney and Premier Robert Bourassa are pummeling characters representing the various provinces— another testimony to the ambivalence Quebecois feel toward the initiative intended by Ottawa to satisfy their aspirations.

At Taschereau, the train stops long enough for me and the train crew to dash to a little supermarket and get munchies for the rest of the ride. In the store I'm surprised to find an American couple deliberating over which cheeses their guests back at camp would like. Then it's more slow trekking at twenty-five miles per hour over incredibly straight track through forests relieved occasionally by river crossings.

At a lonesome stop called Norembega, the conductor explains to me that this is the only train that uses these tracks, so they aren't maintained very well. Any track problems would be discovered by our derailing; we are traveling today the way trains did in pioneer days. This has always been such a railway, since the eastern extension of the National Transcontinental never generated enough traffic to justify its construction and would have been torn up long ago but for the dependence of a few little outposts along it and the symbolism of a route linking the interiors of Quebec and Ontario.

The eastern extension of the National Transcontinental Railway was cursed from the very start—just getting it across the St. Lawrence at Quebec City turned out to be a problem. The St. Lawrence presented a special challenge to early railway builders, not only because of its width, but because of the need to allow clearance for shipping. In the winter of 1880 an unusual expedient had been tried at Montreal when two railways, one north of the river and one south, wanted to connect but were refused access by the Grand Trunk Railway to its Victoria Bridge. After determining that the ice was anywhere from two to four feet thick, the outfits laid a crib of twelve-by-twelve-inch timbers across the ice and then put down light ties and rails. With a small locomotive weighing about twenty-five tons pulling two flatcars equipped with seats, the "Montreal Ice Railway" safely replaced the rail ferry during the icebound season for three years.

The NTR had grander plans for its crossing at Quebec City. In 1898, a bridge was authorized at a point a few miles upstream from the city, and Theodore Cooper, a respected American engineer, was hired to execute the project. A bit of a visionary, Cooper believed in the elegance of the cantilever design, in which the outer ends counterbalance the center. This type of bridge could be built with far less steel than was customary, and Cooper's blueprint called for a bridge of radically lightweight construction in which a webbing of brilliant engineering compromises would create something almost out of nothing. Critics, ranging from leading British engineers to the Caughnawaga Indians who worked high on the girders, warned that the bridge was too light, but because he was doing the work for a nominal fee, Cooper was able to shout them down.

In 1907, the suspended central span was under construction when a work train halted at its end. With a snap the bridge broke and collapsed, killing seventy-four workers. The ensuing investigation treated Cooper kindly, but he was taken off the project and the new bridge was built to double the weight of Cooper's plan.

In 1916 the central span was ready to be hoisted into place. A crowd gathered to witness the operation in which four powerful jacks would lift the four corners of the span into place. With the structure thirty feet above the water, the frame of one of the jacks buckled and its corner of the span dropped, twisting the whole structure till it fell and plunged into the water. Witnesses described workers falling like apples from a shaken tree. Ten of them died.

Finally, the next year a new central span was successfully hoisted into place and the bridge has served safely ever since. But the railway, intended to link the far extremities of the nation by way of Quebec, has never drawn traffic and is today one of North America's great white elephants. Born a child of politics, the Quebec extension of the National Transcontinental Railway hobbles along today as a geriatric—still a ward of politics.

At Cochrane, I and the elderly lady who wouldn't talk to me are the only passengers to detrain. Thus it's a surprise to find a bustling little station that seems to be the heart of a thriving town, which extends up a hill to the northeast. There's a restaurant in the station and a postal center. Two other passenger trains come through here by different routes, each train considerably more important than the one I have just ridden. The *Northland*, a route run jointly by VIA and the Ontario Northland Railway, comes up on the Ontario Northland tracks from North Bay and Toronto and switches here to the old National Transcontinental line west to the paper mill town of Kapuskasing.

The other train is the Ontario Northland's *Polar Bear Express*, which departs from Cochrane for Moosonee to the far north on James Bay—thus the large polar bears painted on the platform concrete. I will ride that legendary train on a subsequent trip.

Cochrane is also a northeastern Ontario town where English meets French meets north. After a hike to my motel on the highway at the outskirts of the city, I walk back into town looking for dinner and evening conviviality. These strolls are my first introduction to one of the oddities of many of Canada's northern communities. One might think that towns virtually laid out from scratch in these climes would be compact, with minimal walking distances between heavily frequented haunts, but often it is just the opposite. Whether planners were intoxicated by the expanses of space they had available or optimistically convinced that subsequent growth would fill in empty territory, I don't know when I visit Cochrane. But northern Canadian towns generally are not laid out for the committed pedestrian.

The weather has turned, and by the time I reach Thibs Tavern, a place recommended by the train conductor, I am windblown and bone-chilled this early September evening. The place is warm and hearty. It has a hunters' ambience, with trophy heads hanging from the walls and a selection of hunting gear for sale. There's an inner room with a pool table, and the outer room is divided by a partial wall into two sections that have equally good views of the TV over the bar where "Hockey Night in Canada" is on the air.

When I first enter, all eyes focus on the stranger. The clientele seems to cross age boundaries; older working couples crowd the bar along with the younger singles who usually dominate these places on Saturday night. After I have a sandwich and strike up a conversation, the eyes seem to accept me by ceasing to notice me.

At the bar a friendly fellow in his twenties spots me for a traveler and offers that he is one, too. He invites me to join him and his friends, Medora and Danielle. Jeff, a handsome, blond, muscular but almost hippyish-looking fellow, and the only native English speaker in the group, has recently spent six months traveling the United States on his motorcycle.

Danielle teaches at the Catholic school in Iroquois Falls. She comes to Cochrane to let down her hair and "do the kinds of things a Catholic schoolteacher can't do in the town where she works." Jeff is eloquently bilingual, while Danielle's English is serviceable.

Medora speaks only French, but Danielle says it doesn't matter because she's not going to talk to me anyway. She's working on getting picked up by a tall lanky fellow at the bar who reminds me of a French cowboy. So it's really just the three of us.

Jeff is a student who took a year off for his United States odyssey by Harley-Davidson—27,000 miles he says. His travel formula was to head toward each big city and then skirt it. With the exceptions of San Francisco, New Orleans, Washington, and Boston, he kept to his itinerary and is glad he did.

What Jeff was really after were the small towns. He felt he knew American cities well enough from the television shows that are pumped over the border, and he didn't like what he had seen. He hoped to find better neighbors away from the bright city lights.

"Did you?" I ask.

"Not always," he says. "I got hassled a lot. People thought I was 'Easy Rider' delivering drugs. I got the shit beat outa me several times—in Texas, Indiana, and Georgia. Some American small towns don't accept strangers very well. How about you in Canada? Any trouble like that?"

I explain that I really haven't stopped off in very many small towns like Cochrane, but that I am going to frequently in the "up north" journeys.

"Well, I expect you'll do better than I did. First, you're not riding a Harley. And second, I really think Canadians in small towns have a different attitude toward traveling strangers. There's nothing Canadians respect more than people making long journeys. It's part of our heritage, eh?"

"So you didn't like America very much?"

"Oh, no. I didn't say that. One on one, small-town Americans are the friendliest, most big-hearted people I ever met—especially the younger ones. Once I got a chance to break the ice with people, they would do anything for me—feed me, fix my Harley, give me a bed." And then, in a conspiratorial whisper to tease Danielle, "And the girls, man. American girls are crazy, eh?"

Danielle knows exactly what he has said and teases back, "What about Quebecois girls?"

With a wink at me, Jeff comes back quickly, "Oh, just like Americans—better than Americans."

Jeff says Cochrane is a significant rail junction and major outfitters' center for sportsmen. There's a sawmill and a plywood plant, but out of sheer cussedness Cochrane has passed up several chances to be a greater industrial center. "A pellet plant called Bioshell wanted to locate here, but the town felt it didn't have enough land. And the Iroquois Falls paper mill could have been built here, but again the town didn't want to give up the necessary land." Jeff and Danielle agree that some of these northern towns have a warped view of how much open space is necessary to preserve their northern character. I serve on a city council at home and know how the public sometimes tends to discount the importance of preserving space while they still have it. But we measure ours in acres; in Cochrane they talk about square miles.

Danielle likes Cochrane and other northeastern Ontario towns like Iroquois Falls because here French and English mingle and share the small-town ethic of the north and escape from the city. "People in the north don't quarrel about language or religion or politics. I have more in common with the English here than with French-Canadians in Montreal or Quebec City."

Jeff agrees, though he notes that some of the most violent anti-French groups from the Ottawa Valley have weapons cached in hideouts around here for the civil war they believe is inevitable. Danielle shudders when he says this. "If anything like that ever happens, it will be people like me who will be hurt the most. Here along the border you will be expected to choose. And even if I choose Quebec, I will be in trouble because of my time in this part of Ontario." She explains that if she had gone out west, it wouldn't be held against her, but French-Canadians who make a life just over the border in Ontario have a stigma with some people back home.

I observe that it's hard to conceive of a violent French-English split in this town where, tonight, English and French patrons mix and socialize freely and even enthusiastically. Several of the most sociable tables of the married set are mixed groups with English and French intermingling.

Jeff says it's true, but his studies of American history have convinced him that Cochrane and places like it might be the Canadian equivalent of towns in the border states in the years before the Civil War. "There's a lot more tension here than you can see. And there's the third factor—Indians. You spend very much time in northern towns like this and you'll see. Their influence is growing so much that they're gonna take over the politics of places away from the population belt." Danielle agrees, though she chooses to put a positive spin on the issue—if the government holds to its commitment to develop the northlands, then this is where all three races will forge the Canadian future.

Perhaps it is a tendency of the climate in these severe northlands to force men to live in harmonious community. But the histories of the region dwell less on the cold as the element that forged the permanence of these communities than they do on fire.

In the dry summer of 1911, settlers around Cochrane and the mining town of Porcupine to the south busied themselves clearing new land and burning the brush in controlled fires just outside of town. Because of the railways—the National Transcontinental and the Temiskaming & Northern Ontario—these townsites were already built-up with frame houses and shops and hotels. Communication between the towns, however, besides that provided by the railway, was still primitive—just a few rutted roads for horse-drawn carriages.

Settlers were accustomed to the danger of brushfires getting out of control: the air was often fouled with smoke and the hazard was considered one of the trials of wilderness life. But no one was prepared for the sudden blast of forty-miles-per-hour wind that swept up from the south that July.

First it struck Porcupine, where several brushfires were fanned into a broad front of flame that bore down on the settlement faster than men could run. In town, women hanging out their wash noticed the sky darken and the air swirling with more smoke than usual and gray ash. Looking toward the end of the street, they saw the flames and a few men bolting into town just ahead of them.

By the time those in town knew what was happening, the flames had engulfed the outermost houses and were marching from building to building toward the lake. With no time to do more than throw a few precious possessions down well shafts, people fled to the municipal dock at lakeside in panic.

An old photograph in a history of the region tells the story. In the center of the frame, a crowd of people push and shove their way farther out on the dock. The waters of the lake churn with chaotic waves thrown up by the fierce, fire-whipped wind. Overturned boats and canoes with people clinging to them testify to its violence. Trees in the background bend sickeningly in the dark gale and huge fireballs loom beyond. In the foreground, a terrified boy and a dog wade into the water to escape from ominous billows behind them.

The diaries of settlers tell of individual struggles. Some attempted to lead their horses into the water, but showers of sparks terrified the animals so that they broke loose and charged crazily into the flames where they were roasted alive. While the fire storm raged, one young woman gave birth in the lake as men held a wet blanket over her and the doctor. Miners who sought shelter in the shafts all died when the fire sucked out the oxygen. And everyone noted an even greater fear that gripped those who waded into the lake to escape the flames: word went around that the morning train had brought in 350 cases of dynamite, which were now sitting in a freight car not far from the dock.

That afternoon, the dynamite blew. By some miracle the force of the blast was directed mostly vertically, sparing the hundreds of heads that bobbed in the water a few feet away. The blast tore a great pit in the ground, which during later rebuilding efforts became a crucial source of fresh, unspoiled water.

By nightfall, when the fire had spent its rage, survivors dragged themselves back to the ashes of what had been their homes. At least seventy persons drowned or were burned to death. Many of the possessions thrown down well shafts were fire damaged since the flames had followed the wooden cribbing right down to the water, which in some cases had been boiled dry. One woman who had been hanging out her laundry when the fire approached returned home to find her Sunday roast perfectly done in the brick oven amid the ruins of her kitchen.

In Cochrane that morning, no one could know of the horror occurring just a few miles south at Porcupine. But there, too, the usual smell of brushfire smoke suddenly became more pungent, the sky darkened, and a sudden violent wind whipped the brushfires into a conflagration. It wasn't the Porcupine fire, but the same wave of hot wind that had swept over Porcupine earlier.

Cochrane, as a railway center, had more men in town when the fire approached than had Porcupine. And since Cochrane doesn't sit on the shore of a lake, there was greater effort to fight the fire and save the town while women and children huddled terrified in the open space of the rail yards.

But all to no avail—the flames soon engulfed the entire town. With no lake, there would have been far greater loss of life at Cochrane than at Porcupine but for the railway and the heroism of a telegraph operator named Taylor in Cochrane's only brick building, the Union Station.

Frantically, Taylor hammered out calls for help to work trains down the National Transcontinental and T&NO tracks to the east, west, and south. Meanwhile an engine was hauled out of the roundhouse, and with flames billowing all around the yard, a train was assembled. It was quickly filled with women and children and chugged out of town to the west with drivers spinning.

But Taylor's work was not finished. As dispatcher controlling operations on single-track lines, he had to stay at his post amid the flames to direct the running of the rescue trains, now approaching Cochrane from three directions, and to dispatch repair crews to points where waves of fire had melted the telegraph lines. While railway employees frantically hosed down the brick structure, he tapped at his key to keep the trains coming. Twice the heat drove him out of the building, which became a brick oven, to the relative safety of the Y out in the yards, but each time he returned when the railway crews succeeded in hosing down the flames. As a result, Cochrane stayed in touch with the outside world almost throughout the day.

More than two thousand people were evacuated by rail who would have otherwise surely perished. Another few hundred, mostly railway men, stayed behind to fight the fire. By 6:00 P.M. most of the town was gone, but a handful of buildings along the tracks was saved to become the nucleus of the town that would rise from the ashes in the days that followed through the relief efforts of the railway. A thousand people accepted the railway's offer of free transportation to anywhere else; the rest returned and, using the brick Union Station as an emergency headquarters, began rebuilding.

Twice more fires struck the region. In 1916, Cochrane was again burned, though this time there was only one death in town. But in the lumber camps and smaller settlements outside of Cochrane more than four hundred died, many who had sought shelter in wells and root cellars. A group of fifty French-Canadians at Nushka declined the offer of a passing train to evacuate them and all perished in a rock cut where the fire blew in like a dragon's breath. Other settlers in the outlying regions, who had built homes with tin roofs supporting barrels of water that they believed would protect them, stayed inside and endured the horror of watching their children slowly cook.

In 1922, the third great northland fire left six thousand homeless farther to the south in communities along the shore of Lake Temiskaming. Through all these fires, the brick station at Cochrane came to symbolize the railway's heroic role, and it is still the focal point of the community. Eventually laws regulating the burning of brush were successful enough that the histories label the 1922 fire "the last great fire." But the histories will have to be revised. Another thousand miles down the rails, I will meet heroes and personally survey the carnage of the greatest fire of them all—the

Manitoba fire of the summer of 1989. Again the flames would forge bonds of community between two races and a railway would save the day.

In the morning at the West Way Motel, I open my eyes to a strange light in the room. I can hear the tinkling of the electric baseboard heaters, and even before I realize what has happened, I feel a thrill of excitement, like a child on Christmas morning. There's a wet sound emanating from the traffic of trucks passing on the highway outside, but it's not raining. I jump out of bed and pull back the thin curtains. Snow—just an inch or so but enough to whiten and invigorate the world.

I have time for a leisurely breakfast at the station restaurant in the same brick building where Taylor tapped out his frantic dispatches in 1911, and then it's out on the platform in the fresh snowfall air to catch the train heading back to Senneterre and Montreal.

It's already sitting grumbling on the tracks when I finish breakfast—the strangest-looking train I ever rode. Pulled by a VIA F-7 and a steam car, the consist includes two coaches, three CN GP-30 diesels, and a caboose. The freight units are deadheading to Senneterre. This time there will be more passengers—at least the deadheading crew that goes with the CN engines. I'm the first one aboard so I sit close to the door where I can check out who gets on. Soon we are moving and no one else has boarded yet. Perhaps I'm early and the train has some more switching to do before most of the passengers board. But then we're picking up speed and a conductor comes through. *"Billet, s'il vous plait."*

It's true. Today I'm the only passenger on train 144 for Senneterre. For six hours it's just me, rolling at twenty-five miles per hour down the arrow-straight corridor of the old National Transcontinental.

12

Walden North

TORONTO TO KAPUSKASING
TO MOOSONEE
ON THE *NORTHLAND*
AND THE *POLAR BEAR EXPRESS*

I'M back in Toronto, after a desultory daytime ride on one of VIA's LRC (light, rapid, comfortable) corridor trains from Montreal. Whoever said that the style of airplane interiors was worthy of emulation? I always thought the antiseptic architecture of airplane cabins was necessitated by the engineering demands of flying people through the air thousands of feet above mother earth, but in its corridor trains, VIA has re-created the interior and regimens of airlines, right down to the pressure to stay in your seat and the stainless steel carts wheeled up the aisle for drinks and meal service.

You meet a different kind of Canadian on these trains. My seatmate was a man from Toronto who is a junior executive for a phone company. He dismissed the issues of Quebec and the Canadian search for identity with the economic dogma that once Canadian enterprise is as competitive in the North American system as those of, say, California or New York, such quaint concerns will evaporate.

At 9:30 on a Sunday night in September, the concourse of

Toronto station is empty and lonesome. The shops in the main hall and down in the commuter mall are all closed. The night custodian with his broom makes the loudest sounds tonight in this place in which I have witnessed gales of laughter, loud talk, and the noise of baggage handling in prime hours.

In the alcove at gate 10, less than half a dozen people wait for the departure of VIA's *Northland* bound for the remote northern Ontario pulp mill town of Kapuskasing by way of the Simcoe-Muskoga resort country, the Temiskaming mining region, and the rail crossroads of the northern clay belt, which I have already visited, Cochrane. My itinerary will take me to Kapuskasing on this train and then back to Cochrane, where I will catch the *Polar Bear Express* for Moosonee on James Bay.

Waiting for the train with me are a sleepy family with kids and a couple of elderly ladies. Another young voyageur—a young woman in her early twenties wearing a Hard Rock Cafe sweatshirt, worn dungarees, and a leather jacket—sits with her head pillowed on a large, ratty denim duffel bag on her lap. From time to time, she looks up with a startled look in her eye as if she is freaked out to be where she is. When the call to board is announced, I am disappointed that there are no native people and no resort-bound millionaires in the queue.

As the train pulls out of the station, I follow my usual routine and hike the length of the train. In the food service car, one with the little lunch counter, the young voyageur I saw in the station is sitting on one of the swivel stools sipping coffee. Accustomed enough now to the instant intimacy of train encounters, I sit down with her and ask where she's going, why she's going, and why she doesn't look very happy about it.

Elizabeth Walsh was born in Cleveland, Ohio, but her family moved to Fauquier, Ontario, when Elizabeth was twelve years old. Her father had war buddies in this small northern town and saw the place as a refuge where he could raise his family in a place far from the troubles of big cities. The critical point had been the evening he watched a TV news report and first heard of the murder that had occurred on the street corner near his home earlier in the day.

Elizabeth grew up "a happy small-town girl with lots of boyfriends," but her family was nagged by a sense that they had failed some kind of test, especially her mother. "Mom felt like we had run away from the world. She wanted us kids to be ambitious and not settle for life in Fauquier."

When Elizabeth finished school it was assumed that she would go off to a city and prove that she could make it on her own. She took the train to Nova Scotia and got an apartment in Halifax. "That's when I discovered that I had inherited my father's phobia about cities. I stayed in all the time, didn't even go out to look for a job."

It wasn't that she was lazy, she insists, but just plain scared. "I hated having to crowd on a bus with strangers and walk down the street seeing no familiar faces. And on the TV news every night I'm watching murders and rapes, right there in the place where I lived!"

Now she's in flight back to Fauquier. Her mother will be disappointed, but Elizabeth doesn't care. She just wants to marry one of those nice small-town boys and try to have babies.

"*Try* to have babies?"

"I had cervical cancer, from the pill, they told me. And I'm afraid the doctors screwed me up." She says that's one of the drawbacks of life in the northern towns. Though Canada's health care system is in many ways a model for societies everywhere and has much better statistics (birth mortality, life expectancy, and so on) than the United States, Elizabeth describes a situation that the AMA would seize on as an argument against the Canadian national health care system. She says that in Canada the doctors in remote northern towns tend to be rookies still learning the art, often doing a field-work equivalent of residency. "People in northern towns can tell you all kinds of horror stories about unnecessary operations and people sewed up with forceps inside them." She knows something went wrong in the operation, which the doctors claimed successfully removed her cervical cancer without a hysterectomy. "They were whispering all kinds of stuff and giving me some double-talk about how I shouldn't expect to be able to have kids easily, after they had told me beforehand that if the operation went well, that would never be a problem. Besides, there are ways—you know—a girl can tell every month if her body's working right. And mine isn't."

As the evening rolls on, the *Northland* is a quiet train, about half-full with families, elderly, young working guys, and a few college students heading to North Bay, Cochrane, and Kapuskasing. Elizabeth tells me a few more local stories—about a fellow named Camille Poisson who was such a partying man that he became a legend and died of a heart attack at age forty-two; about Mayor Roger Dugray of Smooth Rock, who will tell me if I ask him that Elizabeth is a heartbreaker; and about the town of Moonbeam through which we will pass tomorrow morning. Its name is a local joke and has nothing to do with a shaft of lunar light, as described in Coo and other tourist guides. What really happened, according to Elizabeth, is that a man was sitting on a beam at a construction site and looked up and marveled at seeing such a bright full moon. The next day he pointed out to his fellows the beam from which he saw such a good view of the moon. Ever since, the building he was working on and the town that grew up around it have been known as Moonbeam.

By 11:30, when the train stops at Washago, Elizabeth is fading fast and heads off to her coach seat to try to sleep. Thus far we have followed the same route from Toronto as the *Canadian*, which I rode at the beginning of this journey; we passed Lake Simcoe in the dark earlier. But at Washago the *Canadian* transcontinental route splits off to the west, and now we are headed north into "Canadian dream" country.

The route of the *Northland* spans the tracks of several railways built to exploit that dream. Before the first transcontinental, before the Intercolonial, before the Grand Trunk, citizens of Canada's second city despaired of ever seeing their vision of an English metropolis rivaling Montreal come to fruition unless something could be done about the damnable roads. Known as York, before the change to the Indian name of Toronto, the city hoped to anchor a future northwestern empire. But as long as the thoroughfares out of town consisted of swaths of knee-deep mud during the warm season, and blowing snowdrifts the rest of the year, the dream was a joke.

The railway fever that swept the continent after 1850 put an end to that. A number of routes were conceived and some were actually built, but two of the most successful were the Toronto, Simcoe & Lake Huron Railway and the Northern Railway. As ships at sea in those days hopped from island to island to minimize the length of their leaps over empty water, so did the early Ontario railways step from lake to lake. Lake Huron seemed like a good place for a railway to go, with the possibility of connections by steamers that could cruise to anyplace along the vast shores of the northern Great Lakes. To get there, these routes crossed the farm country north of Toronto to Lake Simcoe, then headed northwest for ports on the shore of Huron's Georgian Bay. A branch line, operated as the

Toronto, Simcoe & Muskoka Junction, split off at Washago and ran to Lake Muskoka and Lake Vernon.

While the lines to Huron had obvious possibilities, the connections to the Muskoka region were based on a flimsier proposition. Since 1815, when the federal government bought these lands from the Chippewa for the then sizable sum of $20,000, it had been hoped they would attract settlers who would farm. No one knew what might be the northern limit of the kind of pioneer expansion that built places like Ohio or Indiana; there was little understanding then of the geological and agricultural implications of the voyageurs' travails.

When the Ontario, Simcoe & Lake Huron made its maiden run in 1853, a handful of families began to scratch at the earth in this region that was undoubtedly one of the most beautiful places men had ever been offered free land. But the scratching didn't go very well. What made this land so beautiful, with deep pristine blue lakes and rolling forested hillsides, was the fact that here the rich agricultural earth of the Ontario plain encounters the first rocky shoulders of the Great Precambrian Shield. Within a few years, the settlers all packed it in and went away.

Then came the rich Americans. W. H. Pratt, a New York millionaire, had heard about a fantastically belaked empire of fish and game in northern Ontario where nobody lived but that had its own railway. In 1870, he opened a first-class resort on Lake Rosseau, where for the sum of $5 a day, American plan, the wealthy of North America could escape to a wilderness where no amenities were overlooked. Other establishments followed, and soon the Muskoka Lake region boomed as a playground of the captains of the continent. Special trains carrying as many servants as passengers transferred their prestigious riders to luxury steamboats at Gravenhurst on Lake Muskoka. Many of these lakes are interconnected by little wilderness waterways so that the steamers enabled the vacationers to network with those at other resorts. There were other smaller rail lines, too, such as the *Portage Flyer*, the world's shortest at one and one-eighth miles in length, transferring passengers from the Fairy Lake steamer to the Lake of Bays boat and the famous Bigwin Inn.

Today some of the resorts are still in business and the *Segwun*, the last of the luxury steamers, still makes its hundred-mile cruise through the Muskoka lakes. But the real significance of these routes is their extension by the twentieth century to North Bay on Lake

Nipissing and a junction with the CPR. Eventually they would be rolled into the new Canadian National system and North Bay would become the jumping-off point for a great provincial railway that would open the far northlands of Ontario and create its own home-grown millionaires in the process.

In the morning, I'm surprised to see farms, brick houses, hayfields, deciduous trees (now leafless), and gently rolling open hillsides. The conductor explains that we are entering the clay belt, the agricultural region I visited at the end of my run through Quebec. It is actually a ridge of fertile glacial deposits dumped in a long depression in the otherwise inhospitable rock of the Great Shield.

At Porquis (pronounced Pork-us and named to represent the towns of Porcupine and Iroquois Falls) we meet the Ontario Northland's southbound *Northlander* (not to be confused with VIA's *Northland*), a day train rumored to have the best dining cars in Canada. The train has Swiss equipment with European-style compartments and venetian blinds at the windows. I had toyed with the idea of taking that train instead of the one I'm on, but since it terminates in the gold mine town of Timmins, it doesn't go to Kapuskasing or connect with the Ontario Northland's *Polar Bear*.*

We stop for twenty minutes at Cochrane and the snow I saw here a few days ago is gone. Then we pull out onto the east-west tracks of the old National Transcontinental and pass in the later morning through Elizabeth Walsh's territory, the clay belt towns of Smooth Rock, Fauquier, and Moonbeam. By noon we are at the end of the line—Kapuskasing.

The station in Kapuskasing is located right beside the huge Spruce Falls pulp mill. Running at full capacity, I'm told, the plant sends a single towering white plume into the crystal blue northern sky this fine September day, and I don't smell anything like what I encountered out west in Prince George. The air is chilly, but there is no breeze and the ultraviolet-laden northern sun heats up the dark-colored jacket and pants that I have been told to wear in these climes.

I was first attracted to this town by its reputation as a successful planned community and by a picture in Bill Coo's *Scenic Rail Guides*, which showed the Tudoresque Kapuskasing Inn across a

---

* Since the 1990 cuts in VIA service that eliminated VIA's *Northland*, it now does connect with the *Polar Bear Express* at Cochrane.

body of rock-bordered water. Off the train, I leave my bags with the stationmaster and head off in search of the picture.

It's not far away and lives up to its photographic image. It looks like an old English inn plunked down in very un-English surroundings—an outcropping of shield granite.

But there is another picture. From the inn's side of the millpond, the view is of the rail yards and the Spruce Falls pulp mill. In fact, I discover by walking around the shoreline of the pond (really merely a backwater bend in the Kapuskasing River) that the pristine view in Coo's rail guide can be seen from only one spot—anywhere else the industrial nature of the town predominates.

Inside, the inn is quiet and reserved. No rowdy young people, no noisy families with children. The dining room is filled with well-dressed people who look as if they are here for a convention and older couples who seem like regulars. The menu is, by back-country Canadian standards, expensive—nothing less than twelve dollars.

I'm hungry for a more common touch of the city, so I hike several blocks and eventually find myself in John's Grill, the kind of corner diner that often is the most eloquent spot in town.

John Sabovitch was a bush pilot in the years following World War II when the opening of the northlands seemed like economic Shangri-la. He came to Kapuskasing because his wife, Chris, got a job at Spruce Falls. For him, Kap was a good forward base for his work as a pilot.

He sits down beside me at my table while I saw on my open-face pork sandwich and his wife leans across the counter. For ten years, life here was perfect. "I flew everybody into the wilderness. They were after the mystery of the north and they were willing to pay more and more to experience it." His wife earned good money at Spruce Falls, one of the highest-paying employers in all of Canada.

And then one trip he crashed his plane. "I had a heavy load and the engine quit over a resort lake. I couldn't put down in the bay because of the swimmers, so I crash-landed along the shoreline." It wasn't some isolated snowbound northern lake that did him in, but a vacation spot too full of people.

John was astounded at the pile of capital the insurance and their combined savings amounted to. He bought the grill in 1956, Chris quit her job at Spruce Falls, and they have both been sorry ever since. "It was good at first. But we were stupid to open this business. If I'd stayed at Spruce Falls, today I'd have a pension and could relax," says Chris.

John and Chris certainly look tired. He mumbles so badly that talking seems to be an effort; she has the watery eyes of a woman who needs at least a week of rest. They work long hours because there isn't enough business for them to hire any help.

"We used to get enough people in here every day after work that we could save and build our own pension," explains Chris. But mechanization at the plant has cost jobs, lots of them, particularly among the young single men who would eat their meals on their way to and from work at a diner like John's. "There's a whole generation missing in Kap," says Chris. "The town seems prosperous because the jobs that remain pay well. But there's no one here between the ages of twenty-five and thirty-five."

After lunch I head back to the park by the river for a nap on the grass in the sun. The feeling in the air this September day reminds me of balmy Indian summer days back home—a last chance to squeeze some pleasure out of the dwindling sun. I begin to doze off wondering about the "mystery of the north." Kapuskasing seems about as exotic as Dubuque, Iowa. Without the mystery, why should people live here on this barren pool-table landscape light years from the usual haunts of men? I imagine my usually tolerant wife telling me, "If you want to live in Kapuskasing, Ontario, go ahead. But you'll do it without me." I try to explain that I have no such intention. My kids cry, "Daddy, don't leave us. Mommy, don't let him go." Traveler's guilt.

Then there's another voice saying, "Are you all right, hullo, are you all right?"

I open my eyes and hear the sounds of a radio dispatcher. Standing over me is an officer of the Ontario Provincial Police; his car is parked nearby on the grass.

"Are you all right?" he asks again. He explains that he got a call about a body lying in the grass by the river. It didn't sound good, so he checked it out.

Impulsively, I ask him, "You're a cop, you could get work in lots of places. Why did you choose Kapuskasing?"

He responds matter-of-factly while squinting up at the dwindling September sun, "Kap chose me. I was born here. Got family, roots. And it's not a bad place to be a cop. Not a lot of trouble, you know, and people respect the law." No mystery of the north here.

He directs me to City Hall, where Pierre Millette, a town public relations official, invites me to his office for a chat. He has no idea who I am or what I'm doing here, but my camera and notebook attract his professional attention. When I explain myself and my mission he relaxes and says that it's too bad the mayor, Theodore K. Jewel, is out of town during my visit. Jewel is a rail fan, fighting hard to prevent the imminent cancellation of the VIA route I rode to get here. He is also a black man, a fact which Millette handles delicately with an American. I ask why and he explains he has met American industrial reps who have been put off at finding a black mayor in this northern town.

I ask Millette about the reductions at Spruce Falls. He confirms that the work force has declined from 4,500 to 1,500 in the last twenty years. It's mechanization, not economics. The plant has had steady uninterrupted growth throughout its tenure, but it keeps finding ways to make more paper with less people. Kap, progressive in so many ways over the years, has only recently found the religion of economic diversification. COB Manufacturing, which makes custom furniture and kitchen cabinets, has been one recent catch. And KapTest Engineering has capitalized on the local climate to build a thriving cold-weather testing center for automobiles and anything else that has to work in frigid weather. General Motors has recently established a site to do all of its winter testing here.

Millette says that the economic issue around these parts now is expansion of hydropower facilities. The two big eastern hydro-generating provinces, Ontario and Quebec, erred in the eighties in overcommitting to the United States. "We thought we had this gold mine for international trade with your country. But we forgot that the economic boom here in Canada would need more power to take care of itself." All the mills in the region are scheduled for expansion and modernization that will consume more power, "so now Ontario has to build new dams and we've already dammed most of the non-sensitive sites. We've got a serious public relations challenge on our hands as we get into rivers that involve more serious fish and wildlife and Indian issues."

"Kap," as it is known locally, is the most northerly city in eastern Canada—population near thirteen thousand. In 1911, the National Transcontinental Railway reached the site from the east. West of here, almost all the way to Winnipeg, lay the most rugged stretch of the Great Shield. Kap's first role was as the jump-off point for the railway's leap across the rocks. During surveying, the clay belt was discovered and Kapuskasing became the site of the first experimental clay belt farms. The government hoped to develop hardy crops that could withstand the severe weather in these latitudes and play a key role in realizing the Canadian dream of the north.

Then came the First World War and another use for the place was discovered—as a prison camp for German aliens and POWs. The railway provided a convenient means of transporting prisoners to their incarceration, while the remote location guaranteed that escapees weren't going anywhere. And the prisoners, as slave labor, could work the experimental farms that were a poor draw to Ontario farmboys more interested in enlisting and fighting in Europe.

As many as twelve hundred Germans who had settled in Canada before the war were confined here with another thousand true POWs from Europe. In 1916, they served heroically in the fight against that year's horrendous forest fires, but there were strikes and violence. Despite the thousand-mile barrier of bush country, escape attempts were more common than anyone expected, and three escapees actually made it all the way back to Germany. There is a small, modestly marked plot across the road from the public cemetery where thirty-two Germans who died during incarceration are buried.

When the war ended and the prisoners departed, the Ontario provincial government hit on a tidy solution to the manpower problem by offering free land to war veterans for settlement. Training was provided in the agricultural methods best suited to this latitude and, for a time, with dormitories and regular instruction sessions, the future town of Kapuskasing resembled a remote agricultural college. Settlers worked at clearing the first ten acres of their own lots while boning up on frost dates, insulating mulch, and hardy varieties.

By 1920 the colony was failing and, with the exception of nine families, the novitiate farmers all left. In the meantime, pulp producers had invested heavily in the surrounding timberland. The Kimberly-Clark Corporation of Wisconsin formed the Spruce Falls Company and eyed Kap as a site for a huge pulp mill, if only it could find backing to hedge against the huge risk. In Canada that meant government partnership.

If the rich but hostile northlands of Canada were to be developed, it would require the same kind of intervention by government that had helped build the original transcontinental railway. The province that took the lead in this great enterprise would become the pilot of national destiny. In 1921, in cooperation with Spruce

Falls, the Ontario government laid out Kapuskasing as Canada's first planned community.

Initially the Spruce Falls subsidiary of Kimberly-Clark produced a standard pulp used in a variety of paper applications, but in the mid-1920s, the *New York Times* was casting about for a reliable source for its exponential expansion. They found it at Kapuskasing, and to this day, the *New York Times* is printed on Spruce Falls paper.

Another product grew out of the needs of World War I. In response to a shortage of cotton needed in hospital applications, Kimberly-Clark developed a process that produced cellucotton, a pulp-based artificial cotton substitute. After the war, it didn't take the company long to find a peacetime use for the material. Thus the world was introduced to Kotex disposable sanitary napkins and Kleenex facial tissues. The plant at Kapuskasing now had a diversified product base that might protect it from fluctuations in the demand for newsprint. When the Great Depression struck everyone else in North America, the Spruce Falls plant at Kapuskasing continued operation at full capacity. Between newsprint, Kotex, and Kleenex, the plant had a market that simply didn't diminish in hard times.

Boosters rejoiced. If an essentially single-industry community could thrive here even during the Depression, what might be possible throughout these lands during good times?

In World War II the little city again became a site for a POW camp and for another of Canada's acts of shame. Thousands of Canadian-Japanese were forcibly transported on CN trains from British Columbia and imprisoned here.

Determined that this would never become one of the ghost towns so prevalent in northern Ontario, a string of local governments have since aggressively built and developed a social infrastructure that includes a sports palace, three TV stations, an eighty-six-bed hospital with many state-of-the-art technologies, a nursing home, an extensive recreational department, a downtown nine-hole golf course, six separate schools offering a range of alternatives from exclusive private to public to special education, a mall, and extensive convention facilities at the Kapuskasing Inn. Many Canadian towns have these kinds of facilities, but none so far north and few where their existence is so much a result of local government initiative. And in this town, nobody complains about local taxes. If they go up, people assume the town government is pursuing some new initiative to "keep Kap on the map."

Despite the departure of its young people, Kapuskasing seems indeed to be the model of what can be done with planned communities in the Canadian northlands, and, thanks to the state-of-the-art technology of its pulp mill, it doesn't even smell. But as I will discover farther down the tracks, the trick has been difficult to duplicate elsewhere, especially in provinces that don't have the resources and power that Ontario commands.

At 5:40 P.M. of the same day I arrived in Kapuskasing, I catch the *Northland* headed out. No northern mysteries here—just a cold place to make a decent living surrounded by particularly unpromising horizons.

Back in Cochrane, I spend another evening at Thibs Tavern and the West Way Motel. The mood is different at the tavern tonight— less friendly. I notice that a trucker who has pulled in distributes handfuls of white pills to girls hanging around the bar. Several of the married couples I recognize from the other night get up and leave with tense glances toward the trucker. I follow their lead, but when I ask them about the trucker outside in the street, they shrug their shoulders and have nothing to say.

In the morning, I finally board the *Polar Bear Express* headed for Moosonee on James Bay. There are actually two different *Polar Bears*, depending on the season. In the summer, Ontario Northland runs a fancy *Polar Bear* with a classy dining car like that on its *Northlander*. In the off-season the railway runs what is called the *Little Bear*.

I expect something homely, maybe a few ragtag coaches on the back end of a freight. I'm right about the freight—our train does indeed get switched on behind a dozen heavily loaded freight cars, several of which are flatcars laden with lumber—otherwise the six cars of the passenger section seem new, clean, and state-of-the-art. We have no formal dining car, but there is a pleasant cafeteria-style luncheonette and bar, three coaches with wonderfully comfortable reclining seats, two open baggage cars that you can wander through (I wonder why at first but soon find out), and a trailing generator car with a diesel engine that makes electrical power for the train— REP, Rear-End Power, instead of HEP, Head-End Power.

At least half of the passengers who board at Cochrane are Cree natives, and as the ride progresses more get on, till they come to dominate the ambience of the train. One family in particular catches my eye because they are all so handsome—father, mother, a daughter, and two sons. Like virtually all the native people who ride this train, they are well dressed: colorful ski parkas or school-style jackets, brand-name jeans, and athletic shoes.

I ride for a while with the conductor after he has collected tickets. It's a cold, steel-gray day outside but warm and cozy in the train where he says we have a hundred passengers. With a crew of four—engineer, assistant, conductor, and baggageman—the train, with thirteen freight cars and six passenger cars, moves pretty fast for what is basically a freight—fifty miles per hour. There are no other freight trains supplying Moosonee, and there are no highway connections either. This every-other-day train is it.

The conductor explains that this month there has been a heavy ridership of Indian college students, who are taking increasing advantage of their constitutional guarantee of free education. Many of them attend public colleges currently shut down by a teachers' strike, and they're on the train heading back home to wait and see what happens on their campuses.

The point the conductor is most anxious for me to understand is that the ONR is just about the only railway in North America that is actually expanding track mileage today. It is picking up lines cast off by CN and hopes to compete with the two giants, CN and CPR, within the province. Traffic to and from hydro and pulp mills is what will make all of this possible. "We're one of the few companies nationally doing more than giving lip service to the dream of developing the north," he says with pride.

By 1902, there were tracks all the way north from Toronto through the resort country to a junction with the CPR at North Bay on Lake Nipissing. At Sudbury, the CPR had already shown how a railway could exploit mineral wealth. Out west, railways created economic empires. A final definition of Ontario's border with Quebec in 1884 had extended the province of Ontario all the way to James Bay. In this vast frontier, Toronto saw the potential of backyard empire.

Alarmed by the encroachment of Quebec Catholics, English settlers along the west shore of Lake Temiskaming were crying for a railway. The province of Ontario commissioned the Temiskaming &

Northern Ontario, whose purpose was to provide transportation for settlers in what was now called "New Ontario," but some in the provincial government had a larger vision. The twentieth century would surely create fantastic demands for lumber, and there might even be untapped mineral wealth in the rocks of the region. There was also the fantasy of a tidewater port on James Bay, which might shift the balance of economic power between Ontario and Quebec forever in favor of Ontario.

The Temiskaming & Northern Ontario Railway got off to an inauspicious start. The European laborers were not welcomed by the heavily Orange settlers, who referred to Greek and Italian workers as dagos and contrasted their ways with those of "white men." Soon the usual problems of political patronage in government-sponsored projects threatened to scuttle the promoters' aspirations.

Then a legend intervened. One moonlit night in 1903, a blacksmith in the town of Cobalt thought he saw the eyes of a fox or a wolf gleaming in the dark. He threw his hammer at the two sparkling spots, it struck rock, and the eyes never moved. He marked the place and investigated in the morning. It was silver, the tip of the world's richest vein.

Another version credits the same man with discovering silver flakes on rocks as he crouched to relieve himself in the woods. Even earlier, two railway employees searching for timber to make ties along the shore of Cobalt Lake noticed metallic gleamings in the sand. Hunks of shining metal protruding from rocks were so pliable that they could bend them with their teeth. It was all silver, the outcropping of what would become famous as the McKinley-Darragh mine.

The Cobalt region boomed, and humble settlers and railway workers, as well as the usual prospectors, became mining millionaires overnight. In some locations, huge slabs of solid silver could be pulled off veins with bare hands, "like boards from a barn." By 1907, the Temiskaming & Northern Ontario ran trains to Toronto every bit as opulent as those inaugurated earlier to serve the Muskoka resorts. Now the region had its own homegrown wealth.

But the fast-buck opportunities created mining boomtowns that contrasted sharply with the genteel establishments to the south, though sometimes the leading lights of both places were the same men. Gambling halls, prostitution "hotels," and "blind pigs" (illegal establishments serving liquor) became the focal point of towns like Cobalt. Brawls and knife fights were common.

Today it's difficult to judge just how much of a problem liquor really was. Most of the noise generated over the issue came from prohibitionist Orange Protestant voices, to whom any appearance of "demon rum" spelled ruin and doom. One telling diary entry by a pioneer woman describes the return of her previously teetotaling husband from a visit to the tent of a "Polack" family who fermented their own wine. "And he come home, this was about nine o'clock for his supper, and talk? He talked like a streak . . . all it done for him was make him talk . . . like a gramophone."

Boosted by the money generated by the silver mines, the Temiskaming & Northern Ontario built north of the lake toward a junction with the east-west National Transcontinental at Cochrane. And silver was only the beginning. A prospector clambering over the rocks in the Porcupine area slipped and fell, stripping a layer of moss off the rocks as he went down. He screamed to his companion, a few yards away, who rushed to his side thinking the man had injured himself. Instead they both gazed upon a dome of pure gold atop a quartz outcropping. Three months later another prospector pulled the moss off a ridge of quartz and found golden deposits, like "the droppings of wax from a burning candle," for sixty feet.

When the word got out, poor prospectors clambered aboard T&NO trains and detrained at wilderness points closest to the gold fields. Halfway houses to accommodate them were quickly established, where for fifty cents the traveler could avail himself of the "soft side of a three-foot plank and a pair of blankets." More gold was discovered at Kirkland Lake and then copper at Rouyn-Noranda. In 1922, with the little provincial railway flush with mining wealth, the commissioners hatched a new scheme. The T&NO would not stop at Cochrane, it would push on to the bay.

The first British settlement in Ontario wasn't Toronto or any of the other bustling towns along Lake Ontario but the trading post established by the Hudson's Bay Company at Moose Factory on James Bay in 1673. Thus history as well as the Canadian dream and Ontario's own fantasy of having a saltwater port loomed in the minds of provincial commissioners in the early twentieth century. Surveys showed that a route could be built at reasonable cost, also that there was no sign of valuable minerals, just some gypsum and lignite. The scrub forests of the James Bay watershed would never form the basis of the kind of timber industry found a little farther south. There was the promise of vast supplies of hydropower along the fall line where the north flowing rivers dropped into the James Bay basin; transmission wires, not railways, were needed to exploit this resource.

Boosters were undeterred by these facts, remembering that no one had foreseen much economic potential for the original T&NO route. The building of the line from Cochrane to Moosonee was largely an act of faith. The province had once been rewarded when it invested in tracks leading north; surely something would turn up to make another miracle.

Instead the Great Depression struck, and the T&NO quickly attracted desperate, out-of-work men who became the hobos of legend. It wasn't simply that the jobless saw the mobility of train-hopping as a means to scour the countryside for work—somehow the railway itself, with its noise and motion and productivity, offered an illusion of hope.

Boosters of the James Bay extension now found a new argument for their cause. Why not make that illusion into something real? Governments were going to be called upon to create make-work projects to employ the jobless anyway. Why not employ them to build a railway that might someday net the province an actual profit?

Thus, while railway building elsewhere was halted by the Depression, it was the Depression that actually got the route to James Bay built. The line was finished in 1932; the name for the terminus and future "port," Moosonee, was taken from a Cree word meaning "at the Moose."

The railway and the tiny new town settled back to await the miracle that would enable the extension to pay for itself as silver and gold had done for the main section of the line. The name of the railway was changed to the Ontario Northland in 1946 to herald its role in the realization of the Canadian dream. While the original southern section continued to earn its way and the nickname "Ontario's Development Road," the link to Moosonee looked as if it would be lucky to do as well as the CN's *Skeena* route to Prince Rupert, or the eastern section of the National Transcontinental.

Recently, an economic boomlet has shown signs of making the line productive, and this time it's not silver, gold, or timber that has been the impetus. It's waterpower, hydro generation on the rivers along the route of the *Polar Bear*—Canada's most recently realized and vastest source of wealth. The trains of the Ontario Northland support the construction, supply, maintenance, and manning of the power plants. Millionaires aren't being made here, but a thriving local economy that primarily benefits native people has developed. And the passenger train is nothing like those underutilized routes preserved by the federal government as "essential routes" to remote regions elsewhere. The *Polar Bear Express*, even the *Little Bear* in the off-season, is packed with paying passengers.

For a while out of Cochrane, we roll through clay belt farm country, and then suddenly the traces of people disappear and it's hard-core Great Shield terrain. By noon, we're into a new milieu entirely, gentle canyons cradling rivers running straight north—the approach to James Bay.

Enjoying a hot dog in the cafeteria car at Fraserdale, the only stop listed on the timetable, I note with satisfaction the end of the highway north from Cochrane. From here on it's nothing but rail.

Beyond Fraserdale, we are passing through dense wilderness when suddenly the train stops in a man's front yard. Out of the woods emerges a well-watered lawn where a house faces the tracks; there is no road, no garage, and no vehicles. There is a beautifully maintained vegetable garden and a trellis—and strikingly vivid stuffed figures of a man and woman and two dogs facing the tracks. The real man who has just detrained waves and then embraces his real wife who has come out into the yard to meet him while a real dog bounds about. Fifty yards beyond their yard we are in deep wilderness again.

I'm resisting the urge to drift off into a nap—for fear of missing any more sights like the wilderness lawn—but the day is November gray, and the train is so cozy and warm that I succumb. After a time, I awake to the sound of barking dogs. It's a stop at Moose River, just a little clapboard shelter and a few humble dwellings tucked into the trees beyond a small clearing. Outside it's like a holiday; native families come down woodsy paths to meet loved ones getting off the train. Moms, dads, and grandparents exchange hugs, and swarms of children and dogs romp.

A teenage girl and her mother board and join the handsome Cree family I noticed earlier. I follow the father and one of the teen girls to the cafeteria car, which is jumping with sociability by this afternoon hour. At some tables native kids huddle over Cokes and pizza or hot dogs and giggle. At others married couples guzzle beer and carry on boisterous conversation. There are a few single guys, but generally everyone on this train seems to be part of a family.

It's crowded enough that, after ordering a Coke, I can sit down with the father and his daughter without seeming pushy. His name is Joe, but he asks me not to print his family's name. No particular reason, just Cree humility. If his friends in Moosonee ever read my book and saw his name, he would be accused of seeking publicity or being a show-off.

And there is a good chance his friends would read the book. Many of the families of his acquaintance have college-educated members, and being well read is highly valued. His daughter is a sophomore at the University of Toronto.

Joe confirms what the conductor has told me about the young natives on this train. "They should call this the college train. It would make more sense, since it doesn't go near any polar bears, but it sure carries a lot of college students," and he adds with pride, "Cree college students."

Joe works for the railway as a section foreman. His family doesn't all live in Moosonee anymore, but anytime someone is coming home from somewhere, as his daughter is now, that's where they all gather. That's why his family's contingent on this train has been growing with every stop as we approach Moosonee.

As delicately as I can, I make the observation that the native people riding this train don't conform to the modern image of a people struggling not very successfully in a world that cares little about them.

"It's not like this everywhere, you know," Joe confides. "There are Cree and Chippewa out west in Manitoba who are really hurting. But here in northern Ontario, we do all right. There's work, either for the hydro companies or the railway, or as outfitters, pilots, guides, and things like that. And our people are better educated. We have managers, teachers, professionals, even a few capitalists. But even here I could show you places of hopelessness and anger."

I wonder why it is better for native people here. He isn't anxious to give the provincial government too much credit, though again he compares it favorably with Manitoba. "Many tribes have to choose between their ancestral homelands and finding decent work. Here we can have it both ways. So our families stay together, we keep our identity, and people go for things like college educations."

I ask him what he thinks of the quarrel over Quebec and Meech Lake, and he frowns.

"Quebec 'a distinct society,' 'English and French, the two found-ing peoples,' eh? Well, what the hell are the Cree, the Chippewa, the Inuit? Let me tell you, if that thing passes, you're going to hear a lot more about distinct societies in Canada. All this effort to set things right with the French. What about us?"

The train has stopped at several spots not listed on the timeta-ble, but soon we halt at a place where there is no shelter, no clearing, no sign that this is a place where anyone would expect to catch the train. I head toward the front of the train where I can get a look at what's happening, and here I find four hunters and two trainmen lugging a huge moose carcass into the baggage car. I'm surprised to find the car already contains two other carcasses, several ice coolers full of fish, piles of camping and canoeing gear, and a wire-and-wood cage holding a beautiful malamute. In conver-sation with the hunters and the conductor, I learn that this routine is not uncommon.

Sportsmen come up on the train from Toronto with a "portage" at Cochrane (the transfer of their baggage—canoes, outboards, camp stoves, tarps, coolers, lamps, fuel, and guns) from the *Northland* to the *Polar Bear*. Some are only after fish, dropped off by the train in fishermen's heaven, where they need only to hang a coat on a stick by the tracks at a river crossing to stop the train and bring home their catch (sturgeon, pike, bass, walleyes, and trout). They usually come for outings of three to fourteen days and, according to the vehement testimony of the conductor and the two hunters, most of them are activist conservationists. "We're not like your airplane hunters, who land on the lakes, raise hell with the local herds or fish or what have you, and then they're gone leaving their trash behind. Sportsmen who come in by the railway and then hike or canoe themselves the rest of the way really are different. We don't come here for the trophies or the photos, we come here for the experience."

At Moosonee station, there is a great scramble for taxis, some-thing I didn't expect at a place not connected by road to anyplace else. I have no idea how big the town is, nor how far my hotel is from the station, so I join the rush and find myself sharing a ride with a salt-and-pepper-whiskered academic with a handwoven satchel, a beret, knickers, and a cane. Bert Gilbert is a retired visual arts professor from the University of British Columbia who is traveling all over Canada by train while he still can. Our taxi is a banged-up old Ford driven by a young Cree, who drives just like any New York cabbie. We roar off down the dirt street, which is the main drag in

Moosonee, so fast that I catch only a blur of a passing town that looks like something from a daguerreotype of the old frontier. We slide around a corner and off to our right we can see the Moose River, crisscrossed by huge motor-powered freight canoes. The taxi screeches to a halt, deposits us in front of the Polar Bear Lodge, and tears off down the road.

The hotel is plain, but it is warm and friendly. There's a dining room, the only place in town that can serve alcohol. Our rooms are Spartan and small but clean and quiet. My window overlooks the public dock on the river.

After settling in, Bert and I venture out to explore the town on foot before dinner. At the dock, we discover that a canoe ride to Moose Factory on one of the many islands in the river delta runs $5 a person. These aren't just for tourists; the canoes perform the same role within the island communities as mass transit in cities. There are also a couple of fishing boats and a police boat circling like a water-borne squad car. You can't see Moose Factory or any of the little native settlements on the islands, which are densely forested with firs and now-leafless northern deciduous trees, but the motor-canoe traffic testifies to their presence. Riders huddle wrapped in slickers or blankets—they look cold.

We hike down Ferguson Street behind the Polar Bear Lodge, past a gas station and a general store. Many of the houses are built of logs. Sled dogs and snowmobiles are parked in driveways, even though there is no snow today.

Emerging onto First Street, the main road we came in on before, we are almost run over by a car driven by a boy who can't be more than ten years old. We find out later that driver's licenses are not required in Moosonee, which has no road connections to the outside world. There are no traffic laws either, besides the orders of the ever-present Ontario Provincial Police. All the cars here have been brought in by rail and serve a purely local transportation function. They seem to be in various states of disrepair.

The prospect down First Street toward the railway station screeches with cognitive dissonance. The dirt street, with no sidewalks or even boardwalks, and the architecture of the establishments along it—several groceries, an HBC store, a lawyer's office, a church, a clinic, the police station, the provincial liquor outlet, a couple of diners or luncheonettes—look pioneer, American wild west. The presence of mostly Indians is consistent, but their dress and demeanor are strictly contemporary. On every corner and around the entrances to the stores and diners, knots of brightly dressed teens congregate, just like their counterparts in any mall in North America. Out in the street those lucky enough to have access to cars or ATVs, or, better yet, motorcycles, attract the envious attention of their pedestrian peers on the corners. One young fellow zips up and down the street with a long-haired honey on the back of his unmuffled Kawasaki. As he passes all eyes follow him. On this Friday night, he is king of the street.

The next largest contingent on the street is OPP cops. They're everywhere, all acting alert and ready, as if expecting imminent trouble. But when I ask a cop, he says there's no specific problem expected tonight. This is just their usual stance in these remote communities on weekend evenings. "Alcohol is the biggest problem, especially among young Indians." The province keeps the lid on with severe restrictions: no bars, no public consumption. Liquor can be bought in the provincial store but must be consumed indoors, at home.

Back at the Polar Bear Lodge, Bert and I sit down for dinner. The food is rather bland, and Bert is a quiet, deliberate eater. The restaurant fills up during our meal and, in contrast to First Street, the faces are all white. Drinks are ordered and wine is poured. Here the white population has a wet refuge that somehow dodges the local alcohol restrictions.

Bert goes off to bed early, and I'm sipping a cup of coffee when a fellow sitting with two young women at a table by the window asks me to join them. Apparently I have become a bit of a celebrity, "a writer come to Moosonee." The group at the table can't remember that ever happening before, but they think it's overdue. Someone should write about this place.

The guy is Dan and his girlfriend with the short sandy hair is Danna. The other young woman, whom I didn't recognize at first because she previously had her long dark hair tied back in a severe bun, is the waitress who worked my table during dinner. Her name is Fyffe Hunting, and thus she takes the prize for best name of the entire Canadian odyssey.

Dan has two bottles of good red wine and asks what we should toast. Danna proposes her reunion with her old Toronto school buddy. Fyffe has fled her family's affluent life in Toronto for a "place where you can hear yourself think." Danna, heir to a small family fortune and visiting Fyffe, is considering doing the same. Then they ask me for a toast. I suggest the approaching end of my seventeen-thousand-mile journey through Canada. They think that's just great—long journeys and reunions, an authentic Canadian tableau. The wine warms us and I'm grateful to find this little group that welcomes me so heartily this far from home.

But then the manager, Fyffe's boss, tells us he has to close up. Dan and Danna don't mind having the excuse to head back to their bedroom, from which they do not plan to emerge for the rest of the evening. When they're gone, Fyffe asks if I would like to witness a rare occasion in Moosonee. Tonight there is a party, the Oktoberfest, one of several annual affairs where the liquor rules are suspended for a special occasion. There will be a D.J., dancing, and lots of people.

In half an hour, her friends come by in a pickup truck and four of us squeeze into the cab and head for the James Bay Education Center, where the dance is to be held in the cafeteria. Inside, the scene reminds me of a high school mixer. A few crepe streamers, some Oktoberfest posters on the painted cinderblock walls, cafeteria tables bunched at one end of the room to leave a good space for dancers in the center. Beer is served at the kitchen windows, where school lunches are normally distributed. You have to buy tickets for $2 per beer at a separate table. These arrangements and the $15 cover price are required by law and again reflect the official concern about public alcohol consumption in "Indian country."

Yet there are few natives at tonight's Oktoberfest. Fyffe leads me to a group at one table that includes a woman whose husband is a government official and who is part Cree herself. A tall, black-haired woman wearing high heels and a tight miniskirt, the only such outfit in the place (everybody else wears pants), is also rumored to be part Indian, but the scene is overwhelmingly white in a town where earlier today the main drag was overwhelmingly native.

Fyffe tells me that after the dance there will be a fight in the parking lot. "Bad-guy Indians" and "bad-guy whites" will use the dance as an excuse to have a rumble.

But such concerns are quickly forgotten. The keg beer sold at the cafeteria counter flows freely and soon it's a grand party—everyone dances, everyone has stories of family to talk about, and everyone wants to talk to newcomers like me and the young woman in the short dress.

Her name is Kim, and she is a new teacher at the local school. She is from Toronto, where her father is an assimilated Huron Indian, and she is mortified that she has dressed wrong. It's her first social outing in Moosonee and she dressed the way she would have going out in Toronto. She concedes that she has a lot to learn here in Moosonee.

During a break in the dancing, Fyffe wants to make sure I understand why so many people are so happy to live in this remote place. "It's not escape," she argues, "but search." She says that in a way it's unlucky that my stop here coincides with the Oktoberfest. It's antithetical to what people live here for and only happens to satisfy a need to do occasionally what people back in the populated country do. "In Moosonee you can live in a community of people, cops, doctors, grocers—basic survival stuff like that—where it's not hard to see what life is like without any of those things. There's wilderness all around, and Indians who could carry on here if all the civilized stuff suddenly disappeared."

"So why is that a good thing?" I press.

"You learn to pay better attention to your world. I know more about the woods surrounding Moosonee than I ever did about the woods behind my family's suburban house outside Toronto. And the same thing is true with people. I know more about the people I hang out with here than I ever did about friends back home. Somehow when you come here and simplify life enough, it makes a lot more sense."

I ask if she ever heard of a nineteenth-century American writer named Henry David Thoreau. She hasn't. I describe the main points of *Walden*, the belief that in the woods you can learn to live deliberately, that you can discover enough joy in performing basic survival tasks to be happy, that elements of nature provide metaphors that illuminate the most complex workings of the mind, and that the usual role of human society is to cut man off from this natural fount of wisdom.

Fyffe is impressed, not by my ability to recount quotes, but by Thoreau—a first encounter with the cutting edge of great thought. She says that this man wrote about why people come to Moosonee. Maybe he came here himself. With the French name, he must be Canadian, not American. When I tell her that we Americans teach our children in school that Thoreau's thought is part of their heritage, she scoffs. "You gotta be kidding. From what you've told me, that man is about everything that America isn't. Americans never stand still long enough to appreciate the mysteries of the north. But he does sound like a Canadian—a Canadian who can put into words what a lot of us feel."

Afterward, there is no sign of the impending rumble in the parking lot, but there are bright green and scarlet streaks rippling in the blackness—northern lights—and several of us revelers from the Polar Bear silently walk back to our lodgings. With no street-lamps and only a dim glow from an occasional window, I feel a bit disoriented with darkness immediately around our shuffling feet and the crazy tilting planes of color up above. It seems as if there are unseen cobwebs drifting across my face and settling coolly under my collar. Then we round a corner into the glow of a solitary streetlamp and suddenly the light reveals perfect snowflakes drifting down from the cloudless, starry, auroraed sky. I stop and stand absolutely still. "Where does the snow come from—there are no clouds?" I ask Fyffe.

"No one's ever been able to tell me," she says. "But it happens every once in a while—just a mystery of the north."

At the lodge, I tell Fyffe that I have to catch the train in the morning and then head for my room and tumble into bed. It's going to be a great night for sleeping with the image of the cloudless snowfall so fresh. Just as I'm drifting off, a rhythmical sound on the other side of the wall disrupts me—a squeaking bed and rising gasps of passion; I hadn't noticed earlier how thin the walls are here. It's impossible to ignore and I hear it all, right down to the striking of the match for the postcoital cigarette. Just when I begin to settle down enough to go to sleep it starts again, now in the room on the other side, beyond the foot of my bed. This time I am spared the breathing of the participants, but the rocking of the bed is unmistakable. I think of my wife in New Hampshire, where it's still warm enough that she's probably wearing shorts and sleeveless blouses. I finally put myself to sleep repeating the absurd phrase, almost like a mantra, "Down south in New Hampshire."

Bang, bang, bang. I am roughly awakened from fitful sleep by a pounding on my door. The light at the window is still weak. "Your train goes in twenty minutes." I recognize Fyffe's voice. It's a foggy scramble to rise and get my things together to depart. Fyffe drives me, Dan, and Danna to the station through an early morning frosty fog. I tell them all about the disturbances to my sleep last night. Dan and Danna disavow responsibility. Fyffe laughs that the Polar Bear Lodge is renowned for its squeaky beds—"It's one of those facts of life that you face head-on in the wilderness."

I ride with Dan and Danna back to Cochrane and then Toronto. En route we encounter a real blizzard, the year's first. There's nothing but a white void outside the windows. During the ride Danna deliberates whether she really wants to move to Moosonee. Fyffe has told her this morning about the wonderful author I was quoting last night. She asks me to quote Thoreau some more. In her travel notebook, she writes in huge flowing red letters, "I went to the woods because I wished to live deliberately."

At Cochrane the snow is a foot deep. It has come so suddenly that the highway and airport are closed, but our train connection to Toronto, the *Northland* from Kapuskasing, now packed with travelers, pushes through the snow right on time. We head back to the city on a train blasting its way through the drifts while drivers and flyers sit stranded all across the north.

13

Trouble on the Tracks

SUDBURY TO WINNIPEG
ON THE *CONTINENTAL*

I'VE been in Sudbury before, back at the start of my journey. My train from Toronto, the *Canadian*, has arrived here on time, so those continuing west to Winnipeg on the *Canadian* have an hour to kill while they wait for the tardy connecting train from Montreal. Tonight I'm going to Winnipeg via the CN's *Continental* route, the northern line over parts of the old National Transcontinental and the Canadian Northern through the heart of the Great Shield.

If you choose that route to the west, you are bused from the Sudbury station to the nearby town of Capreol, where you board the CN train. The bus and the train will hold for the connection from Montreal, as the *Canadian* must do, but we don't know how long, so for a while I hang out at Sudbury station with acquaintances I made on the ride up from Toronto, waiting for an announcement.

One of these fellows is Olivar Ilovar, a Yugoslavian American from Brooklyn, a big good-natured man with bushy black hair and a thick black moustache. Oli is traveling because he has been thrown out of his house by his wife—"too much of this, not enough of that." Since he is between jobs and has a little money, he figured, "What the hell. If I'm going to go through the shit of a separation and maybe a divorce, then I might as well do something crazy I've always wanted to do—like cruise Canada by train." Besides the fact that Oli is a great traveling companion, his first-generation American status almost makes him one of the international voyageurs, who have fascinated me throughout these travels.

Oli asks me, "What do you do in a place like this when you're waiting for a late train?" I point to the Ledo Hotel across the street and Oli groans that it looks like the kind of place he came to Canada to get away from. I tell him it's like lobster—the outside is pretty ugly, but the stuff inside is succulent.

"Okay, let's go." But then comes the announcement calling for riders of the *Continental* train to board the VIA bus that has just pulled into the parking lot. The Montreal connection is going to be late enough that the *Continental* is not going to wait for it.

So it's *au revoir* to Oli, who is booked on the *Canadian*. He has a VIA Railpass and doesn't know where he'll go after he hits Winnipeg. I suggest Churchill, my eventual destination. Maybe we can find some polar bears. Oli is intrigued but more interested in testing the waters as a newly single male and cold Churchill doesn't seem like fertile territory. He heads across the street to find out why I recommend the Ledo and I board the bus for Capreol.

It's a short ride and there is only a handful of passengers. I can see the red lights on the towering Inco smelter stack at Sudbury all the way to Capreol. Up the bank from the parking lot at the Capreol station, a tiny train awaits us—just an F-7 diesel, a weird combination baggage and sleeper car and one coach with a takeout counter. That's it for nearly a thousand miles to Winnipeg. I board feeling envious of Oli and the sumptuous environment of the big train he will ride tonight. But as my little train speeds out of Capreol over the fast track of modern CN's main line, I console myself with the thought that I should be in Winnipeg when I'm supposed to, while Oli and riders of the *Canadian* appear to have one hell of a delay to face.

We start out with only a few passengers—three native mothers with babies, a pair of backpacking European girls and half a dozen voyageur guys vying for their attention, and three older fellows who just ride and read without talking to anyone. The conductor says that we will pick up a lot more passengers as the train rolls along, especially during the day tomorrow. This train serves almost a commuter function between the string of northern Ontario communities that lie along its route. We'll see lots of people get on, ride for an hour, and get off.

Outside I can see snowflakes whipping by the coach windows. I'm unusually sleepy tonight, so I head off to my roomette in the strange baggage-sleeper car. It's actually an old crew car, left over from the days when long-distance trains provided separate sleeping facilities for employees working the whole run. I drift off to sleep to the pleasant sounds of the tracks rattling steady and fast beneath the car.

After the late night in Moosonee and my layover in Toronto, I sleep in. I wake in the late morning to the blue-white light of a cloudy, snowy morning flooding my compartment. The track rattle continues at almost the same rhythm I felt as I fell asleep last night, maybe a hair slower. I feel great, rarely have I slept so well on an overnight train, almost as if the train had spent much of the night parked in a station or on a siding with no rocking motion to exercise my body in sleep.

The timetable says we should be approaching a place called Ferland, but as the train slows for a stop, the sign I see outside my window reads HILLSPORT. According to the timetable, we should have been here over four hours ago.

It's true. The conductor comes by my room with the bad news that we are way behind schedule. We sat for half the night waiting for work crews to make emergency repairs to a bridge that had been damaged by a freight derailment earlier in the day. There is a good chance that I will miss my connecting train to my ultimate goal of Churchill, Manitoba, way up north in the tundra on Hudson Bay.

All day long the *Continental* winds through the undulating rocks and meandering lakes of northern Ontario shield country. I don't know if it's the touch of snow, or a unique texture to this land, but this ride seems particularly picturesque, despite the fact that by now I should have had more than my fill of shield terrain. There are countless lakes tucked into the most fascinating crannies in the granite and bush forest. For the first time I notice that the lake color varies considerably, from deep blue, to aqua, to pea green, to rusty brown. I speculate that it's a question of depth, since the green and brown lakes often have dead trees sticking out of them.

Part of the appeal of the ride is the occasional isolated work of the hand of man, an abandoned sawmill, a white church on a far shore, a fishing boat on an otherwise deserted lake, a dirt level crossing, the trusses of railway bridges, a yellow church with a teepee nearby, tiny clusters of log cabins, a wilderness neighborhood of modern houses, and finally the striking Tudor-style station at Sioux Lookout, a town of some three thousand with a Main Street and cars and stores with neon signs.

The route of the *Continental* spans what was once known as the "thousand-mile gap" across the northern Great Shield between the settled regions of the east and Winnipeg. By the turn of the century, when railways were proliferating wildly in both the east and the west, the gap had been bridged only once, by the CPR along the shore of Lake Superior. It wasn't just the difficulty of construction that made the gap so intimidating to railway builders. It was the likelihood that the vast wasteland would never generate any business along the way. In the wheatfields of the prairies, competing transcontinental lines running through different localities could pay for themselves with shipment of local produce, but in the empty miles north of Superior the building of two more competing transcontinental routes was little short of madness. Yet in the years between 1908 and 1915, when the rest of the Western world was embarking on a different kind of insanity, this is what Canadians were busy doing.

I related earlier the story of how the Laurier government came to be entangled with the competing transcontinental schemes of Mackenzie and Mann's Canadian Northern and the Grand Trunk Railway (GTR), GTR President Hays's disastrous bluff leading to the NTR project, and the eventual government acquiescence in the construction of both lines. Once the two projects were under way, the competing outfits pursued very different theories of eventual success.

Mackenzie and Mann were daring opportunists operating on the principle that their aggressive acquisition and construction campaigns would create conditions from which they could somehow profit. With little concern for what it would take after construction was completed to guarantee successful operation of a line in competition with two other railways, they cobbled together a long, meandering route built to low construction standards.

No matter how much Mann and Mackenzie were loved in Manitoba for breaking the Canadian Pacific monopoly, Laurier had no intention of dealing with men he viewed as flim-flam operators. If the government was going to be partners in a transcontinental project, it would be with the GTR. For its part, the GTR simply wanted to buy out Mackenzie and Mann, not just the gap but the whole system. Once Hayes saw that his bluff to build to the Pacific had doubly misfired, failing to intimidate Mann and Mackenzie and inciting the government to offer partnership in making good on the pledge, he began the kind of speculation that Mann and Mackenzie never indulged in. Just what would it take to make a third route across the gap competitive enough to be viable?

First, it would have to be the fastest and capable of carrying the most tonnage. Thus the planners drew a line on the map between Winnipeg and the Maritimes and came up with the nearly arrow-straight National Transcontinental route across the shield country of Ontario and Quebec. By bypassing not only the Lake Superior ports but also Toronto and Montreal, they were making a daring and desperate gamble—that there would be enough prairie grain shipments bound for Quebec or Maritime ports to support a railway with little internal traffic over a nearly two-thousand-mile (counting the eastern section) run. This bet relied on the fatal assumption that no cheaper means of getting grain out of the midwest would appear.

In the spring of 1905 surveyors began laying out the route. Until the rails began to advance, their provisions moved the old-fashioned way—by canoe up tortuous rivers. In the twentieth century, there were fewer men with the skill to execute these journeys without mishap.

Many of the men were French-Canadians with dim memories of the skills of their ancestor voyageurs. In the early days of railway building, the priests of Quebec had discouraged French-Canadians from working on the railways in a foolish attempt to protect them from knowledge of the world and keep them home in their parishes. Out west, William Van Horne and other superintendents of the CPR had such a jaundiced view of French-Canadian workmen that relatively few ever worked on the pioneering railways. As a result, what might have provided a link of continuity between the voyageurs and the French-Canadian railway builders of the twentieth century was abrogated by prejudice and the Church.

Parties forced to fend for themselves for a time in the wilderness fared poorly. Swollen spring streams or fires, often started by the packers themselves, cut them off from their destinations and/or their embarkation points. Men had lost the ability to cope with the swarms of blackflies and flesh-eating moose flies that could turn a white shirt red with blood in a few minutes, and so worked with their skin lathered in a hellish mixture of tar and grease. And the modern assumption that the best thing to do with an injured or sick person is to evacuate him often backfired when the rigors of removal wasted a victim who might have survived with proper care in the bush.

Many quit the work as soon as they could, but of those who stuck to it, surprisingly few expressed frustration in their field notes or journals. Instead they wrote of the excitement of being part of a pioneer experience in modern times, of their undoubted confidence that these lands would soon be conquered by settlers as had the western lands in the days of the Pledge of the Twenty, of a patriotic feeling of identity, and strange intimations of a spiritual presence in the wilderness. In this work they were participating in the fundamental Canadian experience—the conquest of the north.

By 1915, both the NTR and the Canadian Northern routes were complete, but then the war brought down the financial roof. The war, by itself, probably would have doomed the financially shaky Canadian Northern, but before the NTR, the Grand Trunk Railway was fiscally sound. Because of the extraordinarily high standards of construction called for (no curves greater than four degrees, no grades greater than .4 percent, no wooden trestles or bridges whatsoever), the NTR was a bottomless hole into which the GTR poured more money than its government partnership could begin to offset. Costs had exceeded estimates by 200 percent, and new shipping facilities on the Great Lakes and at Montreal promised a cheaper water route for grain. By the close of the war the end was in sight for the GTR, and by 1923 both the Canadian Northern and the GTR were gone, casualties of the race to build across the gap.

For a while Canadian National President Henry Thornton continued both routes but eventually moved to consolidate the advantages of each. Thus evolved the main line of the CN over which I am traveling and which probably should have been the only route built across the gap in the first place. It has thrived as a competitor with the CPR for what cannot be shipped cheaply by water, but the harsh lands along the route have never been settled and developed as they have been in the east and the west. Today Canada's main artery of transportation still runs through country that has changed little since the days when surveyors first cursed it.

At Sioux Lookout we stop for a crew change and I step off for a breath of northern fresh air and the opportunity to meet the new conductor. On the platform, I spot the new guy standing with an old Ojibway by the station bell. The conductor is a pretty good lookalike for Robert Redford. The Ojibway, a man named Big John, has been stationmaster here for twenty years. The new conductor, Dennis Huska, says that Big John has rung the bell for every single train that has passed through here during those years. "He's the only thing around here that's always on time."

When it's time to go, Dennis gives Big John a little salute and then Big John puffs up his chest, solemnly approaches the bell rope and begins a rhythmical yanking—ca-lang, clang, clang, ca-lang. . . . People passing on the street respond to the bell and pause to watch the train pull out. Big John keeps pumping on the rope, even after we have boarded and begun to roll away from his station.

On board, I ride with Dennis, who is pleased to share with me the lore of his train. Though the route is the main line of the CN, the remote country it passes through makes the passenger run "lively." Because of the clay belt, the north-south highway, and Ontario Northland Railway connections to Toronto, the country I recently visited around Cochrane is settled and civilized. Ironically, here where the railway thrives as the national main line, the country we pass through is wilder and more untamed.

"There's a myth you know, of railways having a civilizing influence over the country they pass through. But that only works where the country attracts settlers. It never worked out that way here," Dennis explains. Freights just highball through without stopping except for refueling. Sioux Lookout, which is no metropolis, is the only community of any size along the route. "We got regular riders here who are characters right out of the old frontier. You may meet some of them."

Another trainman passes by in the aisle and Dennis yanks on his sleeve and asks him to join us and fill me in about the rough characters who ride this train. Bill Hoole says it's not just the lack of big communities that has kept this country relatively lawless, by Canadian standards. "You've probably heard about Al Capone using Moose Jaw out west as his hideaway. Well, there were a lot of lesser American gangsters who set up hideouts with the Ojibway Indians in this country during the twenties and thirties. They took up with

Ojibway women, and to this day, their half-breed descendants are clustered in little communities hereabouts. A few of 'em seem to have inherited an outlaw gene."

Some of these folks aren't criminal, they're just strange—like the one-eyed, one-legged Tommy Quist who has been run over by the train twice. "He gets on and jokes with us, 'Hey, you guys ain't got me yet.'"

Then there's a character named Sinclair who has a nasty habit of reaching for the bowie knife he wears in his belt whenever he finds himself in a situation that confuses him.

But Dennis and Bill agree that their strangest rider is a fellow they call the "Rifleman," a member of a Jukes-like clan descended from a gangster and an Ojibway woman. Despite the lack of any convictions, he is widely believed to have killed seven men. The man has become such a legend that Dennis and Bill refuse to vouch for the veracity of any of the stories about him. Since everyone in the territory believes them to be true, it doesn't matter whether they are or not when it comes to dealing with this fellow.

Supposedly, he shot his father in bed and then his brother-in-law and five other guys who crossed him. "He crawls into a house through a back window, does his work, and gets out without leaving enough evidence for a jury," says Bill.

Dennis wasn't always a railway conductor. He used to work for the Hudson's Bay Company buying furs, "the second-oldest profession in the world," based at Norway House and Trout Lake. Because of the growing worldwide distaste for the fur trade, the value of most pelts has declined since he was in the business. The exceptions are of course those of rare species, lynx in particular, which has gone from $10 a pelt to over $400.

There's a trapper riding the train now, and Dennis leads me to the front of the coach to introduce me. Bill Zarecki lives in Sioux Lookout and takes the train out to jumping-off points for his trap lines. He might be in his sixties, though it's hard to tell whether he is a well-preserved older man or a wilderness-bitten younger one. Whatever his age, he is a leathery, rugged fellow with a voice like sandpaper. He explains to me how the trapping business works in modern times.

First you have to get a license to work a certain territory. Most of the land out here is public—frontier. There are no private property owners except a few forest products companies, and even they no longer bother to actually own the land they work. They acquire rights to harvest timber and move on.

But it's not a wide-open opportunity for newcomers. Most of the territories are licensed to individual trappers whose rights are exclusive. Trappers tend to be in the business for life, so openings of license rights to territories are rare.

Once you have your territory, you go to work cutting your trails and stocking your equipment caches. There's no way that a trapper can carry all of the necessary equipment every time he goes out, so he has to establish sites where he buries equipment for safekeeping. And on long lines, where his trek will involve overnights, he must build cabins for shelter during the cold months, which are often the best trapping seasons.

A former CN conductor, Bill has worked his territory largely as a hobby for forty years and has accumulated over ninety traps, four cabins, and a ton of other gear out over his lines. Today he is returning from Ghost River, just in from checking trap lines that he wants to use this winter. He hacked through the growth over his trail and dug up and checked his equipment, always hoping to find lots of rust on his traps. "It neutralizes the human scent." He says trapping gets harder for him every year, but he can't afford to sell his license yet. When he does, the license, his territory, and equipment, minus the cabins, should fetch about $7,000.

I ask if the old story about trapped animals gnawing their legs off is true. "Yep, though often you find just a leg bone in a trap because something else ate the animal it belonged to." But Bill can confirm the story because he has trapped animals that had already gnawed off one leg. "Just another case of how slow learners don't survive," he chuckles. Trapping is not for the squeamish. Bill has found trapped animals that have ripped their bellies and eaten their own entrails. Bill insists you can see all kinds of grisly things in the north woods that have nothing to do with trapping. "The animals are a hell of a lot more unkind to each other than trappers are to them."

There is one trapping practice in particular which Bill and Dennis agree is beyond the pale of civilized trappers, because the cruelty of it shows in scuffs and welts on the pelt and lowers its value. It's called snaring, and it's a favorite of some of the tribes hereabouts. Loops of fine wire or nylon line are hung up to entangle animals working through their paths. Larger animals like moose get their horns tangled in it; smaller ones get their limbs and claws hooked. Since the snare doesn't deal any immediate trauma of bleeding wounds or broken bones as does a steel trap, it takes much longer for the animal to die. He usually thrashes himself till he dies of self-inflicted injuries, exhaustion, or a burst heart. "But always you have a damaged pelt. That's the only sensible measure of cruelty in this country, when the thing you're after—the thing you need for your own survival, which is the reason you do these things to the animals—when that thing has little value because of the method you used."

The car is lively with little knots of passengers engaged in a variety of conversations as the afternoon rolls on. All seem to involve north woods inhabitants enlightening sojourners like myself from down south. I hear a man behind me proclaim that his hometown of Armstrong "isn't the asshole of the earth, but you can see it from there." A Cree man is explaining to a visiting fisherman that sled dogs are different from Fido back home. "The only kindness they know is someone throwing them a frozen fish or kicking them out of the way. You don't reach out to pat them or you lose your hand."

And then, at a little place called Allanwater Bridge, the train stops, a grim-looking man gets on, and all conversation ceases. As the man picks out a seat, his coal-black eyes dart about, and the tawny skin of his face is tight with muscular tension underneath. His hair is short and graying under a baseball cap and he wears a gray windbreaker. He is not a big man, but he exudes an aura of danger.

He tentatively sits but doesn't settle in, and when another passenger returns from the bathroom to sit in the seat in front of him, he nervously gets up and moves to another seat where there is nobody immediately in front of or behind him.

When the train gets under way, and the track rattle takes some of the edge off the unnatural silence, Dennis whistles, "Jeezus, he is tightly wound today." And then he leans over to me and whispers, "The Rifleman."

Another furtive man we didn't notice before now emerges from the vestibule and stonily sits down beside him without saying a word. They both stare straight ahead.

"And Sinclair. Jeezus, we got the squirrels today."

Now Dennis assumes a posture I haven't seen on him before. When he stands up to collect tickets, he draws himself up taller, stiffer, and forms a thin smile of authority before stopping at the seats of the new arrivals and saying firmly, "How are ya today, tickets please." The fellows produce the monetary equivalent quickly and I imagine that I detect a slight bodily relaxation and relief in Dennis's stance. "Have a good one," he says, and heads back to the takeout counter.

The two ride one stop and then get off—without speaking a word to each other or anyone else—at a place called Savant Lake. I catch up with Dennis at the takeout counter, where he is having a cup of coffee. "We give guys like them a lot of space," says Dennis. "You know, we don't even have any weapons on these trains."

I ask if he thinks the Rifleman and Sinclair were armed today. "I don't know, but you saw how uptight they were. They get like that when they're up to no good. And they're out of their territory. We usually pick them up further east. Shit's gonna hit the fan back there at Savant Lake tonight."

Dennis invites me to take a ride with the engineers in the cab, an invitation I never turn down. I've made this trek through the engine room of diesels several times, but I never get used to the intimidating violence of the sixteen-cylinder engine just a few inches away from my ears, even when the engineer has it throttled back for our passage. In the cab, engineers Bob Town and John Sutherland invite me to sit in the fireman's seat and Dennis hangs around for a few miles.

Dennis tells them that we had "some of our strange riders" today. Bob says to me, "Has he been telling you all that rough stuff about our local outlaws? You oughta tell him some of the good stories about our run."

So before heading back to the coach Dennis tells me one last story. His train was headed east one summer and he stopped to unload six college guys and their canoes for a trip up the Sturgeon River route. Twenty miles down the run, the train stopped at a bridge over another leg of the canoe route where he encountered exactly six attractive college girls canoeing in the other direction. He told them about the guys headed their way and vouched for their good character and the girls giggled, "Right on." When the train pulled out the girls were paddling frantically with squeals of delight in the direction of the oncoming guys.

"When we came back west two days later, we picked up the guys at the end of their trip. They swore on their mother's honor that they had met up with the girls, that they sorted themselves out and paired up, and that night, to a man, they all got laid all night long somewhere out in the wilderness."

Bob says that the mating instinct is a powerful thing in the wilderness. When the railway switched from steam to diesels, there was a terrible slaughter of female moose on the tracks. It was the air-driven horns—the tone exactly mimicked the sound of the moose mating call. It took several experiments with horns of different timbres before the carnage was stopped.

Today's CN main line through the northern shield country is a marvel of railway engineering, and Bob and John are happy to show it off. They show me a number of places where you can see the cuts of the original line peeling off into the bush in spots where the route has been straightened or the curves opened. Though straightaways are rare, somehow the length of this winding route is only sixty miles more than a ruler line drawn on a map from Longlac to Winnipeg—lots of little curves, no major meanderings. It is rare to ride over a stretch of track that isn't either in a cut or on a fill; bridges are incredibly frequent.

On most North American railways with this kind of ruggedness, the maximum speed would be thirty miles per hour, or at tops forty, yet despite several slow orders, we barrel along at over fifty, sometimes seventy. It makes the ride, especially in the rumbling stiff-springed engine, a bit like one at an amusement park. We plunge blindly into curving cuts and over hilltop crests, where we can see nothing of what might lie out on the track ahead.

"This is Canada's main line of transportation," says Bob. "The CPR makes a big deal about carrying a third of the nation's rail transport, but the fact is, we carry most of the rest, over half of all rail transport nationwide. And one of the busiest routes in the system is this stretch right here. Everything moves fast through here."

When the dispatching system works properly, as it does 99 percent of the time, the operations are perfectly safe. But when there is a breakdown of some sort in communications, the winding route of the *Continental*, where engineers have little opportunity to see what is ahead of them by more than a few feet, can be very unforgiving.

I ask about the recent head-on crash of a VIA passenger train with a CN freight, and it's clear that my hosts would rather talk about disasters from times past.

"Oh, they just blame whoever's dead," says John. In the case I mention, as it often is, it was the engineers who died in the crash. John invokes the locally famous Dugald wreck of 1947. He says that was a clear case of dispatcher's error, so much so that the RCMP arrested the offending operator on the spot. "But after the investigation, they pinned the blame on the engineer who died in the crash for following a procedure that, though it proved to be faulty, had been established for years and was followed by every engineer throughout that time. If a wreck had happened involving an engineer who didn't follow that procedure, it would have been even more clear-cut—the engineer was to blame."

As we careen into another cut, where we cannot see more than fifty yards ahead of the train, Bill tells me about one of the CN's most famous wrecks that occurred here back in the fifties, the latter days of steam. The dispatcher ordered the eastbound 403 to meet and pass the westbound 404 at the stop of McIntosh. Something interrupted his attention and then he sent out a message to the westbound 404 to meet the eastbound 403 at Canyon. Since McIntosh is east of Canyon, this created what is known in the railway business as the dreaded lap order, when two trains headed toward each other think they are to meet farther down the line than they actually will. The situation is virtually impossible today with radio communications available from cab to cab, but on that day in 1952, two trains hurtled toward each other with the engineers thinking they wouldn't meet until the next station and no radio communications to correct the error.

The dispatcher who made the error recognized it a few minutes after he had sent his orders. Frantically he sent new orders to the stations where the trains were last stopped, but both had pulled out and were beyond reach.

The dispatcher now frantically sent messages calling out the hook-and-rescue trains. He checked to see if there were any work sites hooked up to telegraph along the way where he might be able to send a warning, but there were none. Between McIntosh and Canyon, the two trains would highball toward each other confident that dispatching had given them clear track.

Now the dispatcher turned to his maps to calculate where the two doomed trains would meet. He hoped that it might be at some straightaway stretch of track where a visual sighting might avert disaster. He calculated their routes several times and always came up with a meeting in a blind curve-cut where neither would see the other coming till the last fifty yards. Unless one train or the other was somehow blessedly delayed, that is where the tragedy would occur. He contacted the rescue train again and told them just where to look for the wreck that still hadn't happened. Then he penned his resignation, but he stayed by the key to await developments.

The two trains met in the blind curve-cut we have just passed through as Bill has told me this story. They were both traveling at just a little less than the fifty-five miles per hour we maintain as we roll through. The cut is narrow, with rock walls just ten feet from each side of the train. The two engines collided at full speed, no time whatsoever for any application of brakes—only enough time for the engineers to know that they were going to die, no chance even to jump.

Yet even in this case, with the distraught operator tearfully confessing his error, the investigation laid part of the blame on the deceased engineers. One or the other should have known that the prescribed meeting point was one stop too far down his line and should have proceeded with caution.

We run along the south shore of Canyon Lake and I marvel at the spectacular ruggedness of the terrain. There aren't any high mountains or deep canyons here, despite the regional name, but the land ripples and folds in tight undulations. Besides the rail bed, there is no place you could set a glass of water and not have it tip over.

Bill points out a slope above a cut that was once crowned with a balanced boulder the size of a barn, too big to move without some serious and expensive blasting. When the railway was first built here, it was thought that the boulder could be left where it was for a time. A Cree Indian was hired to monitor its alignment every day and to alert railway officials if and when it ever shifted.

The man conscientiously performed his duty till one rainy day when he decided to go out and get drunk. That was the day that the rains eroded the soil under the base of the boulder, enough that it did more than just shift; it tumbled down onto the tracks, blew up an oncoming steam engine, and killed a train crew heading a freight through the cut at that very moment.

During the afternoon's ride, we have rolled past numerous lakes with little or no sign of human settlement, but passing the lakes approaching Farlane, I begin to note little cabins and occasionally some larger establishments. Bill explains that we are entering the "cottage country." As the Muskoka region in north-central Ontario constitutes a northlands getaway from Toronto, this region serves a similar function for Winnipeg.

"It's the dream of every Canadian, rich and poor, to have a cottage on a remote northlands lake," says Bill. "These places are the real thing, no electricity, no roads, the only way in is the train or seaplane."

The region has spawned its own subculture, complete with its own magazine, *Cottage Life*. Bill has a copy with him and shows me an article titled "The Only Train to Malachi." It's about this train and its importance to cottagers as "the campers' special." Though the government lists the line as one of the protected routes through remote regions, there are fears that it might renege and cut off the campers from their summer vacation getaway. The CN has never been very happy about cluttering up freight schedules on its main line with passenger trains that stop every few miles.

Even though it's late September, smoke still rises from the chimneys of some of the cabins we pass, people sitting on little front porches wave to us and at stops we begin to take on quite a few campers returning to the city. John says the season never really ends here. For many the fall foliage is a bigger draw than summer warmth, and some even come out for winter weekends. "A few days in the silence of the snow out here goes a long way toward putting city traffic, business hassles, and trouble with people into proper perspective."

The train has occasionally made things lively for campers. Just before Redditt, Bob points out a lake he calls "Whiskey Lake." Fifteen years ago the tracks we are now approaching were wrecked by a sudden inundation caused by a broken beaver dam on a lake we can't see up the hill to the right. A speed train (what American railroaders would call a hotshot) bore down on the broken tracks with a load of J&B whiskey, Jamaican rum, fabrics, and a million-dollar package of diamonds. The train went over the side into the lake and quickly sank into the bottomless muskeg beneath the water.

None of the shipment was insured, and curious cottagers, who didn't know about the diamonds, gathered from miles around and watched puzzled as railway search crews scoured the bottom and carelessly stacked up hundreds of cases of whiskey and rum along the shore. When the searchers departed the cottagers began helping themselves to the whiskey and rum. After the track was repaired, train crews riding through noted the general jollity of the campers and at stops people would walk along the train and cheerfully hand up grain sacks filled with bottles of whiskey.

The campers eventually found out about the diamonds, and some mounted their own expeditions to dive and explore the muck in the bottom of Whiskey Lake, but as far as anyone knows the diamonds have never been found. They are probably still somewhere down there—or possibly in the safe-deposit box of some lucky, discreet camper who found something more substantial than whiskey and had the good sense to keep his mouth shut about it.

By sunset, when we should be in Winnipeg, we are still 140 miles away, parked on a siding while two freight trains are sorted out. It's a good time to return to my compartment where a new conductor says that my train from Winnipeg to Churchill will not wait for our arrival, but that VIA will "do something to take care of me."

Through seventeen thousand miles of rail travel across Canada, I have witnessed these kinds of things happen to other passengers. Now just one debarkation away from my ultimate destination, it's my turn. I remember Linda Melillo, way back on my first trip across Canada on the *Canadian*, say, "You have to laugh a lot and just roll with what comes. Things always work out."

When the train finally pulls into Winnipeg near midnight, I'm tired, depressed, angry, and frustrated. In the station there are perhaps a dozen others like me who have missed connections headed west. I seem to be the only one headed north.

That means I'm the last one the harried stationmaster attends to. After a hassle of paperwork, the others are sent off in a van to a local hotel where they will stay till tomorrow, when the next trains going west leave. The stationmaster doesn't quite know what to do with me and finally sends me off to the nearby Louis Riel Hotel with a voucher and instructions to return in the morning when he will think of something. It's not a good night for sleeping. All I can do is obsess on the image of my train hurtling farther toward the Arctic and Hudson Bay while I'm stuck here in Winnipeg.

Hudson Bay—the name enchants with the spell of a different strand of history that unifies Canadians, rather than divides them, in which geography becomes a helpmeet rather than a foe and in which they find their greatest challenge and truest identity.

Native peoples all over North America hold one common belief, that the Great Spirit conceived living things in the far north. The migrations of birds, buffalo, and caribou seem to confirm an instinct in all life to return in the warm season to its northern roots. Ancient legend harks back to the migrations of early humans over the Alaskan land-bridge. Canadians of all races are touched by this notion as we who live in more southerly climes can never be. It's one thing to live in Pennsylvania and see Canadian geese winging north; it's quite another to live in Winnipeg or Kapuskasing and see them headed resolutely farther north.

Henry Hudson knew nothing of this when he sailed his ship *Discovery* past Greenland, through an icy strait, and into a vast "Great Bay" on August 3, 1610. He was looking for a route to the Orient, a northwest passage, a shortcut around the massive new continent that earlier explorers had discovered barred the way. He wintered miserably at the mouth of one of the rivers at the southern end of the bay and his crew mutinied in the spring when the ice went out and Hudson insisted on continuing his explorations. The crew put him, his son, and a handful of officers in an open boat and cut them loose on the bay. He was never seen again, but his mutinous crew made it back to England, where all but two went to prison.

These two, Robert Bylot and Habbakuk Pricket, accompanied Captain Thomas Button with two ships on a voyage in 1612 to look for Hudson and continue his explorations. They found no trace of him, but they explored the bay and discovered the mouth of a great river.

The Button expedition settled into the place, but as the long, vicious winter descended, the party was wracked by hunger and scurvy. To prevent his men from going mad in their isolation and idleness Button kept them occupied studying geography and mathematics. When the ice finally went out, he returned to England with no clues to the elusive northwest passage and a warning about the winter harshness of a place he called Nelson.

In Denmark, there were adventurers who thought they might take a crack at finding the northwest passage. With two ships, Jens Munck set out for the bay under the disastrous impression that its climate, lying at about the same latitude, would not be much different from that in Denmark. It was Munck who discovered the big harbor at the mouth of the river, which would come to be known as Churchill, when he hauled one of his ships up on the sand for the winter. The Munck party found no Indians to help them feed themselves and the tundra offered no fuel but for driftwood, which washed up on the shore from faraway wooded places. They shot rabbit and ptarmigan for food and subsisted desperately in forty below zero weather with little warm clothing. Scurvy appeared in January, and by the time the ice began breaking up in June, all of the party but three—sixty-one men—had died.

Munck and the other two survivors prepared for death as the barrens began—cruelly, it might have seemed—to come alive. In their fevers of death, the three became too weakened to hunt meat and began eating the bitter vegetation that now bloomed in the tundra. And then miraculously, they found themselves regaining their strength. They couldn't know that their succor was the vitamin C in the plants they had been reduced to eating, but soon they were strong enough to float their ship and begin one of the most fantastic sea voyages of all time.

With good stocks of rabbit and ptarmigan and a generous supply of the mysterious Arctic shrubbery that had saved their lives, the three men set out to sail a three-master out of the bay, through the perilous Hudson Strait and across the North Atlantic. Incredibly, they made it.

Others followed, but the dream of the northwest passage began to fade. Hudson Bay might have dropped out of history but for a different dream of two Frenchmen, Médard Chouart des Groseilliers and Pierre Esprit Radisson, who in 1661 reached the southern end of Hudson Bay overland and recognized it as the inland sea that had punished seafaring explorers earlier. When they returned to the St. Lawrence with three hundred canoes stuffed with the finest load of furs ever brought out of the northwest and the French governor arrested them for trapping without a license, they turned to England and the die of Canadian history was cast.

Eager to see some good come of the earlier disastrous expeditions to the bay, King Charles II introduced the Frenchmen to his cousin, Prince Rupert, who outfitted them in 1668 with two ships. Though Radisson's ship, the *Eaglet*, had to return to England, Groseilliers continued on the *Nonsuch* and reached the southern shore of the bay in time to prepare for wintering over. There the experienced voyageur established friendly contact with Indians, who enriched the white men's diet with scurvy-preventing foodstuffs. Not a man was lost during that winter and there was even enough time and energy for the frivolous pastime of brewing and consuming a robust ale.

Returning with a fantastic cargo of furs, the *Nonsuch* passed the *Eaglet* heading out for a second expedition. Back in England the effect of the successful project was such that it gave birth to a remarkable, history-making charter. On May 2, 1670, the king granted to "The Governor and Company of Adventurers of England, Trading into Hudson's Bay," a private fiefdom larger than most countries of the world.

Feeling that their contribution was not properly appreciated by their English lords, Radisson and Groseilliers reversed allegiances again, and in 1682, Radisson led a war party from Quebec to the now-established York Factory at the Nelson River. Thus began the years of French and English struggle for the bay. The HBC built fortified posts at Rupert, Albany, and Moose in James Bay, and at York Factory on the great bay at Nelson River. For decades the posts traded hands with the French generally getting the better of the contest.

In response to setbacks at sites along the southern shores of the bay, the British decided to establish additional posts along the west side of the bay, in particular one at the mouth of the Churchill River where Jens Munck had suffered so cruelly years earlier. In 1731, construction began on a massive stone fort at the mouth of the Churchill harbor, Fort Prince of Wales. Three hundred feet by three hundred feet, with walls forty-two feet thick and as impressive an array of cannon as any fort in North America, the bastion was completed after nearly forty years of labor by skilled stonemasons and condemned convicts who suffered horribly in the arctic clime. For ten years it stood with its guns silent as French warships gave it a wide berth.

But on August 8, 1782, acting commander Samuel Hearne spotted French ships entering the harbor. The fort was considered so impregnable that he retired for the night unconcerned, but in the morning, he faced four hundred French troops in battle alignment before the fort. With only thirty-nine defenders inside the fort, Hearne must have panicked, for without further ado he ran up a white flag and the fort fell without its cannon having ever been fired.

The victorious French troops were so sick and weak from their voyage that they could make only feeble attempts to destroy the fort, and it stands today at Churchill, virtually intact.

With the final French defeat in the St. Lawrence Valley, the HBC hold on the bay and the northwest at last was secure. The first Selkirk settlers of the prairies came in by way of York and soon began the steamboat trade down the Red River that foreshadowed the eclipse of the bay and the HBC by the momentous events of westward settlement and nation-building. Then the rails came to the prairie from the east and the silence of the north descended over Hudson Bay, leaving only a residual engram in the racial memory of Canadians now in a lather over east-west development.

In the morning a different stationmaster is on duty at Winnipeg and he greets me with a smile and a fistful of paperwork. He says I must have a friend somewhere in VIA headquarters, because despite the orders cutting the account for providing stranded passengers with airfare, VIA is going to fly me to a place called Thompson. Then he pauses for me to gush thanks and appreciation. What I want to know is, where the hell is Thompson?

He shows me on a map in his cubicle of an office. It's about two-thirds of the way up the rail route to Churchill, about 150 miles north of Lake Winnipeg. I should get there with plenty of time to visit this small planned northern community before my train comes through, and I can board with my bedroom waiting for the second night of the two-day ride to Churchill.

It's a pretty good deal, when I think about it. VIA is paying an expensive airfare without getting back the price of my train fare and bedroom. I still get to ride my train almost half of the way, and, of course, all the way back.

But I'm not an avid flyer, especially on God knows what kind of plane plunging north into the Arctic. I know the statistics show that flying is relatively safe, especially when compared to highway travel, but aerophobes everywhere know that that argument is totally irrelevant. The odds of dying in a plane crash are about as good as getting caught cheating on my taxes. But I don't cheat on my taxes, because the penalty if I get caught is severe enough to discourage me from risking something that is albeit highly unlikely.

It's the same way with air travel for aerophobes. We don't compare the likelihood of disaster to that of other methods of travel. We compare the quality and circumstances of the disasters themselves. In a car or a train, the moment of disaster is likely to be quite brief with the blessed haven of earth just a few feet away and a vigorous fellow like myself having a decent chance of reaching it whole. When the moment comes in a plane, it may quite likely be prolonged, as in, say, a long plunge thirty thousand feet to earth. Cabins are pressurized and sometimes burst, sucking people out into the void. And then there is fire; in a ventilated craft, blessed smoke will not get me before the licking flames do. The horror has no comparison in mishaps on board other forms of travel. I'd rather ride all the way to Thompson on a bus with the Rifleman.

It's been a long time since I've been in an airport. I've become so accustomed to train stations, I have forgotten about the terra cotta floors, the low suspended ceilings, the bright fluorescent light, the clean, sterile construction, and the Muzak. For the first time I notice the most significant difference in the totality of the two environments. Most train stations, with the high vaulted halls, attempt to create an interior dominated by air and vertical space. I suppose this can be traced back to railway architects' desire to suggest the freedom of rail travel in its early days of novelty. Airport design does everything possible to avoid that effect, and considering that the aerophobe's viewpoint is the instinctual feeling of most normally adjusted people before desensitization, I can see why. Airport design creates an environment dominated by floor, great sweeping masses of it. It makes sense—the floor is like the ground, blessed earth. It's all part of the illusion necessary to tranquilize us before we allow our bodies to be flung into vertical expanses where they don't belong.

As I wait for my flight on Canadian Air Lines (acronym of C.A.L.M., now that's a nice touch!), I'm reassured less by environmental design than I am by the company of an old Chippewa who chews and smokes a really smelly cigar right here in the no-smoking area. He doesn't speak any English, but he smiles a lot and keeps offering me another half-smoked cigar from his sweaty pocket. I tell myself that if this man, who is surely much closer to our atavistic roots of human good sense, can fly on this flight, so can I.

Finally the call comes to board. We are directed down a ramp that leads to the airport pavement. Before us stands a huge, gleaming 737. Maybe this won't be so bad after all. For this short flight, a plane like that will begin its descent almost as soon as it has reached altitude. I think I can do it.

But a waving stewardess gesticulates that we are headed for the wrong plane. That one's going to Edmonton. Ours sits out beyond it, so small and insignificant I hadn't even noticed it. It's an old German-built turboprop and it doesn't gleam. In fact, it's quite dirty. The steps up into the cabin creak and sway. My seat is broken and doesn't recline. When the engines start up the whole plane shakes and vibrates madly. Suddenly we are taxiing down the runway and lifting off; below, I can see railway tracks headed out of Winnipeg. They are the last recognizable feature of the land as the plane rises up into white clouds.

14

Fire and Ice

THE *HUDSON BAY*
TO CHURCHILL AND BACK

W E have emerged from clouds into clear sky fifteen thousand
feet above Lake Winnipeg. I can see its huge outline below,
and along its shores a landscape such as I have never seen from a
plane before—country where there simply are no signs of the hand
of man, though at an inlet along the lake's north shore there is a thin
arced peninsula which is so regular it might be a manmade jetty.

A slowing and a tilt to the cabin, and the throttling back of the
noise of the engines tells me we are beginning to descend toward
Thompson. Out the window I can't recognize anything at first, and
then there's a thin line running through the nondescript grayness of
the land below—my railway. We are down on the runway approach
and now I can see fuel tanks, warehouses, streets, and the clusters
of buildings that make a town. In the airport, I call home. The kids,
Molly and Katie, want me to return soon so I can come to their
soccer and field hockey games. My wife, Nancy, is encouraging. Do
what I have to do. Things will work out.

In Thompson one sees the perverse Canadian urge to build
planned communities out of mostly empty space taken to its most

absurd extreme. Founded in 1961 as a model town by the mining company Inco, it was built to support the world's first integrated mining and processing plant for nickel. Today it is home for twenty thousand people and serves as the main supply and distribution point for the central Canada northlands.

The taxi ride from the airport to the railway station takes forever, costs $25, and seems to meander through the town's outskirts. The stationmaster in the little white clapboard structure tells me I can walk into the heart of town in less than ten or fifteen minutes. With a few hours to kill before the arrival of my train at 5:50 this afternoon, I set out on foot to explore.

I soon discover that I did ride through the heart of town in the taxi. It's just that this planned community is so spread out that even the town center looks like outskirts. Cochrane and Kapuskasing were positively compact by comparison. There is only one road, closed in winter to the outside world, but here the automobile is king—great voids of cold, empty space separate residences and business establishments that only occasionally coalesce into little neighborhoods. Nobody else is walking. Several passing cars slow and their occupants call to me and ask if I need a ride somewhere.

The town center is a mall, surrounded by the obligatory open space and buffered further by large, sparsely filled parking lots. Inside the mall, I find the first real signs of community—groups of native teens hanging out, but also older folks gathering here out of the wind to share gossip and drink coffee. Much of the conversation I overhear centers on the local hockey team and its rivalry with the old portage town of The Pas, a few hundred miles southwest of here. There does not seem to be a lot of ringing of cash registers. I ask one man if he knows why the town was planned with so much space separating everything. "Leave room for growth," he says.

The weather turned gray shortly after we landed, but as I hike back out to the station in the late afternoon, the sun comes out again. A few native women and a young backpacking fellow who is not very talkative have gathered to wait for the train. A switch engine out in the yard slams around putting together the little freight train that will make up part of the consist of the train to Churchill.

I don't know if it's the reappearance of the sun or the thought of settling into my snug roomette on the train, but as I pace the platform, I am overcome with a powerful sense of anticipation and excitement. Something good is coming down the tracks with this train.

The train pulls in with great clouds of steam blowing from its generators. In cold weather these arrivals of Canadian trains with their steam heaters running full blast take one back to the days before diesel. The doors open and the conductors let the steps down. The first person off the train is Oli Ilovar, whom I last saw heading for the Ledo Hotel back in Sudbury. The second is Cherrie Gosselin, the young Filipino-Canadian woman who tended bar on the *Canadian* back in June. With them is a little group of young German backpackers.

Oli recognizes me instantly. "How did you get here ahead of me?" he wants to know. I explain my story and then he tells his. When he arrived in Winnipeg and heard that my train wouldn't make the Churchill connection, he thought he'd come this way just to see what I was after.

Cherrie, who grew up here, is subbing for a sick bartender on this run. It gives her a chance to earn some good overtime and to see her mother briefly while the train makes its hour-long stop. The group of Germans, three girls and two guys, were all traveling separately by train through Canada and met up, one by one, forming this little band that now travels as one. Someone said they might see polar bears in Churchill, so here they are.

By the time the train pulls out at 7:30, the seven of us, minus Cherrie, who is on duty in her bar, have gathered at two tables in the diner for a convivial dinner. The car is one of those CN diner-lounge combinations with the coffee shop–style counter and swivel chairs in the center. With two coaches and three sleepers besides this car, the baggage car, and the freight cars up front, this is the biggest train I have been on in some time. It accelerates very slowly up to about thirty miles per hour, and that's it—the roadbed built on top of seasonally frozen muskeg doesn't allow for greater speeds.

Four of the Germans, who don't speak much English, sit at one table and Oli, I, and the fifth, Patricia, who isn't really a German but a Swiss from Geneva who speaks excellent English, sit at another. Dinner is broccoli soup and salmon or shortribs. With the cold landscape of stunted trees and muskeg passing outside in the twilight, and the steaming food, wine, and hearty talk inside, the hour is perfect. I knew this afternoon it would be.

Patricia is pursuing an open-ended itinerary throughout North America. She's already been to Gaspé and Quebec, and after she sees some polar bears in Churchill, she has tentative plans to go to South Dakota where she has friends and then go with them to California and New Orleans. She is one of the few European voyageurs I have met who wants to go south of the border. "I know everybody says don't go to America, but I'm just stubborn and I've been to the east coast before. How could I come this far and not go to California?"

Oli wants to know how she can afford to do this. "What are ya, rich or something?"

"I'm a nanny. Whenever I run out of money I pick up a job taking care of somebody's kids." But Patricia's experience of that life hasn't always been smooth. At her last job, the father came home drunk one day, made advances, and tried to rape her. He told her that none of the nannies he had hired before ever put up such a fuss. He just assumed it was part of the life.

When Patricia tried to blow the whistle on him, nobody believed her, especially the mother. "They all hated me and said they had enough evidence of strange behavior on my part to get me committed or deported if I didn't stop lying." She left that job under a cloud.

In subsequent conversations with other itinerant European nannies, she has heard things that substantiate the man's ideas, at least for some nannies anyway. "Once I told my story to a Swedish nanny and she wanted to know if the guy was attractive. When I admitted that he was, she asked what was my problem. 'That's what nannies do,' she said. 'Feed the kids and fuck the daddy.' " But Patricia has also met nannies who have had experiences like hers. She concludes from the whole episode that some nannies perform auxiliary services that make life tough on others.

"Fact of life, isn't it?" interjects Oli. Patricia doesn't understand. "I mean, you don't have to be a nanny to know that what some girls will do makes guys expect the wrong things with other girls. God knows I been one of those fools."

I want to know where she had that experience. "England, where else? That's the country I tell people not to go to." Patricia thinks England is sad. She's seen New York, Washington, D.C., Philadelphia, and Moscow, but she says there are no cities anywhere as ugly as Leeds in England. "Drunkenness and no work and no state authority forcing you to conform to some level of decency like in Eastern Europe." She believes it goes back further than the Thatcher era—to the dissolution of empire in World War II. "When the English ruling class saw their world so diminished, they bought up all those cute rural towns and hunkered down to let the deluge sweep over the cities." The Falkland Islands war was supposed to revive the country, but it didn't, it just made the lower classes more belligerent and uncivil. Northern Ireland bleeds the country and nobody knows why it matters so much. "Canada, even America, is like a breath of fresh air after England."

Over dessert, we are joined by another man. He is Randy Wasylkoski, a resident of Churchill. We pepper him with questions about bears and he is happy to enlighten us.

Just south of Churchill, there is a peninsula, Cape Churchill, around which the winter ice forms faster and farther out than anywhere else along the western shore of Hudson Bay. The polar bears' favorite meal is seal flesh and blubber, but during the summer months when they are landbound they can't get it. During those months, they live a miserable existence on the pitiful stuff that ordinary bears elsewhere do, berries and carrion and bugs. But when the ice forms they can leave the land and gorge themselves on seals they find at the verge of the ice and the sea.

Thus at this time of year they begin to migrate and congregate at Cape Churchill waiting for the ice. Pregnant females stay inland and wait for their births and then in the spring follow the males onto the ice and teach the cubs to hunt and kill seals.

But Randy warns us to be careful. Polar bears waiting for the ice to form are more aggressive than black bears or even grizzlies. It's not just a matter of avoiding disturbing them in their haunts. "If they're hungry enough and they spot you, they'll come after you."

Late in the evening, Oli, Patricia and the Germans, Randy, Cherrie Gosselin, and I gather in the darkened coach to watch the northern lights. Patricia introduces me to her friends from Munich, Baden-Baden, and Cologne. I hear one of them say something about how glad he is that he decided to travel Canada rather than America and, through Patricia, ask the fellow why. He doesn't know I am an American and he answers that, besides the danger of violence, Americans are obnoxious, pushy. The best that Europeans can say about them is that they are crazy.

Suddenly the sky outside lights up, as if by lightning. Amid the oohs and ahs I hear the German, who has just been told that I am an American, stumbling all over himself to apologize. He pleads that who should know better than Germans that the sins ascribed to a people as a whole do not have to cling to individuals.

But tonight the northern lights, in a display surpassing anything

I have yet seen in these Canadian travels, make the whole question seem trivial. North of the train the heatless flame shimmers and sweeps blue and magenta, playing on our low voices in the coach car—hushed breathing like cosmic lovemaking. Then on the south side, other watchers, an elderly French-Canadian pair, gasp and point out a jagged green streamer touching the horizon like a lightning bolt that stays, hangs, and turns soft with amazing grace. A dozen international faces press against the window glass— German, Swiss, Yugoslav-American, Filipino-Canadian, French-Canadian, and mongrel American—male, female—faces less like strangers when lit by this ice fire in the Canadian commune of glorious empty space.

Over the darkened horizon beneath the half moon that rises like a watchman's lantern just above the muskeg, I know there are the radar installations of the DEW line. And somewhere beneath the ground men in uniforms hunch over screens displaying green images of the top of the world. Despite the glorious news from Eastern Europe, tonight men and women, provinces and nations are still flung apart by the centrifugal force that curses the species.

The northern lights might have made an appropriate coda for the evening, but when they finally peter out and everyone else wants to go to sleep, Patricia still wants to talk. We settle into Cherrie's now deserted lounge, and she asks if travelers my age feel envy toward the freedom of young travelers like herself. I answer that I've encountered a lot of traveling young people whose freedom is weighted with some burden of sadness.

"So you already know our secret," she laughs with a touch of bitterness. And then, compelled by that urge to share secrets with strangers that motivates these young voyageurs almost as much as the urge to move on, she tells her story. Her father is a diplomat in Geneva, one of the people who organize the international events of peace for which Geneva is famous. "Out in the world, he is a saint. At home he is a pig." He cheats openly on her mother, so that her embarrassment is common knowledge in Geneva. He tells her he has married beneath his station and that she should be grateful that he keeps her on. He beats Patricia and declares that she is stupid and ugly and not worthy of his lineage.

"As I got older, I realized that my father simply despised women. He doesn't like their touch, their nature, their smell. He always made gross jokes about fish. I grew up thinking that I smelled like a fish and poured gallons of perfume on myself to eradicate the smell."

She got pregnant to prove to her father that she was desirable and then had an abortion. She shoplifted and made sure that she was arrested. She was at a party one night where all the guys were ignoring her and she became obsessed with the thought that her father was right about her. She was ugly and smelled like a fish. She came home and swallowed all the pills she could find in the medicine cabinet, but she woke the next day in a hospital.

"Father was penitent, diplomatically saying he knew he was at fault somehow." Yet within a few months, Patricia, her sister, and her mother came home early from a weekend outing and found father in bed with a strange woman. "After that, everyone was screaming all the time," and her father would choose Patricia in particular for abuse.

"That was the end of it for me. I took off and have been traveling for three years. I called once and the screaming began so I don't anymore."

Patricia is not ugly, far from it. Under her tousled sandy hair, her eyes are soft and full of hurt, her crooked smile fills her freckled face with the warmest yearning. She likes one of the German guys she is traveling with; maybe he'll come with her to California. But when I ask if she thinks travel can help her make a new life, she says, "No, you take your trouble with you like a snail carrying its house."

In the morning, outside my bedroom window I see only tundra. There is absolutely no vegetation except moss and scrubby shrubs as far as the eye can see. Besides the moss there are pools of water, occasional boulders, and curious tripod telephone poles—and that's it. It was somewhere along here that Farley Mowat saw as a child "*la fou*," the throng of caribou that inspired him to return years later to discover the dying tribes of the inland Inuit and publish the book, *People of the Deer*, that told their tragic story.

Somehow the Ihalmiut never settled near the coast and its rich supply of fat-bearing flesh. They adapted to living in the Keewatin barrens, subsisting almost entirely on the fat-poor flesh of the caribou. Since the metabolism of fat is what keeps the furnaces of their bodies running against the cold of the Arctic, they require fantastic quantities of meat in order to thrive. Even the slightest decline in the caribou population means starvation for them. When the encroachments of white men, including this railway, began to disrupt the caribou, the Ihalmiut faced doom.

Farley Mowat lived with them for two years, recording that apocalypse. He watched children starving on the white man's misguided rations of fatless grain. He observed the practice of the north in which the elderly, least able to contribute to the survival of a dying family, take the "long walk" out of the igloo into the night never to be seen again. He recorded the mytho-tragic story of Kakumee, the shaman whose helpless fascination with the things of the white men led him to become a major factor in the doom of his people. And he saw and felt with his own senses the invisible powers of the north, which the Ihalmiut ascribe more sensibly than we might think to gods and demons. When Mowat left them, the dying tribe numbered less than two dozen.

It's a fantastic place in which to be riding a train. It wouldn't be possible but for the rediscovery in modern times of the once forgotten back door of Canada, Hudson Bay, and the bizarre project of the Hudson Bay Railway.

The idea of a railway to Hudson Bay was born as far back as the day Manitoba entered confederation. Prairie dwellers said they wanted an outlet for trade with the rest of the world that did not put them at the mercies of the bankers back east in the St. Lawrence Valley. But it was more than that. Two thousand miles in the empty heart of a vast northern continent, prairie dwellers were cursed by the price they had paid for their kingdom—separation, isolation, exile from the world. The connection provided by the Canadian Pacific wasn't enough; the railways of Mann and Mackenzie weren't enough.

Perhaps nothing could ever be enough, but they knew that for two centuries the traders of the Hudson's Bay Company had used the "back door" route through the bay. A railway from the grainfields to a bay port would be a thousand miles shorter than the CPR route to Montreal. Why not build it and give the west its own seaport?

For one thing, the rail distance would be almost twice that to Lake Superior, and worse, the line would have to be built across frozen tundra much of the way with either resultant high construction costs or low-quality roadbed. Like the National Transcontinental Railway, the Hudson Bay scheme would be wrecked by any development of the water route through the Great Lakes. Hudson Bay was icebound during the eight months of the year when European demand for Canadian grain would be highest. And finally, no one knew how high shipping insurance might be for voyages, which would have to run a gamut of icebergs even in the best months.

But none of these considerations dampened the enthusiasm of

Manitobans when ground was broken in 1886 and an editor of the *Winnipeg Free Press* hailed the event as "the dawn of a glorious day. . . . With an ocean outlet that will bring the prairie steppes and grainfields of this vast country as near to the British markets as the farmers of eastern Canada . . . the grand obstacle of distance will be swept away by a single stroke."

The promoters built only forty miles before running out of money and handing the project over to Mann and Mackenzie who, as I related earlier, used the charter land grant and subsidy as the foundation of their Canadian Northern to the west. When Prime Minister Laurier commissioned an admiralty study of the feasibility of a Hudson Bay port and learned that it would be serviceable at best only four months of the year, the project was set aside.

During the planning for the National Transcontinental, no less a figure than the settlement recruiter Clifford Sifton urged the revival of the Hudson Bay project as part of the push to develop the west. Convinced that the project was a political necessity for his western MPs in the approaching 1908 election, Laurier reluctantly dismissed the sensible objections to the plan and accepted the scheme as a national responsibility. The bay was described as the "Mediterranean of Canada" and westerners imagined that the map of Canada was about to be redrawn, with the curse of the difficult east-west geography canceled by an opening to the north. The subsequent Conservative government of Robert Borden dared not renege on the commitment.

But no one knew exactly where the railway should go. The two prime candidates were the estuary of the Nelson River near York Factory and the harbor at the mouth of the Churchill River farther north up the west shore of the bay. At Nelson there were serious questions about its potential as a workable port. Churchill had a better harbor, almost ready-made, but ice formed there sooner and, more important, the rail line would have to be built through seventy-five miles of permafrost tundra, something that had never been done before. With railway men dominating the plan in the early stages, the decision was made for Nelson. Just in case, surveyors were sent to stake out those seventy-five miles to Churchill.

Still, little actual construction occurred. Westerners worked themselves into a froth over the foot-dragging of the government. "To hell with Ottawa, we'll do it ourselves!" they cried. A campaign was begun to gather five hundred subscriptions for at least $100 each of stock in "The People's Hudson Bay Railway Company."

Organizers hoped that thousands more small farmers might sign on for as little as $10. Ottawa heard the rumblings of revolt and finally went to work. Another look was cast in the direction of Churchill, but engineers shuddered at the untried experiment of building seventy-five miles of rail line across ice "that had been frozen since Adam was a kid." Port Nelson suddenly came alive with chaotic activity.

Supervision of the project was assumed by Donald McLachlin, who correctly saw that the tides at Nelson would continually deposit silt in the harbor. Already the lack of appropriate harbor conditions had created a mess, with foodstuffs, coal, building materials, and machines in piles along the shore like so much junk. Two ships had foundered on silt-hidden rocks in the shallow channel. When McLachlin complained angrily about the expensive breakwaters and channel work that would have to be done, he was fired.

He ignored his dismissal and continued on for the next twelve years without any official authority. Somehow, perhaps due to the remoteness of the work or the lack of real interest in the project in Ottawa, no one was ever sent to replace him. By 1916, the tracks were laid as far as a point 333 miles northeast of The Pas when World War I put a stop to all work.

After the war a parliamentary inquiry in 1920 actually aided McLachlin in solving his two worst problems. First it was decided to look once again at Churchill, and second, the testimony of Arctic explorers who knew the land better than anyone offered a solution to the problem of the permafrost. It was not necessary to establish a roadbed on underlying bedrock, as with muskeg, they said. The permafrost itself provided a stable foundation for heavy manmade structures. If true, this discovery would eliminate the necessity for dynamiting a virtual canyon through the permafrost so that road-bed gravel could be laid on bedrock.

In the early twenties, a prairie party called the Progressives met in Winnipeg to form an "On to the Bay" association, a modern lobby, which informed Mackenzie King in no uncertain terms that his government's survival was dependent upon the expeditious pros-ecution of the Hudson Bay Railway construction. With this spur to action, Mackenzie King's new minister of railways and canals re-cruited an Englishman, Alfred Palmer, the world's foremost author-ity on ports, to study the terminus problem. After visiting both sites, he exclaimed with disgust, "You Canadians constantly use two words as if they were one—port and harbor. A port is a facility you build to work ships. If you have any damn sense you put them in a harbor." Port Nelson was scratched and Palmer gave his approval to Churchill.

Now, with a properly motivated government and a settled destination, the work proceeded vigorously. In the winter, a sub-bed of logs and brush was laid on the frozen ground and the tracks and ties put down on top of it. In the spring, when the upper few feet of the ground thawed, the brush roadbed sank into it creating a shaky but usable foundation for work, much like what was used to conquer the muskegs. Then the tracks were jacked up above the corduroy roadbed and work trains delicately crawled over them to dump tons of gravel fill down through the tracks and ties. When the fill settled firmly enough on the permafrost underneath, the tracks were lowered onto it and the job for that stretch was done.

One incident revived the engineers' old fears about the permafrost. On a rainy night in the spring a work train crawling along a temporary section of track jumped the rails and plowed into the thawing muck. The trainmen hiked back down the line to the nearest work camp, where they wired for help and spent the night. Late the next morning members of the derailed train's crew accompanied the wrecking train back to the site of the accident. The previous night's rain had ceased and it was a sunny, warm morning. When they got to the site, there was no train. The foreman of the wrecking crew questioned the trainmen severely, suspecting a hoax, but the men were adamant and pointed out a rut of disturbed muck along the tracks that was just a little longer than their work train. Some digging beneath the rut turned up a few small objects belonging to the work train. The wrecking crew dug deeper—more bits and pieces but no train. There was no doubt about it. The massive iron of the train had absorbed enough heat from the sun to sink deeply into the permafrost, like a hot knife through butter. It was never found.

Despite the lost work train, the construction method worked remarkably well, though small fluctuations in the level of thawing year after year have made the track uneven enough to preclude high-speed passenger runs. Today the *Bayline* takes two days to cover the 1,055 miles of the route because of a thirty-miles-per-hour speed limit in the Arctic sections.

The permafrost also presented a challenge to the telegraph men. Thawed permafrost is too viscous to support vertical poles. Thus engineers devised the tripod poles that are one of the most striking features along the route today. The tripods are simply set on the frozen ground in the winter. They sink a few feet in the first spring thaw and then stay there.

At last the rails reached Churchill and port facilities were constructed. As they did with other risky northern railway projects—Prince Rupert, Moosonee, and the NTR—Canadians settled back to await the bonanza of traffic that would justify the gamble. It was October 1929.

As we roll closer to Churchill, the vegetation becomes somewhat more varied, with even a few stunted bushes. The conductor tells me that the region I woke up to is called "The Barrens" and is particularly sterile. Most of the tundra near the coast of Hudson Bay is considerably more interesting—and colorful. In the early morning light, I can see textures and hues in the low vegetation like the scenery in an HO scale rail layout spackled with cheap coloring materials—lots of deep red and dark green, speckles of yellow, orange, and even blue.

The first impression on stepping off the train in Churchill is of the cold. Though I can see water standing unfrozen in puddles, the windchill feels well below freezing. Cherrie, the bartender, is prepared and gets off wearing a long VIA coat. The Germans have pulled parkas out of the bottomless holds of their backpacks. Oli and I, with our light jackets, are shivering just a few steps off the train. "Jesus fucking Christ," curses Oli, "what is this, the goddamn Arctic or something?"

Without even a look at our surroundings we all crowd into the station, which looks more like an old rural hotel than a railway station. Inside, where it's warm enough to think, we make plans. The Germans have wrangled a free tour in a tundra buggy through Randy Wasylkoski. Oli and I want to get our own vehicle so we can be on our own. Cherrie says she knows a fellow at the motel where VIA employees bunk who might lend us his four-wheel-drive van. She promises to try to arrange it and tells us to meet her for lunch at the Churchill Motel and we'll spend the afternoon searching for polar bears.

The next order of business is to locate the mayor, a man named Mark Ingerbrigsten, who Randy has told me knows more about Churchill than anyone. I ask a friendly-looking fellow wearing a flannel shirt and a quilted vest who is working at the baggage window where I might find the man. "Ingerbrigsten?" he says.

"Why do you want to meet that son of a bitch?" He lets me stutter and mumble for an awkward moment or two and then confesses that he is the man I'm looking for. He comes down to meet the train at every arrival, just to help out.

He directs us to a place called the Town Centre where we should be able to find him a little later in the morning having coffee. Oli and I turn up our collars and set out across a ball field toward the largest building in Churchill. Along the way we pass a Hudson's Bay store, a Canadian Legion hall, a school, and a church. Over our hunched left shoulders we can see the dominant landmark of Churchill, the huge grain elevators at dockside. Otherwise there are no buildings over two stories. Though not as compact as I would like it, especially when the wind blows as it does today, Churchill is less spread out than Thompson or even Cochrane. But it's also a lot smaller—far smaller than I imagined, considering its historical importance. You can see the edge of town from just about anywhere.

The new Town Centre is a remarkable public initiative. Housing a school, a clinic, an indoor playground, a library, a hockey rink, a gymnasium, a museum and display area, town offices, and a cafeteria, the structure is an attempt to create a year-round communal focal point in a place where most human intercourse has to occur indoors. Decorated with Indian art, stuffed wildlife (including an eight-foot-tall polar bear), mobiles, and photo posters, the place creates the illusion of the outdoors with huge volumes of airspace, much like railway stations of old. The heating bill in this climate must be astronomical.

Oli and I grab a quick breakfast of bran muffins and Clamato juice (everybody in Churchill drinks Clamato, says the girl behind the counter). Wandering around waiting for Mark Ingerbrigsten to show up, we are drawn again and again to the big windows looking out the back of the building onto the shore of Hudson Bay. The rear doors are all marked EMERGENCY ONLY, but finally Oli just pushes one of them open. No Klaxons sound, so suddenly we are out on the sand behind the building and the only way back in is around to the front.

It wouldn't matter but for the sign that confronts us about halfway between the building and the water. New and freshly planted it reads, POLAR BEAR ALERT, DO NOT WALK IN THIS AREA.

"Jesus," murmurs Oli, "could they really be that bad?" We clown around the sign for a bit and take pictures and then Oli asks, "Well, are we gonna dip in Hudson Bay, bears or no, or what?" There is no surf and the water presents a deceptively benign image. It is clear and inky blue, like a darker version of the water I have seen in Caribbean islands. We doff our shoes, roll up our pants, and charge the bay, getting wet just up to our knees in water that makes the ocean at Maine seem like a sauna. The saltwater will soon be ice—it is already below the freezing point of fresh water. Our feet are numb so quickly we can't get our shoes back on.

Back inside the Town Centre, Mark Ingerbrigsten and a half-dozen other fellows are having coffee around a long table in the cafeteria. Mark sardonically observes, "We just saw a couple of crazy fellows out behind in restricted bear territory. Haven't seen 'em, have you?"

We sit down with them as Mark declares that people hereabouts know well that the polar bear is the only carnivore that will stalk and kill a human without being a freak. Sage nods all around the table. One man says, "I never go out there this time of year without a big gun." More sage nods. Then Mark admits that some of this is teasing, but he insists that if we are intent on finding polar bears by four-wheel-drive van this afternoon, we had better be more careful than we were just now. "They really will eat you. Keep your motor running and your radio playing loud, and don't get too far from your vehicle."

Because of the fires this summer, Mark can't guarantee that we will see any. "The bears are all screwed up and most of them are still much farther inland than they ought to be." This is good for most townspeople, but bad for people like himself whose business is to make sure that tourists see bears. "When the bears come early and get frustrated waiting for the ice, they raise hell with people's backyard garbage, and sometimes even bust into kitchens. They're like six-hundred-pound raccoons.

"In years when the bears come late we don't have any of those problems, they go straight out onto the ice. But then the polar bear tourist trade gets screwed."

Oli wonders if the best place to spot bear might be the town dump. "Not if we can help it," answers Mark. Town dumps are bad news for communities in polar bear country because there the bears get a taste for things that can be found in people's garbage cans and pantries. Also, the bears can't distinguish between seal oil and things like garbage bags, foam rubber, disposable diapers, and even tires. In dumps the bears eat this kind of material and are later found dead because they can't pass it through their digestive systems.

Thus the town burns everything at the dump, sets out huge bear traps to catch furry intruders so they can be transported to sites far from town, and discourages tourists from looking for bears there.

Except for occasional hunts allowed for population control, bear trapping and hunting are illegal for anyone but native people. Guides can take non-native hunters out for bear, but the kill belongs by law to the native and he cannot legally sell it to his customer. Thus there is a thriving black market for bearskins, claws, and teeth. The non-native hunter returns to Toronto or Chicago with a trophy, though not necessarily the same one he actually killed.

When the other fellows around the table get to quizzing Oli about what life is like in New York City, I get my private audience with the mayor. He has lived here for all thirty-nine years of his life. He met his wife, a woman from Kenora, at a health club and never had any thought of living anywhere else. He visited New Zealand once. "It's a lazy country," he says, leaning back in his chair and slowly sipping his cup of coffee. "I had a hard time gearing down from the pace of life in Churchill."

But he has serious concerns as mayor of an Arctic town whose population has declined from 7,000, at the height of the action on the now defunct military base nearby, to the 1,700 of today. Besides the economic struggle to keep Churchill on the map, the biggest local issue is probably trash—"the problem of having a dirty community." Mark says it's a dominant issue in most far northern towns where the environment doesn't clean itself as well as it does in warmer climes. On top of that, people in cold-weather environments tend to have bad habits about garbage and trash. "They live sloppily because anything you throw outside during nine months of the year conveniently freezes."

Of course there is the issue of local property taxes, currently about $1,200 on a $100,000 house on an eighty-by-sixty-foot lot. If tax increases go to developing the town, such as the Town Centre or a downtown beautification project, nobody complains. "They can see where their dollars went. It's when we have to raise taxes to finance things people can't see, like increased administrative or contract costs, that we get heat."

And then there is the pan-Canadian issue of race. In Churchill, bilingualism means English and Cree—or Chippewa or Inuit. "When the Hudson's Bay people decided on this location, they couldn't have picked a better place for intertribal trouble." The territories of Cree, Chippewa, and Inuit tribes border each other here.

Mark explains the local belief that centuries of intertribal hatred are mollified by the white presence. "The Indian tribes won't intermarry with one another, but they will with whites." Offspring have been able to escape tribal entanglements and still assume leadership roles. "Stable white blood becomes the common denominator for peace."

Almost two centuries ago, the HBC figured out that all the energy the Indians put into fighting each other distracted them from trapping, so the fort here policed a peace. Under a tradition established by white men, the Inuit hold the country from the west point of the river mouth northward. The Chippewa have Cape Merry and country west of here till they meet the Athabascans. The Cree have Cape Churchill and territory generally to the south.

I ask about the role of the HBC in modern times. Mark says they still buy furs here and have a near monopoly on supply. "Nobody else stocks what they have at the Bay store. They operate under a simple slogan, 'We screwed your grandfather, we screwed your father, and now we're going to screw you.'"

Mark confesses that Churchill is currently in an economic decline. "We're now getting nothing but the dirty stuff no one else wants to handle—mostly barley." Despite the advantage of being a thousand miles closer to Europe than Lake Superior ports, in Mark's eyes Churchill is still a victim of the same eastern forces that thwarted so long the building of the railway. "When the money men in the St. Lawrence Valley saw that northlands development meant northlands competition, they started a retrenchment on the Canadian commitment to northlands development. This port has never been allowed to live up to its potential."

Despite the devastating effects of the Depression, the first shipment of wheat left the port in a British ship for England in 1931. When the ship arrived in London sixteen days later, its captain declared that the run had been easy and had been accomplished "in record time"—certainly true since no one had ever done it with a ship of similar size and purpose before. Another ship followed and quickly a problem emerged. Insurers set the rates for these voyages six times higher than for similar shipments by way of the Great Lakes.

Ten ships left Churchill loaded with grain in 1932, but one of them never arrived in England. At 4:20 A.M. on October 1, the *Bright Fan* plowed into an iceberg in the Hudson Strait and sank.

Fortunately for the crew, a nearby icebreaker arrived in time to rescue them, but despite the sixty-four successful voyages in the next eight years, the actuaries of the insurance companies never forgot the *Bright Fan*. Ships continued to arrive with cargoes of seawater, since the marketplace never found Churchill as a major passageway for imports.

Then World War II intervened to suspend shipping through Churchill entirely. Canadian and American navies had their hands full keeping the sea-lanes to the eastern ports open, never mind the narrow strait into Hudson Bay. After the war, exports of grain through Churchill resumed and increased steadily but not impressively. But a new confidence was in the air.

On the other side of the globe, Russians were establishing large communities in places like Churchill and even growing produce in them. Surely, not only would the port offer the modern west a window on the seafaring world, but it would also serve as the model and starting point for Canada's long-delayed conquest of its far north. But none of the optimistic northland publicists of the time noted that in Russia, it was done under the lash of Stalin. In Canada free men were not so enthusiastic about generating a latter-day pioneer rush to the north. As late as 1973, Canadian historians were still writing that the Russian example would eventually inspire Canadians toward efforts that will enable the bay railway to justify itself.

In 1969, a government commission issued a report studying the lagging utilization of Churchill and concluded that, despite its mediocre record as a grain port, the place was still the key to developing the north where "the real challenge of nationhood remains—can we occupy and conquer the vast land itself?"

The inexorable mathematics that were once ignored in order to appease western farmers have had their day. Little more than 5 percent of western exports have ever gone out over this route; almost nothing has come in. Despite flurries of enthusiasm over northlands development, such as that stirred by the voyage of America's oil tanker, the *Manhattan*, through the Northwest Passage, the railway's main value is increasingly in the social service role provided by VIA's passenger train for local native people and the handful of others who man a few mining, energy, or communications outposts along the way. It is perhaps the only train route in North America where, in these latter days of travel, the passenger service is its chief reason for being.

Before Oli and I head back to the Churchill Motel to meet Cherrie, Mark poses with the huge stuffed bear in the cafeteria of the Town Centre. Though grain shipments are still a major factor in the local economy, Mark understands the importance of the growing trade of tourists who want to see whales and polar bears, the only growth industry in town. "Bear's my buddy," he says as he hugs the stuffed animal. "He brings me money and feeds my family."

After a heavy northlands lunch smothered in gravy, Oli and I set out with Cherrie in the motel's four-wheel-drive van. The sun has been bright all morning; the wind has diminished and the day has warmed. Cherrie drives while Oli sits in back, on the roof, on the hood, and the bumpers to record our quest with his video camera.

First we drive past the grain elevators to Cape Merry, the northernmost point in Churchill. Across the river we can see the bulk of the ancient Fort Prince of Wales. On our side there is a cairn and a plaque memorializing Jens Munck. Nearby lie the recent ruins of a tribal village, burned-out shacks and rusting auto husks. Everywhere the rocks are decorated with the magnificent low scrub and wildflowers—blue, yellow, orange, and lots of deep red. But—no bears.

We head east on a paved road paralleling the bay and then turn down several dirt roads to the shore, where we find wind, rocks, and breakers. Farther out past the abandoned radar station, we can see the rusting wreck of the *Ithaca*, a nickel ore freighter that foundered just offshore in 1961. We spot huge flocks of Canadian and snow geese, but no bears.

Farther east at Bird Cove, Oli coaches Cherrie on driving over a rocky hummock, and down by the water we see several moving white shapes. Cherrie turns the van around and backs it toward the cove to set us up for a fast getaway. Then we step out, leaving the doors open and the motor running with Cat Stevens loudly crooning from the tape player, "Oh, baby, baby it's a wild world," as we stalk our prey, cameras at the ready.

Closer now, we can see that some of the bears are black and they're all pretty small. Dogs—we are stalking dogs. Some are tethered to stakes in the ground and others run free among them. They are sled dogs. We venture close and they wag their tails with all the friendliness of Fido back home. But I remember the warning on the *Continental*, "Reach out to pat them and you lose your hand." We back off, and then, realizing that we have come quite a distance from the van, break into a jog that, we all agree, is simply a nice spontaneous urge toward good health.

We drive back toward the highway by a different dirt road and Oli grumbles, "Still no bears." Just inland from the cove there is a little pond, one of thousands one can see from high points along this coast. Here we spot two more white dogs, big ones. Cherrie stops the truck and again we venture out. We can't see them from the spot where we have stopped because of an intervening hillock. As we round it there they are, very big dogs, bigger than dogs. Bears. One spots us, stands upright on two legs and looks right at us. It is magnificent, at least seven feet of living three-dimensional white rug. They don't stand up like this in zoos. And they don't drop down and march forward with such purpose as this one does now.

Cherrie is already halfway back to the van when Oli and I lower our cameras and bolt. The bear, now loping, is after us, no mistake. Back at the van, Cherrie guns the engine and it stalls.

"Shit!" she spits.

"Jesus mother . . ." Oli halts in mid-curse, collects himself, and calmly coaches Cherrie on what to do to avoid flooding the engine. It starts and bucks. As we clear the hillock we can see the bear, now posing as for a *National Geographic* shot and sniffing the air.

Soon we are back out on the highway, laughing with bravado about how close we got to the bears, how big they were, and what great shots we must have in our cameras. But privately I wonder, would Mark Ingerbrigsten have too much dignity to bolt for the van as we did, or would he have never been out there in the first place without toting a cannon?

We spend the rest of the afternoon exploring the handful of human marks on the tundra surrounding Churchill. At the abandoned missile launch site where a joint U.S.-Canadian project studied the electronics of the northern lights, Cherrie imagines that the announced purpose was a cover for some sinister CIA scheme. We poke around and find no windows and lots of shiny padlocks on all the doors. Then back through Churchill and out the road along the river we discover an inhabited Chippewa settlement that reminds me of the rural pockets of poverty that we call Appalachia back in New England. Every tattered house has a magnificent rack of moose antlers over the lintel. We don't see a living soul but for a mean chained dog and a furtive face behind a screen door.

We stop at the graveyard and the Eskimo museum where Cherrie buys a carving for her daughter back in Winnipeg. At the Legion Hall we are admitted because we are visitors, and Cherrie whips five of the locals at pool. We have dinner at the Trader's Table restaurant, where we meet up with the Germans from the train. The dining room is a cozy windowless chamber with a crackling fire and trophy heads, guns, and traps hanging on log walls. The Germans tell us about the half-dozen polar bears they followed around for two hours today in the tundra buggy. Their extended bear study makes Oli, Cherrie, and me blush with embarrassment over our panicked fleeting glimpse.

The Germans have decided to stay in Churchill for a few days. Oli is itching to move on farther west. I don't know what I want to do. Back at the railway station, I make a phone call. Nancy sounds tired and cross—some trouble with the kids. It's time.

Oli and I hang out with Cherrie in her bar as the train heads south in the later evening. It's quiet on board, none of the excitement of the trip up. Cherrie entertains us with stories and observations about drunks in her bar. "I'm paid to take all the shit that's fit to shovel."

There's a drunk in the bar now, a young Chippewa who already staggered when he boarded at Churchill. He tries to talk to us, but his speech is so slurred it's hard to comprehend. He's in some kind of trouble for messing around with the wife of a Cree. Cherrie cuts him off and sends him back to his coach seat. His eyes are so thick with drink that they look almost as if covered by an oozy membrane.

Later as Oli and I are about to turn in, he reappears at the door to the coach, his eyes now wild and glazed. Cherrie is in the little closet at the end of the bar and the man lurches down the aisle toward her, threateningly. Oli immediately stands up to block his way. "Whoa, fellow, where ya goin'?" Oli says, firmly gripping him by the shoulders. He falls back against one of the tables and rolls sickeningly toward the floor. Two elderly women who have wandered in for a late night cup of tea stare horrified. Oli lifts the fellow back up and I assist to steer him back to his seat. He never says a word, but in our grip I can feel his body go limp. The conductor comes along and tells us he'll take care of the fellow from here on.

In the morning, we're back in the bush, forested subarctic country, approaching Thompson. I'm having breakfast in the diner with a huge silent fellow who pauses now and then in his meal to stare intently out the window at stretches of forest burned out by recent fires. I never really imagined before what a forest destroyed by fire would look like a few months later. The surprising thing is that it's not open space; the blackened tree trunks are all still there, like a forest of huge carbon finishing nails.

I've ridden through northlands areas touched by recent fires before, but these are particularly extensive. "You worked on these fires, didn't you," I finally say to my breakfast companion.

"Yeah," is all he says. As it happens, I rode with a VIA employee on my earlier trip out west who told me a harrowing story about her experience on this train earlier in the summer.

"I know a service chief, Brigit McDaniels, who was a hero of sorts in those fires," I venture.

"There were lots of heroes," the fellow mumbles in a dismissive tone. "And nobody died, so what the hell. Just a few million acres of trees and bunnies and a summer of hell for some people who were in the wrong place at the wrong time."

"You had some hard times, eh?"

"Hell no, I didn't. I flew a water helicopter for the Department of Natural Resources out of Swan Lake. We bombed it with a mixture of water and detergent—dishwasher stuff. But we couldn't do shit; the fires just popped up somewhere else. Sometimes from the air it seemed like the whole world was burning and me with nothing but a mouthful of soapy spit to put it out. We never would have but for the two and a half inches of rain that finally fell in a week. But the guys who fought it on the ground will never be the same."

I ask him his name, but he sees my notebook and wants no publicity. I ask him if he knows about the role this train played in the rescue efforts and he says, "Yeah. Everybody knows that. Without the train, there would have been hundreds, maybe thousands of dead Indians."

I met VIA service chief Brigit McDaniels returning east from Vancouver on the *Canadian* in early August, but have saved her story till now. Despite her name, freckles, and curly red hair, she is

French, and very noticeably so when she speaks English. Brigit told me about the fires in bits and snatches over the three days of the trip, much of it in her sleeper office while she fussed over manifests and inventories. Intent on the western quest, I wasn't aware at the time of the northland legends of fires, wilderness mystery, or the unfinished conquest of the land. Her story has grown richer with the miles.

As Cherrie is doing on my current run, Brigit had picked up a slot on the *Bayline* to get some overtime when someone called in sick in early July. The train had just left Wekusko on the second day out from Winnipeg and her crew was serving the second sitting of lunch in the diner-lounge. The conductors and brakemen were on meal break, so that nearly all the train crew were gathered in the car when their radios crackled in unison with a startled transmission from the engineers, "Fire up front!"

"How far ahead?" the conductor seated next to Brigit laconically asked into his radio.

"Now!" came the terrified reply.

"Normally the engineer would see a fire miles before we got to it," Brigit explained to me, but this summer's fires burned on the dry muskeg and peat underground, sometimes for great distances and then, kindling some especially flammable vegetation, burst from the earth like volcano fires. Later the engineers reported that they had suddenly seen what looked like a mushroom cloud above the tracks just ahead of them. Before they had a chance to slow down, they were in the flames.

Back in the diner, Brigit and the crew saw tongues of flame outside the windows and then there was nothing but fire. Inside the car, terrified diners and apprehensive crew members could feel the heat through the diner walls. The conductor quickly ordered the engineer to keep going at track speed, better to hope that they could run through this than to stop in the middle of it. Brigit remembered the propane tanks underneath the car and said a prayer.

Smoke was entering the train through the ventilation system and through open vestibule doors, and Brigit ordered her car attendants to close the doors and shut down the fans. A window in the diner cracked from the heat and the floor felt terrifyingly warm, right through the soles of her shoes. Then just as quickly as the flames had appeared, they were gone. The train arrived in Thompson where the talk was of routine fires along the line. The train had just been unlucky and struck a spot where a fire had recently burst. But folks at the station whistled to see much of the VIA blue burned off the railcars in huge black scars.

The remainder of the run to Churchill was uneventful. Brigit checked with VIA car control during the day layover there and was told that her train would go out that night, but only as far as Thompson. No further explanation was given.

When her train arrived at Thompson the next morning, the town was buzzing with crisis. The YMCA, the mall, and hockey arenas were all packed with people evacuated by air from areas threatened by fire. Now it was clear that what the train had passed through the day before was not an isolated thing. Fires had popped up all over central Manitoba. With no rain in almost two months, the flames were consolidating in huge fronts in the dry bush.

The train was delayed and finally canceled at 6:30 that night. Southbound passengers were put on a bus—the highway was still safe. Later in the evening, the road down which the bus had traveled was closed. Helicopters and small planes winged overhead toward the airport. Rumor had it that everything south was aflame.

Official-looking people started appearing in the railway station—managers from the EMO (Emergency Management Organization), officers of the RCMP, agents of Northern Affairs, and doctors and nurses. Brigit overheard a conversation between two men who looked as though they were in charge. "I'll never forget the worry in that man's eyes as he said, 'This is the big one we've always feared. Without rain, there's no stopping it.'"

The EMO officially seized the train and asked for volunteers from the crew. Brigit signed on and was ordered to rest before the ordeal that lay ahead.

The next day the train was sent out to evacuate the nearby towns of Thicket Portage and Pikwitonei. The implications of the assignment "put fear in my heart—Pikwitonei is north of Thompson." She helped to evacuate 180 people, mostly native people, taking names and checking census lists to be sure that no one was left behind.

Back at Thompson at 11:00 P.M., Brigit could smell smoke in the air. She had no idea what further demands would be made on her train, but she and two crew members raided a grocery store just about to close and bought fifteen shopping carts of food and necessities for the train. Sheets, washcloths, and towels that would normally be picked up by cleaners at Churchill or Winnipeg were becoming a problem. Using the same grocery carts, she and her crewmen hauled the linen to the home of a charitable soul who allowed her washing machine and dryer to be run almost all night long. "People have made a big deal about what I did. But even in an emergency, if you knew a lot of people were coming to your house, wouldn't you vacuum the carpets, put out fresh towels, and rush out to the market to stock your refrigerator?"

In the middle of the night, the word came down that the train was being seized again, to evacuate Gillam, a significant town at the turning point where the bay route leaves the Nelson River valley and heads north across the tundra to Churchill.

The switchers had been working all night to put together a train consisting of all the passenger cars that could be scrounged, eight, and another train of fifty boxcars that could carry a thousand if necessary. Brigit's train got through to Gillam with a few brushes with flames, nothing like what she ran through that first day. Besides its usual population, the little town held another two thousand natives who had come in from the bush. "What did your ancestors do when there were fires like these?" Brigit asked an old Chippewa man.

"Burned," he replied. "Sometimes whole tribes."

All day long the trains sat on the tracks in Gillam waiting for some decision to be made. "You couldn't see the sun. The sky was a deep smoky orange, like in the movie *The Day After*." Because the wind kept changing directions, there was a lot of indecision, with the RCMP landing and taking off in their helicopters. At 7:30 P.M. the sirens went off and there was a panic. People rushed the train and tried to board, but the RCMP officers prevented anyone from doing so. The RCMP declared a state of readiness, and the official edict had a pacifying effect on the crowds.

Then came word that Brigit's train was to evacuate Ilford, forty miles to the south, over the same tracks where Brigit had seen fire earlier in the day. The planes and helicopters reported that the line was safe for the moment and had best be used while it could be. A CN official offered to relieve Brigit of her post, but she insisted on going.

Fifteen miles south of Gillam the air around the train became opaque with smoke. Brigit saw bursts of flame near the tracks as trees exploded from their subterranean fuses, "but it still was never as bad as that first day when we didn't know what was going on." The train arrived safely at Ilford and loaded another eighty-seven people to take back to Gillam. Because fires had swept over the tracks and the heat might have expanded and distorted the gauge, a roadmaster rode in the engine to try to spot any irregularities as the train rolled along at five miles per hour. This time there was no trouble.

For the next few days, the atmosphere in Gillam turned festive. Native kids evacuated from outlying areas gathered in little knots at the edge of town to watch the surrounding fireworks, which were especially impressive in the darkening evening. Brigit made another raid on a grocery store, but this time there was little to be had. A Chippewa woman's washing machine and dryer were pressed into service.

Finally it was decided that 240 elderly and children should be evacuated, not to Thompson, but to Churchill, out across the fireproof barrens. The passenger train could not hold that many, so some were packed into boxcars reminding Brigit of films of Auschwitz internees.

It was an easy trip, with no fires in the barrens north of Gillam. Churchill buzzed with emergency operations activity and the train was quickly turned around for further evacuation work back at Gillam.

The train was held by the EMO in Gillam for a week. A few more short evacuation runs were made during that time, but things seemed to be settling down. A northerly breeze cleared the air of smoke and then it rained. Brigit had heard stories of the desperate battles fought by fire brigades out in the bush, and now some of their wounded began to arrive by helicopter in Gillam. "I thought I had been fighting the war, but then I realized that there were those who were closer to the front lines than I had ever been."

Lightning reignited some of the fires, but then more rain, two blessed inches, at last quenched them. More than a thousand square miles of Manitoba had been scorched; more than a thousand people lost their homes. The smoke cloud from the fires tainted skies for nearly a month, and as far away as my own home in New Hampshire.

Still Brigit's train could not go back south. The fires had destroyed a bridge between Thompson and Gillam. "If I had known that before, I might have panicked. Things were pretty scary at Gillam, but you always thought you had two escape routes—Churchill or Thompson. If I'd known that the exit to Thompson was gone, I would have been crazed at any sign of smoke north of town."

While I understood the safety of Churchill out in the barrens by the bay, I asked her why Thompson and its twenty thousand inhabitants were safe, though surrounded by fires on every side.

"It's a planned community," she told me matter-of-factly. "Many of the people who live there don't even know why it's been laid out that way, but it has enough open space, not just around the town but also within it, to prevent it from being burned by any fire from the bush."

Brigit was flown from Gillam to Winnipeg the first week of August. She met a hero's welcome, her train having evacuated nearly six hundred souls from imminent fire danger. Another train working north from The Pas had performed similar service but had never actually run through the fires, as had Brigit's. As the mayor of Thicket Portage, the first town evacuated, declared in a resolution following the conflagration, Brigit's train was the right vehicle at the right place at the right time. "Without them, there would have been a great disaster."

Beyond Thompson, we roll through country I missed before because I flew to Thompson. Much of it is fire-scarred. At lunch I sit with the Chippewa fellow who was so drunk last night. Now he is sober and cleaned up, but he is still a fragile figure. His black hair is cut to that length of indecision—not long, not short. His name is Eddie Brookhouse and he is twenty-two years old. He speaks in clear, though not eloquent, English and apologizes for his behavior in the bar last night. "I made a real ass of myself, but my situation really is desperate. How much did I tell you?"

"Not much," I answer, "except that you are in hot water for messing around with the wife of a Cree."

"That's why I'm on the train, why I had to leave Churchill. The man really will kill me if he finds me. They don't make empty threats."

"What about your family?"

"That's why I had to get so drunk, so I could face them and say good-bye to them. I've never left Churchill before, and now I can never go back."

"Where are you going?"

"I don't know. Maybe The Pas. I have a little money."

"That's Cree country, isn't it?"

"That's what they tell me, but I hear there are Chippewa there, too, and maybe tribal differences don't matter so much in white man's land down south."

At 7:30 in the evening, the train rumbles across the bridge over the Saskatchewan River and into a small modern-looking city. There are pleasant tree-lined streets and well-maintained homes along the tracks, but I also notice something I haven't seen much in Canada—hostile graffiti marring concrete walls.

The train makes a long stop here, over an hour, to hook up with a branch run coming down from the mining town of Lynn Lake. Oli and I want to check out the town; Eddie has a decision to make. The three of us walk from the train station through a prosperous but for the moment rather deserted-looking downtown, past a native people's welfare and cultural center, down to the banks of the Saskatchewan. A brilliant red setting sun glints fire off the still water and we are entertained by magnificent lazy swirls of very big fish sucking up bugs on the surface.

"You gonna stay here, or what?" Oli asks Eddie.

"Don't know, how does it look to you? I never traveled anywhere before."

"There's some anger here," I venture, noting the graffiti we saw coming in.

"There's anger in Churchill."

"There's anger in Brooklyn, so what the fuck," says Oli.

"You saw the welfare center back there?" I ask.

"Yeah, I think I'll go in." So we walk back downtown. Eddie thanks us for the escort into the first town he's ever been to besides Churchill and disappears into the welfare and cultural center.

Oli has spotted a hotel with a bar, the Gateway Inn, and he gestures for me to follow him as he pushes open the heavy metal door. Inside it's loud, smoky, and beery. Twenty faces turn toward us in a motion like the wave spectators perform at football games. The faces are all Indian, they all seem drunk, and they do not appear friendly.

Oli toughs it out, orders two Blues and leads me to an empty table right near the door. Crossing the room I accidentally bump into a hulking fellow who looks up angrily as I pass and mumble, "Excuse me." While we sit guzzling our beers, the man gets up, walks over to the door, and stands there barring the exit.

Meanwhile another man stumbles over to our table and asks if we can help him out with a dollar because someone just beat him up and took all his money. They hit him in the face and it really hurts, he says. A trickle of blood runs from the corner of his mouth. I dig in my pocket and dump a little pile of quarters on the table as we both finish our beers. A third man has led the man I bumped outside. "Now," says Oli, and he quickly gets up and heads for the door with me following. To my horror I see that Oli is clutching his beer bottle at the neck like a weapon.

Oli bangs the door open fast and bolts through. The third man has led aside the man I bumped, but as I come through the door, the big drunk breaks away from him and lunges for me. He staggers, trips, and falls on the step muttering what must be an oath in his native language. Oli and I jog all the way back to the station, where Oli drops the beer bottle in an empty oil drum.

"Well, that sure wasn't the Ledo," he laughs.

I'm having trouble seeing the humor of it, but as we board the train I wonder where Oli was more scared, at the Gateway or out by the pond at Bird Cove with the bears.

"Oh shit, the bears. I'm from Brooklyn, remember."

It's the last evening I'll spend with Oli and Cherrie, my bear-hunting companions. Oli is headed west; Cherrie and I are both going home to our respective kids. We spend the evening playing gin and talking about home and our pasts in Cherrie's nearly empty bar.

Oli lived in Yugoslavia, near Trieste, till he was eight years old. His father brought the family to Brooklyn in 1969 where Oli thrived as one of the biggest kids on his block in the kind of ethnic neighborhood where English was a minority language. "But I always dreamed about Canada and California, I guess the same way my father did about America. It's the wide open spaces I'm after, see. It was crowded in Yugoslavia and it was crowded in Brooklyn."

Like more immigrants than the immigration service would care to acknowledge, Oli has no citizenship papers. "They got lost in the shuffle. All I've got is a driver's license." Traveling now he fancies himself a citizen of the world. When his marriage broke up, he set out to find a good place to live.

"I also wouldn't mind finding a good woman to live with." He met a good candidate late last night on the train after I went to bed. "She was escorting some Indian kids from Churchill to an alcohol treatment center in The Pas. Name's Fi Holland, grew up in South Africa." She didn't have any citizenship papers either, so she and Oli hit it off. She told him the story of her stepfather dragging her to Montreal where she married a man who took her to Churchill and divorced her. She gave Oli her phone number and address. "Maybe I'll come back here after I check out the west. She says she'd love to go to California."

Cherrie loves Oli's story. "That's the best thing about my job—stuff like that happens on my train all the time. So many passengers are searching for something—and sometimes I get a chance to watch them find it."

"So what's your story?" Oli asks her.

"Me, I got the traveler's itch so bad I had to make a career out of it. My husband lives in New Brunswick and I live in Winnipeg, so I guess you'll think that's pretty weird. Everybody else does. But tomorrow's my little girl's birthday, and all I want to do right now is get home to her."

Now Oli turns to me. "And what are you after besides a book to write?"

Nobody has asked me that question since Linda Melillo. "I'm not sure anymore. At the start of the trip, I was disenchanted with what I had seen of my own country. I thought I might fall in love with Canada. But there was something else, too." And then I tell them some of the stories of centrifugal force that have dogged me wherever I've gone.

"Is that what you've learned in your travels?" asks Cherrie.

"Among other things. Back at the beginning, a woman on your train, the *Canadian*, told me that people take marriage too much for granted, kidding themselves that permanent union is the most natural thing in the world. 'But it isn't,' she said. 'It's the most unlikely thing in the world because everything changes and centrifugal force never weakens.' "

"So she didn't believe in marriage?" asks Cherrie.

"That's what I thought at first. But I misunderstood her. She said the best defenses for marriage against those facts of life are our great North American virtues, freedom and truth—and that sometimes the best hope for permanence is a willingness to let things die and be born again."

In the morning, at Winnipeg, Cherrie is gone to her daughter's birthday party and I make a very tight connection to the *Canadian* heading east. Oli will hike around town until the westbound comes through tonight at 9:00. When we say farewell to each other in the station, he recalls the conversation of last night. "I'd still like to get back with my wife. It's like, when I had the chance to tell her, I never had the words. And when I have the words, I don't have the chance. You probably never had that problem, being a writer and all."

I tell him, "Why do you think I write it all down?"

The trip on the *Canadian* back east is one of the smoothest yet— on time at nearly every station, no soap operas, and one good, tough travel companion whose conversation makes the long hours of shield terrain whisk by. He is Will Williams, a Canadian voyageur, a self-described travel addict who has somehow gotten past thirty without kicking the habit. He's done his time in the Central African Republic, Australia, Thailand, Hawaii, and is currently scheming a year in South America. "Yes, I know that most of us do it out of pain, not joy. No, I haven't figured out why I do it yet. And I'm not so young anymore."

"What do you bring back with you from traveling?" I ask him.

"Prejudices," he says. "I don't like Germans. There are two kinds—the spontaneous, crazy ones who will do anything and scare the hell out of me and the uptight descendants of the Nazis who also scare the hell out of me."

And he hates England, despite a strong family heritage. "The working-class squalor there is unbelievable. English rednecks make American rednecks look like paragons of culture and civility."

I tell him about a VIA bartender I know who brings home felicitous memories of people finding their dreams. "Good for her," Will Williams says cynically. "I bring home images of human ugliness." In the Central African Republic he saw a man who had been hanged from a tree without a drop. He was still swinging and his women were keening at his feet. Down the road Will gave a ride to the army man who did it. That time he didn't ask questions.

"In Australia I was in an Abo bar and six white off-duty policemen came in slapping the palms of their hands with their clubs looking for trouble. But when they saw white witnesses present, they left. Later in a different bar I overheard one of them describing what it felt like when an Abo head caved in under his club after 'the white witnesses' had left. I challenged the bastard and he denied what he said. But he added that 'What 'ell ef et was true, they ighnt 'uman, might.' "

Will is just returning from what he calls a "home-stand"—a train trip through Canada. "When I finished at university I had a snotty attitude that Canada was a cultural backwater, a personal embarrassment, compared to France, Germany, England, China, or even America." But after every trip abroad he came back and did a home-stand. Today he thinks Canada looks pretty good, but not out of patriotism. "I don't know either the English or the French words to 'Oh, Canada.' But Canada's good because I don't have to travel to get there. Traveling sucks, it's just a bad habit. You should quit while you still can."

15

Last Train to Toronto

LAST RUN OF THE *CANADIAN* FROM VANCOUVER TO TORONTO

I'M not prepared for the sheer emotion of the gathering at the CN station in Vancouver on the afternoon of January 14, 1990. The crowd awaiting the departure of the last run of the *Canadian* to Toronto numbers over three hundred, half of whom are here to ride the train. Those of us who will enjoy a special status, like royalty, envied by those who will be left behind on the ground. They all want to talk to as many of us as possible. Names and addresses are exchanged. "Send me some pictures," begs an old woman wearing a black armband, and instantly half a dozen others chime in, "Me, too."

As a visiting American I am struck by the lack of the slick, well-rehearsed demonstrations one sees so often in the United States when a special interest group is threatened by government action. But there is protest: it is homespun, individual, and personal.

An old man carries a sign hanging by a string from a stick over his shoulder. He has scribbled his message in red and black felt-tip pens on a one-by-four-foot piece of one-inch styrofoam insulation.

On one side it reads, "John MacDonald gave the CPR 2,500,000 acres including mineral rights and millions of dollars to provide passenger service in perpetuity. So keep our trains rolling." On the other side it reads, "Senior citizens still depend on the railway, we still care and, Brian, we still do remember how to vote."

His name is Arthur Penucci. I ask him if he thinks this decision will hurt the Mulroney government, and he is conciliatory: "Any government can make mistakes. Canada is the best country to live in, in the world. But we're rapidly becoming a second-class nation. Our government has the power to change its course. We citizens have the duty to try to convince them to do that. I just don't want to see the children lose the best life there is."

A Mrs. Eastman has ridden the CPR route regularly for sixty-one years. She has parked her wheelchair by the gate and tells all who pass that she has vowed to live long enough to see the train's return to service.

A young woman, Janice Fossey, has set up a card table and is gathering signatures for her own personal petition. She had a reservation on the last train, but gave it up to spend the vacation time working on her petition. "Someone has to do something. You can't just sit and say someone else will do it. I'm hoping that all across Canada, as people see the train pulling out for the last time, they will do the same thing I'm doing and convince the Mulroney government that it's not just the rail union members and rail fans who are appalled by this historic error."

On the platform a man carries his one-year-old son on his shoulders. Both wear engineer caps and the man explains to his son that this is the last time he will see the train that made his country. The boy's chin quivers in the cold; his sober expression shows that he knows something terrible is going on here—and he will never, never forget.

Besides myself, there are a few other Americans on hand. Some just happened to be in Vancouver on vacation, one was drawn because he is a history professor, and several are the traditional rail fans. There are no loud "ugly Americans" here today; the usually irrepressible American rail buffs stand aside silent and respectful of their neighbor's loss. One, a man from Seattle, says to me with emotion choking his voice, "I never realized how much I loved these people till I see them hurting so much today. They're good people, damned good people, a hell of a lot better than us—and they deserve better from their government than this. They ought to take to the streets and raise fucking hell. But they won't and that's why it's such a goddamned shame."

When boarding begins there is none of the usual scramble to get on. People linger on the platform. The TV crews scurry around, but even they are sober. Over the outside P.A. someone has played the Doors' song "This Is the End," lending the moment an apocalyptic air. "This is the end of our elaborate plans, the end, of everything that stands, the end . . ."

Finally it's time to go. If you could embrace a train, there are hundreds of people who would. There is no band playing, no banners, no official recognition of the significance of the occasion whatsoever. The train, with nothing more than the standard two toots, pulls out right on time.

Outside my roomette window, I see a burly cop standing by his car in the rail yard, waving as the train pulls out. His tough chiseled face is tracked with tears. And there are more—by the hundreds they line the tracks well out into the yards. They take pictures, they wave, some cry, some hold up a raised fist. Now several begin walking, then running beside the train as if they just can't let it go. Two men in dark-blue three-piece suits have clambered up on top of a piggyback freight car with their cameras. A mile out of the station there are still people standing silently in little knots as the train passes.

Past the stanchions where the cars were washed, past the pumps where the trains were fueled, past the idling diesels of this morning's arriving train, past the empty coaches and darkened sleepers, past a switch engine lashed up to a defunct but still gleaming silver Skyline car, and then under bridge after bridge where there are scores more mourners, the *Canadian* glides out of Vancouver for the last time. These aren't rail fanatics. I've traveled the rails enough to be able to spot them a mile away, reciting their litany of train numbers and obscure rail trivia. These are people who know their history, who know that that history was forged by the steel rails carrying this train today.

So I find myself riding the last train to Toronto. It's been nearly a year and twenty thousand miles since I began my journey, and throughout that time my travels have been shadowed by the Mulroney government's intention to radically cut the passenger rail service. Sometime in October a VIA official hinted that I had better make reservations on the *Canadian* leaving Vancouver on January 14, so I did.

But I never really thought it would come to this. Hadn't President Reagan budgeted zero dollars for Amtrak during two of the years I was traveling the U.S. rails? Today Amtrak is expanding. And hasn't my fundamental history lesson of Canada been that this rail route performed a function in the founding of this nation similar to that of the Bill of Rights in the United States? Canada's historian laureate, Pierre Berton, will affirm in Winnipeg tomorrow, as the last westbound passes through, "We have no blood in our history— no searing civil war, no surgical revolution. We are the only nation in the world created nonviolently by the building of the railway."

In the rear Park car lounge I am reunited with friends I made on the trip out a day ago. First there is Bill Coo, retired CPR, CN, and VIA official, author of the *Scenic Rail Guides to Canada* and an undisputed Canadian rail authority. He has traveled out and back with his younger friend, Bill Nesbitt, an insurance man who has probably ridden this train more than anyone else in Canada— seventy to eighty times since his youth when his family shipped him on the train regularly to visit relatives in Banff and Calgary. The two Bills are scheming a classy photo-essay book on the history of the *Canadian.*

Then there is Bernie Goedhart and her fourteen-year-old son, Jordan. Bernie is a free-lance writer who contracts to the VIA employees' newspaper and is documenting this trip at her own expense. On the way out, in Winnipeg, a trainman promised, much to Bernie's horror, to take Jordan down to North Main to teach him the pleasures of the flesh. When everyone reboarded Jordan gathered up his stuff and hid in a part of the train where his mother couldn't find him. Bernie, fortunately, is a good sport.

David Lovelady, of North Yorkshire, England, is a New World enthusiast who rides the trains of North America whenever he can. He takes voluminous notes, far more than I do, but insists that he is just an inveterate scribbler. Bill and Bill and Bernie and I speculate that at some point he will pull the rubber mask off his face and reveal himself as Paul Theroux.

Rich Schnell and his twelve-year-old son, Patrick, are Americans from Plattsburgh, New York. Rich, who runs an inn, wanted his son to witness a piece of history and get to know the neighbors.

Finally there is Chris McMullen, a black photographer from Middletown, Connecticut, who is riding this run in search of historic pictures.

There is no finer setting for good cheer and comradeship than the

341

Park lounge of the *Canadian*. Over cocktails before the call to dinner we reminisce about the trip out.

In Calgary an inspection revealed a bad wheel on the Skyline car in which our meals had been served, as that train had no separate diner. Off came the car and the train stopped at Golden where the crew cleaned out a local fried-chicken house. The birds were delivered to passengers with the legendary VIA courtesy, but some of the meat was not properly cooked and a few people got sick.

There was the snowball fight at Revelstoke where an English girl more than held her own against the entire diner crew amid a perfect snowfall of huge carnation flakes. And there was another scam to rile Bernie; we coached her son to spot bugs and cockroaches under the bed upon arrival at their hotel in Vancouver.

Heading back east we have an operating Skyline car, a full-service diner, extra sleepers and coaches, and Bernie still speaks to us. This train ride is going to be all right.

In the morning my window displays a perfect Canadian Rockies landscape. The Kicking Horse River riffles alongside the tracks with its milky blue glacial water, studded here and there with white mushroom caps on rocks. A million snow-laden Christmas trees sweep down the mountainsides, where huge herds of elk graze in the deep snow beneath the high hanging glaciers and avalanche tracks. There is no road here with quite the same perspective, and unless this train is somehow restored, I am seeing sights that simply will not be seen by travelers in the years ahead.

I ride through this splendor having breakfast with Ian Waddell, NDP member of Parliament from B.C. He has ten thousand signatures on a petition protesting the VIA cuts, which he is taking to Ottawa. He explains that under the Canadian system, the real battle over an issue like this takes place after the government has initially had its way. He cites the cancellation and restoration of the *Super Continental* through Jasper and the *Atlantic* through Maine. "Those are nice trains," he says, "but this is the CPR line that built the nation. Don't turn your attention away too long or you'll miss its return."

After breakfast we stop under the vertical white glory of Lake Louise and Banff and then wind down through the "gateway of the Rockies" to Calgary, where a large number of our passengers detrain, including the TV crews with their bright lights. Here we pick up a souvenir of our trip out, the defunct Skyline car whose wheel has supposedly been replaced. Bill Coo swears the car was in exactly the same place when we left it, and I take a picture of the suspect wheel to send to Bill for close photographic analysis.

On the prairie after Calgary, a cold thick pea soup sets in. All afternoon and into the evening we can't see anything beyond the telephone poles by the tracks.

After midnight at Moose Jaw a large crowd waits on the platform with candles and bagpipes and signs and trumpets. Outside the air is winter balmy, and the mayor, Stan Montgomery, is surrounded by an enthusiastic crowd of over a hundred as he reads his proclamation for the TV cameras and their bright lights. "Since 1884 . . . the Moose Jaw station has served as a friendly stop for settlers, tourists, soldiers, and citizens coming and going on the train. . . . [Today] that tradition is interrupted by an uncaring, unresponsive government. . . . We are here to give witness and declare by our presence that this is not the last train through Moose Jaw—in a democracy the will of the majority must ultimately prevail . . . we owe it to the future of our children and our grandchildren and to the sacrifices of our parents and our grandparents to continue this just cause. We will not fail them."

The bagpipes play "Oh, Canada" and the crowd chants, "Save the train." I ask an elderly woman why the train is so important to Moose Jaw. "I have children and grandchildren in Kingston," she says. "They're not rich and neither am I. We can't afford to fly to see each other and with the climate and the road conditions, we can't drive great distances the way you Americans do. And despite what [Minister of Transportation] Benny Bouchard says, nobody but penniless, footloose youngsters would travel that far on a bus. What it means is that Canadian families who have dispersed across the land, secure in the belief in the government's commitment to transportation, are now going to be separated. I just won't see my children and grandchildren very often anymore. That's what Brian Mulroney has done for me."

After Moose Jaw, I catch a few fitful hours of sleep and then rouse myself at 5:30 A.M. Service chief Gerry Kloss has told me that we are to meet the last westbound somewhere around that time. The crews plan to stop the two trains and meet on the tracks for a last farewell.

In the cafe end of the Skyline car I find the crew in a black mood. An order has been sent out from VIA that there is to be no stopping for a meet with the westbound. The conductor complains that he and the engineers take their orders from CPR, not VIA. He wonders just how much force the order really has. His radio crackles with communications from the approaching westbound train. It is decided that the two trains will slow to a crawl as they pass each other at the siding at Kemnay, just west of Brandon. One has to stop to wait for the other to pass anyway. It won't be hard to observe the occasion without violating the letter of the order from VIA. But still the order rankles. "They want this train's memory to be snuffed right out. You won't let that happen, will you?" a CPR trainman says to me, seeing my notebook and camera.

Leaning out the vestibule window, I can hear the slightly dissonant duet of the two trains' horns as we pull into the siding. There gleam the headlights of the westbound. The brakes of both trains squeal like dying sows as clouds of steam billow up between the cars. The sky has cleared. It could have been the start of a great new day.

I don't see anyone actually step off either train as we inch through at a speed that can be described as just barely not stopping, but crewmen hang out vestibule doors on both trains and a few even lean far enough to slap hands in the space between the trains. It's a quiet commemoration; most of the passengers on both trains are asleep and the participants are subdued and sober. "Have a good last ride," I hear several crew members shout. The engineers of the westbound wave through their windscreen and the brakeman in the rear Park car flashes his light on and off. And then it's gone, trailing a plume of steam from the vent pipe at the rear of the Park car.

On our train it's deadly quiet; no one says a word. Then we accelerate and the last train to Toronto is now truly on its own.

In the later morning the stop at Winnipeg is a big deal. We are delayed because the connection of the *Super Continental* from Edmonton is late. A woman from Vancouver, Vera Severson, has personally collected 41,000 signatures on a petition calling for reinstatement of the train. On the platform she presents it to NDP MP Bill Blaikie from Manitoba. I ask him what he will do with the petition. He says, "This is too good to just be presented in Parliament the usual way. I think I'll plunk these right down on the Prime Minister's desk."

Winnipeg is the end of the line for the crew we have traveled with to Vancouver and back. Gerry Kloss, our excellent service chief, is retiring here and now. There's a party for him on the platform complete with a cake, signs, a trombonist, and singers. They strike up "The Happy Wanderer," "For Auld Lang Syne," and

"Oh, Canada" with passion and tears. Someone says to Gerry, "Look on the bright side." He says, "I outlasted them by one train."

Sonny Restiaux meets his wife and young son here. The kid wears a poster reading, "Brian, you took my daddy's job." Sonny is number 206 in seniority, the cutoff being 199. Gilbert Pouliot of the dining car is 198 and just made it.

In a corner of the station, which earlier this year housed a magnificent museum of immigrant history and artifacts, I find a pile of signs: "Will the last person to leave Manitoba please turn out the lights"; "Thailand $800,000,000, Amtrak $100,000,000, VIA $0"; "Free trade has given Canadians nothing but headaches, heartaches, and empty wallets." In the Winnipeg paper, I read that VIA President Ron Lawless is quoted as saying that rail-travel supporters have "a peculiar mindset, due to romanticism."

Over early Bloody Marys back on the train, Bill Thompson, from Peterborough, Ontario, a tall fellow in his seventies with magnificent white hair and a female travel companion half his age, describes some of his unpatented inventions. Foremost is the drinking machine, made up of a hot water bottle, some tubing, and a clamp. The bottle is filled with rum and the tubing is run up the inside of the jacket sleeve to the hand where the clamp acts as a faucet when the arm is pressed against the side. One orders a Coke in the bar and doses it accordingly. The invention also has possible applications at work, church, driving, and so on.

He tells me about Norris Crump, the CPR president and legendary father of the modern *Canadian*. Crump's idea was to woo people back from the fledgling airlines with travel that offered pleasures the planes couldn't match. Thus the emphasis on a variety of environments in the train, the keys being the Skyline car at the coach end of the train with its second-class lounge-bar, observation dome, and cafe, and the first-class Park car at the rear of the first-class sleeper section with its clubby muraled bar, a "parlor room" with its observation dome at the very end of the train, and the classy diner.

Crump had his offices in Windsor right over the tracks of a train connecting with the *Canadian*, and when it was late, he would know why. Once as an economy measure, Bill saw the traditional roses removed from the diner tables. On his next trip, they were back. He asked why. "Mrs. Crump rode the train," he was told.

Crump died on December 26, 1989, just a few weeks before the last run of his train. Bill Thompson thinks he was fortunate to pass before he had to witness the end of his dream.

After lunch near Beausejours, we pass the wreckage of a recently derailed westbound freight. The train was running at track speed—over sixty miles per hour—and when the derailment occurred, the seventeen lost cars simply exploded off the track. The farmer who lives nearby said that he heard the wreck, knew exactly what it was, and just hunkered down in his bed hoping it would clear him and his house. As we pass today, CPR crews are bulldozing the wrecked earth, retrieving what cars they can, and burning the rest of the mess in a huge bonfire.

A debate develops in the rear Park lounge between two CPR veterans. One argues that a crew in a caboose could have lessened the disaster. Another says it would make no difference. The elimination of cabooses nationwide, following the trend in the United States, is as hot a topic among freight rail people as VIA is among everyone else.

The American, Rich Schnell, suggests that both governments, Canadian and American, make their surplus cabooses available for the homeless in big cities. Riding across the prairie on a train, I think such a scheme could never happen because it makes too much sense. The government spokesmen back in Ottawa and Washington would quickly come out with their reasons why the thing can't be done and that would be that. Thus the making of a prairie populist.

After dinner, I meet Fred Graham, one of the last of the original crew from the first run of the *Canadian*, and Ann Partridge, a fellow traveler also intrigued by his celebrity, in Fred's room for some serious tale-telling. He recalls that there were a lot of media people aboard that trip, July 24, 1955, and he was interviewed several times. But more memorable were people who were called "firsts"—people who made a hobby of looking for first runs of new trains to ride. Today, sadly, there are only "lasts." Firsts were always wealthy and rarely had any particular connection to railroading. They were just connoisseurs of novelty in the age of newness. "Lasts tend to be ordinary folks like you and me mourning the passing of beautiful things."

Fred waves his hand in disgust when I ask how much of the tradition of the original *Canadian* survives today. "Everybody does everything now—jacks of all trades, masters of none. When I began as a steward, you had your own specific tasks to attend to, you were a specialist. And you did your job according to the Little Green Book put out by the CPR, which spelled out exactly how to do everything, from setting a table to presenting a chilled salmon to polishing silver."

Aside from the attention to precise method, the other big difference between then and now was the hardware. "We had to handle much more stuff than today's crews do—separate containers for everything—gravy boats, ice cradles, containers to keep the bakes hot and to keep the salads chilled. All silver or porcelain, of course."

And today's crews get sleepers at the end of the day. In Fred's time, except for the steward, they all slept in the diner. Tables came off hooks on the walls; the carpet would be pulled back to reveal wells where cots and mattresses were kept. A locker at the end of the car held blankets and pillows. Some made chair beds by arranging eight chairs. A rope with a curtain would be strung up from one end of the car to another to separate the sleeping crew from passengers moving through the car during the night.

"The CPR was the best employer you could hope to work for. You always knew your job and exactly how to do it. And you could get fired only for two things—violating Rule G [the ban on drinking] and fraternizing with female passengers." Otherwise discipline was meted out as "brownies"—demerits that could affect your pay. Fred doesn't know when the phrase "brownie points" came to have an opposite meaning from what it did then, but he suspects it must have something to do with avoiding brownies by kissing up to lax supervisors.

For over an hour Fred reminisces fondly—about his favorite train-riding celebrities (George Formby, Katharine Hepburn, Jingles, and Mackenzie King), about the male brotherhood of the dining crew (no women in those days), about the hours (four days on and four off with twelve hours extra layover automatic for any time put in beyond the required four days), and the way the rhythms of the workday became ingrained in his soul.

"To this day I know it's almost time to go to bed when I get an urge to chip ice. I can feel that urge right now." There were no freezers on board in the early days, just huge blocks of ice. The last chore Fred had at the end of every day was to chip ice and pack the Lady Borden ice cream made specially for the CPR.

Just as I am about to take my leave of Fred Graham, the *Canadian* receives the best tribute of the trip yet. We had been disappointed by the lack of any kind of demonstration at the station, but as the train pulls out, we approach the Thunder Bay Fire Department. The air is charged with flashing red light. At first we think there must be a terrible fire, but then we see the four huge trucks lined up facing the tracks with their lights flashing and the ranks of uniformed firefighters behind them standing at attention. In unison the trucks blast their mega-horns as we pass and the firefighters execute a smart salute—exactly the same routine they would observe for the funeral of a fallen comrade. Fred is jubilant and we can hear muffled cheers from the corridor outside his room. No bagpipes and chants at Thunder Bay—just the military-style salute of the toughest outfit this region has to offer.

After saying goodnight to Fred, I head up to the dome car in search of northern lights. There aren't any tonight, but Ann Partridge entertains me with stories of her adventures that are just as good. She is an outdoor education teacher and has spent much of her life exploring far-flung places all over Canada. She has backpacked up the Labrador Coast and canoed throughout the Northwest Territories. Her most epic journey began by train to Lynn Lake in northern Manitoba, and from there she and her party flew with canoes aboard 350 miles north to Baker Lake. The pilot worried that if there were ice on the lake, he might not be able to set his canoe-laden plane down, and he didn't have enough fuel to go back. But the lake was clear and Ann and her group set off for six weeks of canoeing on Arctic rivers scheduled for dam construction.

"We wanted to do the rivers before they disappeared," she says. And now this train. "I guess that's my passion, things that are in danger of extinction. I'm a fanatic example of Fred Graham's 'lasts.'"

At Terrace Bay, huge flakes of heavy snow make the station scene look like one of those glass globes that you turn upside down to create a snowstorm. We step off the train where we confront a charming rough-hewn house with a large sign hung across its gable reading VIA—CANADA'S NATIONAL NIGHTMARE. Inside we can see candles in the windows and old women waving to the train. It's after 1:00 in the morning.

The lack of sleep is finally beginning to wear me down and tonight I tumble into my snug roomette bunk exhausted. The snowflakes whip past the window as the *Canadian* rolls eastward and I drift into dreams of snowy Christmas Eves as a small boy. There's an electric train waiting for me under the tree with a Canadian Pacific steam engine on its head end. There's church and the singing of hymns and carols. The singing solidifies, crystallizes and, waking, I realize that it's real—people just outside my roomette door are singing in the corridor.

I shake off my slumber and check my watch—7:30 A.M. The train is not moving and outside my window there is a crowd of people and a huge sign, taller than the train. We're in the town of Chapleau. Now I recognize the song "Oh, Canada," sung with the words "God save the train."

Another day begins with a sleepy scramble to get dressed and out on the platform before the train moves on. In the pre-dawn gloaming, I can see the huge sign, now leaning against and towering over the Skyline car: BRIAN RESIGN, PUT VIA BACK ON TRACK. There are lots of people with little signs and a man plays "Taps" on a trumpet and then "I Been Working on the Railroad" and finally "Oh, Canada." Some women are passing out black rosettes to the crew. I ask them if they are rail wives or union people.

"No, we're the Chapleau Ladies," a grandmotherly woman says with great dignity. "We're citizens who don't want to see our little town cut off from the rest of Canada. We've lost the battle, but not the war. This train will be running when Brian Mulroney is looking for a job."

At breakfast in the dining car the story of the morning is that the "mynah bird" is on board. In a nation that Americans do not associate with eccentricity, the legend of the mynah bird goes against the grain. I had seen Colin Kerr and his rare Indian bird on the Johnny Carson show once and I saw their picture on the front page of a recent Vancouver paper. They are on the train, with Mr. Kerr happy to tell his story.

He was playing in a professional golf tournament in India, and not doing very well—dead last to be exact—when he visited a little boy dying of leukemia. The boy had this mynah bird, which he claimed brought good fortune. Colin asked him why he was dying if his bird brought such good luck and the boy answered that the good fortune would appear in his reincarnation. Colin touched the bird and returned to the tournament, where he shot two 62s, the best score of the event. He accepted the boy's gift of the bird, Rajah.

Today there are two birds, Rajah and Ranee. They have been formally married by a Toronto rabbi and have figured colorfully in some of Canada's recent history. Rajah had an audience with the Pope and appeared several times on the Carson Show. Colin says that singer Neil Young attributes the success of his career partly to his contact with Rajah. The bird was recruited to lend its aid to the federal cause during the Quebec referendum. Now it is here to help save VIA.

Despite the colorful diversion of the mynah bird, this last day on the last train is depressing. Outside the rain pours down as we roll through the granite ribs and muskeg of the Great Shield. Inside, the only energy I can find is the interaction of a Japanese couple, here to do a free-lance TV project, with a French-Canadian couple and a Mexican man and his son. Despite the language barriers they educate each other about nachos and mañana, meat pie and separatism, sushi and Mount Fuji.

At Sudbury, it's good-bye to Archie, the stationmaster who rescued me from the Ledo Hotel bar twenty thousand miles, eight months, and a world ago. He retired the day the last train came through heading west. He sold himself his last ticket and got on the train for Winnipeg. Now he stands forlornly under the Sudbury station sign beside the tracks where the Montreal train used to connect with this one. Those tracks are empty today—travelers for Montreal are to be bused from here, an eight-hour trip, and they are not happy campers.

After Sudbury the steward comes through the train taking reservations for one last dinner sitting at 5:00 before we roll into Toronto. Normally this sitting is not well attended, most people preferring to wait for a later dinner in town, but tonight is different and the entire dining car is booked for the last supper.

Everyone gathers when the call is made at five—Bill Coo and Bill Nesbitt, Bernie Goedhart and Jordan, Rich Schnell and Patrick, Chris McMullen, David Lovelady, Colin Kerr, Fred Graham, Ann Partridge, Bill Thompson, and dozens of others. The wine closet is cleaned out; the cook scrambles to prepare a variety of meals from the leavings of the three previous day's dinners; some have scallops, some halibut, some Swiss steak, some chicken—it's potluck time. The toasts begin—to the crew from the passengers, to the passengers from the crew, to Bill Coo, and one in jest to Brian Mulroney for making all this great fun possible. The empty bottles of wine are passed around for autographs—mementos of the last supper on the last train.

After the meal, diners linger while the crew rushes about to get the car cleaned up before arrival in Toronto. Our waitress, Josie, a perky blonde who has refused to stop flashing her million-dollar smile, and Dale, the waiter whom I have jostled a dozen times in my efforts to visit with people in the diner, finally collapse at the head table. They are both losing their jobs.

Then we're into Toronto station. On the platform there is a small group of citizens with signs and candles, but nothing like the turn-outs at Moose Jaw or Chapleau. Rich Schnell is pounced on by a CBC television crew and he explains that he is here to be a good neighbor and to show his son the last of the great trains of North America.

I still can't claim to understand fully how the politics of this country work, but amid the babble of voices on the platform, I hear a man shout, "Wait till the next election!" For three days in January of 1990, you could have heard the same thing all across Canada.

Everyone disperses. The good-byes are quick and merciful. And then I spot him, standing under the electronic departures sign in the middle of the now empty concourse. He wears the same black cowboy hat he wore when I first met him on the *Canadian* heading west last summer—John Solaris, the Alberta rancher who, like me, wanted to travel all of the Canadian rail routes while he still could.

When I tap him on the shoulder he turns, recognizes me, and says, "I'll be damned. You did it, didn't you? You rode the last train to Toronto like you said you would."

"Yes," I say. "But where were you? You were going to ride it, too."

"Couldn't get on. All booked up. So I came east a day early on the next-to-last one. Now I'm going out tomorrow on one of the first runs of the new route up on the northern CN line."

John offers me one of his Players, and this time I accept. "The party's over," he says. "Old John MacDonald must be rattling his goddamn bones over what they done to the railway, to this country—it always was one and the same thing, you know."

The great station has become silent; shopkeepers are closing up their stalls, just a rattle of keys echoes down the concourse. "Canada won't be the same. Quebec wants to leave us and Indians are raising hell all over the place. There's talk that the government is going to cancel the rest of the lines when the uproar over this one has settled down. I wonder where all those youngsters we met last summer will go then. I suppose they'll be out on the Yellowhead thumbing again and gettin' hard like me twenty years too soon."

"They already are hard."

"You say that because you're an American. You think to be as free and true as them, you gotta be hard. But see, that's why they come here and why they were wrong about the government canceling the

train. They weren't hard enough yet to know what was coming—
that they could get kicked in the ass here, too, just like in the rest of
the world. Aw hell, it's just too damn bad. Leave it to the kids to
believe in what oughta be. And leave it to the wise old heads to fuck
it up. But hey, you rode the last train to Toronto. It was a grand
party while it lasted, eh?"

Epilogue

The New "*Canadian*" from Vancouver to Toronto

ALMOST a year after the last run of the *Canadian* over the CPR route, I again find myself in Vancouver boarding a train headed across the continent for the east. VIA calls its post-cutbacks transcontinental run the "*Canadian,*" and indeed it is the same delightful consist of cars, minus the dining car in the off-season. But the route is really that of the old CN *Super Continental*, by way of Yellowhead Pass, Edmonton, and then the northern shield country through Sioux Lookout east of Winnipeg. Craigellachie, Banff, Lake Louise, Calgary, Moose Jaw, Medicine Hat, Regina, Thunder Bay, Shreiber, North Bay, and the downtown station of Sudbury are now without transcontinental rail service, most without any rail service at all.

In Vancouver, the railway station newsstand, restaurant, and passenger service facilities are all closed. Though the place is still well lighted, heated, and cleaned, it echoes with ghosts. A lone, aging Burns Security guard prowls where once crowds jostled to board daily trains to the east. Today there is just the thrice-weekly train by the northern route, and few passengers are waiting.

Yet the train is clean, perhaps cleaner than before, and the service crew is attentive to the point of being officious. Clearly a new regime has been established, as crew who were once famous for being "laid back" about rules and regulations now carefully articulate the policy on where smoking is allowed (no longer in the rear Park car lounge and only in the two bars and in certain designated roomettes and bedrooms) and firmly enforce the formerly loose prohibition of coach passengers entering the rear of the train. This is the first ride on a Canadian transcontinental where I receive no invitation to ride in the cab.

The first night out of Vancouver is rain-drenched and I ride with a group of travelers who had earlier tried to get to Kamloops by bus. Mud slides have closed the highway, turning their bus around at Hope and sending them back to soggy Vancouver, from whence they are now attempting to escape by train. During the night we plow through a mud slide ourselves and a boulder damages the lead engine, which must be replaced at Kamloops in the morning. But we are fortunate to get through; the next two trains scheduled to depart Vancouver in the coming week are scrubbed because of devastating mud slides in the Fraser Canyon.

Throughout the first day of the trip I am treated to canyon and mountain scenery I have not seen before. Because I traveled from Jasper to Prince Rupert and then down to Vancouver on BC Rail in my previous trip, I never rode this portion of the old *Super Continental* route (on the former Canadian Northern tracks) between Kamloops and Jasper. Today it is draped with heavy wet snow while gales of freezing rain and sleet occasionally obscure the mountain peaks.

As we round the big turn toward the east and Yellowhead Pass, a propitious gap in the murk and clouds affords a rare view of towering Mount Robson, highest peak in the Canadian Rockies and said to be visible to the top only on a dozen rare days of especially fine weather. It's almost as if the Canadian weather gods are in on VIA's new regime of trying harder. We get our view of the nearly thirteen-thousand-foot peak on a soupy day when the opposite wall of the canyon is often obscured.

The ride through the Yellowhead reveals only the lower slopes of great peaks, Mount Robson being the last whose top we can see. Along Moose and Yellowhead lakes, the wildlife are again especially cooperative—elk, bear, deer, and condors appear with regularity. Then, just as we cross the divide, the weather turns. It is clearly colder outside now. The snow blows powdery and is stacked up in drifts that invoke thoughts of crackling fires and holiday warmth.

At Jasper we have a long stop while the cars that will make up the *Skeena* bound for Prince Rupert are taken off. Outside in the early evening darkness, fluffy snow has accumulated eight inches deep and cheery lights in the village announce the approach of the long Canadian Christmas season. I detrain, hoping to find Bob Barker over at the AthaB, but it's Sunday and everything is closed. Instead I meet a skier who is happy to be boarding a train out of Jasper just as the ski season commences.

Zach Taylor, a college student on what has become an extended break, rode the *Super Continental* from his family's home in Montreal about this time last year to do a little skiing. He came with the best intentions of getting a job to support his habit, but "somehow the skiing was so good and the companionship so convivial that I never got around to it." By April he was broke and his family thought it was time for him to learn some responsibility. "There was no check in the mail."

He has been working at a resort ever since and finally has saved enough to get home. "Back home I used to dream about skiing in the west. Now I've been dreaming for six months of Montreal delis, shows, university rap sessions, and women who wear classy eastern clothes and speak two languages more beautifully than anyone out here can speak one. Home, man. I'm a homesick skier."

At dinner, as the train rolls toward Edmonton, Zach and I are seated with a young mother and her baby who have been receiving sympathetic cluckings from train crew and fellow passengers since Vancouver. It's been quite a struggle for thirty-one-year-old Bonnie Cook. Young Matthew is at that irrepressible age where all his impulses are out of bounds and he pursues them with seemingly limitless energy.

Like Zach, Bonnie is making tracks back home—to Winnipeg after a bad time trying a new life in Vancouver. "I don't care if it's cold; I don't care if it snows. I just want to see the prairie and be with people who don't have umbrellas permanently growing out of their sleeves." Matthew has just decorated the tablecloth with his mushroom soup and my tossed salad. "Dinner is the hardest time," Bonnie appeals, and so Zach and I join forces with her for the duration of the meal to distract Matthew.

After dinner is finished and Bonnie and Matthew have returned to their coach seat (much to the relief of the diner crew), Zach suggests that what Bonnie needs is a baby-sitter and some adult diversion for the evening. At first I think he's joking, but then he reveals a serious ulterior motive. Boarding at Jasper he met a pair of high school–age sisters who are also traveling to Winnipeg. He is quite taken with the elder, who is just a few years his junior, and sees the baby-sitter scheme as a way to separate her from her younger sister. Sure enough, the freshman agrees to baby-sit for Matthew and Zach heads off to the lounge for pizza and Cokes with her sibling.

Bonnie is grateful to be emancipated for even a few hours. Sitting in the rear Park car lounge, where lonely lights of high plains farms drift by outside, she explains that she is a country and western singer who has lost her way. After a life of false starts, she is heading home to begin again. An elderly couple joins us, and when the man makes a comment about how many miles the train must cross before he gets to where he wants to be, Bonnie says, "This time the miles don't mean that much to me."

The man suggests that her answer sounds like a line from a song. And for the first time a broad smile cracks the tired facial expression she has worn so far. "It *is* a song; we should write a song!" We begin to take turns scribbling in my notebook.

As the intervals between lights outside grow longer, we talk about what makes a country and western song work. "I know that people say it's just sentimentality. But rock music is just hormones, so what the hell. At least there's truth at the core of C and W, and the truth is always about the discovery of pain—especially about people who have taken some dangerous step in response to it. Like me. I walked away from a marriage to a wife-beater and then fell flat on my face trying to make it on my own in Vancouver. Now I feel stronger than I ever have because of having failed so badly."

Soon the conductor comes back with the message that Matthew needs more than a baby-sitter's attention. Bonnie's break is over for tonight and she heads back to her coach, and I go to bed with a song in my head.

In the morning, Zach, Bonnie, Matthew, and I step off the train at every stop for fresh air. The prairie is cold and brisk, dusted lightly with snow, and the towns all have a feeling of anticipation. Twice we notice an old man, poorly dressed, who has gotten off the train and lingers around the wheel trucks, sometimes seeming to search for something under the train. At Melville just before lunch we see him again and Zach approaches and asks him what he is doing. The man turns and in his hand is a small brass box filled with gray dust.

"I'm not crazy," he says. "You see, my wife and I rode this train for our honeymoon back in 1938." On the train he tells us that he was a janitor, never made much money. After he retired he and his wife dreamed of taking a trip on the train to relive their honeymoon. "But she was sick, eh. Cancer, and she died two months before we were supposed to leave. So I carried her ashes out to Vancouver and I'm putting them on the tracks all the way back home. Maybe I am crazy, but I don't know what else to do."

As the last miles to Winnipeg click by, Bonnie oscillates between excitement and dread. Out comes the notebook and, in a burst of inspiration, we finish the song. "You probably don't realize how important this silly song is to me. I'm a singer, and now I'm not coming home empty-handed."

At Winnipeg it's farewell to one friend and a reunion with another. Dennis Huska, who told me stories of the Rifleman a year ago, is our next conductor as the new *Canadian* runs on his old *Continental* route east to Sioux Lookout. Zach and I sit with him in the Park lounge and venture that there must be some advantages in having the big train now on his run.

"Well, we never see the crazies anymore. I don't know how they get around now. But we've lost the campers, too. The train runs on the wrong days at the wrong hours. A lot of them are trying to sell their places, but who wants to buy a camp you can't get to?"

"So who rides this division now?"

"Damned if I know. It's always different. A lot more tourists in the summer, people who used to go over the CPR route. But this time of year . . ." He gestures toward the empty seats around us.

In the morning at breakfast, the only other diner besides Zach and myself is a French-Canadian in his thirties. He is headed to Sudbury, where he is a research librarian working on a grant to improve opportunities for French-speaking students in English schools. But Luc LaChance is a true Montrealais, who struggles with living in a place so alien from his roots.

"There is a thriving community of French professionals in Sudbury, but our lives are obsessed with politics because of where we live and work. My friends tell me I'm not radical enough."

"Why don't you go back to Montreal?"

"I wonder the same thing. My political consciousness tells me that somebody has to be out here doing the job. But I'm at the age where I want something more substantial for myself. No one makes a life in Sudbury—just work and fast living and casual relationships. I'd like to get married, have a family. But the only women in Sudbury interested in that kind of thing are English. My compatriots would never forgive me."

And so it goes on Canadian trains—the stranded skier, the trouble-bitten young mother, the old man with his ashes, the French-Canadian attempting to come to terms with his place— the stories of struggle between centrifugal and gravitational forces never end.

After a fourth night (VIA has solved the problem of late trains on the new *Canadian* by adding thirteen hours to the schedule), I arrive in the early morning in Toronto, where I part with Zach and make a quick connection to a corridor train to Kingston for another reunion. Bill Coo picks me up in his car at the station and drives me to his charming country house on a steep ridge just outside of town overlooking Lake Ontario. With an audience of his menagerie of dogs and cats, we sit in his kitchen and reminisce about the "last train," complimenting ourselves on choosing to ride the last east-bound, instead of the westbound. Though virtually all of the articles and documentaries that have appeared were done by journalists riding the last westbound, trainmen on board report that the ride became a media zoo in which the recorders of history crowded out the participants. "It wasn't that way on our train. We had some dignity."

Bill reviews what remains of the VIA system. The real *Canadian* is gone entirely, as are the *Ottawa Valley* route connecting Montreal to Sudbury via Ottawa, the *Evangeline* and the *Cabot* routes in Nova Scotia, the *Frontenac* route connecting Montreal and Quebec City along the north shore, and the *Northland* from Toronto to Kapuskasing (though the Ontario Northland's *Northlander* and *Polar Bear Express* are unaffected). The number of daily trains in the corridor between Quebec City, Montreal, Toronto, and Windsor has been reduced. Everything else survives but only on a thrice-weekly schedule.

I venture that it hasn't been as bad as some had predicted. One can still travel much of "Canada beautiful" the way you ought to, and the new "Of Style and Steel" campaign to finally rebuild the passenger cars of the old *Canadian* is encouraging. VIA is even adding on-board showers. Perhaps, as the government has claimed, its cutbacks are intended to free up the dollars needed to rebuild and save the system. Bill fixes me with a scowl and shakes his head.

"How can they be serious about saving the system with a transcontinental service that departs Toronto near midnight, sits in Winnipeg for over three hours, and takes four nights to get to Vancouver? When they run trains in the corridor so short that people have to ride standing in the aisles? When the train through cottage country runs on days and at hours that leave the cottagers stranded? When they leave Banff, Lake Louise, Calgary, Moose Jaw, Regina, and Thunder Bay off the map entirely?"

"So you still think that the new service is designed to kill off passenger traffic to the point where they can scrub VIA entirely?"

"I don't know. How can they be planning on that when they're putting millions of dollars into rebuilding the old CPR passenger car fleet? It doesn't make any sense. I don't think the government knows what it's doing."

After lunch, Bill drives me back to the station with a slow detour past the house of John A. MacDonald, now preserved as a national monument. The modest homestead is nestled on well-manicured grounds behind hedges that offer teasing glimpses of the windows and walkways. I speculate that maybe the government is taking a page from Old Tomorrow's book. Maybe they're just postponing a real decision till better circumstances prevail. With Meech Lake a wreck and Indians building fortified barricades, they certainly have their hands full.

Bill shakes his head. "With the French and Indians and impossible geography and you Yanks next door, Canadian governments have always had their hands full. I know I'm cynical about the government, but today we can't afford much more bad luck. And there's not much room for error."

Selected Bibliography

Pierre Berton, *The National Dream* (Toronto: McClelland and Stewart, 1970).

Pierre Berton, *The Last Spike* (Toronto: McClelland and Stewart, 1971).

June Callwood, *Portrait of Canada* (Garden City, N.Y.: Doubleday, 1981).

Bill Coo, *Scenic Railguides to Western Canada and Central and Atlantic Canada* (Toronto: Grey de Pencier Books, 1985).

A. W. Currie, *The Grand Trunk Railway of Canada* (Toronto: University of Toronto Press, 1957).

Blair Fraser, *The Search for Identity—Canada: Postwar to Present*, vol. 5 of *Canadian History Series*, edited by Thomas Costain (Garden City, N.Y.: Doubleday, 1967).

W. G. Hardy, *From Sea unto Sea*, vol. 4 of *Canadian History Series*, edited by Thomas Costain (Garden City, N.Y.: Doubleday, 1960).

Sabra Holbrook, *The French Founders of North America and Their Heritage* (New York: Atheneum, 1976).

H. A. Innis, *A History of the Canadian Pacific Railway* (Toronto: McClelland and Stewart, 1923).

Robert Leggett, *Railroads of Canada* (Vancouver: Douglas, David and Charles, 1973).

Andrew Malcolm, *The Canadians* (New York: Times Books [Random House], 1985).

Selected Bibliography

Grant MacEwan, *The Battle for the Bay* (Saskatoon: Western Producer Book Service, 1975).

Grant McClellan, ed., *Canada in Transition* (New York: Wilson, 1977).

Farley Mowat, *People of the Deer* (New York: Penguin, 1970).

Anne Merriman Peck, *The Pageant of Canadian History* (New York and Toronto: Longmans, Green and Co., 1943).

Bruce Ramsey, *PGE: Railway to the North* (Vancouver: Mitchell Press, 1962).

Thomas Randall, *The Path of Destiny*, vol. 3 of *Canadian History Series*, edited by Thomas Costain (Garden City, NY: Doubleday, 1957).

G. R. Stevens, *History of the Canadian National Railways* (New York: Macmillan, 1973).

Albert Tucker, *Steam into Wilderness* (Toronto: Fitzhenry and Whiteside, 1978).

Index

Index